"This is a relevant and timely book that deals with the complex dynamics of family businesses. It showcases an in-depth intellectual analysis of family business insights alongside a comprehensive collection of cases, examples and questions that stimulate discussion and debate. It is a must read for anyone interested to understand more about how family firms function, why they matter and what makes them unique worldwide."

Dr. Allan Discua Cruz, *Director, Centre for Family Business, Lancaster University, UK*

"*Family Business Management* is an essential book that provides a rare insight into the dynamics of family businesses in the Arab Gulf region and beyond. A significant part of the material is dedicated to fundamental matters, such as succession planning, that are often overlooked in the Arab Gulf region. As family businesses continue to gain prominence in local and regional economies, this book offers business family members, economists, and academics a clearer guide to understand these important institutions."

Sultan Sooud Al Qassemi, *Lecturer, Bard College Berlin and Fellow at Wissenschaftskolleg zu Berlin – Institute for Advanced Study*

"Being a third-generation family business executive, I have benefited from Prof. Dr. Rodrigo Basco's advice on numerous occasions regarding succession, governance, and conflict management. I believe this book will help different generations of family members navigate their unique journeys and reflect on the most important issues, such as governance, succession planning, and family transparency, among others."

Saud Majid AlQasimi, *CEO, Al Saud Co.*

"A world-renowned scholar coming from a family business background, Rodrigo Basco curates a thoughtful journey to greatly inspire family business leaders, practitioners, and all other learners. Gradually moving from managing family dynamics to governance and succession, the text demystifies complexities of family businesses and offers critical and actionable insights into planning and strategizing for families in transition. The global selection of real cases, coupled with carefully themed discussions and learning activities, is of enormous benefit to the family business community. This text has my highest recommendation."

Jeremy Cheng, *Researcher, The Chinese University of Hong Kong; Founder, GEN + Family Business Advisory & Research, Hong Kong SAR*

Family Business Management

Family Business Management provides an accessible overview of the core aspects of family business, with an international, practice-based perspective.

Structured in four parts, the book covers key topics such as family firm goals, conflict management, human resources, strategy, financial management, family and business governance, and succession planning. A wide variety of cases and examples are used throughout the book to highlight cultural and institutional differences between family businesses in contrasting contexts. Each chapter offers a detailed case study and boxed examples, illustrating real-life family business situations and stimulating students' critical thinking and decision-making. Readers are further supported by learning objectives, discussion questions, and further reading suggestions. Digital supplements for instructors include lecture slides, a test bank, and additional case studies.

This textbook is an ideal companion for family business courses, catering to both undergraduate and postgraduate students. It offers valuable insights and practical guidance for business families, as well as professionals working in family businesses.

Rodrigo Basco is Professor and the Sheikh Saoud bin Khalid bin Khalid Al-Qassimi Chair in Family Business at the American University of Sharjah, UAE.

Family Business Management

Rodrigo Basco

Routledge
Taylor & Francis Group

LONDON AND NEW YORK

Designed cover image: Ja'Crispy / Getty Images©

First published 2024
by Routledge
4 Park Square, Milton Park, Abingdon, Oxon OX14 4RN

and by Routledge
605 Third Avenue, New York, NY 10158

Routledge is an imprint of the Taylor & Francis Group, an informa business

British Library Cataloguing-in-Publication Data
A catalogue record for this book is available from the British Library

ISBN: 9781032226026 (hbk)
ISBN: 9781032226019 (pbk)
ISBN: 9781003273240 (ebk)

DOI: 10.4324/9781003273240

Typeset in Times New Roman
by Newgen Publishing UK

Access the Support Material: www.routledge.com/9781032226019

Contents

8   Business governance in family business

9   Family governance in family business

Preface

This textbook that you are going to read contains basic ideas to understand the fundamentals of owning, governing, and managing family businesses. My intention was to share what I have learned from being part of a business family, working with family businesses, researching family businesses, and teaching family business courses around the world. Consequently, this textbook is an attempt to organize ideas, personal experiences, research discoveries, and reading materials in a coherent and structured way, making this knowledge accessible to anyone who is interested in family businesses.

This textbook invites readers to navigate the uniqueness of family businesses by learning new concepts, reflecting on ideas, applying models and information to family business challenges, evaluating and judging real family businesses, practicing decision-making in the context of family business, and creating and tailoring solutions for family businesses. Additionally, the journey readers are about to begin is intrinsically marked by my own cross-cultural perspective to understand the specificities of culture, geography, history, and institutions that affect family businesses' ownership, governance, and management.

This textbook is ideal for students who have to approach the family business world for the first time. It contains the basic elements to develop their knowledge and complement it with their own experiences. This textbook can be a reading reference for any family business course at the undergraduate and graduate levels. Consequently, for instructors and professors, it is a unique textbook for creating, organizing, and preparing their classes with concepts, models, examples, case studies for discussion, and classroom exercises.

Business family members can also use this textbook as an introduction to the world of family businesses. This textbook can help family members interpret, understand, and put into perspective their experiences as owners, managers, and/or family members and project them into the future. For senior generations, this textbook can help them navigate the challenge of maintaining cohesive families while running sustainable and profitable businesses. For younger generations, this book can help them develop the ownership, governance, and managerial skills and abilities needed to build the future of their family businesses. Finally, for family business consultants and practitioners, this textbook is a perfect reference to help them structure, complement, and organize their knowledge and extend their vast experience.

This textbook would not have seen the light of day without the professional, educational, and emotional support of hundreds of friends, colleagues, students, scholars, and family business leaders who have inspired me in different ways, extended their hands with generous stories, and shared ideas and discussions with me. I also thank those who intentionally or not put some stone on my path and locked the wheels of my journey due to their own limitations or incompetence; they helped me reinvent myself and double my efforts to keep my curiosity and free mind alive.

I also acknowledge all my own failures that ultimately shaped my ideas, experiences, and mind to perceive and understand the universe of family businesses in my own way.

With this textbook, I wanted to make sense of those talks I had with my mother Ana Maria, who has believed in my personal and professional journey; Pilar; and Mamama to quench their bitterness of not having their Tata to find answers to their questions. I hope this book helps others play their roles in family businesses. My unconditional gratitude to Inga, who loves my limitations and makes them trivial and sharper at the same time. To Une, Vetre, and Balys, who inspire my understanding of being a father and are responsible for, and to some extent suffering from, helping me perform my role as a father every day. To Florentina, Ana Rita, and Lisandro, who have shaped my concept of brotherhood in a unique way. To my father, Hugo, who unveiled the fragile world of being a human. To Ali, for her generosity in editing my ideas in a foreign language, and to Joana, for opening the Vilnius University Library's doors so I could find a den for my desperate inspirations. And to Arpita, for her support during the process of collecting information, reading material, and drafting ideas.

Rodrigo Basco

Sharjah, March 3, 2023

Part I

Introduction to family business

1 Approaching the concept of family business

Learning objectives

- Recognize the differences and similarities between family and nonfamily businesses.
- Understand the sources of family business heterogeneity.
- Classify family businesses based on different types of family involvement.
- Describe the complexity of family businesses across generations.
- Identify the competitive advantages of family businesses.

1.1 Introduction

Our journey starts by differentiating between two main categories of firms in today's economy: private and public companies. A privately held company is a firm that is privately owned, meaning the owners (i.e., the founders, managers, or private investors) own the firm but their shares are not traded publicly. The most common types of privately held companies are sole proprietorships, limited liability firms, and corporations with shareholders but whose shares are not traded on the stock market.[1] On the other hand, a publicly held company is a firm whose ownership is fully or partially formed of shares freely traded on the stock exchange. This initial distinction between the two categories—privately and publicly held companies—is important because both categories differ in ownership structure, governance complexity, tax regulations, transparency, and obligation to disclose financial information, among other attributes. There is a common belief that family businesses are private and small, but empirical evidence shows that family businesses can be private (e.g., Grupo Barilla in Italy, Mars Inc. in the United States, and Mercadona S.A. in Spain) or public companies (e.g., Wal-Mart Inc. in the United States, Roche Holding AG in Switzerland, and Groupe Auchan S.A. in France).[2] So, *what makes a business a family business?*

Another important aspect to understand the nature of any firm is the relationship between ownership and management. Figure 1.1 shows a continuum with two well-known classical relationships between ownership and management. The right side of the figure captures a firm whose owners (i.e., those who have the right to possess the tangible and intangible property of the firm) do not manage the firm. Namely, the owners and managers have different rights and responsibilities. While the owners have the right to invest their money into the firm, receive returns for such investments, and are responsible for the firm's long-term vision and goals, the managers are responsible for implementing the best strategy to achieve the owners' goals and maintain the firm's long-term competitiveness. Wal-Mart Inc. is a good example of this type of firm as the Walton family is still the major shareholder of Wal-Mart Inc. According to public information, the children of Wal-Mart founder Sam Walton own about half of all Wal-Mart

DOI: 10.4324/9781003273240-2

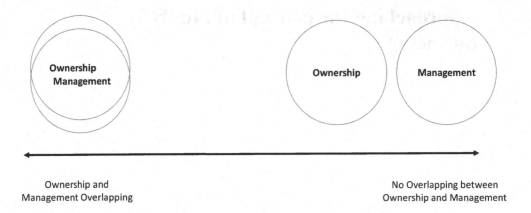

Figure 1.1 Graphical representation of common ownership and management structures.

shares. Doug McMillon is president and CEO of Wal-Mart Inc. "Under Doug's leadership, Wal-Mart is making life easier for busy families and building trust with customers. It is investing heavily in associate wages, benefits, and education—including a debt-free college program and an expanded parental leave policy."[3]

The left side of Figure 1.1 captures a firm in which the ownership and management roles are filled by the same individuals. In other words, the ownership and management roles overlap in one or more individuals, giving them the authority to strongly influence the firm. For instance, in the case of the family-owned firm Emi-G Knitting, Gina took her father and mother's business to a new entrepreneurial level by creating two new brands: Zkano and Little River Sock Mill. Both use organic cotton and sustainable manufacturing processes. Little River was selected as a 2015 American-Made Award Winner by Martha Stewart American Made, which honors American entrepreneurs. The family business defines themselves as follows: "We're a small family business with a passion for making socks. Located in the Sock Capital of the World, Fort Payne, Alabama, we blend years of manufacturing know-how with U.S.A. made craftsmanship to achieve the highest quality products possible."[4]

In between the extremes, there are multiple degrees of overlap. Overlapping ownership and management is more in line with today's entrepreneurial organizations: typically, individuals who own a firm and manage the firm as well. For instance, Meta Platforms, Inc. (informally known as Facebook) is an excellent example as Mark Zuckerberg is co-founder, chairman, CEO, and a controlling shareholder.

Family businesses come in the form of both privately and publicly held companies across all possible ownership and management structures. Family presence in a business makes that business a family business. In simple terms, this book uses the following general definition: a family business arises when two or more family members own and/or manage an organization. In Figure 1.2, family businesses are graphically represented with the addition of a new circle for the family entity alongside the existing ownership and management entities.

On the left side of the continuum, family members are owners and managers at the same time. An example of this type of family business is a "co-preneur" firm—that is, when a couple starts a firm and both family members share ownership and managerial responsibilities. For instance, Beau's Pint Club is a plant-based gelato company founded and owned by spouses Joseph Eyre, who serves as the chief operating officer (COO), and Amber Fox-Eyre, who serves

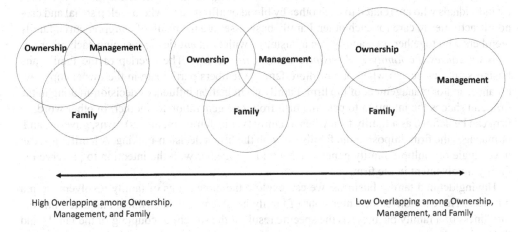

Figure 1.2 Graphical representation of ownership, management, and family structures.

as the chief customer officer.[5] At the other end of the continuum (right side), family members own part of a business, but no family members work in the firm. This is the case in the pharmaceutical group Roche, founded by Fritz Hoffmann-La Roche in 1896. André Hoffmann and Jörg Duschmalé, members of the founding family,[6] are part of the board of directors and are the representatives for the shareholder group with pooled voting rights. The family shareholder group holds a 45.01% stake in Roche AG.

In between the extremes of Figure 1.2, there are multiple degrees of overlap among the three ownership, management, and family entities. The overlapping of the three circles in the middle of Figure 1.2 represents the three levels of overlap in family businesses where family members take on roles as owners and managers. Additionally, on the right side of the overlapping, family members are managers but do not have shares (are not owners yet). On the left side of the overlapping, family members are owners but do not work in the firm.

Family businesses are the most common form of organization in developed, emerging, and transitional economies.[7] Family businesses exist in different sizes, from small companies to big conglomerates, and in different industries, from extractive industries to manufacturing and service industries. It is estimated that family businesses account for a significant portion of the gross domestic products and employment in all types of economies around the world.[8]

The aim of this chapter is to explore, analyze, and understand the fundamentals of family businesses, from recognizing differences and similarities between family and nonfamily businesses to classifying family businesses based on different types of family involvement in firms.

1.2 Family business definition

The introduction of this chapter provided a first, general approach to the concept of family business. However, there are specificities of the family business phenomenon that require attention in order to unveil the different types of family businesses. To define family business in simple terms, we need to consider two different entities: the family and the business. The overlap of these two entities forms a family business. The business entity is composed of individuals who organize and integrate a set of economic activities to achieve specific economic and social goals within the boundaries of a profit-oriented organization. The family entity is formed by individuals who are related to each other by blood or affinity and who develop social and economic activities to care for each other. Family businesses are the result of entrepreneurial family members who together own and/or run a business, with both entities influencing each other.

What causes the family and business entities to overlap? The overlap of the family and business entities occurs when one or more family members participate in the ownership, governance, and/or management of the firm. Family participation influences decision-making in the firm and shapes the intention to pass the firm from one generation to another. In other words, a firm can be defined as a family firm when a family (via its family members) owns, governs, and/or manages the firm, imposing the family view on the firm's decision-making. A family firm can have single or multiple family generations working together with the intention to preserve the family involvement in the firm.

Having defined family business, we can explore the dimensions of family involvement in a business. There are different dimensions of family involvement in a business that determine the familiness of a family business as the specific result of the structural coupling of the family and the business[9]:

- *Family involvement in ownership.* This dimension refers to when a family owns a firm and the family, through its family members, controls the firm. When defining a firm as a family business using ownership dimensions, it is important to differentiate privately held and publicly held family businesses. In the case of a private firm, family members have to have at least 51% of the ownership to control the firm. For instance, Bacardi Limited[10] originated in Cuba; is headquartered in Hamilton, Bermuda; and is one of the largest completely (100%) privately family-owned spirits firms in the world. In the case of public family firms, the family or a group of family members needs to have enough shares to become a blockholder to influence the firm's decision-making through their voting rights. Wal-Mart is a good example of a listed family business as the Walton family owns less than 50% of the shares (through different family members, such as Jim C. Walton, Alice L. Walton, and S. Robson Walton, and a trust called John T. Walton Estate Trust) but still controls the firm because the rest of the shareholders own small fractions of the firm (not organized to pool their decisions into one voice).
- *Family involvement in governance.* This dimension refers to when a family controls a firm's governance and can thus alter its long-term and critical strategic decision-making. Family involvement in ownership gives the family the possibility to participate at the governance level of the firm by appointing their representatives (family or nonfamily members) to the board of directors. The board of directors is a group of individuals representing shareholders' interests with the responsibility of leading the firm and advising and controlling the managerial team. For example, Mars Inc. is one of the largest American multinational food companies and has gained popularity mainly for its chocolate bars. The organization was founded by Frank C. Mars in 1911 and now is owned equally by his grandchildren John Mars (one-third), Jacqueline Mars (one-third), and late Forrest Jr.'s four daughters: Victoria, Valerie, Pamela, and Marijke (one-12th owned by each daughter). The family business is privately owned. Victoria (Forrest Jr.'s daughter) served as the chairperson of the board for three years (2014–2017) followed by Stephen Badger (Jacqueline's son), who served as chairperson until 2021, and now John Franklyn Mars. Jacqueline, John, Stephen, Victoria, Valerie, and Marijke also currently serve on the family business's board of directors.[11]
- *Family involvement in management.* This dimension refers to when there is active family participation in the top management team of a firm. In this case, the family, through one

or more family members, influences the firm's day-to-day decision-making. For instance, Reliance Industries Limited is a multinational conglomerate company with a market capitalization of more than $200 billion and is headquartered in Mumbai, India.[12] It was founded by Dhirubhai Ambani in 1973, but in 2002, he passed away without leaving a succession plan, which triggered a problem between his two sons, Anil and Mukesh. The mother intervened and separated the firm into two parts. Since 2002, Mukesh, the eldest son, has been CEO of the oil and chemical portion of the business. Isha, Akash, and Anant Ambani—the third generation and Mukesh's children—are also actively involved in the business. In 2022, Mukesh Ambani announced that his children Isha and Akash have assumed leadership roles in Reliance Retail and Reliance Jio and that his youngest son Anant has joined the company's new energy business. Anil received parts of Reliance Group with interest in communication, entertainment, financial services, and construction.

- *Generational involvement in the business.* This dimension refers to when family members from different generations (founder and subsequent generations) own, govern, and/or manage a firm. What matters for this dimension is generational involvement in ownership and/or management. For example, Dot Foods Inc.,[13] the largest foodservice redistribution company in the United States founded by Robert and Dorothy Tracy in 1960, is currently managed by the family's second generation. Eleven of Robert's 12 children have worked full time for the family business. Joe Tracy, who is the 11th child of the founder, serves as the firm's CEO and member of the board of directors. His brother, Dick Tracy, who is the 12th child of the founder, is the president of the Mount Sterling—headquartered food industry distribution and Dot Food's board of directors.
- *Family intention to preserve the family as a family firm.* This dimension refers to the family intention to pass the family involvement at ownership, governance, and/or management level from one family generation to the next generation. For example, Guittard Chocolate Company, which defines itself as maintaining a 150-year family tradition of craft and innovation, was founded by Etienne Guittard in 1868. Now, 154 years later, the family business is heading forward with its fifth generation actively involved in the business.[14]

All of the aforementioned dimensions can be used individually or in combination to define what a family business is and to recognize different types of family businesses. Some dimensions are more restrictive than others because they require multiple manifestations of family–business overlapping, whereas other dimensions are less restrictive such that one manifestation of family–business overlapping is enough to consider a firm a family business.

How many manifestations of family–business overlapping does a firm need to be considered a family firm? This is an excellent question to further explore the concept of family business. The answer depends on how restrictive the definition used to define family business is. Specifically, the demographic characteristics underlying the overlap of the family and business entities in terms of ownership, governance, and management distinguish a family business from a nonfamily business and differentiate different types of family businesses. For instance, one may wonder if Ford Motor Company is a family business. By 2015, the Ford family was ranked the 129th richest family in the United States. Through its super-voting B stock, the extended Ford family controls the voting power of Ford Motor Company.[15] Although the family meets the dimension of family involvement in ownership, controversy remains as to whether Ford Motor Company is a family business. One can argue that a listed firm wherein the business family is a simple blockholder is not a real family business because listed firms subject to the market logic (e.g., profit maximization and short-term orientation), so families cannot impose their own logic (the family logic may be driven by other principles beyond profit maximization). This debate opens a new perspective to interpret what a family business is through a behavioral lens.

How do the family and business logics manifest in decision-making? It is important to reflect on the fact that the demographic characteristics underlying the overlap of the family and business entities may have different effects on firms' decision-making at the ownership, governance, and management levels. To define family business, the behavioral lens focuses on the coexistence of the family logic and the business logic. Table 1.1 shows two types of family businesses with different logics. The overlap between the family logic and the business logic emerges in key decision-making areas, such as human resources, finances, strategy, governance, and succession. The family logic alters decision-makers' focus of attention by introducing specific family business goals, including economic goals (profit and long-term survival), social goals (image, tradition, and social recognition), and emotional goals (family kinship relationships and family cohesiveness). Therefore, the behavioral lens helps define family business when the family logic interacts with the business logic in key decision-making areas.

Table 1.1 Family and business logics applied to family businesses

	Family Business with Business Logic	*Family Business with Family Logic*
Logics based on interactions		
Emotions	Aggressiveness—opportunity driven	Submission
Cognitive	Firm as a means to raise entrepreneurs' image, money, visibility	Firm as a means to care for family members, extending the relationship to different stakeholder
Normative	Speculation	Tradition
Rule of justice	Equity	Equity is mixed with equality and needs
Model of communication	Hierarchical communication (written and oral communication) to address specific organizational task issues	Horizontal communication, mainly oral communication, to address specific task issues as well as the emotional, psychological, and physiological needs of individuals
Interaction	Task, function, and chain of command	Kinship and friendship in combination with task, function, and chain of command
External interactions		
Higher-order institutions	Venture capitalist, professional managers, business associations	Family, related social classes, related economic actors
Internal decision-making		
Human resources	Merit	Merit, nepotism, and altruism
Financial	Risk	Conservative
Strategic	Growth	Stability
Governance	Separation of the family and the business with different governance structures	Informal governance structures
Succession	Best candidate (internal or external)	Intra-family succession—nepotism

Source: Adapted from Basco, R. (2019). What kind of firm do you owner-manage? An institutional logics perspective of individuals' reasons for becoming an entrepreneur. *Journal of Family Business Management*, 9(3), 297–318.

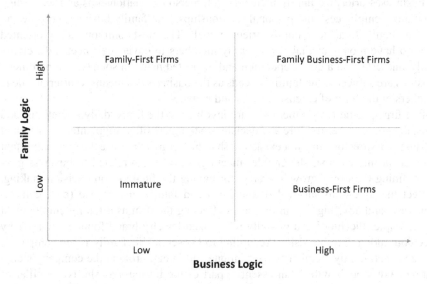

Figure 1.3 Types of family businesses by combining the family and business logics.

1.3 Types of family businesses

Family businesses are not a homogenous group. There are different types of family businesses. The demographic dimensions of family involvement as well as the lifecycle stage of each of the entities (ownership, governance, and management) determine the different types of family businesses. There is a consensus among scholars and practitioners to differentiate family businesses based on how the business and family logics are combined. As shown in Figure 1.3, the intensity of both the family and business logics creates four general configurations of family businesses with specific strategic behavior, governance structures, and performance. Even though these four configurations may not exist in pure form in reality, they help visualize patterns of behavior in family businesses and better clarify the heterogeneity among family businesses.

The family and business logics compete with each other to define owners', managers', and family members' general focus of attention. Key decision-makers' focus of attention determines the essence of a family business—that is, the meaning of the family business for members who occupy different positions across the ownership, management, governance, and family entities. Family owners' and managers' focus of attention defines the family business's priorities, goals, and reference points, thereby influencing the firm's decision-making. For instance, if key family decision-makers prioritize the well-being of family members and the continuity of the family business across generations, the decision-making will be oriented to preserve family harmony and to guarantee the survival of the firm at the expense of decisions to ensure superior short-term performance.

Next, we summarize the most important characteristics for each configuration of family businesses in terms of human resources, strategic decision-making, corporate governance, succession, and performance.

1.3.1 Family-first family firms

Family businesses in the family-first firm group show strong family orientation. The family logic prevails over the business logic, and family values are embedded in the firm. Therefore, these family businesses prioritize family members' interpersonal relationships and well-being as well as nonfamily employees' interpersonal relationships. The family business becomes an instrument for the family to achieve family-oriented goals. The most common family-oriented goals are often to have money available for family members to cover their needs, develop a cohesive family, and establish a good reputation and respected name in society, among others. Business decisions are subject to the family's needs as the business is a means to offer privilege to family members in the form of extensive perks and benefits.

In family-first firms, some family members are involved in the firms' daily operations, and because of this, the governance structure and decision-making are often supplanted by informal procedures. A board of directors may not exist, and shareholder meetings are the most important governance arena. In this context, shareholder meetings cover tasks related to business governance (e.g., defining the firm's growth strategy or having the final say on decision-making, which can affect the long-term survival of the firm) and family governance (e.g., controlling family interests and advising on family topics affecting the firm as a family employment practice). For example, Picchiotti is a globally recognized jewelry brand founded in 1967 by Giuseppe Picchiotti along with his sister. According to Giuseppe, his family is the company's greatest asset, and each family member plays a unique and integral role in the company's day-to-day operations. Giuseppe's wife is an essential part of the business as she is the pillar of the Picchiotti family. Maria Carola, Giuseppe's daughter, also plays a vital role in handling the company's public relations and marketing the brand to a larger audience. Giuseppe's sons, Filippo and Umberto, have worked on procuring gemstones from around the world, which is another key part of the family business's operations. The Picchiotti business model relies on the individual aptitudes and skills of each family member and the role each plays within the context of Picchiotti as a whole. As Giuseppe stated,

> The success of the Picchiotti brand has been due to good communication and that we have always emphasized a family-first mentality. It is a great point of pride to us that we are able to work together so well across generations.[16]

In decisions related to human resources, kinship relationships and length of service are typically the basis for entry, promotion, and compensation policies, with nepotism being the basic principle for decision-making. Human resource decision-making is carried out to increase individual competency (supporting family members' competency development). According to this orientation, people are more important than the business or the focal position. The chairman of Crane & Co, a successful paper mill family business that has had a contract to produce the United States' currency since the 19th century, reflected on this orientation as follows:

> I didn't think when I was growing up that I would play a significant role in the business. I worked in the company when I was young, growing up as a teenager. But, I had a career outside of Crane. However, every generation before me was an active part of the business. My father was involved, my uncles, my grandfather and great-grandfather worked in the business too. Crane & Company was who we were and is who we are. I came to the business from the top, you might say, as I was asked to be on the Board at some point. I stayed on the Board for a while, then I became Chief Executive Officer and now I am Chairman.[17]

Regarding strategic decision-making, in family-first firms, families play an important role in supplying financial (e.g., investments), human (e.g., knowledge and nonpaid family work), and social (e.g., social and economic connections) resources for their businesses. The competitiveness of family-first firms comes from these unique resources, which are difficult to imitate by competitors. Alejandro Diaz Carlo, owner of Carabalí Rainforest Park in Puerto Rico, which is a premier tourist destination, reflects on the resources his family invested to ensure the business family remains resilient across generation. Specifically, talking about tacit knowledge, Alejandro noted the following:

> We have learned from our grandparents and parents how to prepare for severe and extreme weather, and drawing off the experience and support of other family members, both past and present, is one of the main advantages we have as a family business.[18]

Finally, in these firms, management and ownership succession decisions are not explicitly defined until something occurs because of the number of family members involved, directly or indirectly, in the business. In this sense, the continuity of family involvement in the business depends on how the family organizes around the business to remain competitive. Hence, succession is the result of internal activities/actions designed to groom the future successor and accommodate the rest of the family members in different positions by maintaining family harmony. For instance, this is the case of the first ownership and management transition in Mitchells clothing store, a family business founded by Edwin William Mitchell and his wife in 1958 in Westport, Connecticut. The brothers Jack and Bill came into the family business in the late 1960s and assumed ownership and leadership in the 1970s.[19]

In terms of firm performance, although family-first firms are frequently not as profitable as their competitors (regarding business performance), sunk costs (family assets such as time, lower agency costs, communication, and loyalty) often keep these businesses alive. For example, Levant is a manufacturing family firm in Morocco that is in its second generation. During the peak of the COVID-19 pandemic, the company's turnover had dropped by around 50%. Despite a significant decline in revenue and the pandemic's negative impact on profits, the Levant family firm did not reduce its labor costs, and none of the employees were made redundant, ensuring their salaries were paid in full. The message that the family sent was "employees are considered as family members and solidarity is our intrinsic family firm value."[20] In turn, the employees' loyalty will have a long-term impact for the Levant family—survivability is the key performance measure.

1.3.2 Business-first family firms

Family businesses in the business-first family firm group show a strong business orientation. The business logic prevails over the family logic. A business-first family firm makes decisions based on what it needs to do to compete successfully in the marketplace. The role of the business is to achieve competitiveness and sustainability. Business-oriented goals are important in terms of financial and economic performance, productivity and innovation, and stakeholder relationships. The family brings significant assets into the business, but the assessment and use of these resources are based on parameters of merit, productivity, and competitiveness.

In business-first family firms, family members may or may not be involved in daily firm operations. The top management team of such a firm, regardless of whether it comprises family and/or nonfamily members, is responsible for implementing the firm's strategy, which may respond to the owners' goals. In this context, the firm's governance structure plays an important role as this is the arena in which the family and business entities confront their differences and tie their destiny. The board of directors exercises the traditional business roles of control (overseeing the functioning of the firm), support (assisting and advising the top management team), and connection (linking the firm with its environment to get strategic resources). Depending on the complexity of the family, the family governance structure can also play an important role in influencing how family and business issues affect each other. For instance, Alessi, a family-owned Italian design and manufacturing firm founded in 1921 by Giovanni Alessi, has its own charter defining the conditions under which family members can join the firm. At age 18, Matteo Alessi, a member of the fourth family generation, signed the charter to explicitly recognize and adhere to the rules that any Alessi member has to meet to join the firm. He also adhered to other conditions to work in the family business such as have a master's degree, speak a second language, and have at least two years of external experience. After achieving these requirements, Matteo joined the family business and is now the chief commercial officer.[21]

Regarding human resource decisions, the skills, abilities, and capacity of both family and nonfamily members are important in defining entry, promotion, and compensation policies. Another important characteristic in the human resource area is the freedom that managers have in decision-making. Nepotism is less evident in business-first firms because there are typically few family members working in these firm, and those family members who are employed are surrounded by nonfamily members who are professionals, thereby increasing competition and equal treatment across all organizational levels. The S.H. Kelkar Group[22] is one of the largest family businesses in India and is a good example of a business-first firm. The company, a manufacturer of fragrances, was founded in the 1920s. The third-generation member Kedar Vaze worked in various departments to prove his capabilities and then assumed the position of COO. Kedar could have assumed the position of CEO. However, he believed he did not have execution capabilities to manage the business, so he and his father Ramesh (managing director until 2019 and then nonexecutive director and chairman of the board) brought in an experienced nonfamily member professional, B. Ramakrishnan, to manage and lead the group in 2010. After working as COO for four years, Kedar succeeded Ramakrishnan as CEO in 2015. Meanwhile, Ramakrishnan took up a consultancy role.[23]

Regarding strategic decisions, the complexity of their businesses and the business orientation of business-first family firms make the competitive advantages of their businesses less dependent on family resources (financial, human, and social resources). However, the family still provides fundamental resources, such as family legacy, stability across generations, social networks, and long-term vision, among others, which make business-first family firms competitive and different from nonfamily firms. These family businesses are generally run by professional nonfamily members, while family members manage the family brand and wealth via the family office, such as the case of the Walton family as a blockholder of Wal-Mart.

In terms of succession, family influence in the business makes the transfer of ownership and management an important issue for business-first family firms. Regarding ownership succession, even when it could be constrained by the legal context, the concentration or dispersion of family ownership across generations could affect the future development of the family business and the way the family executes control over the business. Intra-family management succession is not as important as in other types of family businesses. The family accepts nonfamily leadership within an adequate family and business governance structure. Therefore, in business-first family firms, succession is understood via a broad perspective, which requires preparing the next generation of family members to assume different responsibilities within the family, ownership, and/or management entities. For example, Marta Ortega Pérez is the daughter of Spanish tycoon Amancio Ortega, founder of Inditex, the parent company of world-renowned fashion brands like Zara, Massimo Dutti, and Pull & Bear. Marta has always been a part of the company, working different roles in the background. She worked her way up to becoming chairwoman of the board of directors in 2021. She decided not to assume the CEO position, leaving it instead to a nonfamily member.[24]

In term of business performance, business-first family firms tend to be more successful in terms of economic and financial performance than other types of family businesses. However, their likelihood of failure is higher than family-first businesses. Since business families in business-first family firms tend to have diversified wealth, their commitment to family business survival could be less important than for business families of family-first businesses. If the traditional family business is no longer profitable, they are able to pivot across their multiple investments.

1.3.3 Family business–first family firms

Family businesses in the family business–first family firm group show a strong intention to balance business and family orientations and preserve both the business and family logics within the family business system. Family business–first family firms make decisions based on both family and business goals. When making decisions, leaders recognize what the family and the firm bring to each other and what they need from each other to keep both entities healthy—a competitive firm and a cohesive family.

In a family business–first family firm, corporate governance comprises the family governance structure and the business governance structure. Both governance structures are linked to support the firm's strategy. The aim is to formalize family and business corporate governance—namely, to coordinate their activities, needs, and mutual support. The family develops its own governance structure (e.g., family meetings or family council) to address family issues that emerge from family involvement in the firm. Then, the family uses the corporate governance channel (e.g., shareholder meeting and board of directors) to influence the firm. Governance mechanisms reduce the probability of nepotism and other risky family practices (e.g., favoritism toward some family and nonfamily employees) and minimize family conflicts that can affect the competitiveness of the firm. At the same time, however, family governance helps the family preserve the unique resources and capabilities that provide a competitive advantage for the family firm. Mitchell Stores in the United States moved from a family-first business in the first two generations to a family business–first business from the third generation on. The family council plays an important role in achieving family harmony and reaching consensus while maintaining their customer-oriented business strategy.[25]

Human resource decisions in terms of entry, promotion, and compensation are based on a combination of person-based characteristics, such as trust, tenure, and loyalty, and position-based characteristics, such as capabilities and the ability to accomplish the tasks required by the focal position. Nepotism pervades human resource decision-making, but its influence is attenuated by the business logic. Meaghan Thomas, the co-owner of Pinch Spice Market founded 2012, summarized the idea of hiring family members as follows:

> You've worked really hard to get your business where it is today. You need to be able to trust that your family member takes it as seriously as you do. If you hire a family member that ends up being a bit of a mooch or a slacker—or, on the flip side, you end up being a mean, unsupportive boss to them—you're going to have problems that could seriously hurt your relationship.[26]

Family business–first family firms take a holistic perspective when it comes to succession and are committed to ensuring ownership and management succession. Succession decisions involve a mixture of direct and indirect practices ranging from grooming future management successors to developing responsible owners and family members who understand the balance between the family and the firm. An example is the leading global beauty brand Estee Lauder,[27] which was founded in 1946 by the visionary woman Estee Lauder. Family members see themselves as a family in business rather than a family business.[28] Estee Lauder could be considered a family business–first family firm because the company attempts to keep a balance between the family and business logics by carrying forward the founder's legacy and vision to have the most inclusive and diverse beauty company in the world. It maintains a high family influence in the business as family members are actively involved in firm operations.

1.3.4 Immature family firms

Immature family firms are those without a dominant family or business logic. These firms are typically traditional "mom-and-pop" businesses, which have a very specific niche of local consumers. Family members act in their own interests, providing their skills and knowledge to keep the business alive. There is no formal structure or governance mechanisms. Informal relationships, personal communication, and commitment and loyalty among family members and among family and nonfamily members are key elements to maintaining the ownership, family, and management entities. These businesses are small and profitable only if family members are engaged in the day-to-day operations. Succession is generally a consequence of social norms to transfer the business from one generation to another. Several of today's leading family businesses started as immature family businesses. For instance, Karl and Theo Albrecht took their mother's small grocery shop in Essen, Germany, and converted it into ALDI supermarket, one of the largest supermarket chains in the world.[29]

However, succession can also be triggered by the collapse of the relationship between the family and the business because of the complexity of the family (new participants are incorporated into the family business). In this context, for instance, the family business could go bankrupt, it could be sold, or one family branch could acquire the power to restore meaning to the family business.

1.4 The importance of studying family business governance and management

Family involvement in a business creates conditions for the business to behave in a particular manner and, consequently, has implications for its performance. Therefore, the aim of studying the fundamentals of family business is to understand how family affects the way a firm is owned, governed, and managed. Understanding the nature of family businesses, we can create knowledge and tools to improve their productivity and competitiveness while keeping the associated families cohesive.

The particular behavior of family firms emerges from two unique effects from family involvement in businesses: family goals and family resources. First, the family alters business goals. In general, firms are conceived as economic organizations that define their own strategies and structures to maximize economic (e.g., return on investment) and noneconomic goals (e.g., sustainable development). However, family involvement in businesses imposes additional goals related to the family—namely family-oriented goals, such as having money available for the family, creating job opportunities for family members, and maintaining the family legacy across generations, among others. Combining business and family-oriented goals implies that family businesses have a different reference point when evaluating their decision-making. Depending on the importance of the business- and family-oriented goals, family business decision-making may or may not differ from that of nonfamily businesses.

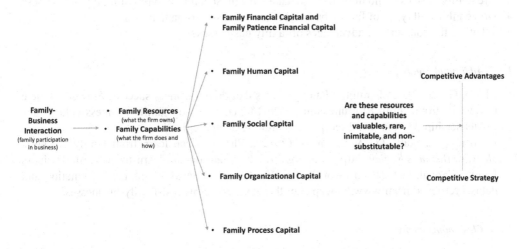

Figure 1.4 The origins of family business competitive advantages.

For instance, a new investment or strategic movement in a nonfamily business is analyzed from an economic perspective by considering the return of investment for shareholders and the economic implications for the firm. However, in the context of a family business, the same investment could have different evaluation criteria because of the reference point, which includes business- and family-related goals. The final decision related to a new investment or strategic movement should satisfy (not maximize) both the economic return and the family-oriented goals, for instance, ensuring that the final decision will not jeopardize family control over the firm.

In addition to the family-oriented goals imposed by the family that affect firm decision-making, the family also supplies resources (assets, knowledge, and skills) and creates capabilities (e.g., processes to effectively use resources). A firm's possession and creation of strategic family resources and capabilities can provide a competitive advantage over its rivals and superior performance. In the case of family businesses, this happens when the family resources and capabilities are valuable (help exploit opportunities and minimize threats), rare (competitors cannot possess them), difficult to imitate (hard to copy), and non-substitutable (no equivalent alternatives). Family resources and capabilities emerge from family participation in the firm (see Figure 1.4) and include *family financial capital*, such as family savings; *family patience financial capital*, such as less pressure to maximize the return on investment; *family human capital*, such as the loyalty and commitment of family employees and managers; *family social capital*, such as family members' network relationships that enable access to critical resources and the family's name in society and their specific location; *family organizational capital*, such as family stewardship toward the family, employees, and the community, the family business culture, and the family governance structures; and *family process capital*, such as knowledge transfer from one generation to another, family communication, and family leadership.

1.5 Additional activities and reading material

1.5.1 Classroom discussion questions

1 What is your perception of family businesses?
2 What are the most common dimensions that define a firm as a family business?

3 Are family businesses homogenous? What are the most common types of family businesses?
4 Do you think all types of family businesses are successful organizations?
5 What are the competitive advantages of family businesses?

1.5.2 Additional readings

1 Chiesi, G. (2022). La Famiglia: Family values that drive business success. *Fortune*. Article retrieved from https://fortune.com/2022/04/02/chiesi-group-family-business-values-succ ess-leadership-pharma-health-corporate-culture-giacomo-chiesi/
2 Kachaner, N., Stalk, G., & Bloch, A. (2012). What you can learn from family business. *Harvard Business Review*. https://hbr.org/2012/11/what-you-can-learn-from-family-business
3 Family Capital. (2022). The world's top 750 family businesses ranking. Information and dataset retrieved from www.famcap.com/the-worlds-750-biggest-family-businesses/

1.5.3 Classroom activity

Aim: Have students reflect on the family and business entities.
Material: White A4-sized paper, colored pencils, and Post-it Notes.
Running the classroom exercise:

- Step 1: Ask students to make a graphic representation of the meaning of family on the white A4-sized paper, giving them enough time for their creativity. After five to seven minutes, ask students to describe the meaning of family in one word.
- Step 2: Ask students to turn the piece of paper over and make a graphic representation of the meaning of business. After five to seven minutes, ask students to describe the meaning of business in one word.
- Step 3: Initiate a discussion about the meaning of family and business while allowing students to share their creativity.

Discussion: Before starting the discussion, create three columns on the whiteboard: (1) At the top of the left column, write "family"; at the top of the right column, write "business"; and at the top of the middle column, write "family business" (this column should not be filled with information until the end of the discussion). Ask students who would like to share and explain their drawings on the meaning of family and business. Start with the family. Let students explain their drawings and stick the words (on Post-it Notes) on the whiteboard. Repeat this step with the business drawings and words by sticking students' Post-it Notes on the business side of the whiteboard.

Takeaways: From the discussion, the different logics governing the family and business entities will emerge—that is, how students perceived the meaning of the family and business entities! This is a good opportunity to recognize similarities and differences in the goals, processes, and decision-making of each entity. These two perspectives are part of the family business (middle column). Therefore, it is time for students to reflect on family business. Open the discussion and let students explain their interpretations of family business. Family business means managing the paradox between these two entities!

1.6 Case for analysis I: Birla—An entrepreneurial family[30]

The Birla family has been an entrepreneurial family since 1857, when Shiv Narayan laid the foundation for the House of Birla and started trading in cotton. In 1919, he formed

Kesoram Industries Limited, which had three major divisions (tires, cement, and rayon). In 1947, Shiv Narayan's grandson Ghanshyam Das Birla carried forward the family legacy by founding Grasim, a textile manufacturer. In 1956, he acquired Indian Rayon Corporation, which is known as Aditya Birla Nuvo, and later, in 1958, he established Hindalco, which took metal production in India to another level of success. Ghanshyam Das Birla also tapped into the education sector by founding the Birla Institute of Technology and Sciences (BITS) in 1964. As time passed, Ghanshyam Das's other sons, Krishna Kumar Birla and Besant Kumar Birla, took over the leadership of other firms in the group. The family's entrepreneurial spirit continued into the fifth generation (see Figure 1.5) with Aditya Vikram Birla (son of Besant Kumar Birla), who was an ambitious and visionary businessman. He joined the family firm at the age of 24, having responsibility for Hindalco, Grasim, and Aditya Birla Nuvo firms, which formed the basis of the family business's global conglomerate, Aditya Birla Group. Aditya Birla fulfilled his dream of transforming his Indian business group into a global business empire under his leadership. His companies ranked as the world's largest producer of viscose staple fiber, the largest refiner of palm oil, the third-largest producer of insulators, and the sixth-largest producer of carbon black. Unfortunately, Aditya Birla was diagnosed with cancer and died in 1995 at the age of 51. Given the untimely death of his father, Kumar Mangalam Birla, a sixth-generation family member, took over his position. Kumar Mangalam then consolidated all the companies under the umbrella Aditya Birla Group. Kumar Mangalam has taken his father's endeavors a notch higher as today the Aditya Birla Group has grown into a global powerhouse in a wide range of sectors—metals, pulp and fiber, chemicals, textiles, carbon black, telecom, cement, financial services, fashion retail, and renewable energy. Over 50% of the group's revenues flow from overseas operations that span 36 countries in North and South America, Africa, Asia, and Europe. Kumar Mangalam states that the Aditya Birla Group is professionally run, and he is happy that his children are working to follow their own passion and dreams.

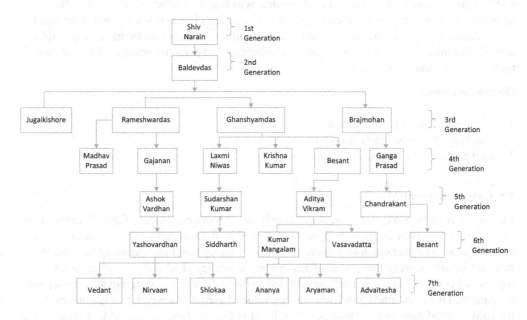

Figure 1.5 Birla family tree.

Discussion questions:

1 Why is Aditya Birla Group a family business?
2 What type of family business is Aditya Birla Group?
3 What do you think makes Aditya Birla Group unique?

1.7 Case for analysis II: Chick-fil-A—A family serving quality and tradition[31]

Chick-fil-A is a popular family-owned fast-food chain that runs across the United States, selling its famous fried chicken sandwiches. The fast-food chain was founded by S. Truett Cathy in 1967 at a mall in Atlanta, Georgia, and since then has grown to more than 2,700 independent restaurants across 47 states, Washington DC, Puerto Rico, and Canada. The family business was successfully taken over by Truett's three children—Dan T. Cathy as chairman, Donald (Bubba) M. Cathy as executive vice president, and Trudy Cathy White as ambassador—after his death in 2014. Dan's son Andrew, a third-generation family member, is also actively involved in the family business. Andrew serves as the CEO. The Cathy family has been in business for more than 70 years, and like Andrew, other third-generation family members are also carrying forward their grandfather's (Truett's) legacy. To name a few family members, Mark, the eldest son of Don (Bubba) Cathy, operates a Chick-fil-A in California, and Angela White, the daughter of Trudy Cathy White, operates a Chick-fil-A with her husband in Birmingham. To join the Chick-fil-A family business, family members have to fulfill two main requirements: (1) have a college degree and (2) have two years of external working experience. Chick-fil-A is willing to embrace family members and to embed them in the firm tradition. For instance, when Cathy family offspring are in school or college, they are welcome to work part time at Chick-fil-A restaurants. The fast-food chain is privately owned, and the family has no plans of making an initial public offering as the founder, Truett, agreed to a contract with his children stating that the family business could be sold if required but could never go public. The Cathy family has a strong foundation of preserving family values, which is also reflected in the way they run their successful business and in their mission to be America's best quick-service restaurant. The Cathy family believes in giving back to the community, which they do by increasing employment opportunities and supporting employees' education and personal emergencies by means of their fast-food chain Chick-fil-A.

Discussion questions:

1 Why is Chick-fil-A a family business?
2 What type of family business is Chick-fil-A?
3 What do you think makes Chick-fil-A unique?

1.8 Case study: Wal-Mart[32]

Walton family history. A little boy named Samuel (Sam) Moore born in Kingfisher, Oklahoma, in 1918 was the first born of the Walton family followed by his younger brother, James Lawrence (Bud) Walton. The Waltons had a lower-class family background and managed to make ends meet financially. During the course of his academic journey (high school and college), Sam worked several jobs, including selling and delivering milk, eggs, and newspapers to support his parents. This work made him learn the true value of earning money. Upon graduating from the University of Missouri in 1940, Sam was hired in the retail industry at a J.C. Penney store in Iowa as a sales trainee. He was a good salesman but not the best at paperwork as he did not believe in making customers wait during the paperwork process. He always was a man of customer service.

In 1942, he served in the US military during World War II. After the war, Sam had a wife, Helen, and a son to support, which is when he put his entrepreneurial and leadership skills to use and purchased the first Ben Franklin franchise store in Arkansas with his $5,000 savings and a $20,000 loan from his father-in-law. The first Ben Franklin franchise store was a success for Sam. He also employed his brother Bud at the store, who also served in the military during World War II. Gradually, the Ben Franklin store became a huge success for Sam, so he went from owning 1 to 15 Ben Franklin franchise stores, which generated over a million dollars annually. In 1950, Sam went on to open another franchise store named Walton's Five and Dime in Bentonville, Arkansas, where Sam introduced the concept of customer self-service, saving customers time because they did not need to seek assistance from a clerk.

How it all began. Sam knew that the future prospects for variety stores were limited. He wanted to expand his stores to rural areas by offering products at affordable prices. Sam thought that being a franchise company would not enable him to have full control over the business, and as a result, he gave up the Ben Franklin franchise. In 1962, with his brother Bud Walton, Sam established Wal-Mart, which is one of the largest retailers in the world today. As a co-founders, Sam Walton served as chairman and CEO, while his brother, Bud, served as senior vice president.

The first Wal-Mart opened as Wal-Mart Discount Center in Rogers, Arkansas. The concept of discount stores was new and Sam Walton did not have a vision, as he stated, "I had no vision of the scope of what I would start. But I had confidence that as long as we did our work well and were good to our customers, there would be no limit to us." The launch of the first Wal-Mart store was received with skepticism toward its discount store concept, as evidenced in the candid impression of David Glass (who joined Wal-Mart 14 years later) when he attended the launch of the Wal-Mart Discount Center in 1962: "It was the worst retail store I had ever seen."

Rise of the Wal-Mart empire. Seeing the success of Wal-Mart Discount Center, two years later, in 1964, Sam expanded Wal-Mart chains to other cities with the hub in Bentonville. Wal-Mart managed to give underserved, rural communities access to products at affordable prices. One newspaper reported, "Cost of living goes down in Claremore, Oklahoma!" indicating that Wal-Mart contributed to lowering the cost of living in the state. As years passed by, the company officially incorporated as Wal-Mart Stores, Inc.

By 1970, Wal-Mart's success was skyrocketing, with 38 stores opened across the United States and more than $44 million in annual sales. However, in order to expand the Wal-Mart chain of stores, Sam and Bud Walton had heavy liabilities as they had debts to pay to almost every bank in Arkansas and southern Missouri. The Walton brothers decided to offer public stock as this was the only option they thought would enable them to repay their debts. In October 1970, Wal-Mart was taken public, offering 300,000 shares at $16.50 per share. In less than two years, the Wal-Mart stock had quadrupled in value, and in August 1972, the company was listed on the New York Stock Exchange. Wal-Mart opened its first pharmacy and established the Wal-Mart Foundation to fulfill philanthropic priorities in 1978 and 1979, respectively.

Chasing rapid growth and success, in 1980, Wal-Mart reached $1 billion in annual sales, faster than any other retail store at the time. Wal-Mart had 276 stores employing 21,000 associates. There was no looking back for the Waltons as they kept reaching new heights of success by always improving and upgrading the Wal-Mart chain. In 1987, Sam and his wife

Helen Walton inaugurated the Walton Family Foundation, which is a family-led foundation dedicated to giving back to the community.

By 1990, Wal-Mart was America's number-one retailer, and the company was taken global in 1991 through a joint venture with a Mexican retail company, Cifra. In 1992, Sam wrote a book *Made in America*,[33] in which he stated,

> The larger truth that I failed to see turned out to be another of those paradoxes—like the discounter's principle of the less you charge, the more you'll earn. And here it is: the more you share profits with your associates—whether it's in salaries or incentives or bonuses or stock discounts—the more profit will accrue to the company. Why? Because the way management treats the associates is exactly how the associates will then treat the customers. And if the associates treat the customers well, the customers will return again and again, and that is where the real profit in this business lies, not in trying to drag strangers into your stores for one-time purchases based on splashy sales or expensive advertising. Satisfied, loyal, repeat customers are at the heart of Wal-Mart's spectacular profit margins, and those customers are loyal to us because our associates treat them better than salespeople in other stores do. So, in the whole Wal-Mart scheme of things, the most important contact ever made is between the associate in the store and the customer.

Death of the Walton brothers. In 1992, Sam Walton passed away, leaving his eldest son Robson Walton to take over as chairman until 2015. A few years later, in 1995, Bud Walton also died. The two brothers' relationship was very loving and loyal, instilled in them since childhood as their mother Nancy Walton always encouraged them to stay close to each other. When the brothers reflected on their relationship, they said it was a great professional and family relationship where the key element was respect for each other.[34]

Leadership

- *Chairman.* Following the death of Sam Walton, his son Robson Walton served as the Chairman until 2015. The same year Gregory B. Penner was elected as chairman of the Wal-Mart board of directors. He is the third person to serve in this position, following his father-in-law Rob Walton and founder Sam Walton.
- *CEO.* David Glass, who was named CEO in 1988, worked his way up from the time he joined Wal-Mart in 1976 as executive vice president and was elected to be on the board of directors a year later in 1977. He was then promoted to become the president of the retailer in 1984. He retired from the CEO post at Wal-Mart in 2000 but remained on the company's board of directors, where he chaired the executive committee until 2006. In 2000, H. Lee Scott, Jr. succeeded David Glass as CEO followed by Mike Duke, who became the next CEO in 2009. In 2014, Doug McMillon succeeded Mike Duke as CEO, and he currently holds the position.
- *Walton family members today.* The Walton family is one of the richest families in America with a net worth of $212 billion according to *Forbes* magazine. Sam Walton had four children (see Figure 1.6): Samuel Robson (Rob), John Thomas, James (Jim) Carr, and Alice Louise. Unfortunately, John passed away in a plane crash in 2005. Bud Walton had two daughters: Ann and Nancy. Today, to name a few Walton family members, Rob, Jim, Alice, Christy (John's wife), Lucas (John's son), Ann, and Nancy own almost half of Wal-Mart's shares according to the Bloomberg Billionaires Index. The Walton family members who serve on the Wal-Mart Inc. board of directors are Rob, Steuart (Jim's son), and Gregory B. Penner (Rob's son-in-law). As mentioned previously, the Walton family has other

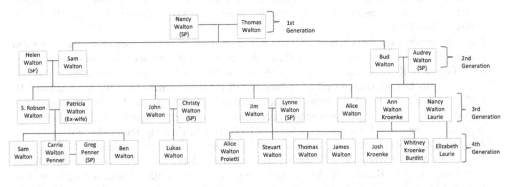

Figure 1.6 Walton family tree.

established ventures to take care of: Jim serves as chairman of Arvest Bank, and a few third-generation family members—Annie Proietti (Jim's daughter), Carrie Walton Penner (Rob's daughter), Lukas (John's son), and Thomas (Jim's son)—sit on the board of directors of the Wal-Mart Family Foundation.

Discussion questions:

1 Why has the Wal-Mart family business succeeded?
2 What are the family resources and capabilities that Wal-Mart has possessed across generations?
3 How difficult could it have been for Wal-Mart competitors to replicate Wal-Mart's competitive advantages?
4 Considering the different types of family businesses, how has the Wal-Mart family business evolved across generations?

Notes

1 The classification presented here is general and could vary from one country to another based on the legal system.
2 More information about the world's top 750 family business ranking can be found in Family Capital. Information retrieved from https://www.famcap.com/2022/08/the-worlds-top-750-family-businesses-ranking-2022/
3 Wal-Mart website. Information retrieved from https://corporate.walmart.com/leadership/doug-mcmillon
4 Emi-G Knitting, Inc. website. Information retrieved from www.emi-gknitting.com/
5 Food Matters Live. (2021). From the world of finance to award-winning plant-based gelato makers. Article retrieved from https://foodmatterslive.com/podcast/from-the-world-of-finance-to-award-winning-plant-based-gelato-makers/
   Devlin, E. (2021). Beau's secures £400k to bring vegan ice cream to wider audience. *The Grocer*. Article retrieved from www.thegrocer.co.uk/fundraising/beaus-secures-400k-to-bring-vegan-ice-cream-to-wider-audience/655368.article
6 More information about the board members can be found on the Roche's website: www.celebratelife.roche.com/explore/culture/moment-with-hoffmann-duschmale/

7 Basco, R., Stough, R., & Suwala, L. (Eds.) (2021). *Family Business and Regional Development*. Retrieved from https://library.oapen.org/bitstream/id/d815531f-58f4-4cb3-9493-ad4e795525b0/9780429058097.pdf

8 For more information about family business impact at regional and national levels the reader can explore the following publications: (1) Basco, R. (2018). Family Business in Emerging Markets. In R. Grosse & K. E. Meyer (Eds.), *The Oxford Handbook of Management in Emerging Markets* (pp. 527–546). Oxford: Oxford University Press. (2) Pieper, T., Kellermanns, F. W., & Astrachan J. H. (2021). Update 2021: Family businesses' contribution to the U.S. Economy. Family Enterprise USA. Report retrieved from https://familyenterpriseusa.com/wp-content/uploads/2021/02/Family-Businesses-Contribution-to-the-US-Economy_v.02202021-FINAL.pdf. (3) Bjuggren, C. M., Johansson, D., & Sjögren, H. (2011). A note on employment and gross domestic product in Swedish family-owned businesses: A descriptive analysis. *Family Business Review*, 24(4), 362–371. (4) Basco, R., Ghaleb, F., Gómez Ansón, S., Hamdan, R., Malik, S., & Martínez García, I. (2020). Ownership Concentration in Listed Firms in the Gulf Cooperation Council: Implications for Corporate Governance. *Family Business in the Arab World Observatory*. American University of Sharjah, Sharjah, UAE. Report retrieved from https://familyfirmblog.files.wordpress.com/2020/09/ownership-concentration-report.pdf

9 Frank, H., Lueger, M., Nosé, L., & Suchy, D. (2010). The concept of 'Familiness': Literature review and systems theory-based reflections. *Journal of Family Business Strategy*, 1(3), 119–130.

10 Information retrieved from www.gotrum.com/editorials/exclusive-interviews/exclusive-interview-with-eduardo-bacardi-ron-del-barrilito/ and www.forbes.com/sites/taranurin/2019/04/28/members-of-the-worlds-biggest-rum-family-work-to-preserve-a-centuries-old-competitor/?sh=5deb94b34348

11 Information retrieved from several website's sources: (1) www.businessinsider.com/mars-inc-family-fortune-net-worth-lifestyle-snickers-twix-2019-3, (2) www.forbes.com/profile/jacqueline-mars/?sh=60f877af5f9b, (3) www.mars.com/news-and-stories/articles/leadership-life-lessons-stephen-badger, (4) www.bbh.com/us/en/insights/private-banking-insights/110-years-of-family-business-ownership-a-conversation-with-victoria-mars.html, and (5) www.scmp.com/magazines/style/celebrity/article/3140034/meet-mars-family-notoriously-private-billionaire-heirs?module=perpetual_scroll_0&pgtype=article&campaign=3140034

12 Information retrieved from https://sg.finance.yahoo.com/news/roles-and-responsibilities-of-the-ambani-kids-105911442.html?guccounter=1&guce_referrer=aHR0cHM6Ly93d3cuZ29vZ2xlLmNvbbS8&guce_referrer_sig=AQAAANt34JnIBTC5Y37-5xDiMixUXVK_Em1gQS-S3POLnhZ6P_xe_0Gbhbx1xL1rQngLxcGw7SxIAbK5Q8ZMimtT-sJyjJZlLiJGLw3_rY-MLOteRUhcGwo2TqpJ8OKq9FORCMzz-xMsPAf3iHFO3lzjduISa1wlwxerE-FoYe4vlq0n

13 To know more about Dot Foods Inc. you can explore their history in this website www.dotfoods.com/about/dot-foods-history/the-dot-foods-timeline/

14 *Tharawat Magazine*. (2017). Guittard Chocolate Company—The happy balance between innovation and tradition. Article retrieved from www.tharawat-magazine.com/pursuit-of-happiness/guittard-chocolate-company/. Additional information can be found on the Guittard Chocolate Company: www.guittard.com/our-company

15 Grzelewski, J. (2021). Ford shareholders OK new generation of family members for board. *The Detroit News*. Article retrieved from www.detroitnews.com/story/business/autos/ford/2021/05/13/ford-shareholders-ok-adding-new-generation-family-members-board/5070922001/
Additional information retrieved from www.forbes.com/profile/ford/?sh=68a9a0ff2ae3

16 *Tharawat Magazine*. (2018). Picchiotti—Success by Design. Interview with Giuseppe Picciotti. Interview available in the following website www.tharawat-magazine.com/roles-in-the-family-business/profiles-picchiotti-jewellery/. More information can be found on the Picchiotti website: www.picchiotti.it/en/heritage/

17 *Tharawat Magazine*. (2017). Crane & C0. 0 Mills, Money, and Mindfulness. Interview available in the following website www.tharawat-magazine.com/pursuit-of-happiness/crane-and-co/

18 Hoverd, L. (2020). Carabali Rainforest Park: Sharing Puerto Rico's beauty and resiliency with the world. Article retrieved from www.tharawat-magazine.com/stories/carabali-rainforest-park/

19 Sekulich, T. (2019). Mitchell stores: Putting people first and the science of hugging. *Tharawat Magazine*. Article retrieved from www.tharawat-magazine.com/hiring-firing-43/special-features-hiring-firing-43/jack-mitchell-hug-people/

20 Basco, R. et al. (2021). Weathering the storm: Family firm strategies in the midst of growing uncertainty. STEP Project Global Consortium. Report retrieved from https://familyfirmblog.files.wordpress.com/2021/09/covid19_report___middle_east_and_africa-v5.pdf

21 *Tharawat Magazine*. (2016). Innovation: Alessi—A family business designing the future. Issue 29. Article retrieved form www.tharawat-magazine.com/emotional-intelligence/alessi-future-design/

22 For more information of Kelkar Group the reader can explore the following website: (1) www.business-standard.com/company/s-h-kelkar-co-23313/information/company-history and (2) Viera, W. (2015). Hope for the best, prepare for the worst—The difficulties of succession. *Tharawat Magazine*. Article retrieved from www.tharawat-magazine.com/sustain/succession-difficulties/

23 Viera, W. (2015). Hope for the best, prepare for the worst—The difficulties of succession. *Tharawat Magazine*. Article retrieved from www.tharawat-magazine.com/sustain/succession-difficulties/. Additional information can be found on the following websites: (1) www.business-standard.com/company/s-h-kelkar-co-23313/information/company-history, (2) https://economictimes.indiatimes.com/industry/cons-products/fashion-/-cosmetics-/-jewellery/family-owned-fragrance-maker-sh-kelkar-company-gets-outsider-on-board-as-ceo/articleshow/16536262.cms, and (3) www.forbesindia.com/article/hidden-gems/sh-kelkar-co-infusing-fragrance-in-lives/38260/1

24 Lipsky-Karasz, E. (2021). Why Marta Ortega Pérez is the secret to Zara's success. *The Wall Street Journal Magazine*. Article retrieved from www.wsj.com/articles/why-marta-ortega-perez-is-the-secret-to-zaras-success-11630413099

25 Information retrieved from www.tharawat-magazine.com/hiring-firing-43/special-features-hiring-firing-43/jack-mitchell-hug-people/ and www.familybusinessmagazine.com/proceeding-cautiously-family-hiring-0

26 Kuligowski, K. (2022). The right way to hire and work with family. *Business News Daily*. Article retrieved from www.morningdough.com/business-marketing/how-to-hire-and-work-with-family-survive/. Additional information can be found on website: https://pinchspicemarket.com/about-us/

27 To know more about the Estee Lauder visit the following website: www.elcompanies.com/en/who-we-are/the-lauder-family

28 Explore why Lauder family is a family in business in the following video: www.elcompanies.com/en/who-we-are/the-lauder-family/a-family-in-business

29 Hevesi, D., & Ewing, J. (2014). Karl Albrecht, a founder of Aldi stores, dies at 94. *The New York Times*. Article retrieved from www.nytimes.com/2014/07/22/business/karl-albrecht-a-reclusive-founder-of-aldi-dies-at-94.html

30 This example discussion is developed solely as the basis for class discussion. This example discussion is not intended to serve as an endorsement, source of primary data, or illustration of effective or ineffective management.
     Ninan, T. N. (1986). Birla group divides business, Aditya's branch of the family gets lion's share information retrieved from. *India Today*. Article retrieved from www.indiatoday.in/magazine/economy/story/19860930-birla-group-divides-business-aditya-branch-of-the-family-gets-lion-share-801286-1986-09-30.

31 This example discussion is developed solely as the basis for class discussion. This example study discussion is not intended to serve as an endorsement, source of primary data, or illustration of effective or ineffective management.

32 This case study discussion was developed solely as the basis for class discussion. This case study discussion is not intended to serve as an endorsement, source of primary data, or illustration of effective or ineffective management.

33 Walton, S., & Huey, J. (1993). *Sam Walton: Made in America*. Bantam Books, New York.

34 Information retrieved from www.youtube.com/watch?v=gc5oVVF7Vu0

2 Family business dynamics

Individual needs, goals, expectations, and emotions

Learning objectives

*   Distinguish among individuals' needs, goals, expectations, and emotions in family businesses.
*   Understand the dynamics of family businesses by focusing on individuals and their interactions.
*   Recognize different family members' roles and their implication for family businesses.
*   Identify the three-circle model as an instrument to explore the complexity of family businesses.
*   Interpret emotions and their importance in family businesses.

2.1 Introduction

In Chapter 1, we learned that family businesses are a unique form of organization because family involvement in these firms affects the way they are owned, governed, and managed. Additionally, after reading Chapter 1, we know that family businesses are not a homogenous group of firms, so we are thus able to recognize different types of family businesses. However, we may wonder about the dynamics of family businesses because these firms are constantly changing and developing across time.

The nature of the family business as a system emerges from integrating three main entities: the ownership, business (also called management), and family entities. It is through these three entities that a patterned network of relationships constituting a coherent whole called a family business emerges. The source of the dynamics of family businesses stems from this interconnected web of relationships. Therefore, any effort to own, manage, lead, or advise family businesses requires understanding various individuals' needs, goals, expectations, and emotions across the three entities.

The aim of this chapter is to gain a deeper understanding of each entity comprising the family business system, their overlap, and the individuals who integrate the system by occupying unique roles across each entity.

2.2 The three-circle model

One of the most important tools to understand the dynamics of family businesses is the three-circle model.[1] The three-circle model is a useful and practical instrument that helps visually interpret and understand the family business concept by depicting the level of overlap between the ownership, management, and family entities (see Figure 2.1). This instrument separates businesses into two different entities, along with the family: ownership and management. Each

DOI: 10.4324/9781003273240-3

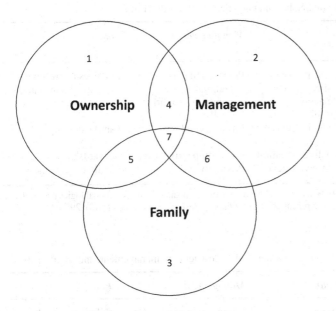

Figure 2.1 The three-circle model.

Notes: The Three-Circle Model of the Family Business System was developed by Renato Tagiuri and John Davis at Harvard Business School, and was circulated in working papers starting in 1978. It was first published in Davis' doctoral dissertation, The Influence of Life Stages on Father-Son Work Relationships in Family Companies, in 1982.

Source: This version of the figure was adapted from Tagiuri, R., & Davis, J. (1996). Bivalent attributes of the family firm. *Family Business Review*, 9(2), 199–208.

entity—ownership, management, and family—has its own logic by which individuals make sense of and develop their activities. Tables 2.1 and 2.2 summarize the main logic of each entity in terms of the characteristics of internal and external interactions and the components of these interactions.

The internal and external interactions in family businesses are characterized by different practices, purposes, strategies, and performance (see Table 2.1). By diversifying their investment portfolios, owners attempt to discover and exploit economic and financial opportunities to preserve and increase their wealth. By creating, developing, and implementing competitive strategies, managers attempt to look for competitive market positions to guarantee firm survival. Finally, by developing a stewardship strategy, family members attempt to preserve personal bonds and relationships that guarantee family stability and cohesiveness.

There are three types of interaction components (see Table 2.2) that define the nature of interactions within each entity. Emotional components are related to the feelings and physiological states that emerge or result from consistent or inconsistent interactions. Cognitive components are related to the memory repository of past interactions that includes beliefs, perceptions, and judgments about the family business. Finally, normative components are implicit or explicit rules of interaction emerging from social standards, cultural influences, and rule of law. The emotional, cognitive, and normative components of family business interactions determine the interpersonal relationships among individuals (behavior) within each entity and with individuals who belong to other entities.

Table 2.1 Differences between the ownership, management, and family entities

Internal and External Interactions	Ownership	Management	Family
Practices	Practices to fund and exploit economic and financial opportunities	Practices to gain and maintain a competitive market position	Practices to preserve personal bonds and relationships
Purpose	Preserve and increase wealth	Firm survival	Family stability
Strategy	Portfolio diversification	Firm competitiveness	Stewardship
Performance	Return on investment	Productivity	Family cohesiveness

Source: Adapted from Basco, R. (2019). What kind of firm do you owner-manage? An institutional logics perspective of individuals' reasons for becoming an entrepreneur. *Journal of Family Business Management*, 9(3), 297–318.

Table 2.2 Differences in the interaction components of the ownership, management, and family entities

Interaction Components	Ownership	Management	Family
Emotional components	Speculative	Competition and aggressiveness	Submission and love
Cognitive components	Firm as a means to increase owners' wealth	Firm as a means to boost managers' image	Firm as a means to care for family members
Normative components	Regulated by the capital market	Regulated by the market (as a place for economic transactions)	Regulated by tradition and legacy

Source: Adapted from Basco, R. (2019). What kind of firm do you owner-manage? An institutional logics perspective of individuals' reasons for becoming an entrepreneur. *Journal of Family Business Management*, 9(3), 297–318.

The overlap of the three entities forms the family business system, which in turn shapes the components of internal and external interactions. The ideal logic of each entity described above is diluted when the three entities overlap. However, the overlap of the three entities varies in terms of degree and complexity from one family business to another. The degree of overlap is determined by individuals who belong to more than one entity simultaneously. Therefore, the overlapping roles that individuals perform create communication channels and, consequently, blurred boundaries among the entities. In other words, individuals can have positions with no overlap (Areas 1, 2, and 3 in Figure 2.1), with at least two overlaps (Areas 4, 5, and 6 in Figure 2.1), or with three overlaps (Area 7 in Figure 2.1). On the other hand, the complexity of a family business is determined by the number of individuals in each of the entities and, specifically, in the overlapping areas. When overlapping areas are filled with new individuals and the number of family members increases, the family business dynamics develop and evolve.

The three-circle model not only identifies the number of key participants in each entity and in the overlapping areas but also reflects the components of the internal and external interactions in the new system called a family business. The emotional, cognitive, and normative components of each entity combine and evolve, together competing to impose their logics by defining the key individuals' focus of attention (the predominant logic) and shaping their behavioral patterns (influencing decision-making). For instance, when a mother is approaching retirement as CEO and has to define her business's ownership and management succession, the family logic and the business logic are likely going to compete (nepotism versus merit pressures from two different entities) in the selection of the best possible successor. One of the logics will have more influence or the logics will combine to define the outgoing CEO's focus of attention and ultimate decision.

It is possible to observe the complexity of family businesses by considering the combined responsibilities, decision-making tasks, and actions of family members due to being part of one or more of the overlapping areas. While some of the responsibilities, decision-making tasks, and actions related to exercising their roles may complement each other, others may contradict each other. For instance, one of a parent's responsibilities is to take care of his or her children and provide them with similar/equal opportunities to achieve their goals independently regardless of their children's skills and capabilities. However, one of a manager's responsibilities is to be transparent with his or her employees and treat them with respect, but the employees' capabilities, skills, commitment, and performance are important elements for promotion and compensation. Having these two responsibilities, how should parents (as owners and/or managers) behave toward their children's intentions to enter the family firm and to develop their careers in the family business? How should parents balance these two responsibilities that have different logics—management and family logics?

In the next subsections, we dive into how roles shape needs, goals, expectations, and emotions to further explore family business complexity.

2.2.1 Roles

Each individual belonging to one of the entities in the three-circle model has particular and unique roles. Every role has responsibilities according to the position an individual has in the family business system. Roles emerge from the position that individuals occupy in the three-circle model. Belonging to one of the three main entities creates specific roles that individuals have to fulfill. The ownership role is to define the long-term vision of the firm and make key strategic decisions without being engaged in the firm's day-to-day activities. The management role is to plan, organize, lead, and control the firm's day-to-day operations by implementing a specific strategy to achieve the organizational (owner) goals. Finally, the family role depends on the position that one has within the family household: parents or caregivers have to assume the role of nurturer, cheerleader, and truth teller, whereas children's role is to participate and indulge in family activities, learn essential values, and care for each other.

While the roles that emanate from each of the entities and the positions within them are important, the most critical aspect of a family business relates to those individuals who have to play multiple roles simultaneously within the family business system—that is, those individuals who belong to the overlapping areas (Areas 4, 5, 6, and 7 in Figure 2.1). The fact that the roles overlap is not a challenge per se since every human being has different roles to play to belong to different societal institutions. However, in family business, these roles have to be performed in situations and places where there is no clear demarcation of what roles individuals should play.

Family members have to understand the complexity of their roles across situations, contexts, and places to avoid a mismatch between their role(s) and a specific context. Performing a role in the wrong context could have negative implications for the stability of each entity and the family business system as a whole. For instance, imagine a family sitting at the dinner table having an intense discussion about the family firm. While the conversation is within the family context, the ownership and management roles of some of the participants may also emerge and could be even more relevant than their family roles. This kind of conversation could be a source of competitive advantage for the family firm by creating agile decision-making, instilling knowledge about the firm in the children, and developing a sense of belonging. However, the mismatch between roles and context could jeopardize interpersonal relationships and create conflict. The father may not communicate in his father role but instead in his managerial role; the mother could assume the family role by defending one party or another (i.e., father versus children) to avoid conflict escalation; and the children, even if they work in the firm, could assume their family role in the conversation. Finally, the conversation could have substantial noise that jeopardizes each individual's understanding.

2.2.2 Goals

Each individual belonging to one or more entities of the three-circle model has particular goals. Goals are aims or targets that an individual wants to achieve depending on his or her position in the family business system. Ownership, management, and family goals define the target individual's plan to achieve in a particular period of time.

Personal goals emerge from the influence of the entities (ownership, management, and family) to which family members belong. In the nonoverlapping areas, each entity exerts a certain pressure on family members to align their personal goals with the entity goals. In other words, the ownership, management, and family logics define individuals' focus of attention and activate their personal goals, which ultimately define their behavior. The primary goal of the ownership entity is to maximize profits while developing corporate sustainability. The primary goal of the management entity is to implement the best strategy to fulfill the owners' goals and preserve business sustainability by satisfying the needs of all stakeholders. Finally, the primary goal of the family entity is to achieve a cohesive, harmonious, and united group of individuals such that each family member can develop his or her economic, personal, and social skills.

As goals emanate from each of the entities, in the overlapping areas, individuals are under the umbrella of two or three institutional logics that compete to influence the dominant goals. It is in these overlapping areas where family members have to deal with different pressures and balance these pressures to prioritize goals. While some ownership, management, and family goals complement each other, other goals contradict and compete with each other. The most difficult challenge for family members whose roles overlap across entities is balancing the different goals they have to achieve and prioritizing them (if necessary) across different contexts and circumstances.

A constellation of goals emerges from the interaction of the family and the business wherein multiple institutional logics (ownership, management, and family) exert their influence over individuals. While the ownership and management logics define the business-oriented goals, the family logic defines the family-oriented goals.

- *Business-oriented goals* are related to the economic/financial aspects of the business, such as meeting or enhancing profit in terms of financial ratios and growing the business by capturing new markets or increasing market share. These goals also relate to the business's stakeholders, ensuring the family business fulfills its ethical, cultural, and social responsibilities for employees, customers, and the local community.
- *Family-oriented goals* are related to ensuring the family's monetary and cash requirements are fulfilled and to retaining firm management and ownership control in family hands. In addition, these goals deal with ensuring harmony between the business and the family in terms of their image, reputation, and communication as well as developing entrepreneurial spirit and interest in the business across generations.

2.2.3 Psychological needs

Family members belonging to one or more areas in the three-circle model have specific psychological needs that motivate them to identify with the family business. There are six psychological needs that motivate identification with the family business: self-esteem, continuity, distinctiveness, meaning, self-efficacy, and belonging. These psychological needs that fulfill individual family members' self-concept are associated with the family business's reputation, image, and shared values. This association is due to the strong emotional and cognitive connections between the family business and family members.

- *Self-esteem*. In this context, self-esteem refers to the confidence family members have regarding their own worth and abilities; it revolves around oneself and a positive emotional status. Identification with the family business may enhance family and nonfamily members' status, prestige, and reputation. Additionally, identification with the family business tends to increase family members' self-esteem because of the common values that both family members and the family firm share.
- *Continuity*. This need is about maintaining a sense of belonging to the past, present, and future within one's self-concept. To fulfill the need of continuity in oneself, the family business plays an important role. Family members' identification with shared values, legacy, transgenerational entrepreneurship, and the family story increases their sense of continuity.
- *Distinctiveness*. This need refers to differentiating oneself from others and looking for uniqueness when constructing the concept of oneself. Identification with the family business makes family members different from other individuals within their networks. For instance, shared values, image, legacy, and a common story are elements that make family members unique and fulfill their need for distinctiveness. Members of a successful family business tend to feel different or special compared to others due to the success of their family's entrepreneurial venture, which gives them confidence, pride, and wealth.
- *Meaning*. Meaning refers to finding one's purpose for existence in the concept of oneself. The need for meaning motivates family members to connect with the family business to look for a meaningful sense for their lives. For instance, the next generation of young family business members at crossroads of either joining the family business or choosing a different career path should consider the career option that would fulfill their psychological need for meaning.
- *Self-efficacy*. This need is about one's belief in his or her capacity to execute a behavior and achieve particular results. The need of self-efficacy could motivate family members in the family business to ensure the continuity of the family business, maintain the legacy of the family, and develop the spirit of transgenerational entrepreneurship.
- *Belonging*. This need is about the feeling of closeness and the importance of maintaining interpersonal relationships. Belonging could motivate the group (i.e., the family and the business) to join forces around common values, goals (e.g., family image and reputation), and identity.

Even though we highlight the positive connection between family members' psychological needs and the family business, in particular contexts or circumstances, psychological needs may not facilitate family members' identification with the family business and could even have the opposite effect by demotivating family members from connecting with the family business. For instance, a recent study showed that less than 10% of students who belong to a business family want to pursue a career within their family firms. When investigating the reasons behind this

Table 2.3 Summary of the main roles, needs, goals, and expectations based on individuals' positions in the three-circle model

Area in the Three-Circle Model	Individual Roles	Individual Psychological Needs	Individual Goals	Individual Expectations
Area 3: Family members who are neither shareholders nor business managers.	Patterns of behavior by which individuals fulfill family functions as grandfather, grandmother, father, mother, son, or daughter to provide moral support, motivation, and wisdom.	Identification with the firm satisfies the needs of belonging and meaning.	Have an intact and cohesive family, maintain harmonious family relationships, and provide support to all family members equally.	Expectations to be respected and loved and to be treated equally compared to all other family members.
Area 5: Shareholders who are family members but are not involved in the family business.	Two roles are combined: owner and family. Owner: oversees the firm's financial performance, monitors the long-term value proposition of the firm and its survival, and controls the risk assumed by the managers. Family: guides family managers and employees to be responsible owners.	Identification with the firm satisfies the need of belonging.	Goals as an owner: maximize the return on investment, guarantee dividends, and sustain the family business's control and legacy. Goals as a family member: Use the family business as a means to fulfill the family's financial needs.	Expectations to influence decisions as a form of power and control and being an owner while also being treated with equal respect and love among peers.
Area 4: Nonfamily employees or managers who own shares.	Participate in important organizational decisions, discuss, and vote for the board of directors (with enough shares), ensure effective and efficient business operations.	Identification with the firm satisfies the needs of self-efficacy and self-esteem as well as the need of belonging.	Ensure high business performance, gain high dividend yields, and maintain a competitive family business across generations.	Expectations to hold management and leadership accountable for successfully implementing a business strategy that maximizes their own returns on investment.

Area 6: Family members involved in the family business without owning shares.	Two roles are combined: family manager/employee and family member. Family manager/employee: participate in daily family business operations while developing their own skills, capabilities, and competencies. Family member: fulfill family functions as grandfather, grandmother, father, mother, son, or daughter.	Family members who are developing a managerial career in the firm embrace identification with the firm to satisfy psychological needs related to their careers (self-esteem and self-efficacy) and more general needs, such us meaning and belonging.	Learn in-depth family business operations, master the skills and competencies to manage the family business, and develop a career path. As a family member, use the family firm to fulfill their professional career path.	Expectations to be a valuable resource for the family business while being respected and appreciated.
Area 7: Family members who are shareholders and involved in managing the business.	Have a 360-degree view of the three systems and perform roles consistent with the context and circumstances.	Since these family members assume three roles, it is expected that their identification with the firm satisfies the need of continuity.	Guide the family business toward success by achieving family cohesiveness, sustainable performance, and a competitive business model.	Expectations to be a leader to ensure the continuity of the family business across generations.

Notes: This table represents a generalization. In the real life, family members' needs, goals, and expectations vary and should be evaluated in each case to understand the consequences for the family business dynamics.

attitude, it was discovered that some psychological needs might also operate as disengagement triggers toward a family business. In this sense, looking for independence from their own family group to fulfill their need for distinctiveness reduces some family members' identification with the family business. In the same direction, high self-efficacy could broaden family members' horizons beyond the family business.[2]

2.2.4 Expectations

Each individual belonging to one or more entities of the three-circle model has particular expectations. Expectations refer to the hope or belief an individual has about something he or she wants to happen. Unlike goals, which require a plan to achieve, expectations are simple feelings that can be related to the outcomes of situations or the actions of people.

Individuals' expectations emerge from a combination of their positions in the three-circle model, the cultural patterns that connect the focal family and business, and the interpersonal interactions among participants. One's role within the three-circle model also generates expectations about oneself and others' expectations for oneself. For example, a parent's role is implicitly associated with expectations to embrace family well-being. Although this concept may seem universal, family well-being could have different meanings, and the way to achieve family well-being could also vary from one culture to another. For instance, in 2015, Eurostat statistics showed that 34% of Spanish individuals between the ages of 25 and 34 admitted they are not independent of their parents. This number contrasted with other European countries, such as Sweden, where young adults left home earlier than those from the rest of the European countries. Expectations about children's independence differ in both countries. Finally, beyond individual roles and cultural differences, interpersonal relationships among individuals who belong to the family business system could alter individuals' expectations of themselves.

Even though all individuals have to manage various expectations, in the context of a family business, the challenge is to simultaneously manage different expectations in the overlapping areas. As mentioned, the parental role has associated expectations to embrace family well-being, but due to their managerial positions, parents also have associated expectations related to the family firm's long-term survival. The challenge is to manage the contradicting expectations. There are two types of contradicting expectations.

The first type of contradicting expectations relates to the alignment of one's own expectations with others' expectations of one's role—for instance, the degree of adjustment between a father's expectations of his role as a father and his daughter's expectations of his role as a father. The second type of contradicting expectations relates to the alignment of one's own expectations with others' expectations about one's expectations. Returning to the father example, this refers to the degree of adjustment between the father's expectations for his role as a father and his perception about the expectations that his daughter has about his role as a father.

2.3 The evolutionary perspective of the three-circle model

The three-circle model provides a static image of a family business's complexity based on the number of key individuals who are part of the family business and their positions across the whole system. The higher the number of overlapping positions within an entity, the more permeable the entity's boundaries, meaning that the ownership, family, and management logics have to be integrated and managed. However, the complexity of a family business can also be viewed as a dynamic process of complexity by taking a look at the lifecycle of each entity across time.

Each entity has its own pattern and pace of development. The family entity evolves from a nuclear family to an extended family, and this evolution affects the family business's complexity. Here, complexity is related to the number of family members (with blood or in-law relationships) who incorporate into the different positions within the family system. That is, as the family evolves, more family members occupy overlapping positions and have to work together to balance the ownership, management, and family logics. In addition to the increasing number of family members within the boundaries of the family business system, the biological, emotional, and psychological changes individuals experience from childhood to retirement also affect their interpersonal relationships and family positions across time. For instance, the father–son relationship typically changes across time as the father becomes a grandfather and the son becomes a father in subsequent stages. Different roles in the family entity mean different goals, needs, expectations, and emotions.

The ownership lifecycle refers to the different stages of development related to the family business's ownership structure. This ownership structure is composed of the rights and duties of individuals who hold equity in the business. Similar to the family lifecycle, the ownership lifecycle is a consequence of the owners' decisions regarding the ownership structure, the inheritance law of the country in which the family business operates, and the evolution of the family lifecycle. Most family businesses start by having high ownership concentration in one or a few family members.

Family businesses then typically move to a sibling partnership (ownership) structure when the number of family members increases in the following generation. A sibling partnership structure means that the ownership is spread out among nuclear family members. The participation of parents and their children at the ownership level increases the diversity of the ownership group in terms of their preferences toward the family business. There is often divergence in opinion regarding strategic direction, goals, and the meaning of the family business for the family itself. In the subsequent stage, known as the cousin consortium, each sibling creates his or her own nuclear family. In the cousin consortium stage, there is a high dispersion of ownership within the family (ownership is fragmented in small parts across family branches and family members).

While the ownership lifecycle could seem like progressive development across stages (lone ownership or couple ownership, sibling partnership, and cousin consortium), in real life, these movements tend to be more complex because of the coexistence of multiple generations at the same time. While the existence of multiple generations is considered a consequence of the natural evolution of a family, the inheritance law, which directs how a person's assets are handed down to his or her descendants, is more restrictive in some countries than in others, thereby shaping the final ownership structure across generations. For instance, Islamic inheritance law establishes that sons inherit twice as much as daughters when one of their parents dies, which has critical consequences for the family business ownership structure in terms of power, rights, and responsibilities. When the inheritance law is less restrictive and there are mechanisms to coordinate the transfer of wealth from one generation to another, family members are able to decide how to distribute the family's entire wealth among descendants, including the ownership of the family business. This gives a business family flexibility to keep ownership in those family branches that are interested in the business while liberating family members who are not interested in the business.

Regarding the business lifecycle, the stages of typical business evolution generally move through startup to growth and establishment, expansion, and maturity. If the business is not able to regenerate its competitive advantages, the final stage is exit. The developmental stage of a family business is a consequence of the family's vision and decision-making. In other words, it depends on the extent to which family leaders are able and willing to navigate the growth process and manage the complexity of the firm.

The family business lifecycle is a tool to better understand the evolutionary dynamics of the three entities that form and are critical to the family business system. There is no one pattern of development; instead, there are multiple combinations across the family, ownership, and business lifecycles. The combination of the pattern of development of each entity has consequences for the way a family business is owned, governed, and managed.

2.4 Emotions in the family business

Emotions play an important role in the family entity because they are the building block of the family entity's existence. Emotional bonding, which is the bundle of subjective feelings that come together to create the bonds among family members, defines the level of family cohesion. Family cohesion is the barometer used to identify how healthy family interactions are in supporting individual independence and family togetherness. In this sense, the level of emotional competence in a family is critical because it represents the ability of family members to understand their own and others' emotions as well as to experience and regulate their emotions in accordance with appropriate roles and general formal/informal societal and cultural rules.

Family members, consciously or unconsciously, have to acknowledge, manage, and accept emotions to achieve a healthy level of family cohesion. A healthy level of family cohesion depends on how family members respond and react to emotions at the intrapersonal and interpersonal levels, which in turn affects their decision-making. Because a family business reflects the family behind it, family members, specifically those who are in overlapping areas, bring emotions that may constrain or expand their behavior and decision-making in the family business.

Contrary to common belief, emotions are not irrational and are actually part of the bounded rationality of one's decision-making. Emotions influence individuals' cognition and, consequently, their decision-making. Emotions represent an important dimension in business because for managers, leaders, and employees to perform their tasks, they have to address, manage, and control their emotions when interacting and engaging with other members. Emotions have intrapersonal effects in terms of individual performance, motivation, and creativity as well as effects on interpersonal relationships in terms of leadership, teamwork, negotiation, and communication. To explore emotions' influence on family businesses, it is important to understand what emotions mean and how they work.

What are emotions? Emotions are strong instinctive or intuitive feelings and momentary subjective experiences stemming from an individual's circumstances or relationships with others and are accompanied by physiological and behavioral changes. In other words, emotions are a psychological state that links an event (external or internal to an individual) to a person's goal-related concerns. In this sense, emotions prepare individuals for actions and responses to events within particular contexts or environments. Even though we can think of emotions as something subjective and intrapersonal, they are also social and interpersonal because emotions are relational. That is, emotions shape and are shaped by social interactions. It is important to differentiate the spectrum of emotions in terms of their time course and to distinguish them from related concepts, such as a person's mood or a trait. While emotions themselves are related to an object, subject, or event and last for minutes up to hours, mood refers to a psychological state that may last for hours, days, or weeks and is objectless. Certain traits can also appear to be emotions, but traits are related to an individual's personality and temperament, are long lasting in the individual, and contain emotions at their core by framing how individuals react to events.

How do emotions work? The framework of emotions in family businesses is shown in Figure 2.2. It illustrates an individual's process of emotions. Emotions emerge because an event happens outside the individual's context/environment or inside in the individual's mind. The event can be anything that happens to the individual and can take different forms, such as changes in the individual's contextual circumstances, changes in his or her relationship with an external object, alternations in the individual's body or thoughts, and results/consequences of an interaction with others or with him-/herself. A person can easily think about negative family events, such as rejection, betrayal, unjust treatment, exclusion or being ignored, and criticism, among others, or about positive events, such being protected, having a respected mentor, being supported and heard, and being recognized, among others. However, emotions are not positive or negative per se. Rather, an individual evaluates (appraises) an event and connects it with his or her own concerns (what matters to him or her). This evaluation links the effect of an event with the individual's objectives and prioritizes the individual's reactions and actions.

An individual's appraisal or evaluation of an event determines whether an emotion is positive or negative. The dichotomous approach to emotions is shown in Table 2.4. When an event happens, the three phases of appraisal activate—the primary, secondary, and tertiary appraisals. The primary appraisal, an automatic evaluation, prepares individuals to respond to threats and opportunities in the environment. For example, is the focal event relevant to one's goals/expectations? Whether or not an event is congruent to one's goals/expectations could generate positive or negative emotions. While the primary appraisal helps individuals recognize whether what happened is good or bad in accordance with their own goals/expectations, the secondary appraisal is socially constructed and reflective. There are eight dimensions of appraisal that can be used to evaluate emotions (see Table 2.5).

The first and secondary appraisals of an event trigger three types of emotional response patterns: physiological, psychological, and sociological. First, the physiological refers to the way the body reacts to an emotion—for instance, bodily expressions affecting one's face, voice,

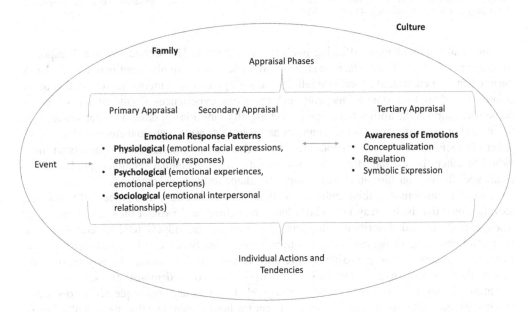

Figure 2.2 Framework to interpret emotions.

Table 2.4 Dichotomous approach to positive and negative emotions

Kind of Emotion	Positive Emotions	Negative Emotions
Emotions related to object properties	• Interest, curiosity • Attraction, desire, admiration • Surprise, amusement	• Alarm, panic • Aversion, disgust, revulsion • Indifference, familiarity, habituation
Future-appraisal emotions	• Hope	• Fear
Event-related emotions	• Gratitude, thankfulness • Joy, elation, triumph, jubilation • Relief	• Anger, rage • Sorrow, grief • Frustration, disappointment
Self-appraisal emotions	• Pride in achievement, self-confidence, sociability	• Embarrassment, shame, guilt, remorse
Social emotions	• Generosity • Sympathy	• Avarice, greed, miserliness, envy, jealousy • Cruelty
Cathected emotions	• Love	• Hate

Table 2.5 Dimensions of appraisal used to evaluate emotions

Attention	Degree to which one focuses on or thinks about an event
Centrality	Degree to which one believes that something is going to happen
Control	Degree to which one can control an event
Pleasantness	Degree to which an event is positive or negative
Obstacle	Degree to which one's objectives are blocked or in danger
Responsibility	Degree to which a person or an object is responsible for an event
Legitimacy	Degree to which an event is fair
Anticipated effort	Degree to which one's resources have to be used to respond to an event

Source: Adapted from Smith, C. A., & Ellsworth, P. C. (1985). Patterns of cognitive appraisal in emotion. *Journal of Personality and Social Psychology*, 48(4), 813–838.

and touch and brain changes affecting one's nervous system. The second emotional response pattern is psychological and relates to an emotion's effect on or involvement in one's mind. On the one hand, an emotional experience reflects the ability to create a mental representation of an emotion based on, for instance, imaginary feelings or past experiences. On the other hand, emotional perception is the ability to recognize and identify emotions in other. In other words, it is the mental process of emotions that connects an event to oneself. The final emotional response pattern is sociological, which is about the relational aspect of emotions that connects an individual to others by defining the nature and quality of interpersonal relationships. Emotions create specific relationships and relationships also shape individuals' emotions.

The tertiary appraisal is about individuals' awareness of emotions as a process of continued reevaluation—that is, the way individuals label, recognize, and explain their emotions. First, when explaining and describing emotional experiences, individuals tend to conceptualize their emotions using verbal language to communicate them. Second, individuals regulate their emotions by distracting, reappraising, suppressing, or controlling emotions. Finally, individuals express their emotions using symbolic expression, such as artistic demonstrations.

Emotions play a role in interpersonal family relationships and, consequently, in decision-making. For instance, succession is a critical event for family members that are part of a family business because it arouses different types of emotions in all participants. Several years ago,

I worked closely with next-generation family member, Amit, who was facing pressure from his father to join the family business. Amit grew up under authoritarian male-oriented leadership. When Amit's father first approached him to discuss Amit's university education and future development, his father discussed the importance of him taking over the family business in the future. Amit had no possibility to express his desires about the future because of the hierarchical culture he lived in and the vertical, one-direction (top-down) communication style of his father. Amit's first reaction was emotional disappointment because working in the family business went against his ambition to live in a Western country and dedicate his life to the arts. From this first conversation, Amit started a process of reflection. The event turned into a central issue for Amit, taking his attention and consuming his time and energy from anticipating the subsequent triggers of succession, all of which intensified the negative emotions around succession. The first and subsequent conversations that Amit had with his father created physiological reactions, such as arrhythmia and sweating. Psychological responses, such as intrusive memories and guilty feelings for not pleasing his father's expectations, also arose. Finally, Amit experienced sociological consequences in his interpersonal relationships. In this sense, Amit found refuge in his sister, who paradoxically wanted to join the family business, but being a woman put her outside the succession career. As a result, Amit and his sister developed a new bond between them. For the next five years, Amit lived the succession process as a chain of small repetitive events that repeatedly triggered emotions that affected his entire life. The consequences of this process affected Amit's personality and his relationship with the environment. Amit assumed leadership of the family business, but he described the future as follows: "I am waiting for my father to die to sell the business to my sister and be liberated from this heavy load after all."

It is important to recognize that the three phases of appraisal define individuals' actions and future tendencies. While emotions help individuals make rapid decisions in threatening or favorable situations and/or contexts, they also help individuals predict future events and their consequences based on past emotional reactions and expressions.

2.4.1 Emotions in family business across contexts

Even though emotions are generally common across all family members, what triggers emotions, how emotions are evaluated, and how family members respond to emotions differ across cultures, contexts, and specific family situations. For this reason, emotions need to be understood across different social contexts. There are several micro-institutions, such as family and religious organizations, and broad macro-contexts, such countries' cultures, that affect the way individuals evaluate events and express, recognize, and rationalize emotions. In the specific case of family businesses, the family context is an important institution in which emotions are created and maintained. Specifically, parents are responsible for socializing their children into familial and societal norms about emotions.

Children learn to discover, understand, regulate, and control emotions in social contexts. The primary socialization process of emotions occurs in the interpersonal relationships between parents and children—namely, in how parents talk to their children about emotions, how parents show emotions, and how parents respond to children's emotions. This means that children are exposed to their parents' emotions and learn how to manage emotions from their parents. The socialization process of emotions helps family members understand their own and others' emotions; interpret which emotions are desirable and undesirable to conform to normative roles, expectations, and values (culture); and express and manage emotions at the intrapersonal and interpersonal levels. In the socialization process, emotional contagion refers to the emotional learning that children undergo based on observing and perceiving their parents' emotions, which leads to the reflexive production of the same behavior in these children.[3] For instance, when a parent develops toxic emotional behaviors, they can negatively influence their children's emotional response patterns and eventually teach them the same toxic emotional behaviors.

2.5 Additional activities and reading material

2.5.1 Classroom discussion questions

1 Why is the three-circle model a useful tool to understand the dynamics of family businesses?
2 Why is it important to understand individuals' roles in family businesses?
3 Why are expectations, goals, and needs important in family businesses?
4 Are emotions rational or irrational?
5 Why and how do emotions affect decision-making?

2.5.2 Additional readings

1 Exter, N. & Turner, C. (2016). The value of family values. *The Guardian.* Article retrieved from www.theguardian.com/sustainability/blog/2016/may/26/the-value-of-family-values
2 Campden, F. B. (2023). Victoria Engelhorn: Becoming more than her family name. Article retrieved from www.campdenfb.com/article/victoria-engelhorn-becoming-more-her-family-name
3 Labaki, R., Michael-Tsabari, N., & Zachary, R. (2013). Exploring the emotional nexus in cogent family business archetypes. *Entrepreneurship Research Journal*, 3(3), 301–330. https://doi.org/10.1515/erj-2013-0034

2.5.3 Classroom activity

Aim: Recognize family members' roles across the three-circle model.
Material: A well-documented family who owns and manages a business with enough information about each member's position across the three entities (ownership, management, family). The instructor could use a case study or a film or could ask students to use their own family businesses to work on this exercise. Additionally, white A4-sized paper, colored pencils, and Post-it Notes are necessary for this exercise.
Running the classroom exercise:

- Step 1: Ask students to draw the three-circle model on a white A4-sized piece of paper.
- Step 2: Ask students to position each of the most relevant family members across the three circles' areas.
- Step 3: Ask students to describe the needs, goals, and expectations of the family members in their positions. The needs, goals, and expectations can be described based on general assumptions by considering the participants' roles, the explicit information coming from the case or film, and/or students' interpretation based on the information provided in the case study or film. For those students using their own family businesses, the needs, goals, and expectations for each family member can be deducted from their own knowledge and experience.

Discussion: Open the discussion so students can comment on their own work. It is important to begin a conversation to show how needs, goals, and expectations change across individuals, their positions, and their generations. Time should be included in this discussion as a dimensions that affects family members' needs, goals, and expectations.

Takeaways: Students should recognize the diversity of needs, goals, and expectations among family members. Additionally, if students are using the same case study or film, the instructor could highlight how one family member's needs, goals, and expectations can appear different to different observers (students). Finally, the instructor should highlight the importance of contextual dimensions, such as time, culture, generation, and type of family, among others, for understanding the needs, goals, and expectations among family members.

2.6 Case for analysis I: Pritzker family across generations[4]

Known to be one of the most powerful yet controversial families in the United States, this family business empire was started by Russian emigrant Nicholas Pritzker, who founded a law firm in Chicago called Pritzker. Eventually, his three sons Harry, Abraham Nicholas (A.N.), and Jack joined the law firm as they were all law graduates. As time passed, A.N. Pritzker got the family into investing. In particular, during the Great Depression, A.N. and Jack built the foundation of the family's wealth by buying real estate and acquiring troubled companies.

A.N. Pritzker and his sons Jay, Robert, and Donald created Hyatt and invested in the industrial conglomerate Marmon Group (acquired by Berkshire Hathaway). After A. N. Pritzker's death in 1986, his eldest son Jay Pritzker took over as chairman and led the family business empire with the support of his brothers, Robert and Donald (died in 1972). Jay was known for being a calm, modest, down-to-earth man who had an eye to acquire businesses that were profitable or that he could help reduce or eliminate taxes.

- Jay had five children: Nancy (died by suicide in 1972), Thomas, John, Daniel, and Gigi.
- Robert had five children: Jennifer, Linda, Karen (with his first wife Audrey), and Matthew and Liesel (with his second wife Irene, now divorced).
- Donald had three children: Penny, Anthony, and Jay Robert (J.B.).

In 1989, Jay made the decision to treat Liesel and Matthew as members of the fifth generation, to whom they were closer in age, not the fourth generation, to which they genealogically belonged. Thomas was the authorized trustee of all the Pritzker trusts, and in 1994, he gave up control of Matthew's and Liesel's trusts to Robert, who emptied out his two children's funds. Liesel and Matthew both had a rough relationship with their father Robert due to his unhappy marriage with their mother Irene.

In 1995, Jay gathered his family members, including his brother Robert, cousin Nicholas J., and four children. They were joined by Robert and Nicholas and six of Jay's nieces and nephews. Liesel, who was then 11, and Matthew, then 13, were not invited. Jay read a letter to them, which was almost like a will, that was signed by him and Robert. The letter stated that most of the family wealth was in trust-owned corporations, which would be distributed to family members to meet their reasonable needs from time to time. The trusts were designed to accumulate wealth to invest in the family business and to improve the family's position in terms of making philanthropic donations. The trusts were not meant to be treated as a source to build individual family members' wealth and make individual Pritzkers billionaires. Moreover, the letter also explicitly stated that the trusts were not to be broken up until the law governing trust perpetuities required it (suggested to be 2042). Jay made his succession plan clear with the letter, declaring that Thomas would step into his shoes as the chairman and head of the family, followed by Penny (Donald's daughter) and Nicholas J. (Jay's cousin, who was closer in age to Thomas and Penny) as vice chairpersons.

In 2003, 20-year-old Liesel filed a lawsuit against her father and the Pritzker family, accusing them of secretly using her trust fund, worth $1 billion, when she was a child. She also claimed that her father looted her trust fund as a result of his divorce from her mother in the mid-1990s. Liesel's elder brother Matthew eventually joined her in the lawsuit, making the same claims. In the suit, the siblings also claimed that some of their assets, including their Hyatt shares, were sold at prices substantially lower than market value to trusts benefiting other family members. Two years of fighting and disagreement between both parties finally resulted in a settlement where all 11 of the Pritzker cousins decided to equally share payments to Liesel and Matthew Pritzker, giving Liesel and Matthew control over about $450 million apiece. However, these allotments are considerably less than the estimated $1.3 billion that will be controlled by each of the 11 Pritzker cousins under a family breakup agreement reached several years ago.

Discussion questions:

1 How can you explain Liesel and Matthew's situation by considering needs, goals, expectations, and emotions?
2 How do you think needs, goals, and expectations have changed among family members across generations?
3 Look for more information about this family business and try to represent the family business life cycle by considering the ownership, management, and family life cycle.

2.7 Case for analysis II: The Henriquez Group[5]

The Henriquez Group was founded by Mario Cohen Henriquez, who was left an orphan along with his siblings at a very young age in Curacao at the beginning of the last century. In order to build a fortune for himself, he left his siblings behind to be looked after by his uncles and aunts and headed to Panama and then to El Salvador, where he started working in a German family-owned retail store. Fast forward to 1926, Mario embarked on his entrepreneurial journey and became the co-owner of the store along with Herbert De Sola. Together, the duo formed a partnership: De Sola–Henriquez. After several years, in 1951, Mario and his two sons Raul and Luis bought out De Sola and formed the company M.C. Henriquez & Co., which continued in the retail sector.

The family business survives today via the second and third generations. The family business does not have a specific core activity but is a holding company that has a portfolio of diverse investments. Mario was adamant about keeping the business in the family, and he knew just how to please his sons to continue in the family business. He knew his son Luis was interested in banking, so he bought shares in a bank, and his son Raul was passionate about coffee and agriculture, so he bought him a farm. In 1971, the civil war in El Salvador drove brothers Raul and Luis to move to Miami, where they had to begin from scratch. Although they got offices and were in search of business opportunities, times were difficult, which made the family, especially the brothers, stick together. Second-generation brothers Raul and Luis had the most loving and understanding relationship and were inseparable. They married cousin sisters who also shared a great bond, so the four of them were very close. Raul and Luis also shared the same bank account until Raul passed away. Overall, the two brothers set a great example on how to love and co-exist with family members personally as well as professionally in a family business. They led the family business in absolute harmony despite having different characters.

Today, the family business is in its third generation. In an interview with *Tharawat Magazine*, Raul's daughter Cristina expressed how it was difficult for her to cope with the deaths of both her parents and how she saw her Uncle Luis in a different light and was trying to understand her uncle's relationship with her father. Cristina's older brother has been involved in the business ever since the brothers had to start over in Miami, but the rest of the third generation is finding it difficult to understand each other and make the family business work. Luis wanted his and Raul's children to share the same bond he shared with Raul, but naturally, great bonds and feelings come from the heart and cannot be forced.

While the third-generation family members were still trying to decide on their level of involvement, Cristina was involved as a shareholder and the family council. The third generation felt pressured and guilty as they were not able to replicate the same love and bond as Luis and Raul shared. Cristina said, "We felt guilty that we could not love like them." Cristina even left the family business for a few years to gain perspective, during which time she became confident in herself and realized part of love is also fighting.

Discussion questions:

1 Why do you think Cristina feels guilty? Guilt is described as self-conscious emotion, so how can you explain her emotion?
2 Should the interpersonal relationships in different generations be the same? Why or why not?

2.8 Case study: Estee Lauder Companies[6]

Little Esty. It all started with a little girl named Josephine Esther Mentzer, who was called Esty. Esty inherited her Hungarian mother's beauty and her Slovakian father's entrepreneurial spirit. Her father was an immigrant in the United States, where he ran a small hardware store. Esty discovered her love and passion for makeup when her maternal uncle stayed at her place for a brief time and created velvety skin creams in the kitchen. Esty learned the art of inventing and applying fluffy skin creams on women's faces.

The journey from Esty Mentzer to Estée Lauder. Fast forward from Esty's youth: she met her husband Joseph Lauder in the late 1920s. The couple then tied the knot in 1930 and moved to Manhattan. Esty was an ambitious young woman who believed in transforming her passion for beauty into reality and took small steps toward her beauty empire by selling skin care products and makeup in beauty salons. Putting her in-born sales skills to use, Esty used to demonstrate her products to women while they were enjoying beauty treatments in salons. She had remarkable innate sales and marketing skills that arose from her knowledge of cosmetics and skin care, which helped her identify what women wanted.

She believed it was essential for her potential consumers to experience the touch and feel of her products on their faces and see the results for themselves. Due to her personal high-touch service, Esty's products received good feedback, which led her to officially launch her company with her husband in 1946. She decided to base her company's name on her name but with a slight variation: Estée Lauder. A year into the business, Esty and Joseph got their first major order: $800 worth of products from Saks Fifth Avenue. After this, they never looked back. Esty set a new benchmark for the "gift with purchase" marketing strategy, which has now become a standard industry practice. In addition, spreading her sales and marketing magic, Esty relied on the most trusted pre-social media marketing method—word-of-mouth campaigns. Her oft-repeated mantra was "Telephone, telegraph, tell a woman." She was confident that women who liked her products would spread the word. She chose the most chic and elegant packaging for her products to signify the sense of luxury her brand offered.

Esty was the ultimate inspiration for women in business. She attended the opening of all her new stores and overlooked each store's sales techniques and merchandise displays. Esty and her husband built one of the most innovative cosmetics companies all while juggling multiple roles as spouses, business partners, and parents to their two sons, who later joined and took over the family business legacy. In 1953, Esty tapped into the fragrance market with her innovative creation Youth-Dew, a bath oil that doubled as skin perfume. Youth-Dew happened to be a game changer for the Estée Lauder company, transforming the startup into a multi-million-dollar business. Esty retired in 1995 and passed away in 2004.

When the second generation stepped in:

Leonard A. Lauder (chairman emeritus). After attending Columbia Graduate School of Business and serving as a lieutenant in the US Navy, Esty's oldest son Leonard joined the family business in 1958, when the company reached annual sales of $800,000. Leonard contributed to increasing the company's sales and profits by implementing innovative sales and marketing programs. He started the first research and development laboratory, which brought in professional management at all levels, and he was the one who took Estée Lauder to the global level by initiating the company's international expansion in 1960 with the opening of the Estée Lauder account at Harrods in London.

Leonard has held several positions since he joined the company and has worked his way up to executive officer positions. He served as president of the Estée Lauder Companies Inc. from 1972 to 1995 and as CEO from 1982 to 1999. He became the chairman of the board of directors in 1995, when his mother retired, and he remained chairman until June 2009. He navigated the company in the right direction, which resulted in the launch of various brands, including Aramis, Clinique, Lab Series, and Origins. During the mid-1990s, under his leadership, the company also acquired brands like Aveda, Bobbi Brown, Jo Malone London, La Mer, and M·A·C. Leonard married in 1959, and his wife, Evelyn H. Lauder, also became part of the family business. She served as the senior corporate vice president for the Estée Lauder Companies Inc. until she passed away in 2011. The couple had two sons, William (executive chairman of the Estée Lauder Companies Inc.) and Gary (managing partner of Lauder Partners, LLC), and five grandchildren. On January 1, 2015, Leonard married Judy Glickman Lauder, an internationally recognized philanthropist and photographer.

Ronald Lauder (chairman of Clinique Laboratories, LLC). Ronald is the younger son of Esty and Joseph Lauder. Ronald married Jo Carole Knopf in July 1967. They had two daughters, Aerin and Jane. Ronald received a bachelor's degree in international business from the Wharton School of the University of Pennsylvania. He also studied at the University of Paris and has a certificate in international business from the University of Brussels. Ronald began his career by working externally at Oevel, a Belgian factory, and later joined the family business in 1964. He was responsible for Clinique Laboratories and worked his way up to becoming the general manager of Clinique Laboratories in 1985. Nine years later, in 1994, he began serving as the chairman of the board, a role he currently holds. Ronald played a vital role in the creation of Prescriptives and served as chairman of Estée Lauder International from 1992 to 2002. He also served as a member of the Estée Lauder Companies' board of directors from 1968 to 1986 and from 1988 to 2009. He was re-elected to the board in November 2016. Ronald also co-founded the Alzheimer's Drug Discovery Foundation with his elder brother Leonard, and together, they serve as co-chairmen of the foundation.

When the third generation stepped in:

William P. Lauder (executive chairman)—son of Leonard A. Lauder. William did not foresee joining the family business until he enrolled into the Wharton School of the University of Pennsylvania. Upon his graduation, he worked at Macy's as an executive trainee and associate merchandising manager for three years. He then joined the family business in 1986 in a mid-level marketing position in the Clinique division. He was 26 years old when he joined the family business, at which point he had to work with his grandparents, parents, and uncle to run a massively successful business empire.

In an interview with *Wall Street Journal*, William described that while being a part of a gigantic successful family business, he also was fighting the perception that his success was only due to his legendary last name. He explained that "leading a public company is a sentence, but leading a publicly held and family controlled business is a life sentence."[7]

With his broad range of experience, in 1990, William successfully began leading Origins—a skincare brand that is a division of Estée Lauder (holding company)—as the president until 1998. Under his remarkable leadership, Origins created a store-within-a-store concept and achieved the highest growth rate among cosmetic companies in the United States. Moving forward, from 1998 to 2001, William became the president of Clinique Laboratories, LLC, where he introduced the brand's first anti-aging product, which was very well received by consumers and went on to win the Cosmetic Executive Women Award for "Best Skin Care Product in Limited Distribution" in 2000. From July 2001 through 2002, he was group president of the Estée Lauder Companies, responsible for the global business of the Clinique and Origins brands and the company's retail store and online operations.

From January 2003 through June 2004, he was chief operating officer (COO). He served as the president of the company from July 2002 until February 2008, and from March 2008 through June 2009, he was the CEO. Despite being a family business, Estée Lauder Inc. is no stranger to hiring external employees for executive positions. During the course of grooming William, Fred Langhammer served as CEO for the company from 2000 to 2004. In addition, in March 2008, a non-Lauder, Fabrizio Freda, succeeded William Lauder as president and COO of the Estée Lauder Companies and then as CEO in July 2009.

In mid-2009, William assumed the position of executive chairman and chairman of the board of directors of the Estée Lauder Companies.

Aerin Lauder (style and image director)—daughter of Ronald Lauder. Aerin joined the family business in 1992 after graduating from the Annenberg School of Communications at the University of Pennsylvania. She has taken on numerous executive roles, including senior vice president; creative director; and style and image director, which she still maintains. She also served as a board member from 2004 to 2016. In 2012, she founded her own luxury lifestyle brand AERIN under the Estée Lauder Companies and is also the creative director for the brand. In 1996, Aerin married Eric Zinterhofer, a private equity financier and founding partner of Searchlight Capital Partners. The couple has two teenage sons as of 2022.

Jane Lauder (executive vice president, enterprise marketing, and chief data officer)—daughter of Ronald Lauder. Jane is a Stanford University graduate who joined the family business a year after her graduation in 1996. She has created and led brands like American Beauty and BeautyBanks. From 2006 to 2008, she served as senior vice president, global marketing for Clinique, where she was in charge of leading the brand's strategic marketing positioning and product category, market, and channel expansion. From 2008 to 2014, she was the president for high-end skincare brands like Origins, Ojon, and Darphin. Jane took all these brands to the next level of success under her leadership.

Jane Lauder has been serving on Estée Lauder Companies' board of directors since 2009. She then served as the global brand president for Clinique (2014–2019), where she switched the revenue stream from low- to high-growth distribution channels and tripled the brand's online business. She also worked rigorously on the efficacy and effectiveness of the brand's skincare products via high-touch service and personalization.

Jane then took on the position of executive vice president, enterprise marketing and chief data officer of the Estée Lauder Companies. With her extensive experience, she combines data-driven insights with creativity and leads the company-wide strategy to leverage business insights and analytics to build digitally directed priorities to accelerate growth.

Jane is married to Kevin Warsh, who she met at Stanford. Her husband is a financier and bank executive and was the youngest-ever appointee to the Federal Reserve Board. The pair is very private about their personal life and are believed to have two children.

Gary Lauder—the younger son of Leonard A. Lauder. Gary is the only grandchild of Esty Lauder not involved in the family business. He is the managing director of Lauder Partners, LLC, a Silicon Valley-based venture capital firm.

Ownership. There are two types of shares: Class A shares have one vote per share, and Class B shares have 10 votes per share, which allows the family to control the company. By 2021, the Lauder family owned approximately 38% of total common shares and held about 86% of the voting power.[8]

Fourth generation tapping in. Daniele Lauder, daughter of William Lauder, granddaughter of Leonard A. Lauder, and great-granddaughter of the founder Esty Lauder, launched her own limited-edition makeup collection called ACT IV in collaboration with Estée Lauder. She is the first member from the fourth generation to enter the family business and is an actress and model by occupation (Figure 2.3).

Discussion questions:

1 Use the three-circle model to position the most important family members across the three entities.
2 Can you describe the differences and similarities in the family members' needs, goals, and expectations?
3 How will the current configuration of the three-circle model change in the next generational stage?
4 Why do you think it is important to understand family members' roles, needs, goals, and expectations using the three-circle model?

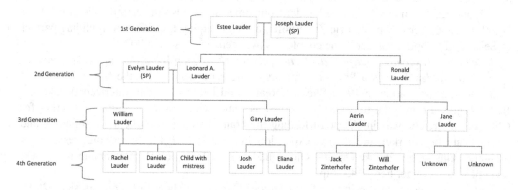

Figure 2.3 Lauder family tree.
SP, Spouse.

Notes

1 The three-circle model, as an instrument to visualize the complexity of family businesses, was developed by Tagiuri R. and Davis J. at Harvard Business School around 1978. In 1996, the article titled "Bivalent attitudes of family firms" published in *Family Business Review* used the model.

2 Basco, R., Hamdan, R., & Vyas, A. (2021). *Succession Intention of the United Arab Emirates NexGens*, Sharjah, UAE. Report retrieved from https://familyfirmblog.files.wordpress.com/2021/08/success ion-intention-report-final-v2-spreads-1.pdf. Basco, R. & Gómez González, J. (2022). Antecedents of next generation succession intention in family businesses: A cross-country analysis. *European Journal of International Management*, online first. Article retrieved from https://doi.org/10.1504/ EJIM.2022.10051782

3 Panksepp, J. B., & Lahvis, G. P. (2011). Rodent empathy and affective neuroscience. *Neuroscience & Biobehavioral Reviews*, 35(9), 1864–1875.

4 This example discussion is developed solely as the basis for class discussion. This example discussion is not intended to serve as an endorsement, source of primary data, or illustration of effective or ineffective management.
Andrews, S. (2003). Shattered dynasty. *Vanity Fair*. Article retrieved from www.vanityfair.com/news/ 2003/05/andrews200305.

5 This example discussion is developed solely as the basis for class discussion. This example discussion is not intended to serve as an endorsement, source of primary data, or illustration of effective or ineffective management.
Story adapted from *Tharawat Magazine*. (2015). A legacy of love—The story of the Henriquez family. Article retrieved from www.tharawat-magazine.com/legacy-love-story-henriquez-family/.

6 This case study discussion is developed solely as the basis for class discussion. This case study discussion is not intended to serve as an endorsement, source of primary data, or illustration of effective or ineffective management.

7 Byron, E. (2008). Family matters: Tensions Roil Estee Lauder Dynasty. *Wall Street Journal*. February 2008. Retrieved from www.wsj.com/articles/SB120406413598194599

8 Information retrieved from the Estee Lauder website: www.elcompanies.com/en/investors/stock-info rmation/ownership-profile#:~:text=The%20Lauder%20family%20now%20owns,has%2010%20vo tes%20per%20share and www.forbes.com/sites/chloesorvino/2016/03/02/estee-lauder-chairman-will iam-lauder-joins-ranks-of-billionaires/?sh=32ae9a6a33bb

3 Interpersonal relationships and communication in family businesses

Learning objectives

- Distinguish different types of interpersonal relationships in family businesses.
- Understand the importance of interpersonal relationships in family businesses.
- Recognize the impact of families' interpersonal relationships in family businesses.
- Identify types of family communication styles and their impact on family businesses.
- Learn how to apply a family genogram in the context of family businesses.

3.1 Introduction

In Chapter 2, we focused on the needs, goals, expectations, and emotions of family members by considering their positions across the ownership, business, and family entities. This represents the first step in our journey to unveil the dynamics of family businesses. We learned that the uniqueness of family businesses emerges because of the different logics (ownership, management, and family logics) that may compete at the individual level to gain an individual's focus of attention, thereby influencing that individual's decision-making when he or she performs different roles simultaneously.

Individuals are the building blocks of family businesses, but interpersonal relationships are the social connections that tie individuals together within the family business system. Interpersonal relationships are the social associations, connections, and/or affiliations individuals have with other people in specific contexts. In a family business, the ownership, business, and family entities represent a context in which individuals with different and overlapping roles relate, interact, and communicate with each other.

The aim of this chapter is to navigate the different interpersonal relationships in family businesses, understand the nature of these relationships, and reflect on the effects of these interpersonal relationships on family businesses. The first approach to interpreting family interpersonal relationships should consider the multiple layers of contexts in which the family is embedded, such as the national cultural context and familial context (religious and specific family values and beliefs). Beyond the multiple layers of context, the communication style that prevails in the family is important to consider because it facilitates interactions and ultimately the mechanisms for problem-solving.

3.2 Interpersonal relationships in the family entity

Interpersonal relationships in families are the central point of departure in understanding the dynamics of family businesses because family relationships tend to affect ownership and

DOI: 10.4324/9781003273240-4

business (work-related) relationships. In other words, family relationships set the foundations and provide the context for family members' emotional, social, and cognitive development. The scope, quality, and intensity of family relationships are important for the rest of the relationships involved in the family business system. Because the family influences the business, what and how interpersonal relationships are built in the family affect the balance between the ownership, business, and family entities.

Even though the concept of family may vary from one cultural and institutional context to another, there are three approaches[1] to exploring and understanding the concept of family. First, the structural approach to family is about the form and hierarchy (objective criteria) of those who are part of a group of people living together and their biological/legal connections (marriage, blood, and adoption). In this sense, the most common way to define family is by considering the family of origin—people living together are connected by blood or affinity. With this approach, it is important to distinguish two types of families. A nuclear family is formed by one or more parents and one or more children, whereas an extended family includes near relatives, such as grandparents, aunts, and uncles, among other relatives, beyond the nuclear family. However, because of cultural changes, new inclusive forms of families have emerged in modern societies. For instance, a family of orientation focuses not only on family formed by people living together who are connected by blood or affinity but also on those who act/live as they if were connected by blood or affinity. In this category, we have families that are different from nuclear and extended families, which can include step-families (e.g., a couple living with children from their previous relationships) and cohabitating families (e.g., unmarried couples who may or may not have children).

Second, beyond the formal structure of a family, it is possible to define a family based on people's behavior within the family entity. The task-oriented approach to family focuses on the functionality of the family by considering how people behave to provide love, support, and care for each other within a specific family cultural framework of values and beliefs. Each family member has specific roles, and their main tasks are related to nurturing and socializing.

Finally, the transaction approach goes beyond the structure of the family and the task distribution of their members and focuses on the quality of family members' relationships in terms of the communication and emotions that connect, establish, and maintain relationships. What makes a family is the quality of family members' interactions to create a home, a common identity, and a shared vision.

Certainly, the three approaches to defining family are important for understanding the family realm and family dynamics because they provide different levels of complexity that intertwine. While the structural and task-oriented approaches are easy to observe and help answer what a family is, the transactional approach digs deeper into what family members do to create a family by exploring interpersonal relationships. Interpersonal relationships are the fundamental micro-foundational mechanisms that give unique meaning to a family.

In the family business context, the scope of interpersonal relationships is determined by the structure of the family, whereas the quality and intensity of interpersonal relationships are determined by the overlapping tasks across the three circles and the communication style used for family interactions. Following this general framework, we next explore the interpersonal relationships among family members (i.e., in couple, sibling, parent–child, and extended family relationships) and how these relationships can shape family business behavior and performance.

3.2.1 Couple relationships and family business

The quality of a couple's relationship affects the rest of the relationships in a family and, consequently, the relationships within the ownership and business entities of a family business.

Sustaining a couple relationship across time is difficult and requires being grounded in three principles. First, the responsive principle requires a couple to respond to one another and attend to each other's needs, goals, expectations, and emotions. Second, the resolution principle requires a couple to accommodate, coordinate, and collaborate in maintaining control under stress, conflict, and friction. Finally, the maintenance principle requires a couple to remain united by continuing to build their affection and commitment. Embracing these principles is important for the well-being of a couple relationship and for the spillover effects on the rest of the focal family's relationships.

Aside from the abovementioned principles, a couple's behavior is an important predictor of their relationship and the quality of their family life and can help clarify family business dynamics. Conflicted couples contaminate family relationships (e.g., sibling and parent–child relationships) with stress and anxiety. There are four toxic behaviors, including both verbal and nonverbal communication, triggered when someone feels anxious or threatened that can damage any couple's relationship. First, criticism behavior emerges in those couples that continuously express irritation, frustration, and complaints by finding fault in each other. This behavior is an attack on one or both parties' character or personality. Second, defensiveness refers to the attitude to counterattack in response to any comment or suggestion made by one's partner. This behavior often manifests as a self-protective attitude via indignation and playing the victim. Third, stonewalling refers to shutting down conversations to avoid conflict and minimize stress. Finally, contempt emerges when one partner feels superior and makes the other partner feel unworthy or less than. Contempt typically manifests as disrespect and mocking with sarcasm, hostile humor, and condescension and is clear evidence that a couple is in trouble. Contempt triggers conflict not only between partners but also among the rest of the relationships that form a family business (Table 3.1).

These toxic behaviors have negative consequences for relationships within a family business when one or more of them become habitual patterns—that is, when toxic patterns of behavior are embedded in a couple's relationship. The real impact of the quality of a couple's interpersonal relationships on a family business depends on the roles that each partner plays in the three-circle model. Are both partners working in the firm as spousal team? What is their ownership participation? Was the business created by the married couple or by one of them, or was it inherited? In other words, to what extent does the role of being a couple in a marriage overlap with other roles (ownership and management) in the three-circle model?

There are different roles that a family business leader spouse can play in a family business,[2] and their patterns of behavior matter for understanding the implications for family businesses.

- *Business partners*. Life partners who decide to also become business partners need to have positive communication patterns to sustain their personal and professional interpersonal relationships. A couple's positive interpersonal relationship can birth and sustain a successful business and a cohesive family. Take, for example, the successful couple business partnership, Mama Earth, an Indian brand for babies co-founded by spouses Ghazal and Varun Alagh. The couple established the brand because the baby products available in the Indian market were not suiting their son. That is when the couple decided to put their research hats on and produce natural products for babies. The brand is estimated to be valued at $750 million. Ghazal believes the couple's relationship has grown stronger after becoming business partners, and they work really well together.[3]

  On the other hand, if a couple does not have a healthy interpersonal relationship, business continuity may be jeopardized. For example, the famous American fashion designer duo

Table 3.1 Examples of toxic behaviors

Toxic Behavior	Example in the Family Entity	Example in the Business Entity	Implications for Interpersonal Relationships in the Family Business
Criticism	A situation in which the wife communicates to her husband: "You are not even able to think about your partner. You know why? You are selfish and egocentric! Yes, you are!"	A situation in which the father communicates to his son or daughter: "I do not think your idea to improve the communication between departments is logical. It does not have sense at all! This is a business, not a play room!"	Mistrust, perception of being controlled, fear of being criticized.
Contempt	A situation in which the parents have an argument: "No one in the entire world can have such silly arguments! Sincerely, it sounds childish. Could you be any more pathetic?"	A situation in which the parents share an opinion with children: "If it were as simple as you think, I would leave this position and give it to a child. You still have lot of things to learn. Now I am too busy to follow up on your ideas."	Not feeling equal; subordination; fear of expressing feelings, ideas, or thoughts.
Defensiveness	A situation in which the parents' reaction is to be defensive as a strategy to deal with a conflict: "I did not have time to stop at the children's school today. I am busy at my job. I am sacrificing by working and spending time for you and the children. All of you have the best because of my hard work!"	A situation in which the parents provide feedback to the children at work, and the children feel threatened: "What do you think, I can do everything here? I am not Superman! I have lot of responsibilities. I could have been working at a better place than in our firm."	Lack of openness; fear of expressing feelings, ideas, or thoughts.
Stonewalling	A couple that avoids talking, and when conflict emerges, they prefer to put the conversation aside: "I do not want to continue with this conversation."	A discussion about a business matter becomes a discussion about personal matters: "Yes, you are right, as always! I do not have anything to add. See you tomorrow!"	Lack of communication, not sharing feelings, distant relationships.

Tory Burch and Chris Burch co-founded the clothing brand Tory Burch LLC. They got divorced in 2006, and in 2013, the divorced couple had an ugly fallout professionally. Chris sued his ex-wife for breach of contract and meddling with the sale of his shares, whereas Tory counterclaimed that Chris was at fault as he launched his own line of stores, C. Wonder, which were selling products that resembled her upmarket-boho aesthetic. Although Tory Burch did not disclose many details of the settlement, she did reveal that Chris Burch "will retain at least some of his stake in the business."[4]

While working with one's spouse could be a rewarding challenge because the romantic love, loyalty, solidarity, and care for each other is linked to each partner's intellectual and professional career development, it could entail a potential downside because of the work-family conflict emerging from the overlapping roles that both partners play at home and at work. The difficulty of balancing work and family demands as well as understanding partners' needs, goals, and expectations are even more evident when the family and the business share the same location (e.g., farm family businesses).

- *The chief emotional officer.* Some spouses of family business leaders play the role of maintaining the alignment between the emotional needs of the family and the needs of the business and ownership entities. The main aims of a chief emotional officer are to understand family members' needs, goals, and expectations and act as a mediator, moderator, coach, and/or facilitator to make the interpersonal relationships within the family business more harmonious. This individual's interventions happen behind the scenes, aiming to preserve the cohesiveness of the family. For example, the success of Osmo Suovaniemi, inventor and founder of Biohit, a finish company in the healthcare industry, cannot be understood without considering the efforts of his wife and partner, Oili. Oili not only worked as the company's bookkeeper and chief cashier but also as an emotional partner during the different stages of the family business.[5] However, not all chief emotional officers are equally effective or effective across time. For instance, when a couple relationship develops toxic patterns of behavior, the chief emotional officer could affect the rest of the relationships in the family business and consequently increase interpersonal conflict.

The five functions of the chief emotional officer[6]:

- *Communication facilitation.* The chief emotional officer is the hub of the family, embracing family members and ensuring their bonds through constructive conversations. The family member in this position knows how to approach other family members to have a conversation, knows how to listen, is able to share sensitive information, helps others reflect and interpret situations, and intervenes in conflicts to help resolve them.
- *Stewardship of family culture.* The chief emotional officer has the unique task of keeping and transmitting the family's culture, values, and traditions by creating activities that tie family members with their past and build the future. The chief emotional officer documents the family's story; puts albums together; organizes celebrations; and gathers family members to celebrate traditions, anniversaries, and important family dates.
- *Encouragement of family relationships.* The chief emotional officer plays an important role in helping family members develop harmonious interpersonal and collective relationships by promoting fairness, cooperation, and empathy.
- *Bridging the business and the family.* The chief emotional officer is able to create a bridge of understanding between the family and the firm. The role of this individual is to help family members understand their own roles as owners, family members, and/or managers.
- *Leadership.* The chief emotional officer leads the emotional side of the business family by acting accordingly to inspire and motivate family members to develop a cohesive family.
  - *The senior advisor/keeper of family values.* These spouses help the rest of their family members understand the role of the family in the business, preserve the family business values across generations, support family members' careers within and beyond the family

business, and prioritize the continuity of the family business and its legacy through their interventions. While the role of the senior advisor/keeper of family values is important for preserving the family business legacy and maintaining it as part of the family identity, his or her influence when the couple is engaging in toxic behaviors could easily deteriorate the commitment of the rest of the family members toward the family business and increase interpersonal conflict.

- *The free agent.* The free agent refers to a spouse who is not interested, committed, or involved directly or indirectly with the business. This individual separates his or her role in the family and the family business itself. In other words, the free agent's role in the family is not altered by the family business, and the free agent does not impact the family business either.
- *The jealous spouse.* The jealous spouse is a partner who competes with the business for time and affection. Family businesses are often so important for family business leaders that their spouses feel displaced and relegated. In the long term, this competition becomes negative for a couple's interpersonal relationship, and if the couple develops toxic behaviors, then there is no good prospect for the family business.

3.2.2 *Sibling relationships and family business*

Sibling relationships are one of the most important relationships to guarantee the continuity of family firms across generations because the quality of sibling relationships may impact family business development. There are a lot of well-known stories about sibling relationships in family businesses and their positive and negative effects on these businesses. An example of the positive effects of sibling relationships on a family business can be seen in Damiani,[7] a global luxury brand for jewelry and high-quality watches founded in 1924 in Valenza, the Italian capital of jewelry. The founder, Enrico Damiani, started the Damiani brand with a passion for art and successfully passed down the legacy to his son Damiano, who then passed it down to the third-generation sibling trio (Silvia, Guido, and Georgia). According to the third-generation Damiani siblings, they work well together and are committed to the family business's success due to the values with which their parents raised them. They have been brought up to believe in the strength of a family business. Under the siblings' leadership, the brand undertook international expansion. By the fiscal year ended on March 31, 2022, the group reached exceptional achievements by showing a consolidated revenue of €238 million and a 69% rise over the previous year. The growth is coming from all regions and sales channels, particularly the retail sector, where revenue was up 82%.[8]

McCain Foods Limited is an example of the negative effects of sibling relationships on a family business.[9] McCain Foods Limited is a Canadian multinational frozen food family business founded by the McCain brothers: Wallace, Harrison, Robert, and Andrew. A dispute arose when the surviving brothers Harrison and Wallace (Robert and Andrew passed away by the time of the dispute) had to decide the future successor of the family business. Wallace wanted his son Michael to take over the family business, whereas Harrison wanted their nephew Allison to be the successor. In 1990, Wallace appointed Michael as CEO of the entire McCain Foods US division, a move that disappointed Harrison and the rest of the family members. After a long dispute, Wallace lost his bid for McCain Foods and was removed as co-CEO (retaining his shares in the family business).

Unlike parent–child relationships, sibling relationships tend to be more equal and horizontal. Sibling relationships are often characterized by contradicting love–hate feelings, often including high levels of intimacy, trust, closeness, and affection but also rivalry, competition, and sibling quarreling. The quality of sibling relationships can be determined by analyzing the combination of two dimensions[10]: sibling hostility and sibling warmth. The sibling hostility dimension refers to causing trouble, fights, friction, and disagreements, whereas the sibling warmth dimension refers to sharing, helping, affection, and teaching. The combination of these two dimensions forms four types of sibling relationships (see Figure 3.1).

- *Harmonious relationships* are characterized by a low level of hostility and a high level of warmth. Siblings in harmonious relationships enjoy their partnership (high satisfaction working together), get along very well, and have a low level of conflict. Harmonious relationships increase siblings' self-esteem, which in turn positively affects their roles in the family business system.
- *Hostile relationships* are characterized by a high level of hostility and a low level of warmth. These relationships are highly conflictive with verbally and/or physically aggressive behaviors. Siblings develop perceptions of rivalry in terms of parent attention, respect, and love within the family unit. Hostile relationships affect siblings' social behaviors and reduce their self-esteem.
- *Affect-intense relationships* are high in both hostility and warmth. These sibling relationships fluctuate in terms of conflict and affective connections, making them difficult to manage (control) within the family business system. Conflict between the siblings tends to shift to personal conflict, thereby affecting the quality of business relationships and hindering conflict resolution.
- *Uninvolved relationships* are characterized by low levels of hostility and warmth. The siblings' low interest in each other reduces conflict but also affect. The result is low commitment among siblings to pursue a successful business partnership.

Sibling dyad relationships are not alike, and there are several forces affecting them. First, sibling dyad relationships change based on individual demographic characteristics, such as siblings' gender, siblings' birth order, and the age difference among children. For instance, first-born siblings are typically role models for their younger siblings and are more likely to provide

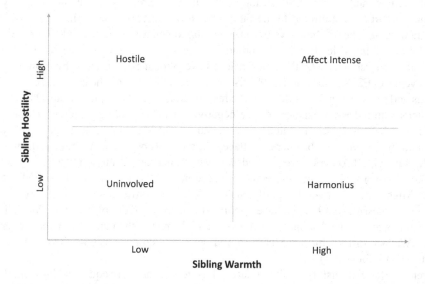

Figure 3.1 Siblings relationships.

Source: The figure was adapted from Wrench, J. S., Punyanunt-Carter, & Thweatt, K. S. (2022). Interpersonal communication. A mindful approach to relationships. Via the Open Education Resource (OER) LibreTexts Project. https://LibreTexts.org.

warmth and nurturing because their parents often assign them to take care of the younger children. Accordingly, first-born, second-born, and subsequent children could have different perceptions of their relationships. For instance, a second-born child may perceive more warmth and less conflict than a first-born child because of the responsibility to be a role model or take care of their younger siblings (culturally) assigned to first-born children.

Second, contextual forces, such as family culture (shared values and principles), family structure (configuration of the family itself), and family dynamics (in terms of task roles and transactional aspects), can strengthen, diminish, and neutralize sibling relationships. In terms of culture, the importance of primogeniture—the right of succession belonging to the firstborn child—in some families could shape the relationships between siblings. For instance, regarding succession intentions in the Arab world, the responsibility the first-born male in a family has in terms of leading the family and the firm shift sibling relationships from being horizontal to more hierarchical. In terms of family structure, the extent to which family positions and roles are clearly demarcated may affect interpersonal relationships among siblings. For instance, the strong educational and caretaking functions of siblings in some societies may be replicated in the family business context when adult siblings use the firm to provide resources to the family and to serve as a source of jobs for all family members. Indeed, siblings in collectivistic cultures (e.g., in Latin America) hold stronger family values and expectations regarding their obligations to assist, respect, and support family members than their European counterparts.[11]

In terms of family dynamics, family relationships could be an important dimension that shapes sibling dyads. For instance, the absence of a parent at home (e.g., when a parent places excessive importance on his or her professional career), which detaches this parent from his or her family role, forces other family members (often siblings) to replace the parent role. Siblings often try to compensate for low-quality parent–child relationships to fill the parental void. Additionally, the quality of parent–child relationships spill over to sibling relationships such that good or bad spousal relationships are often absorbed by children and replicated across the rest of the family's relationships (e.g., in sibling relationships).

Finally, sibling dyad relationships are not stable but are instead dynamic across time. The quality of relationships and siblings' perceptions of them may also change during their childhood, adolescence, adulthood, and elderly years. For instance, there is evidence that sibling relationships tend to become less close later in life when each sibling forms his or her own family. During childhood, siblings spend more time together and engage in prosocial and play-oriented behavior, thereby developing cooperation–competition interactions. During their teenage years, siblings spend less time together, pursue different interests, and look for independence. During adulthood, at the beginning, siblings tend to keep their distance while each forms his or her own family. However, research has also shown that adults feel closer to their siblings than to parents or friends. This closeness becomes important as siblings age because sibling relationships are more likely to provide emotional and social support to each party. The evolutionary development of sibling relationships may also reflect on the family business context. For instance, the conflict-resolution mechanisms that siblings learn during their childhood and teenage years can become important tools to resolve conflicts in a family business. Parents are vital role models for their children, teaching and helping them develop conflict-resolution mechanisms that may remain for the rest of their lives and affect sibling interpersonal relationships. However, most of this teaching and helping is not formal but is informal as children tend to directly observe and interpret how their parents resolve conflicts and learn from their own experience when having problems with their parents.

In summary, the type and quality of sibling relationships matter for the success and continuity of family businesses. Sibling relationships differ depending on the specific circumstances, such as when siblings cohabitate with their parents, have begun to create their own families, or have adult children who show intentions to work in the family business. Sibling relationships are dynamic and should be contextually analyzed because the intensity of their bonds changes across time and contexts. In particular, siblings' goals, needs, and expectations change when new family roles are added to their existing sibling roles (e.g., father role), which in turn engender changes in their management (e.g., assuming managerial leadership positions) and ownership (e.g., become shareholder) roles.

3.2.3 Parent–child relationships and family business

Parent–child relationships are important because they nurture the physical, emotional, and social development of children by creating unique bonds. Parent–child relationships are the foundation of children's personalities and behavior, and consequently, the quality of parent–child relationships may impact the dynamics of family businesses. To analyze parent–child relationships and their effects on children's behavior, we need to focus on the four main parenting styles (see Figure 3.2), which combine the dimensions of responsiveness (the extent to which parents are warm and sensitive to children's needs) and demandingness (the extent to which parents control their children and influence them).[12]

First, the *permissive parenting style* is characterized by high responsiveness and low demandingness. There is open communication between parents and children, and parents let children make decisions by themselves without imposing rules or expectations. Parents look for their children's friendship to avoid conflict.

Second, the *authoritative parenting style* is characterized by high responsiveness and high demandingness. Parents and children have open conversations to express thoughts, feelings, and opinions, but parents set clear rules, guidelines, and expectations, which are accompanied by explanations (communication). This parenting style tends to be supportive and nurturing. If children fail to meet expectations or achieve goals, parents approach them with support rather than punishment.

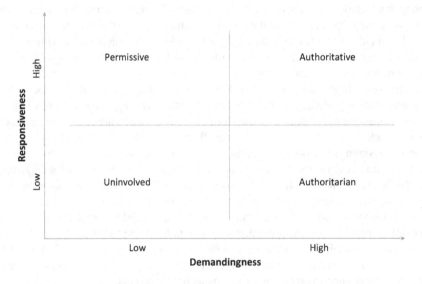

Figure 3.2 Four types of parenting styles.

Source: From Koerner, A., & Fitzpatrick, M. (2006). Family Communication Patterns Theory: A Social Cognitive Approach. In D. O. Braithwaite & L. A. Baxter (Eds.), *Engaging Theories in Family Communication: Multiple Perspectives* (pp. 50–65). SAGE, Thousand Oaks, CA. Published with Copyright permission.

Third, the *uninvolved parenting style* is characterized by low responsiveness and low demandingness; there is little engagement between parents and children. Parents are not demanding and do not discipline their children. Parents are indifferent to their children's needs and thoughts, and they do not implement rules or execute control or corrective actions. Therefore, little nurturing and attention are observed.

Finally, high demandingness and low responsiveness create the *authoritarian parenting style*, whereby parents enforce strict and clear rules but give little consideration to their children's needs, feelings, or emotions. The communication tends to be unidirectional and hierarchical, and children are expected to obey.

Although the authoritative parenting style arguably has the most advantages for children's independence, self-reliance, and social behavior, there is no one-size-fits-all approach, and different parenting styles are often necessary based on children's needs, parents' and children's gender, children's birth order, and the different moments of the family lifecycle.

Parenting styles have implications not only for children's development but also for the interpersonal relationships that children develop in the family business system. For instance, parenting styles affect successors' psychological functioning, well-being, and leadership.[13] The permissive parenting style in the family business context could result in having children who feel entitled to being successors. Entitled children may develop unrealistic expectations that are not necessarily in the best interest of the family business. With time, entitled children can create rights and privileges that are in opposition to the business logic and tend to distort reality. For instance, a comment like "I must be CEO because I am the oldest son" breaks the business logic of appointing the best possible candidate for the CEO position. Parents following the authoritative parenting style would likely expect their children to be involved in the family business and would be willing to have an open conversation if the next generation had any suggestions. If their children are not interested in joining the family business, the incumbent generation would be supportive of their decisions.

The authoritarian parenting style develops obedient successors who follow the rules and traditions imposed by incumbents or family leaders. However, these successors could have less social competence and lower self-esteem. Finally, the uninvolved parenting style develops children without emotional connection with the family business because of the distant relationships, poor nurturing in family business issues, and lack of business-sharing experience. In this context, children may show low interest in the family business and may thus have low self-esteem when engaging in any responsibilities across the business and ownership entities.

3.2.4 In-law relationships and family business

In-law relationships are those that an individual has with someone who is a relative because of marriage. In-law relationships extend the structure of the nuclear family with new members and can include one's partner's family (e.g., brother- and sister-in-law), one's daughter's and/ or son's family (e.g., son- and daughter-in-law), and one's brother's and sister's family (e.g., brother- and sister-in-law).

In-law family relationships play particular roles in families because they are kinship relationships based on affinity. The intensity of in-law relationships depends on the quality of the relationships within the nuclear family and the culture in which the nuclear family exists. An example of an in-law relationship involved in the foundation of a business can be found in Mithila's Pickles.[14] Sisters-in-law Kalpana Jha and Uma Jha started the business in 2009 in the city of Darbhanga, India. Since then, the business has grown rapidly. Mithila's Pickles has become one of the most popular brands of pickles in India. Its success is due to its high-quality products at affordable prices and the harmonious relationship between the sisters-in-law. An in-law can also successfully take over the business, as in the case of Wolf Coffee. In 2018, Rick and Jeanne Mariani, founders of Wolf Coffee in the 1990s, wanted to pass their business on to the next generation, so their daughter Natasha and her husband Nick stepped out of their corporate careers to continue the Mariani's vision of bringing great coffee to Sonoma County.[15]

On the other hand, in-law relationships can have a dark side, such as in the case of the popular British celebrity chef Gordon Ramsay and his father-in-law Chris Hutcheson, who was the chief executive officer in Gordon Ramsay Holdings before he was fired from this position.[16] In 2010, in a public dispute, both Hutcheson and Ramsay accused each other of different offenses. Hutcheson accused Gordon of pitting his daughter against him, whereas Gordon alleged that Hutcheson fraudulently added Gordon's signatures to a north London pub property. The feud escalated in 2011 when Gordon Ramsay decided to take his wife's family to court. In April 2017, Hutcheson and two of his sons pleaded guilty to a charge of conspiracy to hack into the computers of Gordon Ramsay Holdings Limited.

While in-laws are family members through affinity, it is the family culture that offers them greater or less integration into family life and, consequently, into the family business. In other words, considering the dimensions of the family concept, in-laws are part of the family structure (structural dimension) but in-laws' roles (task-oriented dimension) and interactions (transactional dimension) vary across cultures.

There are two hidden mechanisms through which family in-laws affect family business dynamics. The first hidden mechanism occurs when in-laws interpersonal relationships within the family influence family members' needs, goals, and expectations. It is common to hear stories of family business decisions made by nuclear family members being challenged the day after by the same brother or sister who previously agreed on the decision. The change of mind sometimes comes from a conversation with a spouse (in-law). These kinds of implicit influences are difficult to observe, interpret, and anticipate and tend to be harmful.

The second hidden mechanism occurs when family in-laws become owners of the family business. In this situation, in-laws acquire the right over the business and have voice and vote. For instance, imagine a situation in which a member of the nuclear family who participated in family business ownership dies and this person's spouse becomes owner of the company. If the in-law was not socialized and integrated into the family business values and traditions, the in-law is likely going to create friction and conflicts at the ownership level. While in some formal institutional legislation (laws), this is a right that cannot be denied, in other formal institutional contexts, prenuptial agreements can limit it. However, even in this case, most family businesses do not anticipate this issue because of the emotional aspects, the difficulty of talking about it, or a lack of time or because the family's wealth is not significant enough to discuss this issue in advance.

3.3 Family communication

The uniqueness of a family business starts with the family relationships, which shape the functionality and quality of the family entity. In interpersonal family relationships, communication refers to the way family members interact, share, exchange, and transmit information about themselves regarding their needs, goals, expectations, and their emotions. More importantly, family communication is a mechanism that creates meaning in a family.

There are two key dimensions that define the style of family communication—conversation orientation and conformity orientation[17]—which can be used to analyze communication in the family and business contexts. Conversation orientation determines to what degree a family generates an environment that encourages family members to interact and communicate about different and varied topics. In families with high conversation orientation, their members develop activities through which they engage in free, open, and frequent conversations to exchange thoughts, ideas, experiences, and expectations without restrictions. In this context, there is a participative style of decision-making. On the contrary, in families with low conversation orientation, their members limit the frequency of their interactions and restrict the topics of their conversations because ideas and thoughts are considered private. Families with low conversational orientation do not believe that conversation (being open and engaged with one another) is necessary for their functioning (e.g., for children's education and socialization).

On the other hand, conformity orientation is about the degree to which a family's climate encourages conformity, agreement, and alignment regarding beliefs, attitudes, values, and behaviors. In families with high conformity, members cultivate a climate of uniformity. While parents or leaders define guidelines for what to conform to, children and followers have to be obedient. These families avoid conflicts through conformity to keep family harmony. Family members are expected to subordinate their needs and goals to those of the family. On the other hand, in families with low conformity orientation, members accept diversity of beliefs, attitudes, values, and behaviors. They maintain open minds to embrace differences among family members. Children are involved in family decision-making, but these families believe in the independence of family members and the need for members to have their own space, and to some extent, they subordinate family interests to personal interests.

The combination of a family's position in terms of being high versus low in the conversation and conformity dimensions creates four types of family communication styles (see Figure 3.3).

• Families in the quadrant with high conversation and high conformity develop a *consensual communication style* by encouraging open communication but maintaining the family hierarchy (e.g., among parents and children) to control and define guidelines of what is good or bad. In principle, these orientations are in contradiction. Parents spend time explaining their

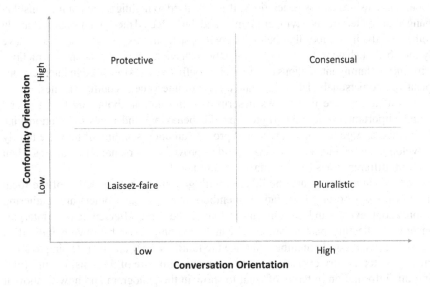

Figure 3.3 Types of family communication styles.

Source: The figure was adapted from two sources: Maccoby, E. E., & Martin, J. A. (1983). Socialization in the Context of the Family: Parent–Child Interaction. In P. H. Mussen & E. M. Hetherington (Eds.), *Handbook of Child Psychology* (1–101). New York: Wiley and Baumrind, D. (1971). Current patterns of parental authority. *Developmental Psychology Monograph*, 4(1), 1–103.

decisions, values, and beliefs, but conflict is not welcome because it can jeopardize the hierarchical family structure.

- Families in the quadrant with high conversation and low conformity develop a *pluralistic communication style* by encouraging open communication but low hierarchy and control by letting family members explore their own limits. Families in this quadrant are not afraid of conflict or disagreement since they develop strategies and mechanisms to address them. Children are more independent and are able to make their own decisions.
- Families in the quadrant with low conversation and high conformity develop a *protective communication style* by defining a high level of obedience among members with minimal interactions. Parents or leaders know what is good or bad for the rest of the family members, and they do not share their reasoning. Families with the protective communication style do not support conflict, and when conflict does arise, they do not have the strategies or mechanisms to handle them. Children may struggle to make decisions.
- Families in the quadrant with low conversation and low conformity develop a laissez-faire communication style by limiting interactions, giving freedom to family members to define their own judgments of what is good or bad, and promoting personal exploration and growth. Family members are emotionally divorced from each other.

Exploring and recognizing these family communication styles could help family business leaders and practitioners understand the dynamics of family businesses in terms of family member' interactions. Each style may explain why conflicts arise and how to use communication as a mechanism to address conflict.

3.4 Family genogram

A family genogram is a tool that business families, practitioners, and business consultants and advisors use to explore and visually present family structures (biological and affinity connections) and interpersonal relationships across generations. It is also used to highlight the main events that could have changed the patterns of behavior in a family and thus affected the dynamics of the family business. In other words, it is a tool that helps interpret past family experience that could have shaped family members' behavior, the family's collective behavior, and interpersonal interactions as well as clarify current family interactions (positive and conflictive ones) and design interventions to engender positive interpersonal relationships and correct or intervene in conflictive ones.

A genogram is a family tree that shows descriptive information about family members' relationships and important events that trigger specific behaviors and types of relationships among family members. A good genogram should provide an understanding of how the family functions to develop potential interventions that could improve interpersonal relationships when individuals perform different roles (owner, manager, and family).

The process of creating a genogram should start with gaining deep knowledge of the focal family structure (who is who and how family members relate to each other) and gathering past information about events and circumstances that could have affected family interpersonal relationships. Collecting past information can be accomplished by having individual conversations with relevant family members to trace the family's story and by referring to archival documents. This step is very critical and requires maximum care of the sensitive information. Managing this information in terms of what to show in the genogram and how to show it is a matter of preserving family cohesiveness.

There is a tradeoff between privacy and the information depicted in a genogram. It is important to recognize the difference between a fact and individuals' interpretations of the fact because the same event could have different interpretations as family members observe and reflect on it. In practice, there could even be more than one genogram. There can be an official genogram that is shared by the family and that serves as an instrument to initiate communication, reflect on inter-personal relationships, and put the past into perspective. Additionally, the published genogram could be used to enhance the family's conflict-resolution skills. Family leaders, business consultants, and advisors could also have a parallel genogram with more details that take into account different family perspectives as well as provide a third view of events and relationship quality. In this case, the genogram can serve as a personal instrument to guide the family with conflict-resolution mechanisms, unify perspectives, share a common vision about the family and the firm, and direct interventions toward healthy family interpersonal relationships.

The first step is to draw the family tree, going several generations back until reaching the founder of the family business. Squares are used to symbolize male family members, and circles are used to symbolize female family members. Couples are connected together, and from the connector, children are linked below. In each square or circle, the most important demographic information should be added: name, date of birth and death, role(s) occupied in the family business, and (if necessary) the numbers of shares held. Additionally, information about careers, ethnicity, religious affiliation, and education can be added to help interpret patterns of behavior and relationships.

Once the first stage with demographic information is completed, the second step is to add the quality of relationships among the most important family members. Based on the information gathered (e.g., based on the individual interviews, group meeting behavior, observational data, and/or archival data) and the interpretation of the data, the genogram should display the emo-tional links of relationships, such as harmony, hate, and distance, among others.

The final step is to add (maybe at the bottom of the genogram) a timeline with critical business information, such as founding date, ownership composition, management leadership, and any other important event that could have altered family interpersonal relationships.

3.5 Additional activities and reading material

3.5.1 Classroom discussion questions

1 Why are interpersonal relationships important for family businesses?
2 How important is the quality of family interpersonal relationships across generations?
3 Do parenting styles differ across mothers and fathers and across the gender (male/female) of target children? Why?
4 What is the importance of communication in maintaining interpersonal relationships?
5 Why and how does a family's communication style affect the functionality of the family firm?

3.5.2 Additional readings

1 Thomas, D. (2022). Split decisions: How siblings succeed—and fail—in business together. *Financial Times*. Article retrieved from www.ft.com/content/5008140b-2ab9-4d0f-ab6e-cc4eb01a901c
2 Lee, J. (2011). Understanding family business relationships. *Tharawat Magazine*. Article retrieved from www.tharawat-magazine.com/understanding-family-business-relationships/
3 SPGC–KPMG (2020). The power of women in family business. A Generational shift in purpose and influence. Report retrieved from https://globaluserfiles.com/media/40495_189802815b1b1b1fe170e38b43f0f3444639e750.pdf/o/GM-TL-01249-PE-STEP-Article-Power-of-Women_v5_web.pdf

3.5.3 Classroom activity

Aim: Recognize parenting styles and their effects on the dynamics of family businesses.

Material: Access two different movies to prepare the exercise: *The Inheritance*[18] and *Entre Les Bras.*[19] Ask students to watch both movies and take notes about the main characters and parent–child relationships.

Running the classroom exercise: The best approach to this exercise is to establish teams of no more than three students. In this way, they can share ideas, knowledge, and points of view. Class time can be divided as follows:

- 10 minutes: Ask students to discuss and describe the parenting style for each family using examples from the movies to illustrate their positions.
- 10 minutes: Ask groups to share ideas while the instructor moderates the debate.
- 10 minutes: Ask students in each group to discuss the consequences of the parenting styles for the businesses, the families, and the next generation of family members.
- 10 minutes: Ask students to share ideas about the consequences of the parenting styles.

Discussion: The instructor should guide the debate and ensure that students do not confuse actions (behavior) and conversations illustrating the parenting style in each family. Students should also identify the consequences for the family, business, and ownership entities and successors' psychology and behavior.

Takeaways: Contrast the two different parenting styles, their effects on the individual and family interpersonal relationships, and the consequences for the businesses and families.

3.6 Case for analysis I: Dassler brothers[20]

Do you know that the two popular rival sports brands Adidas and Puma emerged from a family conflict between two German brothers Adolf (Adi) and Rudolf?

The story begins after World War I. The brother duo established a family business in 1924 named Gebrüder Dassler Schuhfabrik in the German town of Herzogenaurach. Adi, the younger brother, channeled his love of sports by making and selling everyday shoes at reasonable prices. Additionally, he experimented with making sports shoes for his personal use. Gradually, he launched sports shoes in the market following the popularity of sports in the country. As a result of his production skills, Adi partnered with Rudolf, his older brother, who was responsible for the managerial side of the business.

The brother duo worked well together and were able to manage and expand their business. By 1930, they had sold 10,000 pairs of running shoes and 1,850 pairs of football boots. In 1932, Adi fell in love with a 16-year-old girl named Kathe. A third party, an in-law, entered the brother's relationship, which altered the dynamics of their interpersonal relationship. Adi's wife started to get involved in business matters.

In 1936, the company provided a pair of shoes designed and crafted by Adi to the American sprinter Jesse Owens at the Olympic Games in Berlin. Jesse won, and the brothers' shoes reached great popularity, boosting their business. However, World War II stopped the course of the brother's success as their shoe factories were converted into a weapon factories.

After World War II, the brothers started their shoe production again. However, in January 1948, after a period of long-lasting tension, there was turmoil that caused a divide between the brothers. Unfortunately, the brothers' tension shifted into interpersonal conflict and triggered their rivalry, which was never resolved during the course of their lives.

The reason behind the rift is not known even to their children and grandchildren. There are several theories behind their dispute related to stealing, family affairs, political problems, and resentment. The tension between both brothers was so strong that they were not able to stand each other. Consequently, they decided to part ways by dividing earnings, employees, and equipment between each other. After this decision, they never spoke to each other again.

The brothers' split led to the birth of two globally thriving sports brands: Puma and Adidas. Rudolf founded Puma in 1957, and later Adi formed Adidas (a play on his nickname). The brothers sued each other many times for design and trademark issues. Having their production in the same German town, the brothers' rivalry translated to society by dividing the entire town in two: Puma on one side of the Aurach River and Adidas in the other side. Both brothers preserved their hatred in the form of their own business rivalries. Nowadays, neither of the two companies are controlled by descendants of their founders.

Discussion questions:

1 Would you like to share a business journey with your brothers or sisters?
2 What do you think makes a sibling relationship successful or unsuccessful in business?
3 Is there a success or failure case of siblings in business in your family or in your close network? Can you reflect on to what extent their relationship makes the family and business
   successful or not?

3.7 Case for analysis II: The co-preneurs Mr. & Mrs. Hartz[21]

The popular ticketing platform, Eventbrite,[22] was co-founded by the brilliant couple Julia and Kevin Hartz along with their friend Renaud Visage. Eventbrite is one of the best examples of a co-preneur business (entrepreneur couples). Founded in 2006, the online global self-service ticketing platform for live experiences achieved massive success over the course of a decade, and it became a publicly traded company on the New York Stock Exchange in 2018. By 2021, Eventbrite had facilitated tickets for 5.4 million live events globally in nearly 180 countries, delivering more than 291 million total tickets.

The founders identified a gap in the technology market and came up with an innovative idea to make selling tickets hassle free for any type or size of event, ranging from music festivals, marathons, conferences, community rallies, and fundraisers to gaming competitions, with a mission to bring the world together through live experiences. Kevin is currently the chairman and previously served as the CEO of Eventbrite. Prior to establishing the global self-service ticketing platform, he was co-founder and CEO of Xoom Corporation, an international money-transfer company acquired by PayPal in 2015. Additionally, he also served as an early-stage investor and advisor to successful startups, including Airbnb, Pinterest, Uber, Lookout, Trulia, Flixster, Skybox Imaging, and Yammer. Julia currently serves as the CEO of Eventbrite and is the woman behind the platform's vision, strategy, and growth. Under her leadership, the company has become the world's largest event technology platform and has received multiple awards for workplace culture.

The duo harnesses their specific areas of expertise in a way that enables them to comple-ment each other's work rather than causing clashes and conflict. When Kevin was asked about his interpersonal relationship dynamic with his wife in an interview with Silicon Valley Open Doors, he commented that he and his wife found the right operating rhythm, abided by certain principles and rules to divide and conquer, optimized their complementary expertise, and worked in different areas, all of which made them harmonious co-preneurs (cohesive unit) with very little conflict. According to Kevin, since entrepreneurs should have a lifelong pursuit, getting to know one's business partner is important for the success of any entrepreneur, which explains why he is more partial to a couple team or sibling team where there are lifelong relationships.

Discussion questions

1   Why do you think Kevin believes lifelong relationships are important for the entrepreneurial adventure?
2   What makes co-preneurs successful or unsuccessful in business?
3   Would you like to initiate a business journey with your partner?

3.8 Case study: British royal family[23]

The royal "family firm." The British royal family has long been in the spotlight for their historical background and interesting family dynamics. Behind the royal family is a royal firm that controls the British royals. The term "family firm" was attributed to King George IV, Queen Elizabeth II's father, who reportedly stated, "We're not a family, we're a firm." Prince Philip (Queen Elizabeth II's husband) popularized the term. The royal "family firm" consists of more than 400 employees who work in the background to manage the royal family.[24]

The monarchy succession. After Elizabeth II served several decades as queen, Prince Charles was officially proclaimed King Charles III in 2023. The United Kingdom monarchy traditionally follows the primogeniture system, according to which the throne is passed down from firstborn to firstborn and not from sibling to sibling. Therefore, Prince Charles' firstborn, Prince William, is the first in line for the throne. If Prince William becomes king, he will be succeeded by his firstborn child, Prince George. Next in line is Prince George's sister, Princess Charlotte, and continues with his younger brother, Prince Louis. The line then continues with Prince William's brother (the fifth in line for succession).

The troubled marriage of Prince Charles and Princess Diana. Prince Charles was married to Princess Diana from 1981 to 1996, and together they had two sons, Prince William and Prince Harry. The unhappy marriage of Prince Charles and Princess Diana was the most talked-about topic in the media globally. Prior to his marriage to Princess Diana, the Prince of Wales was in love with Camilla Parker Bowles (today's Queen Consort). However, following strict royal family protocols, the Prince had to give up on his love for Camilla and marry Princess Diana, who seemed to be a better fit for the future King. The failed marriage was officially over in 1996 followed by Princess Diana's unfortunate and untimely death in 1997 in a tragic car accident. Later in 2005, Prince Charles finally married the love of his life, Camilla. The early years of Prince William's and Harry's lives were quite difficult as they witnessed how the media contributed to their parents' unhappy marriage, sabotaging their mother's mental health and privacy.

Troubled marriage—troubled children. Growing up, the brothers shared a close bond as they supported each other in coping with the crumbling marriage of their parents and later with the loss of their loving mother at such a young age. Being the older child and second in line to the throne, Prince William was groomed to be more invested in taking on his responsibilities to fulfill his royal duties. Meanwhile, Prince Harry was also taking on his royal duties to represent the queen. However, he was deeply affected by the way the media wrecked his mother's life and the suffering that both his parents went through.

Duke and Duchess of Cambridge. Prince William is the Duke of Cambridge, and as a result, his wife Catherine (Kate) was given the title of Duchess of Cambridge. Prince William and Kate were both students of art history at the University of St. Andrews. Their engagement in 2010 was well received. Kate belonged to an upper working-class British family. Her mother is a successful entrepreneur of a mail-order party supply and decoration company estimated to be worth $40 million, and her father belongs to a wealthy Yorkshire family that had ties to the British aristocracy and was entitled to trust funds that were established 100 years ago, making Kate the perfect fit for the British royal family.

Duke and Duchess of Sussex. Prince Harry is the Duke of Sussex, and as a result, his wife Meghan was given the title of Duchess of Sussex. Prince Harry had several relationships throughout his youth, but everything changed for him upon meeting Meghan Markle, an American actress. The couple was set up by a mutual friend in 2016.

Since both Prince Harry and Meghan were public figures, the couple's relationship started to swirl around the media globally. However, not all of the newspapers and magazines reported their relationship in a positive light. Several newspapers and media outlets reported offensive words directly targeting Meghan. This provoked Prince Harry's reaction, exacerbating his relationship with the media. After a year of dating, in November 2017, Prince Harry and Meghan got engaged. It had been a century since someone in the British royal family was going to marry an American divorcee. Elizabeth II's uncle, Edward VIII, who was previously king, voluntarily abdicated the throne to marry American divorcée Wallis Warfield Simpson.

The couple's wedding was in May 2018. However, the couple was not able to adapt to the royal family's rules, hierarchy, and culture. Additionally, the British media was clearly not a big fan of the Duchess of Sussex, as evidenced by the negative portrayal of her in tabloid headlines and reports that critiqued her every action. This coverage was completely opposite compared to the way the British media portrayed the Duchess of Cambridge, making the media's favoritism of her very apparent. Despite the media's negative projection of Meghan Markle and invasion of privacy, it came as a shock to the world when the Duke and Duchess of Sussex announced their decision to step down as senior royals to move to the United States in January 2020.

Tell-all interview. On March 7, 2021, the Duke and Duchess of Sussex sat down with famous American media personality Oprah Winfrey to reflect on their lives as actively working senior royals. In the candid interview, the couple revealed shocking and disappointing incidents they experienced as senior royals. They referred to the royal family as "the firm." Meghan stated that the family firm and its constituents played an active role in extending false narratives about the couple, which has cost them their mental health and peace of mind. The royal couple brought attention to the lesser-known family firm, which is said to be a part of the royal institution and comprises the royal family members.

The Duke and Duchess of Cambridge also suggested that the firm and the British media have a symbiotic relationship. They have invisible contracts behind doors such that the royal family members give media outlets full access to their lives in return for better, more positive press coverage. The couple claimed to leave due to the invasion of their privacy by the British media and the lack of support from the family firm. Prince Harry stated how more than 72 members of Parliament called out the colonial undertones of articles and headlines written about Meghan. However, he expressed that he was hurt and disappointed in his family for not publicly acknowledging the issue to stand in support of Meghan Markle. Moreover, he mentioned being aware of his family's stance and crediting their silence to their fear of upsetting the British media.

The couple accused family members of having conversations about how dark their baby's (Archie's) skin would be. The couple also claimed that Archie was denied the royal title of prince and was going to be deprived of security, unlike his royal cousins. Prince Harry clarified that he always felt trapped and that it was high time for him to leave in order to protect his wife and son. Chiming in, Meghan vocalized how she tried very hard to make the family firm proud but felt a lack of support.

The couple also disclosed that in the first quarter of 2020, they were financially cut off by the firm and were able to embark on a fresh start with the inheritance his late mother Princess Diana left him. Prince Harry highlighted that the simple reason for them exiting was his fear of history repeating itself. He had witnessed how the media shattered his mother's life, and by that time, he felt the relentless media was doing the same to his wife.

The Duke of Cambridge remarked that it is hard for people to distinguish the firm and family as it is a family business. He also described that the queen and the royal family members were welcoming and supportive when Meghan entered the family but that it was the firm—those operating the family business—that made her feel rejected and isolated. Meghan also described how the family firm never denied false reports about her making the Duchess of Cambridge cry during her and Prince Harry's wedding. In fact, she stated it was the other way around as Kate made her cry but owned up to it and apologized, with all ending well between them. Prince Harry described his relationship with the queen as being warm and loving, but when asked about his relationship with his father, Prince Harry revealed that Prince Charles initially stopped taking his calls as he was unhappy with Prince Harry's decision to leave. According to Prince Harry, his father had recently started answering his calls, and the two had put a lot of work into mending their relationship. Prince Harry stated he felt let down by his father due to his inability to empathize with him given that Prince Charles had experienced similar hurt and pain. In regard to Prince Harry's relationship with his older brother, Prince William, the brothers were taking some space from each other. However, Prince Harry exclaimed how he loves his brother and will always be there for him as they have been through a lot of ups and downs in life together.

When Prince William was asked in an interview if he had spoken to his brother Prince Harry after the Oprah Winfrey interview, he said he had not but that he will. The interviewer also asked if the royal family was a racist family, to which the Duke of Cambridge responded, "Very much not a racist family."

Response from Buckingham Palace. After the tell-all interview, with the intention to settle the matter, Buckingham Palace released a direct and simple statement on behalf of the queen:

ROYAL COMMUNICATIONS

Tuesday, 9th March, 2021

**THE FOLLOWING STATEMENT IS ISSUED BY BUCKINGHAM PALACE
ON BEHALF OF HER MAJESTY THE QUEEN**

The whole family is saddened to learn the full extent of how challenging the last few years have been for Harry and Meghan.

The issues raised, particularly that of race, are concerning. While some recollections may vary, they are taken very seriously and will be addressed by the family privately.

Harry, Meghan and Archie will always be much loved family members.

ENDS

Discussion questions

1 To what extent have past events shaped Harry's behavior? What importance could parent–child relationships have in this case?
2 Do you think Harry and Meghan's communication strategy to give this interview was good or bad for the royal family's interpersonal relationships? Why? What do you think about the official press release on behalf of the queen? Do you think using the media or any indirect form of communication to talk and discuss issues among family members is a good idea and healthy for a family business?
3 What do you think Harry and Meghan wanted to achieve by using the interview as a communication channel among family members, and what do you think they really achieved?
4 Is it easy to change the culture of a family? Why or why not? How can Harry and Meghan rebuild their bonds with the rest of their family members?

Notes

1 Wamboldt, F. S., & Reiss, D. (1989). Defining a family heritage and a new relationship identity: Two central tasks in the making of a marriage. *Family Process*, 28(3), 317–335.
2 Poza, E. J., & Messer, T. (2001). Spousal leadership and continuity in the family firm. *Family Business Review*, 14(1), 25–36.
3 Rajiv Singh. (2022). Varun and Ghazal Alagh's Mama Earth empire is built on the foundation of frugality. *Forbes India*. Article retrieved from www.forbesindia.com/article/unicorn-tracker/varun-and-ghazal-alaghs-mamaearth-empire-is-built-on-the-foundation-of-frugality/79809/1
4 O'Connor, C. (2015). Billionaire Chris Burch's fashion Chain C. Wonder to close all stores. *Forbes*. Article retrieved from www.forbes.com/sites/clareoconnor/2015/01/06/billionaire-chris-burchs-fashion-chain-c-wonder-to-close-all-stores/?sh=a5af38e320f5; www.vanityfair.com/culture/2013/01/tory-burch-chris-burch-fashion-line-lawsuit-settlement
5 Kontinen, T. (2011). Biohit: A global, family-owned company embarking on a new phase. *Entrepreneurship Theory and Practice*, 38(1), 185–207. https://doi.org/10.1111/j.1540-6520.2011.00488.x
6 Dashew, L. (2009). The other CEO. *Family Business Magazine*. Article retrieved from www.familybusinessmagazine.com/other-ceo-0
7 More information about Damiani can be found in its website http://investorrelations.damiani.com/ENG/page/the_group/the_history.php and
   Tharawat Magazine. (2018). Damiani—family, values and jewellery. Article retrieved from www.tharawat-magazine.com/big-data/damiani-family-values/
8 Bolelli, G. (2022). Italian jewellery group Damiani boosts growth, revenue up 69% in fiscal 2021–2022. *Fashion Network*. Article retrieved from www.fashionnetwork.com/news/Italian-jewellery-group-damiani-boosts-growth-revenue-up-69-in-fiscal-2021-22,1454995.html#fashion-week-milan-msgm
9 Several sources were used for this example. Information retrieved from: (1) https://torontolife.com/city/love-and-war-in-the-house-of-mccain/; (2) www.theglobeandmail.com/report-on-business/mccain-brothers-unlikely-to-end-feud/article1035633/; (3) www.nytimes.com/1994/10/30/business/canadian-family-s-feud.html
10 McGuire, S., McHale, S. M., & Updegraff, K. (1996). Children's perceptions of the sibling relationship in middle childhood: Connections within and between family relationships. *Personal Relationships*, 3(3), 229–239. https://doi.org/10.1111/j.1475-6811.1996.tb00114.x
11 Fuligni, A. J., Tseng, V., & Lam, M. (1999). Attitudes toward family obligations among American adolescents with Asian, Latin American, and European backgrounds. *Child Development*, 70(4), 1030–1044.
12 Maccoby, E. E., & Martin, J. A. (1983). Socialization in the Context of the Family: Parent–Child Interaction. In P. H. Mussen & E. M. Hetherington (Eds.), *Handbook of Child Psychology* (1–101). New York: Wiley.

Baumrind, D. (1971). Current patterns of parental authority. *Developmental Psychology Monograph*, 4(1), 1–103.

13 Shanine, K. K., Madison, K., Combs, J. G., & Eddleston, K. A. (2022). Parenting the successor: It starts at home and leaves an enduring impact on the family business. *Entrepreneurship Theory and Practice*, forthcoming. https://doi.org/10.1177/10422587221088772

14 Website: www.jhajistore.com/; additional information about the business: https://sugermint.com/kalp ana-jha-and-uma-jha-mithilas-pickles/

15 Information retrieved from Wolf Coffee website www.wolfcoffee.com/pages/ourstory

16 Information retrieved from www.mashed.com/628064/the-time-gordon-ramsay-feuded-with-his-own-father-in-law/?utm_campaign=clip and www.mylondon.news/news/celebs/itv-gordon-gino-fred-go-21753491

17 Koerner, A., & Fitzpatrick, M. (2006). Family Communication Patterns Theory: A Social Cognitive Approach. In D. O. Braithwaite & L. A. Baxter (Eds.), *Engaging Theories in Family Communication: Multiple Perspectives* (pp. 50–65). SAGE, Thousand Oaks, CA. Communication in the Real World. An introduction to communication studies. Published using Pressbooks University of Minnesota Libraries Publishing edition, 2016. Book retrieved from https://textbooks.whatcom.edu/duttoncmst101/front-matter/copyright-information/

18 More information about the Inheritance: www.imdb.com/title/tt0328844/?ref_=tt_urv

19 More information about Entre Les Bras: www.imdb.com/title/tt2141717/?ref_=fn_al_tt_1

20 This example discussion is developed solely as the basis for class discussion. This example discussion is not intended to serve as an endorsement, source of primary data, or illustration of effective or ineffective management.

This example was built by using different sources. Information retrieved from: (1) https://ghsexplos ion.com/2842/features/adidas-vs-puma-a-history-of-two-brothers/#:~:text=Unfortunately%2C%20so mewhere%20down%20the%20line,success%20for%20their%20own%20brands; (2) www.business insider.com/how-puma-and-adidas-rivalry-divided-their-founding-town-for-70-years-2018-10#after-the-second-world-war-there-was-a-split-between-rudolf-and-adolf-2; (3) www.theguardian.com/sport/2009/oct/19/rivalry-between-adidas-and-puma; (4) www.academia.edu/download/31024471/Northampton_paper_130324.pdf; (5) www.youtube.com/watch?v=Nl0iGMkxwcc, and (6) www.yout ube.com/watch?v=uPCMrllEfSQ.

21 This example discussion is developed solely as the basis for class discussion. This example discussion is not intended to serve as an endorsement, source of primary data, or illustration of effective or ineffective management.

22 Information retrieved from: (1) Eventbrite website: www.eventbrite.com/team/; (2) interview with Kevin can be watched: www.youtube.com/watch?v=utnoPfKI7ck, and (3) Petch, N. (2017). Do life partners make good business partners? *Entrepreneur Middle East*. Article retrieved from www.entre preneur.com/article/297991

23 In collaboration with Arpita Vyas, this case study discussion is developed solely as the basis for class discussion. This case study discussion is not intended to serve as an endorsement, source of primary data, or illustration of effective or ineffective management. Several sources were used to develop the story: (1) www.youtube.com/watch?v=McGQvA3i_IY and www.forbes.com/sites/arielshapiro/2021/03/10/inside-the-firm-how-the-royal-familys-28-billion-money-machine-really-works/?sh=8f1a0 ad2bccf; (2) www.youtube.com/watch?v=w-gkAM0XZMU and www.youtube.com/watch?v=EXpF FFCvcH4; (3) www.youtube.com/watch?v=I1SEDfgNyqM and www.cnbc.com/2011/01/31/Famous-family-business-feuds.html; (4) www.youtube.com/watch?v=-JQOM1foboc; (5) www.youtube.com/watch?v=UMdru3TVOBQ; (6) www.youtube.com/watch?v=46N-bulO-aM; (7) www.youtube.com/watch?v=hVXzTuPNadk and www.townandcountrymag.com/society/a9644632/kate-middleton-fam ily/; (8) www.royal.uk/statement-communications-secretary-prince-harry

24 Landler, M. (2021). In royal "Firm," the family business always comes first. *The New York Times*. Article retrieved from www.nytimes.com/2021/03/09/world/europe/royal-family-firm-meghan-harry.html

Part II

Management in family business

4 Conflict, conflict management, and communication

Learning objectives

- Distinguish different types and sources of conflicts in family businesses.
- Understand how conflicts affect family businesses.
- Recognize how context can affect the perceptions and dynamics of conflicts in family businesses.
- Identify alternative ways to manage conflicts in family businesses.
- Interpret the importance of communication for conflict resolution in family businesses.

4.1 Introduction

In Chapter 3, we learned about the importance of interpersonal relationships in the family business context and how interpersonal relationships affect family businesses in terms of decision-making. We can all agree that interpersonal relationships make up the fabric of family businesses and are what make family businesses unique. When the main interpersonal relationships in a family are strong and healthy, the family business is able to develop competitive advantages (e.g., agile decision-making, extended social capital to leverage economic activities, and a strong social reputation, among others) that are difficult to imitate and replicate by competitors. However, interpersonal relationships are not without conflicts. Conflicts are one of the weakest parts of any family business project because most of these conflicts are difficult to untie due to the emotional load and deep sentiments that interfere with decision-making at the business and ownership levels.

There are two main issues when describing, exploring, and trying to understand family conflicts in relation to the dynamics of family businesses. First, business families and practitioners have to understand the nature of family conflicts by considering how they are linked to the ownership, management, and family entities. Generally, there is no one isolated conflict but instead multiple conflicts that overlap and are intertwined vertically (across levels, such as the individual level and the group level) and horizontally (across the three entities and the external environment). Second, if the "diagnosis" of conflict is correct, business families and practitioners have to design a conflict-resolution approach by embracing the three entities to maintain equilibrium and harmony between the ownership, management, and family entities.

The aim of this chapter is to explore the nature, types, and sources of conflicts that most commonly affect family businesses' decision-making and continuity. Since it is impossible to cover all possible conflicts in family businesses, this chapter focuses on the most important and general conflicts by aggregating them into a coherent framework. The chapter concludes by introducing some tools that business families and practitioners can use to handle conflicts.

DOI: 10.4324/9781003273240-6

4.2 Definition of conflicts in family businesses

We all frequently experience conflicts in our lives. A conflict can be described as having a strong disagreement with someone due to differences in opinions, ideas, interests, and/or discrepancies in the way to approach situations as well as when someone does not have a good emotional connection with someone else or a situation. Although people sometimes try to deny conflicts, they exist and are best approached by channeling, handling, and resolving them. Not recognizing, addressing, and handling conflicts can jeopardize our own emotional and psychological stability and our relationships with others and can damage the social institutions in which we dwell.

It is important to establish that conflicts can occur at both the micro- and meso-levels. First, at the micro- or individual level, there are two types of conflicts: intrapersonal conflicts and interpersonal conflicts. Intrapersonal conflicts are those that arise when an individual experiences a contradiction or feels his or her needs, goals, and expectations are threatened. Intrapersonal conflicts are characterized by cognitive and/affective dimensions—for example, a parent who is uncertain about inviting his or her child to join the family firm. This intrapersonal conflict emerges because of the differences in the parent's roles in the family as a father/mother and in the business as a manager. On the other hand, interpersonal conflicts arise due to incompatibilities, inconsistencies, or disagreements between individuals in a social context—for instance, a child having disagreements with his or her entrepreneurial parents because the child is not willing to gain a few years of external work experience prior to joining the family firm.

Second, at the meso- or group level, we can likewise distinguish between intragroup conflicts and intergroup conflicts. Intragroup conflicts occur when there are incompatibilities, incongruences, and disagreements between two or more subgroups within one larger group (the family)—for instance, when two family branches have different strategic goals and strategic directions for the family business. On the other hand, intergroup conflicts arise when two or more groups of individuals who belong to different entities confront each other or disagree—for instance, when family owners and family managers disagree in terms of distributing profits or reinvesting in the family firm.

Conflicts are difficult to identify. In most family businesses, we can recognize some symptoms of conflicts that manifest at the surface level and are visible. Among the most common symptoms, we can highlight the following:
Individual level:

- *Opposition and rejection behavior* manifest when family members consciously or unconsciously attempt to oppose others' ideas, projects, and goals without clear explanations and convincing arguments for doing so.
- *Indifference* manifests when family members are not motivated to work and participate in family business projects.
- *Irritability, hostility, and aggressive behavior* arise in daily interpersonal interactions among family members and can be seen in individuals' physical movements and posture, voice levels, and facial gestures.
- *Intrigue, rumors, and gossip* manifest in family members' behavior to reduce or denigrate other family members' goals or actions by perpetuating false narratives.
- *Unreasonableness* occurs when family members do not show empathy for others and put their own interests before others' interests and before the family business's interests.
- *Physical symptoms* manifest as insomnia, stomach disorders, chest pain, and/or faster heart rate.

Group level:

- *Fragmentation of family members into different subgroups* occurs when conspiracy and plots manifest at the group level, which results in disseminating misinformation, confusing family members, and undermining trust.
- *Fragmentation of family members and nonfamily members* arises when family members unify against nonfamily members (other owners or nonfamily employees). This problem escalation can create the sense of us versus them.

It is difficult for someone who is involved in a problem (regardless of the level) to recognize the roots of the problem or the triggers. The symptoms tend to be so visible and strong that most individuals focus on them instead. This is akin to focusing on reducing our high temperature when we feel sick instead of looking for the problem that caused the high temperature. For instance, it is often easier for a parent to give a position to his or her child in the family business to reduce the child's irritability and hostility during daily family life than to address the child's lack of responsibility toward the family business. In other words, it is easier in the short term to spoil the child than to address the real problems behind the child's attitude.

Acknowledging a problem is not an easy task because when conflicts become interpersonal, they tend to be an accumulation of several incidents across a long period of time.

4.3 The conflict process in family businesses

A family business is a fertile arena for conflicts because of the overlap between the owner-ship, management, and family entities, which makes individuals have to interact and engage in different activities. To simplify our understanding of conflicts in family businesses, we can apply the five-stage process of conflict:[1]

- First, the potential incompatibilities, incongruences, and disagreements are typically triggered by the focal family's communication, the family business structure, and personal variables, all of which create fertile conditions for conflicts to arise. Communication is the mechanism through which family members interact. The content, channel, and context of communication are subject to misunderstanding because of the overlapping roles of family members. For instance, this is the case when parents communicate to their children as man-agers but in the context of the family when they are supposed to act as parents. Therefore, the content and channel of communication may not match the context in which the commu-nication takes place because they are affected by emotions. The complexity of the family business structure is related to the size of the ownership, management, and family entities such that the more family members' roles overlap, the more the friction among them. Each entity has its own internal hierarchy for family members with role specialization and social status that could generate friction among individuals. Indeed, while the hierarchy in families is assigned based on tenure, in family businesses, it is assigned based on skills and capabil-ities. For instance, take an uncle who is a manager in the family business and a nephew who is the CEO in the family business. In this case, they have two different types of authority: the uncle's authority is cultural and is based on seniority, and the nephew's authority is business related and comes from his position. Finally, the individual-level antecedents for conflicts entail the personal characteristics inherent to any individual, such as individuals' characters, personalities, emotions, or moods.

- The second stage of the conflict process involves cognition and personalization. This stage involves one or both parties recognizing/perceiving the preceding conditions for a conflict. When a conflict is perceived, that means the parties involved experience anxiety, frustration, and/or hostility. At this stage, emotions can play a significant role in how family members perceive, interpret, and feel conflicts. Therefore, since the family is a strong emotional entity, the family logic emerges in family members' cognition as they interpret and understand the situation. Conflicts stay at the intrapersonal level, taking place or existing within the mind of an individual.

- The third stage involves participants' intentions to act in a specific way to handle/avoid the conflict. Intentions are a good predictor of individuals' ultimate behavior. However, intentions condition not only people's behavior but also their inferences of others' intentions regarding the same perceived conflict or their inferences of others' reactions to their behavior. Many conflicts in family businesses escalate because of incorrect inferences of others' intentions or anticipated behavior. For instance, a young daughter may think her mother does not trust her to assume a big responsibility in the family business, but the reality is her mother infers that she is not interested in the business.

- The fourth stage is the behavior itself (statements, reactions, and actions) that one or both parties display to channel, handle, and/or avoid the conflict and entails a process of interaction at one moment in time or across a long period of time. At this stage, the conflict shifts from the intrapersonal level to the interpersonal level and becomes visible. An important aspect of this stage is conflict intensity, which can vary from no conflict at all to minor disagreements, questioning and challenging, verbal attacks and threats, and aggressive positions.

- The final stage is the outcome—that is, the result or consequence of the conflict—which can be positive (functional) or negative (dysfunctional). Conflicts can end up being functional for each individual involved and for groups of individuals (i.e., ownership, management, and family entities). At the individual level, a conflict can improve the quality of decision-making when each party listens to and understands the other's point of view and generates psychological and personal gains. At the group level, a conflict can help a group think about how to integrate the ownership, management, and family entities; challenge the status quo in the family business; and stimulate creative solutions to meet the needs and goals of each entity. Functional conflicts generally improve ownership performance, business productivity, and family cohesiveness. On the other hand, conflicts can be dysfunctional when they erode individuals' trust, reduce the satisfaction of interpersonal relationships, and undermine group unity. In a family business, dysfunctional conflicts reduce the effectiveness of the responsible ownership entity to lead the family business according to its long-term vision, distract managers' attention away from exercising operative strategies, and weaken family ties that affect family cohesiveness. When dysfunctional conflicts in a family business are prolonged over time and become entrenched in the ownership, management, and family entities, they jeopardize the survival of the family business and disrupt family harmony.

4.4 Sources of conflicts in family business

Beyond the antecedent conditions that trigger conflicts described in Section 4.3 (communication, structural, and personal characteristics), it is generally important to explore the specificities of the sources of conflicts in family businesses. It may be difficult to intervene, address, and manage conflicts without knowing the origins that affect interpersonal relationships. The sources of conflicts refer to the causes that trigger intrapersonal, interpersonal, and group conflicts. In family businesses, we focus on the sources of conflicts that emerge from the overlap of the ownership, management, and family entities. In other words, conflicts emerge as a consequence of the multiple roles that family members perform.

Role overlap triggers conflicts because of the contradictions in behavior, perceptions, expectations, and intentions that arise when someone performs different roles (owner, manager, and/or family roles). Role overlap engenders different types of conflicts at the individual and group levels:

- *Circumstantial conflicts* stem from a particular situation in which a mismatch of role and context exists due to a lack of understanding among family individuals who are involved in the situation, which leads to various misinterpretations. Take, for example, a woman who leads a family business who has to perform the roles of mother and manager. When evaluating her daughter or son as an employee, both of these woman's roles could contradict in terms of how to evaluate her daughter or son and how to communicate this evaluation. Being a family business leader, the mother needs to be fair in her employee evaluation. However, if the evaluation happens to be negative, there is a high probability that her son or daughter would misinterpret it as the mother being overly strict and uncaring.
- *Conflicts of interest* are the classic conflicts that emerge when family members have different interests across their overlapping roles. For example, take a family member who is owner of the family business and would like to maximize his or her return on investment to increase dividends to improve the family's lifestyle. The same individual, as a manager of the firm, would like to reinvest the profits to modernize and digitalize the firm.
- *Conflicts of values* emerge when the principles and values associated with different roles contradict or clash. Conflicts of values are common when multiple generations work together, and each generation of family members eases, adjusts, or modifies the original principles and values guiding their behavior and actions. Conflicting values and principles can be related to political values, religious values, work values, moral values, and recreational values. For example, the work values across generations in a family business as well as how family members preserve or change their approach to working together and balancing their work–family time can be a source of conflict. While the founding generation may work more because of their cultural values and personal desire to build the family business from scratch, second and subsequent generations are more likely to find a balance between their work and recreational time.
- *Structural conflicts* emerge at the group level and are related to confrontation among the three entities that form a family business (ownership, management, and family). Each entity has its own logic justifying its existence and tries to impose this logic on the other entities.

Role overlap is a common source of intrapersonal conflicts—for instance, when a family member whose roles overlap has to decide how to behave knowing the contradictions and consequences of his or her actions. An intrapersonal conflict becomes an interpersonal conflict when an individual family member's behavior affects, threatens, or engenders the perceptions or expectations other family members have of him or her.

In addition to the role overlap, another source of conflict emerges according to family members' role perception and expectations:

- *Role perceptions* trigger conflicts when one individual's behavior directly affects someone else in the family business, and the latter person's perception of the individual's initial behavior generates dissatisfaction and negative emotions. In other words, one behavior (an action taken) to perform a role dissatisfies another person in terms of how this person experiences and perceives the behavior itself.

- *Role expectations* trigger conflicts because an individual's behavior affects the expectations of others who hold particular roles in specific situations. While perceptions involve the senses to produce psychological stimuli, expectations are mental ideas and representations of how an individual in a particular role should act or perform. Everyone has in mind what an ideal father, mother, or brother is, and these expectations about roles differ due to family culture and societal traditions. Each role a family member has to perform in the ownership, management, and family entities is socially determined and defines what is good or bad and what is ideal behavior. When individuals' expectations confront the actual behavior of others in their roles, intrapersonal and interpersonal conflicts can emerge.

Finally, how individuals handle negotiation to solve a problem or an issue, how individuals interact to reach agreements, or how individuals communicate common agreements could be the source of conflicts in family businesses:

- *Role negotiation* can trigger conflicts because of the way family members negotiate their place in the family, ownership, and management entities. Such negotiation entails interactions through which family members attempt to alter each other's expectations about their roles (how the roles should be interpreted, enacted, and evaluated). For instance, in the Van Kralingen family business, founded 1926 as a removals company, the second and third generations bargained for their interests to guarantee the family business's continuity. Hizkia Van Kralingen's father always tried to convince his son to join the business. When the time came, Hizkia Van Kralingen negotiated his position and vision by refocusing the company on doing removals for museums, galleries, and collectors—namely, he refocused the family business on the museum logistics industry. Once his father agreed, Hizkia Van Kralingen joined the family firm in 1990. He then went on to change the business's name after himself, Hizkia Van Kralingen, to highlight the new focus of the family business.[2] In this example, the negotiation was well managed by both parties. However, it is during this kind of process that family members may confuse their multiple roles and the negotiation process could lead to an escalation of conflicts because of inappropriate communication and interaction mechanism.

The two generic sources of conflicts—role overlap and role negotiation—can be amplified by the micro- and macro-context in which the family businesses dwell.

4.4.1 Conflict and context

The main sources of conflicts are not conflicts per se; rather, the specificities of the family business are what usually trigger conflicts. The capacity of sources to trigger conflicts is constrained by the context. This means that the context could accelerate, delay, or suppress the trigger effect. The following are the most common contextual elements that trigger conflicts (this list is not intended to be exhaustive):

- *Poor processes and structures* connecting the family, ownership, and management entities may aggravate role overlap and role negotiation as sources of conflicts. A lack of a governance structure for the family and the business with demarcated arenas in which family members can perform their roles and reduce the mismatch between their roles and context increases the likelihood of having conflicts within the family business. In addition, a lack of governance tends to come with a lack of policies that set expectations, which also increases conflicts. For instance, an employment policy can anchor children's expectations in terms of employment and remuneration and can be a means to minimize nepotism and reduce conflicts over role expectations.

- *Family communication style* may contribute to aggravating conflicts stemming from role overlap and role negotiation. Lack of communication, poor communication channels, and one-way communication increase misunderstandings among family members and can potentially scale intrapersonal and interpersonal conflicts. George Bryan, a third-generation family member involved in the Drayton Manor Theme Park family business (one of the most popular theme parks in England, founded in 1950), reflected on the business's transition from the second generation to the third generation, which came with important organizational changes.[3] The four members of the third generation, which consisted of brother William, George and their cousins Edward and Helen, actively worked in the family business. All of them knew that, being the eldest, William would lead the new generation as managing director. When it came time for the transition, George found it difficult to accept because based on external advice, William transformed the family business structure and, consequently, the family and the business relationship. George and Helen moved from their operational roles to board-of-director roles. This change made George feel terrible. George thought that having an open and effective conversation with his family members would have been the best way for him to avoid feeling hurt as he would have been able to understand the practicalities of William becoming the managing director.
- *Generational gaps* are another important conflict stressor. A generational gap refers to the disparities in opinions, beliefs, and values among family members from distinct generations who occupy different roles across the ownership, management, and family entities. Although family members typically grow in a similar cultural environment, each generation has different knowledge, experiences, and time horizons for their decision-making and has lived different disruptive events. Therefore, generational gaps not only affect individuals' expectations for and perceptions of their own and others' roles within a family business but can also influence family communication and consequently trigger conflicts. For example, siblings Şirin and Kerem Çelikel, the second generation of Anel Holding, a Turkish family business conglomerate, highlighted the generational gap when it came to decision-making in their family business. Belonging to Generation Y, the brother and sister are interested in how their decision outputs improve the community, while the previous generation was more concerned about performance.[4]
- *Limited resources* are another common stressor exacerbating role overlap and role negotiation as sources of conflicts in family businesses. Since family business members have their own particular goals but also represent the goals of the family, ownership, and/or management entities simultaneously, scarce resources require negotiation among family members and decisions to balance the entities' needs in terms of resources, particularly financial resources. For instance, there is usually a tradeoff between reinvesting benefits or distributing dividends. During the economic downturn caused by COVID-19, Molson Coors, a Canadian firm still guided by the seventh generation, suspended dividends to preserve the firm's capital and protect its liquidity. Andrew Molson highlighted that the family serves as the presence of a committed, knowledgeable, long-term-minded shareholder sitting on the board, acting in the interests of all shareholders.

4.5 Types of family business conflicts

Not all conflicts that arise in family businesses are alike. There are different types of conflicts, which can be grouped into two categories[5] that may have different outcomes for individuals and groups.

First, cognitive conflicts arise from perceptions of disagreements about differences in viewpoints, ideas, and opinions related to the jobs, processes, or tasks that family members have to perform as a consequence of their roles as owner, manager, and/or member of the family. These conflicts drive individuals to be engaged in their roles, committed to the family business, and less resistant to change. Indeed, cognitive conflicts can enhance the quality of decision-making at the family and business levels. We can distinguish two different subtypes of cognitive conflicts. Task conflict relates to differences among family members in terms of what they think needs to be done, whereas process conflict refers to disagreements about how things should be done. These cognitive conflicts are important for improving group function-ality, such as increasing information exchange, developing collective learning mechanisms, expanding knowledge, generating innovative attitudes, and—ultimately—boosting group performance.

Second, affective conflicts (also called relationship conflicts) arise from interpersonal tensions and are emotional in nature because they entail person-related disagreements characterized by animosity and annoyance among family members. This type of conflict makes family members feel negative, irritable, suspicious, and resentful. Therefore, affective conflicts may blind family members, causing them to make biased decisions due to their emotional ambivalence. For instance, some family members may focus on other people and personalize conversations instead of resolving task or process problems, which may diminish mutual understanding among family members. Affective conflicts tend to hinder the quality of decisions, thereby jeopardizing the cohesiveness of the family and the sustainability of the firm.

Even though cognitive and affective conflicts differ in their nature, in the particular context of family businesses, there is a connection and blurred boundaries between them due to the multiple roles and kinship relationships among family individuals. For instance, a constructive cognitive conflict about how to organize a family business's governance structure could become an affective conflict because of the complexity of each entity and the difficulties of managing family interpersonal relationships across time. A family conflict could have the following sequence. It starts as a minor disagreement in terms of different opinions and the exchange of ideas among participants. The next level is a serious dispute where feelings come into play—personalized attacks, political behaviors, and divergent goals emerge. Next comes a destabil-izing conflict characterized by dogmatic positions, aggressive rhetoric and enemies, and no constructive common goals. Finally, the war stage is a sign of complete disengagement to look for a solution. Each party has its own goals and position, and there is permanent interpersonal relationship damage as well as economic and socioemotional wealth destruction.

The cognitive versus affective classification of conflicts is important because of each type's consequences for individuals who play different roles in the family business system and for the groups represented by each entity (ownership, management, and family). While cognitive conflicts tend to be constrictive at the individual and group levels, affective conflicts tend to be dysfunctional and have serious consequences for interpersonal relationships and entities in terms of ownership performance, business productivity, and family cohesiveness. Table 4.1 summarizes the most important conflicts that could emerge based on individuals' positions and roles across the three entities.

Table 4.1 A summary of the types of conflicts across the overlapping entities

Relationships between Entities	Who Might Be Involved	Conflict Description	Types of Conflict
Family and ownership	• Active vs. passive family owners • Family vs. nonfamily owners	Conflicts of interest: • When both parties have different strategic perspectives about the firm. • When active family owners (or majority family owners) are in a position to gain personal benefits at the expense of passive family owners (or minority nonfamily owners).	• When both parties in a conflict are family members with different roles and positions across the ownership and family entities, the likelihood of having an affective conflict is higher. Additionally, a cognitive task conflict could shift to an affective conflict. • When nonfamily owners are part of a conflict, the conflict is more likely to be a cognitive (task or process) conflict and could be resolved/addressed by improving the functionality of the business system.
Family and business	• Family members employed in the business vs. family members not employed in the business	• Family members with different roles in the business and without active roles could differ on strategic (leadership) and operative aspects, such as family member employment and compensation. • Work–family conflicts because of the demands from each entity.	• Most of these conflicts are affective conflicts in nature and require a comprehensive analysis of the causes. In other words, they tend to be relational resulting from personality clashes and negative emotions. • These tend to be a mix of cognitive and affective conflicts. Depending on the conflict-resolution process, either type of conflict is possible.
	• Family employed and nonfamily employees	• Both parties could disagree about how to accomplish the main organizational goals.	• These tend to be cognitive conflicts as parties have different understandings about the tasks and processes that should be implemented. They can become affective conflicts when the discussion involves family-sensitive issues, such as succession and future leader development.
Family, business, and ownership	• Family members who have roles in all three entities	• Conflicts related to the family business's long-term strategy, leadership, and operational tasks.	• High probability of a cognitive conflict shifting to an affective conflict when the conflict touches upon family issues, such as the next generation of family leaders.

4.6 Conflict management

Conflict management is an important skill for family business leaders to encourage their family members to develop. With this skill, family members can ensure functional conflicts to improve decision-making as well as to handle and minimize the impact of dysfunctional conflicts. For example, Sheikh Sultan Sooud Al-Qassemi, managing director of Al Saud Company in the United Arab Emirates, mentioned that he dedicates a significant portion of his time to handling, addressing, and managing family interpersonal relationships to avoid conflicts. How family business leaders and family members approach conflict and negotiate their goals and needs is important for the quality of interpersonal relationships within each entity and between them.

The conflict-resolution method[6] is an instrument that can help clarify how family members address conflicts. The model has two independent dimensions of interpersonal behavior: assertiveness and cooperativeness. While assertiveness refers to behavior intended to satisfy one's own concerns, cooperativeness refers to behavior intended to satisfy another's concerns. Combining these two dimensions, we can identify five approaches for handling conflict situations:

- The *avoiding* approach (unassertive and uncooperative) occurs when family members recognize that a conflict exists but try to suppress it or avoid it. Family members avoid face-to-face confrontation and discussion. The avoiding approach is not the best way to address conflicts because it procrastinates a resolution (sooner or later, family members should address conflicts), and time could play against participants. This approach can also trigger secondary conflicts with other family members, and it escalates different emotions that can confuse the origins of a conflict with time. However, this approach can be used to cool down individuals' first reactions and postpone conflict resolution (conversation) until participants are in a different context or the focal conflict becomes less important.
- The *collaborating* approach (assertive and cooperative) occurs when family members attempt to satisfy all parties' concerns or demands and look for a win-win solution for parties' goals. With this approach, both parties can get what they want while minimizing negative feelings. The collaborating approach is very important for long-lasting relationships, specifically in the family business context where kinship relationships overlap with work-oriented relationships. It is not always possible to use this approach because the goals and interests of each party could compete.
- The *competing* (assertive and uncooperative) approach occurs when a family member or a group of family members seek to satisfy their own interests, needs, and goals regardless of the impact on the rest of the family members and without considering the balance of the three entities. Parties are more aware about the results of the negotiation than the process itself and the importance of the relationships in the long term.
- The *accommodating* approach (unassertive and cooperative) occurs when family individuals or family groups are willing (even when they do not understand each other) to recognize others' interests, needs, and goals in order to maintain the kinship relationships that tie them together. One party is able to self-sacrifice his or her goals and interests with the intention of satisfying the other's goals and interests. In this case, the party taking the accommodating approach does not care about the result as much as the relationship.
- The *compromising* approach (intermediate in assertiveness and cooperativeness) occurs when family members are willing to accept solutions with incomplete satisfaction for both parties (both parties win and lose something). The aim of this approach is to create a balanced situation to end a disagreement and find a satisfactory resolution for all parties.

Even though one or two of these five conflict-resolution approaches are likely more developed for each of us, it is important to recognize that their effectiveness depends on the specific situation or circumstance as well as the demographic (e.g., age and generation) and personality (e.g., patterns of thinking, feeling, and behaving) of the individuals involved in a conflict. For instance, the generation gap and age difference between parents and children could change the parents' attitudes when addressing conflicts. Young parents may tend to use the competing approach for conflict resolution to impose their vision of and long-term strategy for the family business. This is normal because they have high psychological ownership of the family business and the energy needed to direct its destiny. However, parents who are close to retirement and can perceive that their professional careers should shift from the front line of family business operations will probably use alternative conflict-resolution mechanisms, such as compromising, through which parents embrace their children's needs and goals while preparing them for future leadership.

The conflict-negotiation process can entail several different conflict-resolution techniques, which are further developed in Section 4.6.1.

4.6.1 Conflict-resolution techniques

Conflict-resolution techniques attempt to find ways for two or more parties to find a solution to a disagreement. These techniques can be useful when conflicts reach a high level of dysfunctionality for the group(s) or entities (ownership, business, and family) involved. Learning and applying these techniques can be useful for family leaders to address problems in one entity that may contaminate the other entities in the medium or long term. In the family business context there is a tendency to avoid addressing conflicts or postponing a resolution because of the kinship relationships that tie family members together. For instance, siblings may not talk about situations that affect them because of their emotional affection, the consequences of escalation, or simply the desire to not disappoint other family members. However, the accumulation and overlap of intrapersonal conflicts affect sibling relationships sooner or later, with conflicts that are not addressed today serving as the source of future conflicts over other issues related to succession or parents' inheritance, for example.

There are two general types of approaches to manage conflicts (traditional and complementary), which consist of two main dimensions.[7] The first dimension relates to how to handle parties: separating the parties of the dispute or bringing the parties together. The second dimension relates to the focus of attention: issue related or individual related.

The *traditional techniques* attempt to change the circumstances associated with a conflict by separating/moving family members (if possible) across the three entities or within each entity (positions and roles) and by addressing issues (organizational and structural issues) related to the conflict. For instance, when siblings have problems working together, their parents may opt to move the siblings' positions in the organization to avoid conflicts or avoid conflict escalation. In addition, in the approach taken by many family business consultants, there is a tendency to address conflicts among the ownership, management, and family entities by developing governance structures (separating and demarcating roles and creating structures). Implicitly, this approach considers that conflict resolution in family businesses is, to a certain extent, independent from the individuals involved and is all about the blurred boundaries between the three entities that require governance, regulations, and procedures. Among the most common techniques are the following:

- *Expansion resources.* One way business families solve conflicts is to allocate resources and positions to satisfy the demands of family members or family branches. For instance, a father may decide to separate his business into three sub-businesses, one for each child, to avoid conflicts. Even though this technique could satisfactorily address problems in the short term, it could also postpone or delay the eruption of interpersonal conflicts because resources are limited and should be allocated in the best interest of the whole system. Continuing with the example, sooner or later, the children's paths are going to meet when the father has to step aside and begin delegating and transferring ownership and management succession.

- *Authoritarian approach.* This is a simple method whereby family members execute their power based on the positions they occupy and force a solution within or among groups or entities. This technique for conflict resolution is common in hierarchical business families with vertical decision-making. For instance, this technique may be used when a young "NextGen" is not interested in joining the family business but his father's mandate points him as the natural successor. Because of the family culture, the NextGen is not able to contradict his father's decision. His only solution is to accept the position and hope the future changes the course of his destiny by altering his opinion about the business or providing an opportunity for him to sell it after assuming control.
- *Structural changes.* The structure and processes in each entity and their interactions need to be updated to serve the changing interests of each entity due to the complexity of the family and the business over time. Family businesses use corporate governance to direct and coordinate the dynamics of each entity and their interactions, and in most cases, the creation of and adjustments to governance structures and bodies across time are reactions to solve conflicts and not to satisfy the functional needs of the whole family business system. For instance, Carvajal Grupo in Colombia, which is a centennial firm operating in more than 12 sectors with roughly 26,000 employees, initiated a developmental process for its family governance structure in 1996 (when the third family generation started to think about transferring the firm to the next generation) by creating a family council to formalize and coordinate the family–business relationship.

Even though traditional techniques can be effective depending on the context, the type of conflict, and the time horizon, the main limitation is their lack of consideration of those involved in a conflict. That is, there is no consideration of individuals' interests, needs, goals, and expectations to address and manage conflicts in the long term. Because family members are also linked by their kinship relationships, sooner or later, their lives are going to converge in different situations and circumstances, so inefficient past conflict resolution will most likely result in another conflict.

The *complementary techniques* attempt to deal with family members and the dynamics of the conflict. These techniques are important because merely separating family members in their business positions or adding resources to avoid problems is a short-term solution. Family members are most likely going to carry their conflicts throughout the three entities, thereby causing cross-contamination. For example, even when siblings are separated in the business structure to resolve their conflicts, they also interact in the family and ownership entities and can thus carry their conflicts with themselves. The following are some complementary techniques that can be used for conflict resolution.

- *Discussion and negotiation.* This technique happens in families that are mature enough to engage in a constructive talk-listen approach to find a solution to their problems. This technique is related to the communication style that a business family has developed across time. Business families that balance their conversational and conformity orientations (see Chapter 3 about family communication styles) in a constructive way are able to effectively engage in discussion and conversation.

- *Coaching.* This technique involves a one-to-one process (an external coach and one party in the focal conflict) to help family members sort conflicts out. The aim is to support and help family members reflect on the focal problem and conflict and develop their abilities to engage in, manage, and find sustainable solutions.
- *Mediation.* This technique entails the intervention of an impartial third party in a conflict among/between family members who attempts to help the participants resolve their conflict autonomously. Mediation is applied using communication and negotiation practices that help conflicted participants understand each other's interests and needs and develop constructive solutions.
- *Team development.* This technique involves an intervention process driven by group dynamic practices that is managed by a professional advisor with the purpose of transforming the group of family members into a team. Family team development can improve communication, create and consolidate the family identity, build superordinate family business goals, and enhance cooperation. The importance of the team-development approach lies in preventing conflict more than resolving conflict.

4.6.2 Conflict-stimulation techniques

Conflicts are not always negative in family businesses. Some conflicts can be functional and help individuals, teams, and entities advance their skills, performance, and/or well-being. Indeed, in any organization, lack of conflicts can be a problem in itself, but this issue is pronounced in family businesses where family members attempt to preserve the status quo or where the strong influence of one individual, group of individuals, or entity over another prevents conflicts from emerging. There are different techniques that family businesses can implement to stimulate functional conflicts that can help the ownership, management, and family entities work together harmoniously.

- *Develop channels and arenas for communication among family members.* One may think that family members are able to communicate effectively because they belong to the same family and interact frequently. However, this is usually not the case in most families. Family members do not always talk about important issues directly. While social family meetings can help family members strengthen their familial bonds, they do not necessarily encourage conversations that stimulate conflict. Having channels and arenas to communicate is sometimes an effective means to introduce contradicting ideas and challenge points of view in exaggerated situations to encourage family members to engage in productive conversations.
- *Invite an outside member into the family group or entity.* If the family group or one of the family business entities is stagnant, introducing external individuals (e.g., nonfamily members or members who do not belong to the group) could help family members activate and engage in positive conflicts because external members always cause friction in the status quo of an existing group of individuals and stimulate progression in the conversation. Such an introduction may improve individual performance as well as group productivity.
- *Stimulate competition.* The equal treatment of individuals in families can sometimes paralyze individuals, groups, and entities from confronting ideas or points of view to engender functional conflicts. To break this trend, introducing competition within or among groups or entities can help individuals explore and exploit their capabilities and improve decision-making. Introducing competition in the form of awards or bonuses or just public recognition can create a healthy atmosphere for people to step away from the status quo.

4.7 Additional activities and reading material

4.7.1 Classroom discussion questions

1   What is a conflict, and why do conflicts emerge in family businesses?
2   What are the most common and unique types of conflicts in family businesses? Reflect on your own conflicts and the conflicts you have witnessed in your family business.
3   Why is it important to understand the conflict process? Why do you think context, situation, and personal characteristics matter for conflict escalation?
4   When are conflicts positive, and when are conflicts negative? Can you elaborate about your own personal experience in your family business?
5   What are the best conflict-resolution techniques? Why?

4.7.2 Additional readings

1   Wofford, J. (2022). Building consensus from conflict: Tips and tools. *FFI Practitioners*. Article retrieved from https://ffipractitioner.org/building-consensus-from-conflict-tips-and-tools/
2   Di Loreto, N., & Isaacson, A. (2022). Avoiding conflict will only hurt your family business. *Harvard Business Review*. Article retrieved from https://hbr.org/2022/10/avoiding-conflict-will-only-hurt-your-family-business
3   Wing, C., & Gera, R. K. (2020). Create a culture of generosity and communication in your family business. *Harvard Business Review*. Article retrieved from https://hbr.org/2020/05/create-a-culture-of-generosity-and-communication-in-your-family-business

4.7.3 Classroom activity

Aim: Self-recognition and reflection of how family members address interpersonal conflicts.
Material: In a Word document, list the ten statements below.
Based on your past experience in any past/current role in the ownership, business, and/or family entities of a family business, score the following ten statements by marking the number that best reflects yourself (1 means low and 5 means high).

1. I work to achieve my goals and satisfy my needs no matter what	1	2	3	4	5
2. I put other's needs, goals, and expectations above my own	1	2	3	4	5
3. I like to find a middle way to achieve my goals as well as others' goals	1	2	3	4	5
4. I try not to get involved in conflicts	1	2	3	4	5
5. I strive to explore and recognize issues with others	1	2	3	4	5
6. Once I have a good argument, I never give it up	1	2	3	4	5
7. I work to achieve harmony	1	2	3	4	5
8. I try to achieve some of my original goals when negotiating	1	2	3	4	5
9. I avoid open discussion and controversial topics in discussions	1	2	3	4	5
10. I share information and emotions with others	1	2	3	4	5

Running the classroom exercise: Distribute the pieces of paper with the ten statements and provide students with the following instructions. Ask them to take a couple of minutes to self-reflect on each of the statements and score each of them from 1 (low) to 5 (high). After all the students have completed the task, guide the interpretation of answers.

- First, ask students to sum up the following pairs of questions: 1 and 6, 5 and 10, 4 and 9, 2 and 7, and 3 and 8.
- The sum of Questions 1 and 6 shows the importance of the competing style.
- The collaborating style is the sum of Questions 5 and 10.
- The avoiding style is the sum of Questions 4 and 9.
- The accommodating style is the sum of Questions 2 and 7.
- Finally, the compromising style is the sum of Questions 3 and 8.

Discussion: Give all participants time to reflect on their self-assessments. Ask them to reflect on their own personal experiences to explore how they have reacted to a conflict in the past and what conflict-resolution approach they implemented. Some students will likely be willing to share their ideas publicly. Start the debate with the following question: Does the result of your conflict-resolution self-assessment match your own previous perception about how you handled conflicts?

Takeaways: The highest sum of a pair of questions reflects an individual's primary self-assessed conflict-resolution approach. Even though there could be one dominant approach, the importance and distance of the second and third pairs of questions are also important and can reveal alternative conflict-resolution approaches. This is a good exercise to collectively reflect on the different approaches across contexts and circumstances. It is important to recognize that the context and/or importance of a conflict could trigger different conflict-resolution approaches.

4.8 Case for analysis I: The team is broken![8]

This example illustrates the conflict process in a real situation. To preserve the confidentiality and privacy of the real family members of this case study, all names, locations, and other details have been changed.

Stage 1: Two brothers named Marc (the elder, who does not have a bachelor's degree) and Anthony (the younger, who has bachelor's and master's degrees) ran a successful family business in the United Arab Emirates that sold information technology peripherals, consumer electronics, and mobility products. Both brothers lived together with their wives and children and had a great personal and professional relationship. The brothers juggled their multiple overlapping roles as siblings, business partners, brothers-in-law, and uncles. Marc's and Anthony's wives were not involved in the business, and their relationship was not the best, but they acted respectfully toward each other. Both in-laws had different perceptions about their respective brother-in-law. Each time the wives had the opportunity, they tried to influence their husbands with ideas about the other brother and their interpersonal relationships. For instance, Marc's wife, Sara, used to tell Marc that Anthony looks down upon him because he never went to college. On the other hand, Anthony's wife, Sally, used to tell Anthony that Marc was dominating him and taking advantage of being older.

Stage 2: Disagreements between the brothers were not long in coming, and with them, pressure from their wives increased. Business- and ownership-related disagreements mixed with the wives' pressure. The brother relationship got stuck. Both of them became suspicious about the ultimate intentions of the other. Something broke in their relationship. At some point,

Marc started to believe that Anthony was trying to supersede him because he was more educated than him, whereas Anthony believed Marc was trying to assert his position of being the older brother and dominate him.

Stage 3: Both brothers were developing misconceptions about each other but decided to keep it to themselves as they wanted to avoid creating any sort of a dramatic environment between them.

Stage 4: One day, the brothers had an ugly blowout argument with each other in front of a few of their young employees, which demonstrated how both of them had a negative perception of the other. A technical problem about how to solve a customer's needs by applying new ideas became a personal problem without apparent reason.

Stage 5: The accumulated tension among the brothers across time and the eruption of the intra-personal conflict in front of their employees finally disrupted their relationship. Members from both families were dragged into the situation, and wives and children experienced estrangement in their relationships as well. This situation carried on for years. The level of the interpersonal conflict among the brothers reduced in intensity, so they were able to keep working and assuming their roles in the business entity. However, each of them managed their part of the business independently, and the business suffered. Their family relationships never were the same. Both families kept their distance and only occasionally met for family events.

Discussion questions:

1 Explain the source of conflict and type of conflict among the brothers.
2 If you were a business consultant, how would you address this situation?

4.9 Case for analysis II: Steinberg family business[9]

Many empires rise through time, while others cease to exist. Walmart and Steinberg were two family-owned business empires. The former is now leading the hypermarket and grocery market, while the latter is nowhere to be seen anymore.

Overview. In 1917, the immigrant Ida Steinberg opened her first grocery store in Montreal, Canada. With her persistence; hard work; and support from family members, especially Sam, her second-oldest sibling, Steinberg Inc. was able to expand quickly and exponentially. Within a matter of 20 years, Sam led the company's expansion with ten stores and two supermarkets. By 1960, the company had 92 stores along with some warehousing and real-estate businesses.

However, the years ahead were full of turbulence and conflict for the company. In 1969, Sam passed his role as company president to Dobrin, his son-in-law, but Sam still essentially managed the company until his death in 1978. The company started to experience many problems, including a huge decrease in sales, a decrease in its market share with no proper vision and strategy, and problems with the unions. In addition to the business problems, family problems emerged because of Sam's nepotism and lack of succession planning. When things started to drift further, Irving Ludmer, a former employee at Steinberg, was appointed CEO with the hopes that he would be able to turn the company around. Ludmer led the company from 1983 until 1989 and was successful in reversing the company's growth trajectory. However, his conflict with the board of directors and several family conflicts led the company to a lock-up agreement with Michel Gaucher to buy the company for CAD 1.3 billion. Within three years of the takeover, Gaucher went bankrupt and sold the company in pieces, marking the end of the Steinberg name in the industry.

How did Sam's full dedication to the family lead to its eventual demise?

Sam's leadership. Sam was a persistent, tough, and visionary leader who always made sure family came first. He made time for his family to the point that family calls to his office number were directly sent to him no matter how busy he was or how important the issues were. Sam also kept the family first in his company decisions, which resulted in a nepotistic culture within the company. Knowing that family members were always considered first and were always favored, top talent within the company were always rushing to leave to other competitors because of this culture. As a father, Sam provided his four daughters—Mitzi, Rita, Marilyn, and Evelyn—with a luxurious life and did not encourage any of them to study or work in the company. Mitzi was the only daughter who graduated and worked in the family business of her own will. As the head of the Steinberg family, Sam made sure everyone lived a good life and had a place in the company, and he ensured they met every week following his mother's teachings of always keeping the family first and keeping the family together.

Sam's succession. Sam chose Dobrin, Mitzi's husband, as his successor mainly to keep the family in control of the company. Ignoring Dobrin's lack of leadership skills, Sam chose him as his successor, which was the start of the company's downfall. Sam also made sure that the board of directors mainly consisted of his family members, giving them control of the company. This made it difficult to replace the president at first until the board saw no other way to keep the company alive and decided to hire Irving Ludmer while Mitzi served as vice president. However, Ludmer was not happy with the fact that Mitzi had control over him, and she was eventually pushed to resign from her role as vice president while keeping her shares of the company. This led Mitzi to try and sell her shares of the company, igniting a feud and a lawsuit between her and her sisters. This feud made it difficult for Ludmer to manage the company, so he relied heavily on the support of Marilyn and Evelyn. The support that Ludmer was taking advantage of gradually faded away when he had to fire Billy, Marilyn's son, leading all of the family members to reunite under their shared hatred of Ludmer. Because of this battle of control, Steinberg was eventually sold to Gaucher, marking an end to Steinberg's reign of 71 years.

Discussion questions:

3 Explain the source of conflict and type of conflict in Steimberg family business.
4 How can you describe the conflict management approach in Steimberg family business?
5 What kind of communication style is most dominant in Steinberg?

4.10 Case study: The fate of Gucci[10]

This is the story of an Italian family that managed to transform their family name into the globally renowned luxury fashion brand Gucci. The founding father of Gucci was Guccio Gucci, who was born in 1881 to parents Gabriello (a leather craftsman) and Elena hailing from the Tuscany region of Florence, Italy. Due to the family's weak financial background, at the age of 17, Guccio decided to move to London to make money and found a job as a bellhop at the Savoy Hotel, where he noticed how luggage and bags were an important status symbol for the rich and elite. During that time, he became passionate about pursuing his idea of producing high-quality luggage and bags. In 1901, he returned to Florence to join the leather manufacturer Franzi. During the same year, he also married a women named Aida and went on to have six children with her. Being the son of a leather craftsman, Guccio had strong knowledge of leather and was thus able to launch a line of high-quality bags. In 1921, his vision became a reality with the start of his company La Casa Gucci (House of Gucci). By the 1930s, the brand reached success, gaining traction overseas. In 1953, Guccio Gucci, the founder of one of the biggest brand names in history, died.

Gucci managed to reach new heights of success with significant contributions from the second generation. Even though the third generation also made major contributions, it was the third-generation members who were responsible for the disruption and destruction of the Gucci family business. Unfortunately, today, the Gucci brand is not owned by the Gucci family, and no family member has been involved in the business since 1993. Maurizio was the last third-generation family member; he sold his shares to Bahrain-based investment company Investcorp. Gucci was later bought by the French group PPR, which is now Kering (a French-based multi-national corporation specializing in luxury goods). *What happened in the Gucci family business to make it become a nonfamily business?*

Second generation. Guccio Gucci had a total of six children: a son named Ugo from Aida's previous relationship, whom he adopted, and five biological children—Aldo, Rodolfo, Grimalda (daughter), Enzo (passed away at the age of nine), and Vasco. Except for Grimalda, who did not have shares or a role in the business, Guccio and his sons expanded and grew the Gucci empire.

* *Ugo.* Not much is known about Guccio's stepson; however, it is said that he had a wild life-style as he spent his youth gambling and chasing women. He later went on to join an extreme Italian political party. While Guccio was approaching his old age, he feared Ugo would inherit Gucci shares and misuse them to advance his political career. To avoid that, Guccio offered Ugo a hefty amount of money in return for his future rights in the company.
* *Aldo.* He was the first child of Guccio and Aida, born in 1905, and is credited with the brand's expansion in the international market. Starting in his early school days, he used to accompany Guccio to their first Gucci store to do small tasks like sweeping floors and delivering parcels to clients. As a result, Aldo had a deep connection with the brand and eventually joined Gucci to work full time after gaining a degree in economics. The iconic Gucci logo that we still see today is also the work of Aldo's creativity, which was introduced in the 1930s. Aldo had the vision to expand and make Gucci products available to customers in different parts of Italy and ultimately overseas. He served as chairman from 1953 to 1986, and in 1953, he accomplished his goal of expanding internationally by inaugurating Gucci's first store in New York. Guccio was not very supportive and was reluctant about the idea of international expansion. Guccio remarked to Aldo, "Risk your neck if you must, but don't expect me to pay for it. You may be right. After all, I am an old man, I'm old-fashioned enough to believe that the best vegetables come from your own garden."[11] Aldo envisioned the expansion and opened several stores in different cities across various countries, such as Hong Kong, Japan, and many more. Aldo passed away in 1990, leaving behind four children: three sons with his wife Olwen Price, Paolo, Roberto, and Giorgio, who inherited a total of 50% (each given 16.6667%), and a daughter Patricia from an extra-marital affair, who did not inherit anything.
* *Vasco.* He is the second son of Guccio and Aida and was born in 1907. He married Maria Taburchi in 1933 and joined the family business in 1938 to support Aldo in production and design. He passed away in 1974, after which Maria is said to have sold the shares she inherited from Vasco to Aldo and Rodolfo as Maria and Vasco had no children.
* *Rodolfo.* Born in Italy in 1912, at the age of 17, he was spotted by a film director who cast him in a movie as a supporting character. In the same year, he bagged another role—this time as the protagonist—which became a huge success. With the passing years, he chose acting as his profession and became one of the most charming and popular actors. His wife, Sandra Ravel, was also an actress. The couple got married in 1944 in Venice, Italy. Four years later, in 1948, Rodolfo and his wife welcomed their only child, Maurizio. In 1954, Sandra passed away, leaving behind six-year-old Maurizio and husband Rodolfo. Upon the death of his

father Guccio, Rodolfo joined the Gucci family business to support his brothers Aldo and Vasco. Aldo and Rodolfo bought out Vasco's widow, split the shares, and became 50/50 owners. However, Aldo's children were not happy with this arrangement because Rodolfo did not contribute significantly to growing the Gucci empire. After Rodolfo's death in 1983, Maurizio inherited his father's shares in the company, becoming a majority shareholder.

Third generation:

- *Giorgio.* Giorgio is the eldest son of Aldo Gucci and is said to have contributed to some of the significant designs of the Gucci label.
- *Paolo.* Born in 1931, Paolo is the second son of Aldo and Olwen. Paolo and his brothers were encouraged by their grandfather Guccio to work in the family business in their early years and were given small chores like wrapping and delivering packages. Growing up, Paolo did not share a close relationship with his father, so he worked under his Uncle Vasco in the factory, where they both discovered Paolo's talent for design. He leveraged his design skills to design a full Gucci line. With his passion and dedication to design, he deservingly secured the position of chief designer by the 1960s. As the late 1970s approached, Paolo bagged the position of vice president after gaining sufficient experience working as chief designer, but after a point, he felt that his promotion was a strategic decision to deprive him of the opportunity to lead the Gucci empire. In other words, he believed it was a way to keep him out of the way of his father and uncle. "I wanted to expand," Paolo told *People* years later, "to bring in other financial backers and make the business run on more modern lines. But the Guccis have medieval concepts of business. So, I became the black sheep." Paolo's vision for the Gucci empire was neglected, which made him resent his family, especially his father. In order to attain his vision, Paolo secretly launched his own fashion line without addressing or discussing it with his father or uncle. As a result, he was fired and stopped working in the family business in 1980. By 1987, he sold his remaining Gucci shares for $45 million. The following years were difficult for him as he declared bankruptcy in 1993, having debts of approximately $90 million.
- *Roberto.* He was the youngest son of Aldo, and the only known business-related fact about him is that he helped set up the first Gucci store in Belgium. He was married to Drusilla Caferelli, and they had six children together.

The dynamic couple: Maurizio and wife Patrizia (in-law). Maurizio was the only child of Rodolpho, who was not very interested in the Gucci family business in his early years as he wanted to make an identity of his own. One night, at a party, he met a young, witty woman named Patrizia, who belonged to a small business family. There was an instant spark between the two, which increased on Patrizia's end when she found out that he belonged to the prestigious Gucci empire. The couple fell in love and reached the point where Maurizio introduced her to his father, Rodolpho, who thought Patrizia was a young woman who did not love Maurizio but only loved his money. Being in love with Patrizia, Maurizio disregarded his father's remarks and went ahead to tie the knot with her. They decided to lead a simple life away from the glitz and glam of the Gucci empire, which Patrizia wholeheartedly supported. A few years later, upon his father's (Rodolfo's) death, Maurizio was very interested in leading and taking full control of the family business. In the background, Patrizia motivated him to become the face of Gucci as she always wanted them to enter Gucci and take the brand to another level. However, with the time, Maurizio started to feel that Patrizia was trying to put him against his family. Maurizio drifted apart from Patrizia and had an extramarital affair with his childhood friend Paolo Franchi. In 1993, Maurizio was struggling to run Gucci as he went over budget and squandered money on

Gucci's headquarters in Florence and Milan, which then led him to resign and sell his shares to Investcorp marking the end of the Gucci's family connection to the business.

Conflicts:

Maurizio, Paolo, and Aldo.[12] In 1985, Maurizio wanted to oust his Uncle Aldo from the family business in order to gain full control and leadership of the business. Maurizio made a deal with his cousin Paolo, who agreed to vote to oust Aldo from the chairman position in return for having his new designs launched under his label Paolo Gucci as he already resented his father and held a grudge against him. Maurizio achieved his goal as Paolo voted for him to be chairman and reported Aldo to the Internal Revenue Service (IRS) for tax evasion, putting Aldo completely out of Maurizio's way so he could gain full control of the family business. In a statement about Maurizio and Paolo, Aldo stated, "Some have done their duty … others have the satisfaction of revenge. God will be their judge."[13] Moreover, Paolo started his own fashion line under his label, but he and Maurizio eventually started to have evident issues with each other such that both have called each other out in public interviews. When Paolo was asked if Maurizio was fit to run Gucci, he chuckled and expressed his negative views: "Absolutely not! He can't because he dreams every 5 minutes; he doesn't think, he dreams!"[14] In an interview in which Maurizio was asked to respond to Paolo's remarks, he replied,

When we took the responsibility of Gucci America, it was doing a business of $54 million with a profit of $6 million. Today, we do a business of $138 million …with $18 million profit. If this is the answer to a dream, I accept it.[15]

Maurizio deceived Paolo by having him arrested during one of Paolo's fashion shows in Rome for breach of contract for Paolo's collection.

Aldo and Paolo. The father–son duo did not have a very strong interpersonal relationship, and Paolo replicated Guccio's parenting style, being quite harsh with Paolo. In 1980, infuriated by his family's ignorance of his vision to run the Gucci empire in a different way, Paolo went ahead to launch his secretive fashion line under the Gucci brand name. The senior family members were furious, and as a result, the board (headed by Aldo) decided to fire him immediately, suing him for trademark infringement of the Gucci brand. The elder Gucci family members were so vexed that according to ABC News,[16] they issued warnings to their suppliers saying that working with Paolo would mean saying goodbye to doing business with Gucci.[17] Two years later, in 1982, Paolo was taken back by the family business and attended a board meeting with a tape recorder. He used the recording to sue his family members, alleging that he was physically attacked during the board meeting and suffered emotional trauma. Paolo took complete revenge on Aldo in 1986 by reporting him to the IRS for tax evasion.

Maurizio and Patrizia. Patrizia was devastated by Maurizio's betrayal of her and their children and did not take the divorce well. She reached an extreme phase of depression, sadness, and anger, which made her want to see Maurizio dead. As a result, she hired a hitman and had Maurizio murdered outside his residence.

Fate of Gucci. Gucci's brand value remains strong today despite not having any Gucci family members working in the business. What had once started off as a family business is now owned by the French group Kering. We saw the Gucci family empire fall apart as the family members sold their shares one by one.

Discussion questions:

1 What kind of conflicts appear in the Gucci story?
2 What roles did emotions play in the family interpersonal relationships?
3 How did conflict escalate?
4 Could this ending have been avoided?

Notes

1 Robbins, S. P., & Judge, T. A. (2007). *Organizational Behavior*. Upper Saddle River: Prentice Hall.
2 *Tharawat Magazine*. (2016). Hizkia Van Kralingen—Turtles, art, and the family business. Article retrieved from www.tharawat-magazine.com/future-industries/hizkia-van-kralingen-family-business/
3 *Tharawat Magazine*. (2018). Drayton Manor—Roles, relationships, and rollercoasters. Article retrieved from www.tharawat-magazine.com/roles-in-the-family-business/special-features-dray ton-manor/
4 Information retrieved from www.tharawat-magazine.com/geny/beyourself-anel/
5 Jehn, K.. (1995). *Affective and Cognitive Conflict in Work Groups: Increasing Performance through Value-Based Intragroup Conflict. Using Conflict in Organizations*. In De Dreu and Van De Vliert (Eds.). London: SAGE.
6 Thomas, K. W. (1992). "Conflict and negotiation processes in organizations," In M. D. Dunnette & L. M. Hough (Eds.), *Handbook of Industrial and Organizational Psychology* (Vol. 3, 2nd Ed., pp. 651–717). Palo Alto, CA: Consulting Psychologists Press.
7 Proksch, S. (2016). *Conflict management*. Cham, Switzerland: Springer.
8 In collaboration with Arpita Vyas, this example discussion is developed solely as the basis for class discussion. This example discussion is not intended to serve as an endorsement, source of primary data, or illustration of effective or ineffective management.
9 This example discussion is developed solely as the basis for class discussion. This example discussion is not intended to serve as an endorsement, source of primary data, or illustration of effective or ineffective management. Henriques, D. B. (1991). Wall Street; A Steinberg extended family affair. *The New York Times*. Article retrieved from www.nytimes.com/1991/11/17/business/wall-street-a-steinb erg-extended-family-affair.html
10 In collaboration with Arpita Vyas, this case study discussion is developed solely as the basis for class discussion. This case study discussion is not intended to serve as an endorsement, source of primary data, or illustration of effective or ineffective management.
11 Quote retrieved from www.grunge.com/825096/the-untold-truth-of-aldo-gucci/. It comes from the following book: Forden, S. G. (2002). *House of Gucci: A Sensational Story of Murder, Madness, Glamour and Greed*. William Morrow Paperbacks.
12 Information retrieved from www.youtube.com/watch?v=byh09ojFQrQ
13 Fitzgerald, R. (2021). Sex, lies and dirty money: 7 things you didn't know about the Gucci family. Article retrieved from https://medium.com/the-glitter-gold/sex-lies-and-dirty-money-7-things-you-didnt-know-about-the-gucci-family-e3f81721bad5
14 Everett, V., & Bentley, L. (1982). Move over, 'Dallas': Behind the glittering facade, a family feud rocks the House of Gucci. Article retrieved from https://people.com/archive/move-over-dallas-behind-the-glittering-facade-a-family-feud-rocks-the-house-of-gucci-vol-18-no-10/
15 Information retrieved from www.youtube.com/watch?v=byh09ojFQrQ
16 Moore, C. (2001). PrimeTime: Gucci, glamour and greed. *abcNEWS*. Article retrieved from https://abcnews.go.com/Primetime/story?id=132294&page=1
17 Information retrieved from www.grunge.com/838151/the-untold-truth-of-paolo-gucci/

5 Human resource management in family businesses

Learning objectives

- Distinguish between human resource management for family and nonfamily employees.
- Understand the effects of nepotism in family business human resource management.
- Recognize the different faultlines in family business human resource management.
- Identify the origins of asymmetric treatment and its consequences in family businesses.
- Interpret the effects of fairness and justice in family business human resource management.

5.1 Introduction

Human resource management refers to the set of practices of recruiting, hiring, deploying, training, and managing nonfamily and family (who are actively or non-actively involved in the business) employees. That is, human resource management entails not only nonfamily employees but also family members who work in the focal family business. In the family business context, human resource management also includes practices that regulate the relationship between the family and the business—for instance, the entrance conditions (hiring selection criteria) for family members in the firm.

There are several reasons to understand the uniqueness of human resource management in family businesses. First, human capital is a source of competitive advantage for some family businesses because of the people-oriented perspective used to embrace employees and engage them with family business projects. For example, the SABIS education network is a 130-year-old Lebanese family business that owns and operates schools in 20 countries across 5 continents. Victor Saad, the fourth-generation family member who serves as the vice president and board member, noted that "as a family business, SABIS benefits from the loyalty of its family members who have an emotional attachment to the company, and are always more inclined to persevere and 'go the extra mile.'"[1] Second, family involvement in a business creates a unique form of family human capital characterized by a set of knowledge, abilities, and skills that is transmitted from one generation to another and is difficult to imitate by competitors. For example, Crane & Co is an American family-owned paper mill business, founded in 1801, that has a contract with the government to produce the United States' paper currency, which they still retain today. Sixth-generation Crane family member Charlie Kittredge, who serves as the chairman of the board, highlighted this advantage:

> I didn't think when I was growing up that I would play a significant role in the business. I worked in the company when I was young, growing up as a teenager. But, I had a career outside of Crane. However, every generation before me was an active part of the business. My

DOI: 10.4324/9781003273240-7

father was involved, my uncles, my grandfather and great-grandfather worked in the business too. Crane & Company was who we were and is who we are.[2]

Finally, beyond its positive view, human resource management is also a source of negative effects on employees and on firm performance (productivity) because of nepotism, emotions, and the unequal treatment that family and nonfamily employees often receive. For example, Shine Light LLC, a family-owned business based out of the United Arab Emirates that sells electrical light fittings,[3] has a culture that promotes unequal treatment among family and nonfamily employees in terms of working hours and monthly salaries. Family employees have the flexibility to start working when they prefer and receive higher salaries compared to their nonfamily member employee counterparts. Consequently, human resource management in family businesses should maximize the strength of family and business relationships while minimizing the weaknesses of such relationships.

The uniqueness of human resource management in family businesses emerges because of the scope and scale of the practices involved. The scope of human resource management is related to different sets of knowledge, abilities, and skills that family and nonfamily employees bring to and create within a family business. In this context, asymmetric treatment between family and nonfamily employees is necessary for consolidating the competitive advantages of family and nonfamily human capital. While this asymmetric treatment can be good, too much of a good thing also can be bad. For instance, this asymmetric treatment, which tends to favor family members over nonfamily members, jeopardizes competitive advantages when it boosts employees' perceptions of unfairness. On the other hand, the scale of human resource management is related to the level of application, not only in the business entity but also in the family entity. Specifically, the treatment that family members receive to develop their professional careers in the family business system is a source of human capital that affects the competitiveness of a family business.

The aim of this chapter is to shed light on how human resource management in family businesses deals with the paradox that emerges from the lack of/blurred boundaries among the three entities. This paradox tends to erode authority and responsibilities, creating alternative guidelines to manage human resources and the competing logics (i.e., the ownership, management, and family logics) that reflect different guiding principles, for instance, loyalty versus merit, need versus equality, nepotism versus fairness, and entitlement versus competition.

5.2 Nepotism

In the family business context, nepotism is defined as a form of favoritism that is granted to relatives, loyal employees, and family friends in the form of specific positions and differential treatment in their career paths in the focal family business. Nepotism is considered the prevailing logic that most family businesses use in their human resource management. However, it can have negative consequences for family businesses because hiring and promoting individuals with poor skills deteriorates decision-making, increases interpersonal conflicts, reduces employees' morale by boosting their perceptions of unequal treatment, and signals that merit is not important in the organization. However, nepotism can have positive consequences when it is exercised to support and leverage the competitive advantages of family businesses. These consequences relate to the social, human, financial, and entrepreneurial resources brought by families to their firms. For instance, the preferential treatment that family members may receive to enter, occupy, and rise through a family business's hierarchical structure strengthens the family–business relationship, increases the family's commitment to the business, guarantees the continuity of the founder's values, and transmits tacit management knowledge from one generation to another.

The problem that most family businesses have is recognizing when and how to draw the line between "good" nepotism and "bad" nepotism. When is hiring and promoting children good or bad for a family business in terms of firm productivity and competitiveness and family cohesiveness? For instance, someone may wonder if the appointment of the 38-year-old Marta Ortega as nonexecutive chairperson of Inditex[4] was an act of nepotism? The answer could be yes: Marta got this position because she is the daughter of Amancio Ortega, the founder and a major shareholder of Inditex fashion group. There was not a fair process to select the best candidate in the labor market. The answer could also be no: by the time of her appointment, Marta had developed a successful professional career in the business over more than 15 years, starting as a sales assistant and gradually working her way upward. She did possess the knowledge and skillset to be a suitable candidate for this top position.

Judgments and questions were inevitably going to arise regarding the quality of the decision to appoint Marta Ortega as nonexecutive chairperson and the main strategist of Inditex group who would have to confront the challenges of the new digitalization era. It is possible to analyze this situation by considering the two types of nepotism[5] based on the principle of reciprocity in family relationships. First, *restricted reciprocity* in family relationships is based on the principle of quid pro quo, which is characterized by low trust and equality of exchange. The logic is "give and receive" or "something for something." Second, *generalized reciprocity* in family relationships is based on the indirect principle of reciprocity such that individuals do not expect to immediately receive something from the other party. Generalized reciprocity is built on family trust.

When nepotism occurs within a culture of restricted reciprocity in family relationships, a system of patronage emerges whereby a group of family members interacts via the mutual and direct exchange of things, such as positions, money, legitimacy, and even emotional support. In this context, entitlement nepotism is characterized by family members putting their own personal goals before comprehensive family goals, so family relationships are built around asymmetric information and a low level of trust. One family member or a group of family members tends to exploit the family business resources for their own (or their family branch's) benefits. On the contrary, when nepotism occurs within a culture of generalized reciprocity in family relationships, a steward system emerges. In this context, family members align their goals and act in the interests of the family business, embracing all individuals across the ownership, management, and family entities. The family business is an instrument through which the family stays together. In this context, family members are pro-organization, developing a high level of trust, and nepotism is the mechanism to materialize the family's desire to control and manage the firm across generations.

Since family businesses are susceptible to nepotism due to the kinship relationships that serve as the foundation for interactions among the ownership, management, and family entities, it is important to evaluate and understand the consequences of different types of nepotism for human resource management.

5.3 Human resource approach

As stated earlier, one of the main characteristics of human resource management in family businesses is the degree of asymmetric treatment that employees and family members may receive. The degree of asymmetric treatment is created by the extent to which faultlines exist that divide employees and family members within a family business. Faultlines are hypothetical dividing lines that split people into two or more subgroups based on their alignment with one or more individual attributes.

Figure 5.1 Types of faultlines and human resource management approaches in family businesses.

There are two common faultlines in family businesses. The first attributes that may divide employees are based on their family or nonfamily status. There is a natural separation between family employees and nonfamily employees in family business that is called the intergroup faultline. Family members tend to be a more cohesive group of individuals with a common identity, and they are the owners or ipso facto owners and thus have a high sense of psychological ownership over the business. These characteristics differentiate them from the rest of the employees. The second attributes emerge within the family members themselves. Even though family members tend to be a cohesive group of individuals, differences among family members do exist that could split the group into different subgroups, which results in an intragroup faultline. The most common attributes are employment status, ownership status, different family branches, birth order, gender, and generation.

Combining the notions of intra- and intergroup faultlines in family businesses, it is possible to create four main human resource management approaches. These approaches affect the asymmetric treatment described earlier differently, which may impact human resource practices and eventually firm competitiveness and family cohesiveness (Figure 5.1).

- *Intra-family asymmetric treatment:* There is no different treatment between family and nonfamily employees when human resource management practices are applied. However, the treatment that family members receive or the treatment among different groups of family members is not equal. There is a perception that human resource management discriminates against one group of family members over others, which materializes as asymmetric treatment of family members in terms of hiring, promotion, evaluation, and remuneration. The uniformity of the human resource management practices in the business entity guarantees a low level of conflict and the possibility to create and develop valuable, rare, and inimitable human capital. However, the asymmetric treatment that individuals receive in the family entity increases the perception of unfairness and, consequently, the probability of family interpersonal conflicts, which may erode the competitive advantage that the family brings to the business. For instance, a family branch, a group of family members, or an individual may receive special treatment to access a management position or extra benefits that the rest of the family members working in the firm do not receive. In some cultures, this is the case for the eldest male: he has the responsibility to assume the leadership position in the future and thus receives special treatment. Such asymmetric treatment of family members weakens family cohesiveness, which translates into poor decision-making and inter- and intrapersonal conflicts and affects business competitiveness in the medium and long term.

- *Inter-family/non-family asymmetric treatment:* There is a distinction between family and nonfamily members that results in asymmetric treatment when human resource management practices are applied. The two main rationalities that enhance this asymmetric treatment are entitlement and altruism. While a culture of entitlement emerges from the belief that family members who work in the firm deserve a certain level of privilege to keep the business in family hands, altruism is the act of promoting someone else's welfare at the risk or cost of the family itself. The difference between entitlement and altruism is that while the former is part of a culture of privilege that carries on from one generation to another, the latter is often a behavior on the part of the incumbent generation to develop the next generation's skills, abilities, and capabilities and ultimately to give children job opportunities. A culture of entitlement may have more harmful impacts on employees' perceptions of fairness than altruistic behavior. However, altruism can have a dark side, such as the free-riding behavior of children who may abuse their parents' benevolence, trust, and love and take over the parents' roles by reducing their responsibilities in the business, reinterpreting rules to their own benefit, or simply taking unilateral advantage.
- *Fragmented asymmetric treatment:* This approach combines the two fractures that divide individuals and creates asymmetric treatment between family and nonfamily employees and among family members. When fragmented asymmetric treatment is institutionalized, it can have a potentially destructive effect on the firm because the perceptions of unfairness among employees and family members prevent them from building and consolidating competitive advantages around human resources. It also has harmful consequences in terms of building trust and developing a common vision around the business.
- *Equal treatment:* There is no faultline dividing nonfamily and family employees, and a clear and uniform approach is taken with all employees. Human resource management is highly professionalized, which helps develop equal treatment for all employees regardless of their status as family or nonfamily members. Perceptions of equal interpersonal treatment increase employees' job satisfaction, fairness perceptions, and long-term commitment.[6] The risk that this approach could have is a lack of interest among family members (mainly observed in the next generation of family members) to develop affective commitment to the business and to pursue a learning process within the boundaries of the business.

5.3.1 Origins of asymmetric treatment

One consequence of a family being involved in a business is that the family affects business decision-making. Therefore, asymmetric treatment of individuals or groups of individuals in the business is a reflection of the family's values and beliefs, family members' interactions, and the family structure and communication. In other words, asymmetric treatment reflects family dynamics in terms of functionality. Using the Circumplex model[7] as an instrument to understand family dynamics based on the dimensions of cohesion and flexibility, it is possible to link and infer the origins of asymmetric treatment inside the business entity.[8]

The Circumplex model of the family system is a tool for diagnosing the functionality/dysfunctionality of families in their interpersonal relationships. The functionality/dysfunctionality of a family is a function of the family cohesion dimension, which is the emotional connection that family members have with one another, and family flexibility dimension, which is the amount and types of changes (e.g., in roles, leadership, rules, and regulations) that a family experiences. Family cohesion ranges from high to low. *Enmeshed families* at a high level of family cohesion and *disengaged families* at a low level of family cohesion are unbalanced families that may develop patterns of dysfunctionality. In both types of families, the extreme characteristics of closeness, loyalty, and dependence could be the consequence of pathological family behaviors. For instance, having too low or too high affection or intimacy in a family could affect family members' self-esteem, communication, and psychological issues. Children who do not live in a healthy and positive environment tend to have low self-esteem and feel more hostile, aggressive, and antisocial. On the other hand, growing up in an environment with too many emotions can be counterproductive because it can link or bond family members with unhealthy emotions, reducing family members' independence and forcing them to display fictitious loyalty. The effective functioning of families is in the middle of both extremes—the family finds a balanced equilibrium. Family members feel connected and can find support in each other but, at the same time, are independent enough that they are responsible for their behaviors. Family members are able to develop their own interests while having common interests that link and unite them.

The dimension of flexibility also ranges from high to low at both ends. Highly flexible families are chaotic and tend to lack self-regulation as a system to develop common norms and values. There is no clear authority, and roles are extremely diffused, creating an environment that lacks discipline. Chaotic families are dysfunctional due to the lack of stability that any system needs to ensure healthy bonds and interactions characterized by norms and values. When norms and values are too flexible and/or not clear, there are no boundaries for family members' behavior or realistic anchors for their expectations. On the other hand, rigid families are extremely reluctant to accept changes that may jeopardize their existing values, beliefs, and rules as well as their authority and hierarchy. In these types of families, stability and strong leadership under clear rules translate into a strict environment of discipline. Family members know their roles and what is expected from them, but they cannot question or move away from what the system imposes on them. Rigid families are dysfunctional because of their lack of adaptability to internal and external forces and shocks. At the middle point of these two ends, we can find balanced families (flexible and structured families), which are more functional in nature. While recognizing and accepting authority, rules, and regulations in family life, family members are willing—based on a participative approach—to reach consensus to readjust these characteristics across the family lifecycle.

The characteristics that each family displays as a functional/dysfunctional system can be connected to the asymmetric treatment observed among family members and between family and nonfamily members in a family business (see Figure 5.2).

- The nature of chaotic enmeshed business families, in which family members are close and loyal to each other and are highly dependent, is reflected in their businesses as accommodating and satisfying family needs and expectations. Businesses influenced by enmeshed families tend to have unclear leadership and business discipline, but family members rely on each other even when these families go through changes (e.g., generational changes) that in turn alter the business rules. In these family businesses, there are few faultlines among family members, but the real difference among groups is between family members and nonfamily members. Human resource practices are consistent among family members and among nonfamily members but not between these two groups because these businesses' human resource practices tend to favor family members as the nepotism approach is strong in directing human resource actions.

- The nature of chaotic disengaged business families, in which family members are not close to each other and are highly dependent, manifests in businesses as no clear leadership to execute the vision of the family in the business, thereby leading to several contradicting goals. Family members' lack of discipline causes them to disrespect roles and blur the boundaries between the ownership, management, and family entities. Additionally, changes in these families happen quickly, and there is often no stability for these businesses to consolidate procedures and routines as family members attempt to quickly harvest achievements. In these family businesses, faultlines among family members frequently emerge based on family branches or personal interests creating constant disputes. Therefore, human resource practices are unformalized, inconsistent, and ambiguous because they are exposed to and reflect the changing logics governing these families. Asymmetric treatment among family members is more important and salient than asymmetric treatment toward nonfamily employees, who are subordinate or aligned with one family branch or family group of power. Consequently, there are high perceptions of unfairness.
- The nature of rigid disengaged business families, in which family members are not close to each other and are highly independent, is reflected in their businesses as authoritarian leadership (incumbent generation) and strict rules that everyone has to accept. The high level of discipline forces family members to align their vision of the family business with the vision of the dominant leader or group of leaders. In these family businesses, asymmetric treatment could be directed toward family members and nonfamily members because of the authoritarian leadership. Fragmented asymmetric treatment is a common modus operandi in these family businesses, generating high unfairness perceptions in family members and nonfamily members.

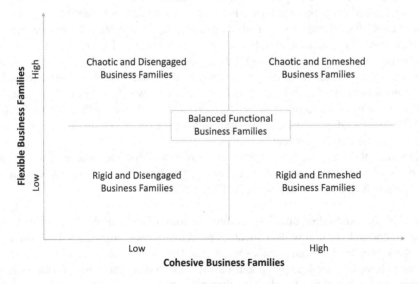

Figure 5.2 Types of functional and dysfunctional family businesses.

Source: Adapted from Olson, D. H. (2000). Circumplex model of marital and family systems. *Journal of Family Therapy*, 22(2), 144–167.

- The nature of rigid enmeshed business families, in which family members are close and loyal to each other and are highly independent, is reflected in businesses as a high orientation toward the family as well as a high authoritarian leadership style that aligns family members' goals to stay together and be loyal to the family. Family members receive preferential treatment compared to nonfamily members. These businesses often have an "us versus them" culture. Perceptions of fairness among nonfamily members may impact the effectiveness of human resource practices.
- Balanced business families, which appear in the center of Figure 5.2, are functional families and are, to a certain extent, the ideal type of family. The nature of balanced families is reflected in businesses as consensual human resource practices among family members and accepted practices among nonfamily members. Even when asymmetric treatment could appear to favor family members or nonfamily members, the reasons for such practices or actions are explained and communicated to the rest of the participants. For example, when the family wants a specific potential candidate to continue with the family's management legacy, the preferential treatment that this candidate receives does not create damage across the family and business entities if the reason for the election is justified. In these family businesses, the importance of just procedures guides the distribution of justice in achieving high levels of fairness.

5.4 Justice/fairness

Organizational justice is about individuals' perceptions of fairness in a context of interaction, such as their workplace or family environment. This definition has two important elements for understanding the concept. First, justice is socially constructed such that individuals interpret fairness. Second, the implicit concept of fairness refers to impartial and just treatment without favoritism or discrimination. It is important to understand that the construction of perceptions of fairness should be interpreted within the logic of each entity because what is fair in the family may not necessarily be interpreted as fair in the business. To explore justice in family businesses, we first have to understand the four different types of organizational justice.[9]

Distributive justice. This type of justice is about perceptions of fairness that employees and family members have regarding the distribution of outcomes (what they receive or the outcome of a decision). In this sense, it is important to explore the three parameters that employees and family members develop around their perceptions of fairness. Each parameter may lead to a different fairness perception for the same situation.

- *Equity* is the justice principle that employees and family members use to define their fairness perceptions based on the ratio between their own inputs and the related outcomes or results they obtain. They then compare this ratio with that of relevant other employees or family members as a reference value. Equity is an important justice principle in the business entity because of the idea that efficiency prevails as the main business logic to compete and survive. Business rules and procedures are created in an attempt to follow this principle such that the human resource compensation system is linked to employees' productivity and achievement. In the ownership entity, equity is also an important principle as shareholders receive dividends based on the proportion of the company they own. However, without clear boundaries, the principle of equity is subject to bias based on individuals' own interpretations of equity (which are affected by specific circumstances). This bias is particularly evident in the family context when interpreting equity. In the family, there are no clear rules and procedures to help participants reduce their biased interpretations of equity. For instance, what is fair in terms of equity for parents is not necessarily fair for children.

- *Equality* is the justice principle that employees and family members use to define fairness perceptions based on the assumption that everyone should receive the same outcomes regardless of their inputs or needs. Equality is an important justice principle in the family entity because parents typically attempt to treat their children equally by avoiding discrimination and giving them all the same opportunities. The equality principle is embedded across different cultural contexts as well as formal institutional contexts. For instance, in some countries, children receive equal inheritances regardless of their birth order or gender. Equality is more difficult to apply in the business entity, and when this principle is applied, it generates discrimination in favor of mediocre employees. In family businesses, equality as a justice principle tends to be used among family members who work in the family firm—for instance, all family members from the same generation earn the same salary regardless of their positions and inputs.
- *Need* is the justice principle that employees and family members use to define fairness perceptions based on the assumption that those who need more have to receive more. Need is also an important justice principle in the family entity, where parents, for instance, tend to adjust their decisions based on what their children need or how they can compensate for their children's weaknesses. In family businesses, the principle of need is applied to promote and accelerate family members' professional careers because they could be potential successor candidates, but the need principle is also applied to favor family members at the expense of nonfamily members.

Procedural justice. This type of justice is about fairness perceptions related to how people are treated or the decision process that results in the distribution of certain outcomes. In other words, employees' and family members' perceptions of fairness based on procedural justice are built when individuals consider the existence of a consistent process applied across people and time. Such a process is free from bias when it is based on accurate information, includes feedback mechanisms to rectify inconsistencies, respects ethical and morality principles, and ensures the participation of all interested groups (those that could be affected by the decision or outcome). Fair processes are important for employees to commit to the family business, for family members to trust each other, and for the three entities to increase their stability. Additionally, when individuals feel that processes are fair, the probability of perceiving distributive justice as fair increases.

Interpersonal justice. This type of justice is about fairness perceptions emerging from the treatment employees and family members receive when a decision is implemented. This means that employees and family members are treated with politeness, dignity, and respect. Even though it is possible to consider interpersonal justice as part of procedural justice because interpersonal relationships are key dimensions in understanding family cohesiveness and business sustainability, interpersonal justice plays an important role in building fairness perceptions. When family members are not able to understand and align their multiple roles and the contexts where roles are performed, interpersonal justice could be jeopardized. For instance, in a family business in which several family members are involved, one of them could feel like he or she is not being treated with respect when the decision about who the next leader should be arises. It is common to hear, "My father did not treat me as I deserved when promoting my sibling to the CEO position." In this example, the next-generation family member is confused by what respect means in light of his or her family and business roles due to ownership perceptions.

Informational justice. This type of justice is about fairness perceptions emerging from the information received by employees and family members about the procedures used or the outcomes distributed in a certain manner. Information gained via formal and informal mechanisms is important for employees and family members to understand the rationality of decision-making, which could affect their daily work and roles or their expectations about their future in the family business. For instance, in a family business, the communication style within the family is often transferred to the business side. When the family's communication style is characterized by few conversations, business decisions are likely poorly communicated in the family business, and the resulting lack of information could lead family members to create their own interpretations, thereby increasing their unfairness perceptions.

5.4.1 Levels of justice

There are three levels of justice to be managed in family businesses that shape fairness perceptions. First, the fairness perceptions in each entity (ownership, management, and family) need to be managed according to the different institutional logics used to interpret fairness. That is, what is fair in one entity may not be fair in another entity. Second, the blurred fairness perceptions of family members in the overlapping areas create different interpretations of fairness that need to be managed. Third, the fairness perceptions among different subgroups within each entity (e.g., family and nonfamily employees) need to be managed. Family and nonfamily employees in a business tend to set up different mechanisms to build their perceptions of fairness. For instance, the informal communication mechanisms that exist among family members could increase their fairness perceptions based on informational justice. However, because these mechanisms are not available for nonfamily members, their fairness perceptions are likely lower.

Therefore, the challenge for family business leaders is twofold. First, they have to recognize three levels of justice through which perceptions of fairness emerge and then manage these perceptions of fairness in each level to minimize interpersonal conflicts. Second, they have to understand that asymmetric treatment is intrinsically part of human relationships and is even more salient in the family business context where kinship relationships comprise the building blocks that link the ownership, management, and family entities. Therefore, the aim is to manage the approach to asymmetric treatment to keep the family in control of the firm while avoiding jeopardizing the competitive advantages stemming from human resources. For instance, we cannot change the current generation's intention to appoint one of their children as the future CEO just because this is asymmetric treatment against nonfamily members. The current generation has to manage (using the proper procedures to increase the level of information exchanged and to maintain respectful interactions among key participants) this situation to minimize potential unfairness perceptions in the three levels of justice.

Avoiding unfairness perceptions among family business participants helps family businesses consolidate their human resources as competitive advantages on which they can build cohesive families and sustainable businesses. However, one may wonder how family business leaders (in any one of the entities or at their intersections) manage asymmetric treatment. Independent of the nature and complexity of each entity, the main instrument for family members to manage and address perceptions of fairness is communication, through which family members can exchange information and have their voices heard. For instance, in the family entity, distributed justice could be based on needs, equity, or equality depending on the circumstances, but mixing different distributive justice principles may be a problem in the ownership and management entities. While the ownership and management entities also require communication as a mechanism to gather information and hear everyone's voice, it is important to ensure that the regulations that govern human resource practices (e.g., hiring, training, and compensating) are applied consistently across individuals and time.

Failing to manage justice will likely lead both family members and nonfamily employees to develop unfairness perceptions and consequently leave the family business. This could have important negative consequences for family businesses when their competitiveness is built on tacit knowledge, social connections, and employees' commitment. However, the most damaging effect is when unfairness perceptions create dysfunctional behavior that jeopardizes family cohesiveness and business sustainability.

5.5 Dysfunctional behavior

Managing a family business means administrating asymmetric treatment in the best way to avoid violations to the institutional logics that are part of each entity (ownership, management, and family). The aim of leaders and those whose decisions affect others is to maintain the equilibrium of fairness/unfairness perceptions because high unfairness perceptions over time lead to dysfunctional behavior among family members and nonfamily employees. Dysfunctional behavior, defined as an impairment or disturbance of an individual or group of individuals to develop proper relationships, manifests as poor communication, frequent conflicts, emotional and physical abuse, and unhealthy patterns of interaction.

The ultimate expression of dysfunctional behavior in a family business is the Fredo effect.[10] The Fredo effect occurs when "a family member's incompetence, opportunistic behavior, and/or ethically dubious actions can impede the firm's success"[11] and family cohesiveness. This effect is not only about having an incompetent family member in the top management position or as a potential successor who feels smart, demands respect, and has high expectations to lead the family firm but also about having someone with irrational behavior seeking what they consider to be right, important, or desirable for the future of the firm and the family without taking into consideration different stakeholders' goals, needs, and expectations.

Perceptions of unfairness contribute to creating the Fredo effect in individuals who feel displaced from important managerial positions or not taken into account in the decision-making process compared to other family members. However, unfairness perceptions alone do not create the Fredo effect since it is usually accompanied by experiences, traumas, and syndromes (e.g., the silver spoon syndrome). For instance, this effect can arise in the context of authoritarian parent–child relationships in which children are not able to differentiate themselves[12] via a natural and progressive process starting in the early stages of their lives but in which differentiation instead explodes with unpredictable behavior and attitudes to release pressure and demonstrate independence. Additionally, in the case of entitled children, who emerge from the nepotism approach of parents providing positions and salaries that do not align with their children's capacities, they often do not understand their positions and demand leadership roles. Another example is the case of children who experienced altruistic behavior (being selfless) from their parents to preserve family harmony, which can damage children's perceptions of reality (in terms of effort and rewards) and create mental problems in an overprotective family environment.

Beyond specific disorders that family members can develop (e.g., personality disorders, traumatic-stress disorder, and bipolar disorder), it is important for family businesses to recognize signs of dysfunctional behavior that can lead to the Fredo effect in the long term— for instance, family members who deny responsibility for their behavior; use intimidation to achieve their goals; exploit emotions to manipulate situations; maintain a high level of secrecy about family interactions, thoughts, feeling, and emotions; and have poor communication to set rules of coexistence.

Although one may think that the Fredo effect only arises among those family members who work in the focal family business, it can also be found among family members who are influential enough to affect the whole system. Take, for instance, Edgar Bronfman Jr., grandson of Samuel Bronfman, founder of the Seagram Company. His ambition to work in Hollywood led to the squandering of his family's fortune. Samuel Bronfman's economic activities were related to the alcoholic distilled beverage business as he founded the Seagram Company. The company expanded and diversified to oil, gas, petrochemicals, and entertainment. Edgar took over the business after his father's death in 1971. Edgar handed control to his son Edgar Jr. in 1994. To conquer the entertainment sector, Edgar Bronfman Jr. sold almost 25% of Seagram's ownership in DuPont to buy MCA (Universal Pictures) without considering that DuPont made around 70% of Seagram's income. The story continued with other questionable decisions, such as when Seagram was sold to Vivendi for shares in Vivendi whose value then plummeted. The downhill slide for Seagram was unstoppable.[13] This demonstrates the dysfunctional Fredo effect when family members are not able to align their personal goals with the family business goals by building a better tomorrow for all stakeholders.

5.6 Additional activities and reading material

5.6.1 Classroom discussion questions

1 Why is human resource management different in family businesses than in nonfamily businesses?
2 How can parental favoritism influence human resource management?
3 Are nepotism and altruism the same concept? What are the effects of nepotism and altruism in family businesses?
4 Can you describe the different forms of asymmetric treatment in family businesses? What is the impact of asymmetric treatment on family businesses?
5 What is the Fredo effect? How can it develop in family businesses?

5.6.2 Additional readings

1 Kidwell, R. E., Eddleston, K. A., Cater, J. J. & Kellermanns, F.W. (2013), How one bad family member can undermine a family firm: Preventing the Fredo effect. *Business Horizons*, (1) 5–12. Article retrieved from www.sciencedirect.com/science/article/pii/S0007681312001 19X
2 Douglas, M. (1997). A family business that tries to treat workers like family. *The New York Times*. Retrieved from www.nytimes.com/1997/04/02/nyregion/a-family-business-that-tries-to-treat-workers-like-family.html
3 Sullivan, P. (2018). Family businesses hire a new type of executive: Chief referee. *The New York Times*. Article retrieved from www.nytimes.com/2018/07/06/your-money/family-busin ess-conflict-resolution.html

5.6.3 Classroom activity

Aim: Reflect on justice and fairness in the context of family businesses.
Material: Share the story below with each group of students based on the assignment of roles within the groups:

- Mark is the eldest son in the family, and he has worked closely with his father for several years. He studied business administration and received an MBA from one of the most prominent business schools in the country. He feels confident about the future of the company and strongly believes that his father's vision should be respected. He thinks he is ready for new responsibilities and, eventually, to lead the firm. Additionally, he thinks his sister's shares should be passed to him as he has been the main support for this firm.

- Maia is the middle child in the family and just one year younger than Mark. She got married not long ago and has been on maternity leave for almost a year. Before taking maternity leave, she worked in the company in different positions but never felt confident with any of her assigned jobs. In her last conversation with her father, she declared her desire to join the family business as a top manager or even as a board member because she wants to maintain her status as a family member of the family business. Otherwise, she would like to exit the family business and sell the 33% of the shares she possesses.

- Chris is the youngest of all his siblings, but he knows he has the strongest entrepreneurial spirit. Since the early stage of his career, he developed a career outside the family business with independence and a long-term vision to prove himself and gain legitimacy. He sold his unicorn startup not long ago and saw an opportunity to turn the family business into a tech firm. He thinks it is for him "to go back to the origins" and run his family business and give a lift to the family legacy. If his sister sells her shares, he would have enough to control the firm.

Running the classroom exercise—first part: Divide the class into groups of four members each. Ask the students in each group to assign the following roles: (1) Mark, the eldest sibling; (2) Maia, the middle sibling; (3) Chris, the youngest sibling, and (4) the business consultant. Ask each student to reflect on the character they represent by thinking about additional arguments to support their own point of view. Ask each sibling to have a private conversation with the business consultant (for a couple of minutes) to present his or her demands. Ask the business consultant to reflect on the demands/position of each sibling. Question for the business consultant: How you describe each of the siblings considering the distributive justice principles? After the consultant's reflection, ask the following question: What is the solution for this case?

Takeaways: Any decision made by the business consultant and, ultimately, the parents will not be a fair solution for any of them (siblings) because they are applying different principles of distributive justice. The best way to address this issue and the potential problems that this situation could cause for the family business is to develop a decision-making process that is clear for all participants and helps them navigate their personal positions by considering what is best for the family and the business.

Running the classroom exercise—second part, assignment: Ask each group to design a decision-making process to address the issues among the siblings. The participants should keep the roles they represent to come up with a final solution.

5.7 Case for analysis I: What a mistake![14]

Can hiring relatives bring positive results to a firm? Many people might think so, yet others think that it might have detrimental effects on a well-functioning firm and on family relationships. For Liza, hiring her stepson came with many unexpected consequences and one important lesson. Liza and her husband, Karl, run a small advertising agency. One day, Karl invited Mathias, Liza's stepson, who was looking for a more meaningful and rewarding future, to join the couple-controlled business.

Liza thought it would be great to have Mathias join the business to make the family relationships stronger, experience something new with her partner's family, and—ultimately—have someone to pass the business to. Liza interviewed Mathias as if he was a potential candidate for the new position they had. Liza assessed his skills and felt he had the ability to perform the job. However, because of her family relationship with Mathias, she neglected to ask him important questions to determine his motivations and explore other psychological aptitudes.

Mathias turned out to be a child of entitlement. He always focused on working toward his own personal agenda and did not care much about the legacy of his family and the firm. Because he was not given authority in the firm, Mathias was impatient and went off to promote himself without Liza's or his father's knowledge. For instance, Mathias spoke with employees as if he owned the firm, which led one of their professionals to leave the firm because he could not stand Mathias. The situation turned worse when Mathias initiated an affair with one of the company's employees. Intrigue and rumors moved around the rest of the employees' conversations. This triggered Karl to finally fire his son. Interpersonal relationships in the family became difficult. Mathias was very frustrated with his father's decision and lashed out about how they never supported him and how they never gave him a management role, blaming it all on Liza.

Mathias decided to open a competing advertising agency firm. This was the moment when Liza realized that she made another mistake. She assumed a noncompete agreement was not necessary with her husband's son. Liza realized that she made a painful decision in hiring Mathias without following a strict hiring approach similar to the one she uses with other (nonfamily) interviewees. She also realized that it is not right to assume someone's motives even if the person is a family member and that asking standard impersonal questions is very necessary even when hiring relatives.

Discussion questions:

1 How can you describe the asymmetric treatment in this family business?
2 Use your knowledge of justice and fairness to explain Mathias' behavior.
3 Do you think it would have been possible to correct Mathias' behavior? Why?

5.8 Case for analysis II: Embracing nepotism[15]

Can there ever be a positive side of nepotism? Ivy Molofsky, the director of human resources at Thomas Publishing Co., has argued that nepotism yielded great results for her firm. Harvey Thomas founded Thomas Publishing over a century ago in New York. The company is currently managed by two cousins who are Harvey's grandsons: Tom and Jose. Nepotism is embraced throughout the company as many members of the company have hired other family members, making the company a place where fathers, mothers, sons, daughters, sisters, brothers, and many other relatives work together.

Everyone in the company understands that nepotism can help their relatives get an opportunity at Thomas Publishing, but there are no favors involved during their employment journey at the firm. Family members are selected for the jobs that match their skills and qualifications, are paid the same salary as other nonfamily employees performing a similar job, and are rewarded based only on their performance. All employees are subject to biannual performance reviews that are done fairly and can determine their future in the company for good (raise and promotion) or for bad (firing).

Since everyone in the company understands that no special treatment is given to any employee, family members do not speak resentfully or cause any sort of trouble when a family member is fired because they are aware that the decision has a legitimate reason. Everyone in the company is treated equally to pursue their careers and to adopt an entrepreneurial mindset in solving problems and tackling challenges. This gives all employees the chance to showcase their capabilities and get a fair shot at leading different teams and eventually leading the company.

Molofsky stated that there are many advantages associated with adopting nepotism in the company's hiring decisions. One of these advantages is a shorter learning curve as new family members who are hired are usually aware of the company's culture and expectations. Loyalty is another advantage that she mentioned, which is mainly due to the older generation feeling confident about offering opportunities to their own family members (younger generations) to work in the firm. As a result of their trust and faith, the younger generation becomes more loyal to the family business. New family hires try to deliver exceptional performance as individuals feel a sense of extra pressure to prove they were hired because of their skills and not because of their relatives. When nepotism is successfully practiced in hiring, employee turnover is significantly reduced.

Given her experience with nepotism at Thomas Publishing, Molofsky has argued that nepotism can truly bring positive results to firms if it is practiced properly. Nepotism can be a very successful human resource practice. A family business is nepotistic by nature, so adopting a successful nepotistic hiring framework can lead to improved job satisfaction, productivity, and loyalty among family and nonfamily employees while yielding positive results for the overall family business.

Discussion questions:

1 What are the negative consequences of nepotism?
2 What do you think family entrenchment is?
3 Why can some family businesses make nepotism an advantage?

5.9 Case study: It is just a scandal or the scandal[16]

In November 2022, a group of four independent members of the board of directors established a commission to review the conduct of the chief financial officer of Tyson Foods, a listed company in the United States. The chief financial officer was charged with public intoxication and trespassing. The police report stated that they received a call from a woman who reported arriving home and finding a semi-naked unknown man sleeping in her bed. When the police arrived, they found John Randal Tyson, the chief financial officer of Tyson Foods, intoxicated (drunk), and they struggled to wake him up.

John Randal accepted the situation and publicly said, "I apologize to our investors as I have to our employees. This incident was inconsistent with our company values as well as my personal values. I am committed to making sure it never happens again."

The independent commission has to analyze this event, consider the consequences for the company's image, and decide what action to take with John Randal. Recently, the company faced another public incident with a high senior executive. Doug Ramsey, who was chief operating officer at Beyond Meat, left the firm after being arrested for assault. Ramsey was suspended and left the company.

Discussion question:

1 In your opinion, how should the independent board commission proceed in this case? Should John Randal be fired?

Tyson Foods, Inc. John W. Tyson started his entrepreneurial journey at the beginning of the 1930s during the Great Depression by delivering chickens around the Midwest. He saw an opportunity and, with one truck, moved a load of live chickens to Chicago. Since then, the family has been in the food-production business. During World War II, food was rationed;

however, poultry was not. The business grew along with the demand for chicken in the American diet. By the end of the 1940s, the company provided three services: the sale of baby chicks, the sale of feed, and logistics. In the early 1950s, John's son Don joined the company and took it to become a listed company in 1963. The company's major expansion came when Don convinced his father to build their own processing plant, a decision not without friction because of budget issues. The company followed an inorganic growth strategy under Don's leadership. Don became chairman and CEO when his father and mother had a car accident. The company continued growing and internationalizing, and by 1989, it doubled its size in just five years.

By the end of the 1990s, Don Tyson formally retired, but he remained actively involved in the company at the governance level as part of the board of directors until 2011, when he died at the age of 80. His son John H. Tyson, the third generation of Tysons, took over as chairman of the board of directors. He also served as CEO from 2000 until 2009. Today, the CEO is Donnie King, who started his professional career and leadership within the company in 1982 in the poultry segment.

Tyson Foods is an American multinational corporation and one of the world's top-three largest processors and marketers of meat (chicken, beef, and pork). It is a listed company and is ranked among the Fortune 500 largest US corporations. The company is controlled by the Tyson family through super voting shares.

John Randal Tyson, the fourth generation. *John* Randal Tyson is the son of John H. Tyson. He is developing a meteoric career in the family company. Some analysts and business columnists think that his career is going too fast to be real and that his last name helps him. A Credit Suisse analyst said that such big companies usually hire executives with experience who are well prepared to assume the responsibilities of top management positions, such as those of the chief financial officer. However, the company executives defended John Randal because his education and experience support his career trajectory. For instance, Donnie King said, "John Randal has had experience outside of Tyson, escalating levels of responsibility in banking and venture capital, and within Tyson, for the last four years, he's led M&A strategy, ventures and other areas of the company."

In 2020, John Randal said to the *Wall Street Journal* that he always intended to get involved in the family business: "I've been involved in some capacity my entire life."[17] He also mentioned spending his childhood at the company headquarters with his father and grandfather as a way to show his identification with and commitment to the company. In 2019, at the age of 29 years old, John Randal Tyson joined the company as chief sustainability officer to address issues related to resource conservation and food waste. In September 2022, he was promoted to chief financial officer. He studied economics at Harvard College and got his MBA from Stanford University. He worked for JPMorgan Chase as a private equity investor and as a lecturer at the Sam M. Walton College of Business.

The board of directors. The board of directors comprises 13 members. Some of them are family members, as is the case of Barbara Tyson and John Tyson; some are executives, such as Noel White and Donnie King; and still others are independent, such as Kevin M. McNamara, who is the lead independent director.

The current CEO stated that the review of John Randal would be conducted by the board's governance committee, which is composed of directors who are independent of the family. However, the journalist Douglas A. McIntyre questioned the independence of the board of directors by pointing out that the board is filled by individuals who are Tyson friendly.[18] The journalist cited the case of Noel White, who used to be CEO and was the lead independent director until 2007.

Discussion questions:

2 If you were part of the commission to review John Randal's behavior, what would be your position? Please, justify your behavior.
3 Based on your previous answer, please write a press release to announce the final decision and the justification and rationality behind it.
4 Write an email to the 139,000 Tyson Food employees to explain the situation, the decision, and the reason for the final decision.

Notes

1 *Tharawat Magazine.* (2016). SABIS®—130 years of innovation in education. Information retrieved from www.tharawat-magazine.com/future-industries/sabis-innovation-education/. Additional information can be found on the SABIS website: www.sabis.net/
2 *Tarawat Magazine.* (2017). FEATURES: Crane & Co.—Mills, money, and mindfulness. Information retrieved from www.tharawat-magazine.com/pursuit-of-happiness/crane-and-co/. Additional information can be found on the Crane & Co. website: www.cranecurrency.com/company/locations/
3 Although this example describes a real family business, names and other important details have been changed to preserve the anonymity of our interviewees and sources.
4 Inditex Group comprises Zara, Pull&Bear, Massimo Dutti, Bershka, Stradivarius, and Oysho, among other brands. It is one of the world's largest fashion retailers, with 6,477 stores worldwide in 95 markets. The Inditex group reported revenue of €27.72 billion (£23.3 billion) for the 12 months ending January 31, 2022, an increase of 35% year over year. Net profit increased by 193% to €3.24 billion (£2.7 billion).
5 Jaskiewicz, P., Uhlenbruck, K., Balkin, D. B., & Reay, T. (2013). Is nepotism good or bad? Types of nepotism and implications for knowledge management. *Family Business Review*, 26(2), 121–139.
6 Waterwall, B., & Alipour, K. K. (2021). Nonfamily employees' perceptions of treatment in family businesses: Implications for organizational attraction, job pursuit intentions, work attitudes, and turnover intentions. *Journal of Family Business Strategy*, 12(3), 100387.
7 Olson, D. H. (2000). Circumplex model of marital and family systems. *Journal of Family Therapy*, 22(2), 144–167.
8 Daspit, J. J., Madison, K., Barnett, T., & Long, R. G. (2018). The emergence of bifurcation bias from unbalanced families: Examining HR practices in the family firm using circumplex theory. *Human Resource Management Review*, 28(1), 18–32.
9 Colquitt, J. A. (2001). On the dimensionality of organizational justice: A construct validation of a measure. *Journal of Applied Psychology*, 86, pp. 386–400. https://doi.org/10.1037/0021-9010.86.3.386
10 Based on the *Godfather* films of Francis Ford Coppola and the novels of Mario Puzo and Mark Winegardner, the Fredo effect refers to the incompetent middle brother, Fredo Corleone, who was denied the leadership role in favor of his younger brother Michael. As a result, Fredo engages in irrational behaviors and ultimately betrays his family.
11 Kidwell, R., Kellermanns, F., & Eddleston, K. (2012). Harmony, justice, confusion, and conflict in family firms: Implications for ethical climate and the "Fredo Effect." *Journal of Business Ethics*, 106(4), 503–517.
12 Based on Bowen theory, family members vary in their susceptibility to the group effect exerting conformity control over their thinking and behavior. A person with a well-differentiated self has realistic dependence from others to hold his or her own opinions; defend them; and address conflicts, criticism, and feedback by separating facts and emotions.
13 Leonard, D. & Burke, D. (2002). The Bronfman Saga from rags to riches to… CNN Money. Information retrieved from https://money.cnn.com/magazines/fortune/fortune_archive/2002/11/25/332573/. Green, H. (2021). When billionaires battle: The fall of Seagram sheds light on the role blood

plays in family-controlled firms. *Toronto Star*. Article retrieved from www.thestar.com/business/opin ion/2021/11/13/when-billionaires-battle-the-fall-of-seagram-sheds-light-on-the-role-of-blood-in-fam ily-controlled-firms.html . Salter, J. (2013). Charles Bronfman opens up about Seagram's demise: "It is a disaster." *The Globe and Mail*. Article retrieved from www.theglobeandmail.com/report-on-busin ess/careers/careers-leadership/charles-bronfman-opens-up-about-seagrams-demise-it-is-a-disaster/ article10816816/

14 This example discussion is developed solely as the basis for class discussion. This example discussion is not intended to serve as an endorsement, source of primary data, or illustration of effective or ineffective management.

15 This example discussion is developed solely as the basis for class discussion. This example discussion is not intended to serve as an endorsement, source of primary data, or illustration of effective or ineffective management.

Story created based on information retrieved from Ivy Molofsky (1999). Why we like nepotism. *Family Business Magazine*. Article retrieved from: www.familybusinessmagazine.com/why-we-nepotism.

16 This case study discussion is developed solely as the basis for class discussion. This case study discussion is not intended to serve as an endorsement, source of primary data, or illustration of effective or ineffective management.

Foley, S., & Chávez, S. (2022). Tyson Foods launches board review over new CFO's arrest. *Financial Times*. Article retrieved from: www.ft.com/content/12a3baaa-b035-4000-ac97-ccf99 0ff8523.

17 Bunge, J. (2020). Tyson Scion to lead sustainability push. *The Wall Street Journal*. Article retrieved from www.wsj.com/articles/tyson-scion-to-lead-sustainability-push-11579606201

18 McIntyre, D. (2022). Tyson's John Tyson needs to be fired. 24/7 Wall[St]. Article retrieved from https:// 247wallst.com/consumer-products/2022/11/15/tysons-john-tyson-needs-to-be-fired/

6   Strategic and financial management in family businesses

Learning objectives

- Distinguish the different types of family business goals.
- Understand the effects of family business goals on decision-making.
- Recognize the importance of reference points and endowment bias for decision-making.
- Identify the main resources and capabilities that families create and develop in their businesses.
- Interpret the effects of market and nonmarket strategies for firm performance and survival.

6.1 Introduction

Family embeddedness in a business affects strategic and financial management decisions, which implies setting high-level goals, analyzing the competitive environment, coordinating internal organization, implementing and evaluating market and nonmarket strategies, and allocating resources accordingly. Family participation is not what makes a family business's strategic and financial management unique; instead, the uniqueness stems from the types of goals that the family imposes on the business that alter decision-making.

Family businesses combine business-oriented (traditional business goals) and family-oriented goals. The incorporation of family-oriented goals, which are not necessarily economic in nature, alters the reference point in the decision-making process and creates potential biases that can affect final decisions. In other words, decisions are made based on the extent to which the expected outcomes will contribute to both business goals and family goals. Decisions should satisfy the demands of the business to maintain its competitiveness but also the demands of the family to maintain its cohesiveness, which ultimately ties individuals to the business.

Additionally, from a strategic and financial point of view, family involvement in the business contributes to the creation and development of unique and difficult-to-imitate resources and capabilities, which represent the competitive advantage for most family businesses. Family involvement in the business creates, develops, and preserves specificities across the business's financial capital, social capital, human capital, and reputational capital. These endowment resources need to be handled in a unique manner that ultimately supports and leverages the combination of market and nonmarket strategies.

The aim of this chapter is to explain how the existence of family-oriented goals affects family businesses' decision-making and the extent to which families can create and develop bundles of resources that they can use to leverage their strategic position.

DOI: 10.4324/9781003273240-8

6.2 Family business goals

Family businesses are typically not profit-maximizing organizations. This does not mean that family businesses are not profitable or competitive. For family businesses, profit is as important as in any other organization because it represents an indicator of success and the source of capital to sustain and expand their operations via reinvestment of profit. However, because of the family's effect on the business, family businesses tend to be guided by a profit-satisfaction orientation rather than by a profit-maximization orientation. Profit maximization refers to efforts to select the best possible strategic and operational options to earn as much money as possible, whereas profit satisfaction refers to efforts to select good options that can satisfy different types of stakeholder goals. A profit-satisfaction orientation emerges from the internal forces of the three entities; the nature of the goals that each family member has based on his or her owner, manager, and family roles; and the external forces stemming from the interaction between the family business and its context.

Internal and external forces materialize in interpersonal relationships. Interpersonal relationships happen among family and nonfamily members within the family business boundaries across each entity (ownership, management, and family) and beyond the family business borders with external individuals and economic agents (external environment), both of which define the existence of multiple goals in family businesses.

At the individual level, each role is associated with specific goals, and when individuals hold multiple roles at the same time, goals may contradict each other. For instance, the profit-maximization goal of an owner could differ from and contradict a father's goal of creating an organization that can be transferred from generation to generation. This is the first source of coexisting goals. However, group goals also coexist because family and nonfamily members with specific roles in different entities often try to impose their interests in a family business, and groups from different generations may do so as well. For instance, the next generation of family managers' goals could reflect their vitality and energy to develop aggressive growth strategies. Such goals may contradict with the incumbent generation's goals, which may be more conservative regarding the business to ensure family cohesiveness.

One way to visualize the multiple goals in family businesses is to classify them using two dimensions. First, the entity with a higher influence on the dominant family group of decision-makers defines the firm's focus of attention. The family and business entities compete to impose their own logics and define the focus of attention of key decision-makers. In addition, there are family-oriented and business-oriented goals. Family-oriented goals are those related to the family's economic, affective, and psychological needs, whereas business-oriented goals are those related to the business's economic and financial achievement and other stakeholder needs. Second, the economic nature of the goals dimension which differentiates goals as economic goals, which are related to profit achievement and financial needs, and noneconomic goals, which are related to satisfying social, cultural, and religious needs.

The combination of the family-/business-oriented dimension and economic/noneconomic dimension creates a configuration of four types of goals[1] (Figure 6.1).

- *Business-oriented economic* goals are those related to the business's economic and financial performance, which is generally measured with objective ratios (e.g., return on assets), and business growth, such as its market share, new market, and business portfolio.
- *Family-oriented economic* goals are those related to the family's cashflow needs to satisfy the family's lifestyle and are measured as the transfer of cash from the family to the firm and as the family's control over the business's ownership, governance, and management.

- *Business-oriented noneconomic* goals are those related to other stakeholders' needs, such as employees (e.g., working environment), customers (e.g., customer experience), suppliers (e.g., ethical behavior), and communities (e.g., commitment to the local economic and social environments).
- *Family-oriented noneconomic* goals are related to the family's social and emotional needs (e.g., providing jobs for family members and having a name in society).

The interpersonal interactions between and among family and nonfamily members shape the web of family business goals. Because of the negotiation process by which family business goals arise, these goals are not static but dynamic and in constant change. For instance, a generational change alters the main family business goals because the succession process and the bargaining power of the incumbent and next generations tend to shift the dominant group and define a new focus of attention for the family business. As an example, the Canadian family business AtoZ Logistics started off in Toronto in 1990 as a trucking company by the first-generation family business member Bob. Initially, the family business goal was to establish a small- to medium-sized enterprise transportation company. However, the goal changed upon the entrance of the second generation—Bob's sons Greg and Mike—who transformed and expanded the transportation business into a logistics business. As the third generation stepped in, cousins Sara and Jake shifted the business goal to expanding the business nationally.

The individuals who belong to the dominant group and are willing and able to influence decision-making have a higher probability of defining the prevailing family business goals. In other words, the dominant group defines the focus of attention to determine the family business's aspirations (what the family business wants to achieve). This is important because the family business's aspirations serve as the compass for family members' behaviors and thus shape the business's strategic decision-making.

Figure 6.1 Family business goals configuration.

Source: Adapted from Basco, R. (2017). "Where do you want to take your family firm?" A theoretical and empirical exploratory study of family business goals. *Business Research Quarterly*. 20(1), 28–44.

6.2.1 *Family business goals as reference points*

Goals that define the family business's aspirations are important because they are the reference points for decision-making. From the behavioral economic perspective, a reference point determines how an outcome or a potential outcome is perceived as a gain or loss, which in turn influences decision-making. Therefore, goals can help us understand why decision-making in family businesses is unique and sometimes different from that in nonfamily businesses, specifically regarding strategic and financial decisions. There are three main characteristics of family business goals that make decision-making unique in family businesses: goals as reference points, loss aversion, and diminishing sensitivity.

Goals become reference points because the decision-making of the dominant group encompasses two distinct phases: the editing phase and the evaluation phase. During the editing phase, family members define their strategic and/or financial options using the information available to them. During the evaluation phase, family business goals become reference points for decision-makers and alter the value of outcomes.[2] Namely, the value of a decision is related to the original reference point such that the dominant family group compares where the family business is or where the family business should be with the outcome offered by a particular strategic or financial choice.

If the family business's reference point is to preserve the family's control over the business, then strategic and financial decisions are directed to keep the business under the family's control even at the expense of having a less profitable business in the short term. In other words, the dominant family group in the family business compares the expected outcomes of strategic and financial choices with their respective reference points (family-oriented and business-oriented goals) to decide if the family business is in a gain or loss position. In this case, a reference point divides the space of an outcome of a strategic or financial decision into regions of gain and loss (success and failure or positive and negative). Therefore, the dominant group evaluates outcomes as gains or losses relative to neutral reference points.

Another characteristic of goals as reference points in the value function[3] is the dominant group's loss aversion (the value function is steeper for losses than gains) (Figure 6.2).

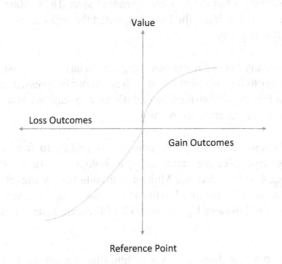

Figure 6.2 Shape of the value function in family businesses.

Specifically, losses are typically more painful than similarly sized gains are pleasurable. In other words, the dominant group in a family business is typically more sensitive to losses than to equivalent gains. When the expected outcomes of strategic or financial choices are below the respective family business goals, the situation is perceived as a loss relative to the goals. The dominant group is likely going to try harder to change this situation or to assume more risk (risk taking) than when expected outcomes are above their respective goals.

The final characteristic is that the impact of gains and losses relative to goals as reference points present diminishing sensitivity. That is, outcomes have a smaller marginal impact when the distance between expected outcomes and goals, as a reference points, is higher (Figure 6.2). This pattern arises because the value function is concave above the reference point and convex below it (Figure 6.2). Members of the dominant group are willing to exert less effort as they move away from their goals but more effort as they approach their goals.

6.2.2 Socioemotional wealth as an endowment effect

Family business goals, which define a family business's aspirations, are related to the business's economic, social, and emotional endowments. For the economic endowment, it is easy to understand that when firms achieve their economic goals by engaging in productive activities, profits accumulate and generate economic wealth. In a similar way, when the social and emotional aspirations of the dominant group in the family business (as reflected in family-oriented goals) are achieved, the stock of socioemotional wealth accumulates. Socioemotional wealth is defined as "non-financial aspects of the firm that meet the family's affective needs, such as identity, the ability to exercise family influence, and the perpetuation of the family dynasty."[4]

Pursuing family-oriented goals increases the family business's socioemotional endowment, which manifests in four dimensions.

- The first dimension—*transgenerational family control and influence*—is not only about the stock of capital to exert control over the business but also the intention to pass ownership from one generation to another by establishing the family legacy. For instance, Au Gant Rouge is a Lebanese tableware and decoration family business operating since 1875. Maria Fatté, a fifth-generation family member who continues the business, stated the importance of continuing the family legacy in the following way:

  Once you've owned and managed a company over so many generations, you have a responsibility to keep it going. It's in our character to be hard workers, to believe in our business, and to believe in our country. Our belief in this family business is that it's here to stay. We want to take it further, as far as possible for future generations to enjoy.[5]

- The second dimension—*the psychological level of having control*—is related to family members' emotional attachment, cognitive-affective state, and psychological ownership from being part of the family business. For instance, the Maison Tamboite luxury bicycle family business founded by Léon Leynoud in Paris closed in the 1980s. However, his great-grandsons wanted to reestablish the family business legacy, with CEO Frédéric Jastrzebski expressing the following:

  My brother and I both felt the need to pay our dues. That's a feeling that was transmitted through our family values. Even though the family business had closed down in the 80s, we still felt that sense of heritage. We wanted to restore Maison Tamboite to its former glory. Our wives are also involved, so we're really back to being a family business. Our cousins are also welcome to come to join us if they wish to in the future. The young generation is also getting more and more active. That feeling of belonging is there in all of us. We really feel like the custodians of the brand, keeping it safe for the next generation.[6]

- The third dimension relates to *family members' identity* with the firm as well as the *reputation and social status* that being part of the business family confers to family members. For instance, the British family business Sparks Clothing, which offers a wide range of personalized gifts and clothing, was founded by Deborah (mother) and Verity (daughter) Sparks almost a decade ago and was rebranded as Sparks & Daughters to reflect the origin of the business and the long-term commitment. Verity and her husband, Lex, took over the business when Deborah retired in 2019, keeping the family ethos at the core, so their brand identity represents trust.[7]
- Finally, the fourth dimension—*social ties*—refers to the connections family members create through the family business with customers, suppliers, and other stakeholders, which are characterized by trust, support, and loyalty. For instance, the Luen Thai Group, is an almost six-decades-old Chinese family business with a wide portfolio that started off as a shipping agency and trading business and has expanded into apparel manufacturing, fishing vessels, airline cargo, hospitality, and real estate. The youngest son and chief financial officer of Luen Thai Holdings Limited highlighted how their family business has a culture of giving back to the community and the environment and how they work with their customers and stakeholders to impact the local community in terms of their social responsibility standards.[8]

These four dimensions of socioemotional wealth produce noneconomic utility (value) that family members receive from the business. Family businesses' stock of socioemotional wealth is important for understanding their strategic and financial decision-making because family business members' psychological ownership and loss aversion (i.e., their tendency to prefer avoiding losses to acquiring equivalent gains) trigger the endowment effect. The endowment effect is a bias that occurs when family members overvalue something they own regardless of the possible objective market value.

6.3 Strategic and financial behavior

There is a general public opinion that family businesses are conservative in their strategic behavior and that their strategic behavior differs from nonfamily businesses, but this is not the case for all family businesses. Family businesses' strategic and financial behavior depends on the coexistence of multiple goals and their socioemotional wealth endowment. The more the family business goals are business oriented and the lower a family business's socioemotional wealth accumulation, the more similar the strategic and financial behavior of family and nonfamily businesses. However, the uniqueness of family businesses' strategic and financial behavior emerges when family businesses incorporate family-oriented goals in their aspirations, which in turn affects the value of gains and losses of expected outcomes as well as whether and when the socioemotional wealth endowment generates emotional bias.

Take family businesses' diversification strategy as an example. Family businesses diversify less than nonfamily businesses even when families with concentrated wealth in their businesses would benefit from such diversification. That is the case when the expected outcomes of implementing a diversification strategy are evaluated as losses relative to the reference points in terms of family-oriented goals, such as potential loss of control over the business. The consequences of not implementing a diversification strategy are less profit and/or more risk for owners' wealth. What happens when the reference point is altered? For instance, it could be that the expected outcomes of not implementing a diversification strategy are evaluated as losses relative to the reference point in terms of reputation or social legitimacy. In this situation, family businesses will be willing to implement a diversification strategy. Losses are painful, so in this case, their loss aversion pushes family businesses to take action and diversify even when diversification could be a risky strategy because of, for example, a lack of international experience and the need for excessive capital to achieve positive results.

The same analysis is applicable to any kind of strategic decision in family businesses, such as investment in research and development, divestment, internationalization, and selection of and collaboration with suppliers, among others. It is important to consider different elements when analyzing why and how family businesses make decisions.

First, it is important to consider the reference points defined by the dominant coalition as a mix of business-oriented and family-oriented goals. The importance of decisions depends on the nature of the decisions themselves and the likelihood of gaining or losing relative to the family business goals (reference points). Family businesses are not static, and the importance of family business goals can change depending on the context. The particular moment in time that decisions have to be made, the generation(s) involved in the decision-making process, and the family and business governance structures are the three contextual dimensions that constrain business-oriented and family-oriented goals within the family business boundaries. External dimensions are related to the economic, legal, and social contexts and how their dynamics influence family business development. Second, family businesses are loss averse because they prefer avoiding losses over acquiring equivalent gains and want to maintain their level of socioemotional wealth. The latter increases the dominant coalition's emotional bias regarding the family business. Finally, the diminishing sensitivity in family businesses means that when expected outcomes are close to their respective reference points, they have a stronger effect on the action/decision to be taken than when they are farther from their reference points.

This approach can also be applied to analyzing family businesses' risk behavior. While it is common to hear that family businesses are naturally risk averse, this is not really the case for most family businesses. Family businesses' risk behavior is linked to their reference points to determine whether the expected outcomes fall into the gain or loss category. Family businesses tend to be risk averse when the expected outcomes are within the gain category but risk taking when the expected outcomes are within the loss category. Additionally, beyond that, the shape of the value function (Figure 6.2) makes family businesses loss averse, and their socioemotional wealth endowment frames family members' emotional bias toward their firms, meaning that family members value their firms higher than market value.

6.4 Strategic management in family business

Any family business that strives to survive and achieve its goals has to define a strategy to compete. A strategy combines two domains: the market domain and the nonmarket domain.[9] In the market domain, based on their internal and external competitive advantages, family businesses define how they are going to compete and how to position their products or services. On the other hand, in the nonmarket domain, family businesses establish social, political, and familial actions to support their overall strategy.

6.4.1 Market domain

6.4.1.1 Internal competitive advantages

A firm has a competitive advantage when its value-creating strategy is not simultaneously being implemented by its competitors.[10] From the resource-based view perspective, resources and capabilities play a key role in a firm's ability to develop and maintain a competitive advantage when they are heterogeneous and immobile. Resources and capabilities must have four attributes to be considered strategic; namely, they should be valuable, rare, difficult to imitate, and nonsubstitutable.

A family business's competitive advantage emerges from the strategic resources and capabilities stemming from the relationship between the family and the business. Beyond the traditional resources (tangible) and capabilities (intangible) that any firm can convert into something valuable, rare, difficult to imitate, and nonsubstitutable, in the family business context, family presence (throughout the ownership, governance, and management) is the main source of strategic resources to develop a competitive advantage over competitors and have superior performance.

The interaction between the family and the firm generates unique types of resources and capabilities that are together referred to as familiness.[11] Family presence in a business not only brings but also creates strategic resources, such as financial, human, reputational, and social capital.

- *Financial capital.* The financial capital that the family provides to the business across the lifecycle (during the entrepreneurial, growth and maturity, and decline stages) can be a strategic resource for several reasons. The family's amount of money, even when it is limited, is adjusted to business needs over time. That is, the family is able to adapt its financial needs to meet the financial needs of the business by transferring resources. The cost of the family's money is lower compared to other alternatives in the market (e.g., bank credits or external investments, among others). Family capital is characterized as patient capital because family members have a longer time horizon when making a financial investment in the business than nonfamily members (investors) or other institutions (banks or other financial institutions). The imperfect contract underlying family financial capital based on trust and confidence confers flexibility in terms of payment, rules, and renegotiation. The meaning of this capital was well summarized by Charles Kittredge, sixth-generation chairman of the board and former CEO of Crane & Co., a US paper company founded in 1801, when he said, "As a family business, we don't need to see the return next quarter; we can invest longer term."[12]
- *Human capital.* Families in business are able to develop knowledge, skills, and capabilities by creating a specific work environment in which it is possible to align interests between individuals (family and nonfamily members) and the family business itself. When the dominant family group intends to pass the firm from one generation to another, internal formal and informal mechanisms are put in place, such as training and development, protection of individual knowledge, and interactions that consolidate knowledge spillover, among other mechanisms, to guarantee the transmission of business-specific knowledge across generations. Indeed, long-tenured and committed family employees guarantee and preserve the economic value of experience and skills. For example, the Gynella brand, which falls under the umbrella of its parent company Heaton Healthcare Group, is one of the largest Czech family businesses. It has been successfully running for 20 years and was established by co-preneurs, Jaromír and Jaroslava Frič, who continue working in the family business

but have handed it over to their children: Jaromír Frič Jr. and Natália Kazíková. The second-generation sibling duo wants to preserve and continue the business empire that their parents have built. They are also interested in further developing and growing the business and intend for their children to take over but without any pressure.[13]

- *Social capital.* Family presence in a business not only shapes the structure of the social capital but also the cognitive (subjective interpretations of shared understanding) and relational (feelings of trust shared by participants) aspects of social capital. The family brings a new network of relationships in which resources and capabilities are embedded that the family business can use for its own benefit. In this context, social capital is strategic due to the accessibility of resources and capabilities beyond the boundaries of the firm that would not be available to the family business otherwise. Additionally, families create and nurture unique cognitive and relational features with customers, suppliers, and other local organizations to access actual or potential resources, exchange information, and develop long-lasting relationships. They are able to do so because family members, who are usually locally embedded, are able to grease their network of relationships with shared language and interpretations as well as common values and beliefs to develop trust, shared norms, and obligations within the network. For example, in Wal-Mart, Sam Walton's culture remains at the heart of the family business by serving customers' needs first, and by doing so, the company serves its associates, shareholders, communities, and other stakeholders.[14]

- *Reputational capital.* The long-lasting relationships between the family and the business, the family's commitment to the business, and the family name associated with the business create a family business's reputational capital,[15] which demonstrates that it is reliable and trustworthy in its specific market and local community in general. Reputational capital is an important intangible asset for interacting with stakeholders—for instance, to control prices because customers are willing to pay extra; to overcome external economic and financial shocks because employees are willing to support the business; or to consolidate the supply chain with mutual confidence in terms of quality, delivery timing, and other product/service characteristics. HiPP is a family-owned company that produces organic food for babies and children. Today, the company remains committed to the principle of organic farming with a network of more than 8,000 selected farmer and strict standards and procedures to guarantee the quality of suppliers. The company is the world's largest processor of organic raw material. Claus Hipp stated, "We will be in the right place in the future if we carry on the way our predecessors have so far. That means we'll put the interests of our customers first and do everything to make sure they're happy."[16]

Family presence in a business also serves as a resource configurator[17] of organizational abilities by putting the financial, human, social, and reputational resources to use in an effective and efficient way to support the family business's strategy and guarantee long-term survival and performance. When the configuration of resources and capabilities is effective and efficient, the family's presence in the business becomes a specific strategic resource to support the business's competitive advantage.

- *Evaluating, storing, and shedding resources.* Family commitment, the long tenure of family and nonfamily managers, stable family and business cultures, and the transmission of knowhow from one generation to another help family business management develop and store strategic resources. For instance, Antonio Dominguez, the third-generation family

CEO of Le-Vasalle, a medium-sized Peruvian family business, explained, "The successor choice among my children was done by considering the ability of my middle son to manage relationships instead of using other characteristics such as the entrepreneurial spirit of the offspring or the primogeniture principle."[18] As this example shows, network relationships embedded in the current and future generations are a unique and difficult-to-imitate resource that family managers know how to develop, preserve, and transmit. Additionally, the intangible resource accumulation and its use are additional competitive characteristics of family businesses. For instance, family businesses are able to activate their critical recovery memory to overcome crisis. Critical recovery memory is the tacit organizational knowledge gained from past crises that businesses employ to tackle new unexpected ones.[19]

- *Building resources.* Building resources refers to creatively using resources, combining different resources, and ensuring agility when allocating resources to support the family business's strategy. A family business's ability to build resources is possible because of family and nonfamily members' engagement in the organizational culture (commitment, trust, common stories, and community sense) and long-term vision. For instance, family business managers' ability to reconfigure resources was well appreciated by many firms during the COVID-19 pandemic, which produced a strong external shock that directly affected firm revenues and jeopardized firm survivability. For instance, Udo J. Vetter, chairman of Vetter Pharma in Germany stated,

Our supply chain is comprised primarily of other family companies and all the family owners came together to make sure the supply chain wasn't interrupted. Non-family businesses generally don't maintain such close relationships and by business families coming together in the supply chain, we were able, collectively, to keep our businesses running and make arrangements for employees to be able to come to work.[20]

- *Leveraging resources.* While evaluating, accumulating, and building valuable, rare, inimitable, and non-substitutable resources are important to develop core competencies, family businesses need to use resources to positively contribute to and consolidate their competitive advantages. The superior performance and longevity of family businesses are due not only to their different resources but also to differences in how they leverage their resources to expand, create, and renovate their products or services, develop their business portfolios, and/ or rebuild the foundations of their business models. For instance, an informal communication channel in a family business may grant it a high level of flexibility and low bureaucracy to make agile decisions in terms of innovation or internationalization. In any organization, the process to leverage strategic resources depends on characteristics that are traditionally common in family businesses, such as patient capital, long-term vision, and firm-specific tacit knowledge. For instance, Fitzers Catering in Ireland had to transform and add to the business by leveraging its competitive resources during the COVID-19 crisis. CEO Sharon Fitzpatrick explained,

Our company has been a culinary innovator and leader in the Irish hospitality industry since 1986. For sheer survival, we had to make a 180-degree turn and develop an e-commerce business from the ground up. Only that way could we bring our expertise to people's doors with food boxes that are easy to order, prepare and serve at home. We will actually come out of the pandemic stronger than before, with two entirely new businesses as well as a cookbook that I didn't have the time to write in the past.[21]

It is important to highlight that financial, human, social, and reputational capital as well as family business management capabilities can contribute to family businesses' competitive advantages but also to competitive disadvantages. This is the case when a family business's social capital dominates how the business functions without expanding relationships beyond kinship and close network relationships. The lock-in effect prevents family businesses from going beyond their trusted networks, leading them to fail to discover, create, and appropriate new opportunities and introduce new knowledge for future potential innovation. All family businesses should examine how their competitive advantages are built on unique resources as well as the disadvantages that could create. This is the case of the Bancroft family, which was no longer able to act together and unite against Rupert Murdoch, so his media empire was able to acquire Dow Jones Co. (the company that publishes the *Wall Street Journal*) (Table 6.1).

Table 6.1 Resources and capabilities that form from family presence in a business—
Advantages and disadvantages

Resources and Capabilities	Advantages	Disadvantages
Financial Capital	Constant (slow/medium) growth from using profit reinvestment and family money to support the family firm. It is about a long-term perspective of growth and is generally related to organic growth strategies.	Not having enough resources to grow, internationalize, or expand the business. Being dependent on reinvestment and family money could significantly damage the family business's ability to explore and exploit growth strategies (appropriate opportunities).
Human Capital	Family businesses rely on family and nonfamily employees to develop competitive advantages. Human capital is an important asset for family businesses during crises (internal or external) to support and help them survive.	Being highly dependent on kinship and friendship for developing the family business could have long-term consequences related to nepotism, favoritism, and other practices that can harm family businesses.
Social Capital	Family social capital helps family businesses access information, news, technology, and other resources that would be inaccessible otherwise.	When family social capital is too strong, it can lock family businesses into a small network structure, preventing them from incorporating new critical ideas, information, and resources, which are necessary to innovate.
Reputational Capital	Family reputation is an important intangible resource that family businesses are able to create and preserve across time and helps them maintain long-lasting relationships with customers and suppliers. Trust-based relationships when doing business are a value added for family businesses and their networks of stakeholders.	Building competitive advantages on reputation is a risky strategy for family businesses because it is a fragile asset. It takes a long time to build but can be destroyed quite quickly. Additionally, it is important to put reputational capital into perspective across generations (reputation-reality gap) and to monitor brand expectations among customers and suppliers.

6.4.1.2 *External competitive advantages*

Family businesses have to find and create profitable and sustainable business models within the sectors in which they compete. Like any other organization, family businesses evaluate the competitive environment in terms of Porter's five forces[22]—namely, threat of new entrants, supplier power, rivalry among existing firms, buyer power, and threat of substitutes—to determine the best strategy to exploit their competitive positions. There are two generic strategies: cost leadership and differentiation. The cost leadership strategy refers to when family businesses' production costs are lower than their competitors, whereas the differentiation strategy refers to when family businesses develop and deliver unique products and services compared to their competitors. For either of these generic strategies, family businesses have to develop their own competitive advantages.

The main challenge for family businesses is to know how to use their strategic resources and managerial capabilities, which emerge from family involvement in the business, to sustain their generic strategies. It is important to highlight that merely being a family business does not predispose a family business to apply a particular strategy or to have a priori advantages from using one strategy over the other. Many family businesses have been able to successfully deploy cost leadership strategies, as in the case of ALDI supermarket, which started as a small grocery store in Germany and has grown to a giant retailer with more than 12,000 stores around the world. On the other hand, other family businesses have been able to implement differentiation strategies, as in the case of Eswaran Brothers Exports, a Sri Lankan tea export family business. Operating in a competitive industry, the family business identified the need to apply a differentiation strategy in terms of being the most sustainable tea company in the world. Family business leaders have to develop and leverage resources and capabilities to sustain a cost leadership strategy or a differentiation strategy.

One strategic characteristic that most family businesses have in common is their customer orientation behavior. Regardless of whether family businesses follow a cost leadership strategy or a differentiation strategy, their customer orientation behavior is a salient strategic posture.[23] The link between customers and family businesses' intentions to closely understand them to satisfy their needs enhances family businesses' generic strategies. For example, Mitchells is a multigenerational family business specializing in men's and women's stores.[24] The family ensures value and maintains every relationship with mutual respect. The organization's culture is such that employees know customers well, including their personal details like their birthdays, hobbies, and—at times—even their pets' names.[25]

6.4.2 *Nonmarket domain*

A nonmarket domain is a set of actions and activities beyond the marketplace related to the social, cultural, political, legal, and familial contexts that support a firm's competitive strategy. In this sense, there are four pillars comprising a family business's nonmarket domain: corporate social responsibility, corporate geography responsibility, corporate political activities, and corporate family responsibility. Corporate social responsibility, corporate geography responsibility, and corporate political activities are three common elements that firms use to support their main competitive strategies. However, corporate family responsibility is a unique pillar in family businesses' nonmarket domain based on the overlap between the family and the business. The four pillars of family businesses' nonmarket domain are directly or indirectly connected to the market domain to support firms' competitive strategies and can boost or hinder firm performance and the likelihood of firm survival.

- *Corporate social responsibility.* This pillar refers to actions that attempt to integrate social concerns in their business operations and interactions with their stakeholders. For instance, philanthropic actions or practice that firms use by donating money to support worthy causes within the local community.

- *Corporate geography responsibility.* This pillar refers to practices and policies intended to have a positive influence on society or a group of stakeholders. There are two main reasons family businesses have high incentives to invest in corporate geography responsibility: locality and family identification. First, families are locally embedded, which links a family business with the local community. Second, the family's high identification with the business pushes family businesses to be good corporate citizens. For instance, the Zott family business was founded in 1926, and as one of the leading dairy production companies in Europe, it serves as a relevant social and economic player in Mertingen, Germany. In collaboration with the Ministry of Construction in the Free State of Bavaria, the family business is attempting to implement corporate initiatives to revitalize the town center and turn it into a lively, attractive place for the local community.[26]
- *Corporate political activities.* This pillar refers to actions that attempt to shape public policy, influence public institutions, and create a political family network for family businesses to achieve their goals. For instance, the European Family Businesses (EFB) is an institution that actively lobbies for changes that support family businesses.[27] On the EFB LinkedIn page, the organization self-defines as follows: "European Family Businesses strives to make political decision makers aware of the contribution of family businesses to society and to promote policies that are conducive to long-term responsible entrepreneurship." Therefore, the European family businesses that belong to this organization are able to actively outline their corporate political activities.
- *Corporate family responsibility.* This pillar refers to the overlap between the family and the business. The family's influence on the firm can be seen as a continuum moving from weak to high influence and affects the business's decision-making philosophy related to succession, human resources, and governance. As described in Chapter 1, there are three main associations between the family and the business: family-first, business-first, and family business—first orientations. For instance, in 2014, the founder of Luxottica,[28] Leonardo del Vecchio, moved back to the front line of the business at age 79 after 10 years of having a nonfamily CEO. He created a new structure that would allow his children (six children from three marriages) to enter the business's management structure.

6.5 Combination of market and nonmarket domains as a determinant of performance and survival

Strategic management in family businesses is about the combination of their market (generic strategic posture) and nonmarket (idiosyncratic family characteristics derived from the family's influence on the firm) domains, which makes these firms successful and survive longer. That is, there should be complementarity between how a firm organizes the relationship between the family and the business (nonmarket domain) and the strategic behavior the firm takes to compete (market domain). Recent studies show that family businesses perform better if they follow a differentiation strategy and balance their family- and business-oriented decision-making (family business first) or if they follow a cost leadership strategy and put the business first in their decision-making (Figure 6.3).

On the one hand, family businesses that deploy a differentiation strategy benefit more from having the family embedded in decision-making because doing so complements a business-first orientation by incorporating family needs, family objectives, and family resources. A family business—first orientation creates unique resources and capabilities that support and leverage

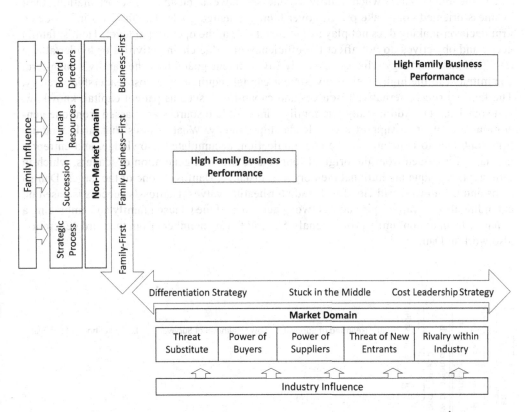

Figure 6.3 Combination of market and nonmarket domains and family business performance.

Source: Basco, R. (2014). Exploring the influence of the family upon firm performance: Does strategic behaviour matter? *International Small Business Journal*, 32(8), 967–995. https://doi.org/10.1177/0266242613484946 with copyright permission.

a differentiation strategy. For instance, the family's long-lasting relationship with the firm and family members' commitment can support innovative activities that require time and patient capital to produce benefits. For instance, W. L. Gore & Associates, Inc. is a multinational manufacturing firm specializing in products derived from fluoropolymers and was founded in 1958 by Wilbert Lee Gore and his wife in the United States. This family business gives employees the chance to innovate by giving them time once per week to come up with innovative ideas to improve products and processes. The firm's website defines the company culture as follows: "Built upon the principles of freedom, fairness, commitment and respect for the enterprise's waterline, Gore has a distinctive company culture in which highly motivated people thrive."[29] Additionally, via their social capital, families can often easily create and develop external stewardship relationships (e.g., with suppliers, banks, and communities, among others), which reduce transaction costs (because of trust-based relationships) and improve coordination among economic actors (e.g., to quickly respond to customer needs in collaboration with suppliers). For Gallager, a New Zealand family firm started in the 1930s by Bill Gallagher that is one of the most technologically innovative businesses in the country today, the central "part of their commitment to innovation is listening to the customers all the time and feeding their views back to the company at all levels."[30]

On the other hand, when family businesses have a business-first orientation, their business-oriented goals take priority over family-oriented goals. The family's influence on firm decision-making does not play a significant role at the operational level. That is, family needs and objectives do not affect the efficiency of value chain activities or hinder/alter a cost leadership strategy. However, family involvement guarantees the family's long-term commitment to the high level of investment capital required by a cost leadership strategy. The family brings alternative resources and capabilities, such as patient capital, knowhow, and social capital. Additionally, the family's intangible resources are passed from one generation to another to support a cost leadership strategy. What ensures that such a family firm continues to innovate are the communication, accumulated knowledge, and entrepreneurial spirit passed from the original founders to the next generation of leaders, which in turn create a unique institutional memory. For instance, Danfoss is one of the largest Danish firms and is known worldwide for its radiator heating valves. Danfoss's success is based on extending its innovative spirit across two generations of the Clausen family and embracing a dynamic team of nonfamily professionals. Several family members from the third generation also work in Danfoss.[31]

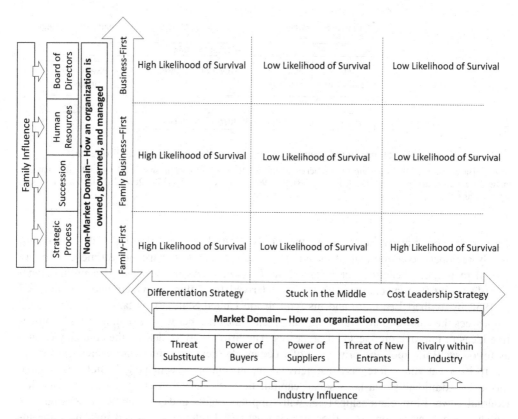

Figure 6.4 Combination of market and nonmarket domains and family business survivability.

Source: Adapted from Basco, R. (2014). Exploring the influence of the family upon firm performance: Does strategic behaviour matter? *International Small Business Journal*, 32(8), 967–995. https://doi.org/10.1177/0266242613484946 and Basco, R., Rodríguez-Escudero, A., Martin Cruz, N. & Barros-Contreras, I. (2021). The combinations of market and non-market strategies that facilitate family firm survival. *Entrepreneurship Research Journal*, 11(3), 245–286. https://doi.org/10.1515/erj-2019-0258.

Even though current evidence shows that the combinations of a business-first orientation and a cost leadership strategy and a family business-first orientation and a differentiation strategy are the most profitable, they do not necessarily increase the likelihood of family business survival. A longitudinal study[32] showed that a differentiation strategy is the best strategy family businesses can use to ensure long-term survival. A differentiation strategy can be used with any type of family–business relationship (family-first, family business-first, or business-first orientation) in the nonmarket domain (Figure 6.4). Family members involved in the business are well positioned to develop and exploit resources and capabilities to support a differentiation strategy by, for example, focusing on customers who are willing to pay a premium for unique products and services, being close to customers' needs, showing flexibility to adapt to the external environment, and maintaining a resilience capacity to absorb external shocks (crises). For instance, Sir William Gallagher, CEO of Gallagher, stated, "The benefit of a private controlled family business are numerous, and include the ability to make fast decisions and to play the long game"[33]—two characteristics that make family businesses more capable of developing and implementing a differentiation strategy.

6.6 Additional activities and reading material

6.6.1 Classroom discussion questions

1 Why do family and nonfamily businesses differ in their decision-making?
2 Are family-oriented goals an advantage or disadvantage for family businesses? Can you provide some examples that support your position?
3 What are the competitive advantages of family and nonfamily businesses?
4 Why do family businesses develop specific nonmarket strategies in relation to the family?
5 What are the most successful combinations of market and nonmarket strategies in family businesses?

6.6.2 Additional readings

1 Barrett, E. (2022). Patagonia's founding family gave away company profits—but it still controls the retailer's future. *Fortune*. Article retrieved from https://fortune.com/2022/09/21/patagonia-family-control-shares-charity-climate-change/
2 Ward, J. (2002). How strategy is different for family business. *Campden FB*. Article retrieved from www.campdenfb.com/article/how-strategy-different-family-businesses
3 *Tharawat Magazine*. (2016). Financial strategy for family businesses in troubled times. Article retrieved from www.tharawat-magazine.com/financial-series/financial-strategy-family-business/

6.6.3 Classroom activity

Aim: Reflect on family involvement in business and its effect on strategic and financial management.

Material: Ask students to watch the documentary *Entre Les Bras* directed by Paul Lacoste before coming to class.

Running the classroom exercise: Break the class into groups of four students each.

- Each group of students should reflect on the Bras family's important and critical decision-making. Ask each group the following questions:

1 To what extent was the decision influenced by family-oriented goals? What kind of family-oriented goals influenced the decision?

2 Do you think the decision would have been different for a nonfamily business?

• Each group should analyze the types of resources (financial, human, social, and reputational capital) that the Bras family has developed so far. Ask each group the following questions:

1 Is the bundle of resources a source of competitive advantage for the family business? Why or why not?

2 To what extent and when could the bundle of resources be a source of competitive disadvantage?

Takeaways: There are several decisions in the family business that have been affected by family-oriented goals, and the aim of the exercise is to have students reflect on them and visualize the importance of the family's influence (explicit or implicit) in the decision-making. The type of firm, industry, and family are contextual elements that define the importance of family-oriented goals and their effects on decision-making. The contextual elements should be considered when generalizing this analysis to other types of businesses, industries, or families. Additionally, the discussion could focus on predicting or forecasting the future of the family business if family-oriented goals are allowed to influence business-related decision-making. The second part of the exercise is to reflect on the capital endowments that the family has created, developed, and maintained in the business. How and when do capital endowments become competitive advantages, and to what extent can these competitive advantages be scaled to grow and expand the business?

6.7 Case for analysis I: ALDI and the power of family ties[34]

Many family feuds lead to separation, along with many associated business problems, but some family problems can actually bring about positive change in a business. The ALDI brothers, Karl and Theo Albrecht, were two Germans that took over their mother's grocery business in 1946. Within two decades, the brothers were efficiently operating more than 300 stores in Germany thanks to their complementary business skills.

The brothers were frugal, and they shared the same business values, which mainly revolved around their belief that people should get high-quality food at very low prices. This belief dominated their business strategy, leading them to incorporate low-cost strategies within their stores. For example, they focused on selling a select number of products at lower prices, which helped them focus their business operations to increase efficiency. They also used a word-of-mouth strategy to avoid spending money on advertising. In addition, the limited products sold by ALDI also helped it reduce its real estate by limiting its store size to 12,000 square feet compared to 145,000 square feet for its competitors.

Most of the select number of products were exclusive private-label brands, a strategy used to maintain high profit margins. The limited products offered by ALDI also increased inventory turnaround, which led customers to make fast choices. ALDI also hired employees who could engage in multiple roles in order to further reduce its operational expenditure and be able to offer great products at very low and competitive prices. This approach was unordinary and helped the brothers grow their business for decades, but it was not enough to keep them together forever.

In the early 1960s, the brothers eventually split up due to some private problems that were not officially disclosed but were most likely linked to a disagreement over selling cigarettes. The split between the brothers also led them to split the brand into what it is today: ALDI

Sud (South) led by Karl and ALDI Nord (North) led by Theo. The two brothers honored their agreement to operate in certain geographies to avoid directly competing with each other, and they also maintained very close coordination, especially during supplier negotiations.

Within the next two decades after their separation, ALDI was able to expand into three major markets: the United States (split between ALDI Sud and ALDI Nord), the United Kingdom (ALDI Sud), and France (ALDI Nord). The brothers were able to enforce a model whereby they could operate separately but still coordinate together, leading ALDI to its tremendous growth as it now operates more than 10,000 stores with a combined turnover of more than €50 million.

ALDI was able to adopt a cost leadership strategy mainly because it was led by two brothers who shared the same beliefs and values. Having grown together with a frugal mindset, both brothers believed it was crucial to provide high-quality food at low prices, and they always acted based on this belief. Even after their separation, they still united when negotiating with suppliers for better prices, and they both maintained their price competitiveness in each of their respective territories.

Discussion questions:

1 How do you think ALDI combined market and nonmarket strategies to compete?
2 What critical resources and capabilities do you think the ALDI brothers developed to consolidate their low-cost leadership strategy?

6.8 Case for analysis II: Feetures case study[35]

Every great business starts with finding a real opportunity that triggers the interest of the entrepreneur. This is exactly what happened with Hugh Gaither, the founder and CEO of Feetures, who spent around 27 years working for Ridgeview sock and hosiery company. His passion, creativity, and long experience in the field allowed him to believe in the power of technology and to design an innovative sock with a seamless toe and snug fit using fibers that conformed to the foot to enhance runners' performance. Hugh's motivation to help people, particularly athletes, perform their best and bring change to the sports tools and equipment market made him work to achieve this primary goal by creating these pioneering socks, which became a necessity in many athlete's gym bags. The uniqueness and value of the product resulted in an international and national portfolio of 4,500 stores.

Subsequently, many followers tried to imitate the features of the sock. However, Feetures maintains its dominance in the market as it enjoys a lot of other strengths that its competitors' business models lack. The management structure of the family business alone was an unbeatable competitive advantage for the firm as it generated exclusive strategic resources and capabilities. John Gaither, the eldest son, became the chief operating officer of the company and was with his father since the inception of the firm, supporting logistics and planning inventory. John witnessed the power of being the first movers in the market, the initial buzz the product created, and word of mouth by celebrities. These factors were John's main motivators to work harder on planning for the future, setting long-term goals, and strengthening his commitment to the business as the family name is associated with the brand, an attachment that will remain forever. John believed in his father's vision for creating value in the sports industry. As a result, all the income, regardless of the amount, was reinvested based on business needs to foster growth and to kill the competition by creating strong barriers to entry. The strong sense of trust and belonging and the prioritization of business interests over personal interests were the main causes of Feetures' quick international expansion, unlike competitors, which were forced to share profits with investors.

Eventually, John became more involved in the development phases of the product when it came to designing and marketing. Most of the company's investments were toward enhancing the product's design and communicating the new features to targeted segments. Additionally, he was responsible for building the customer experience before, during, and after purchasing. According to John, clients are not only the people who buy Feetures' products but also the company's internal people who take care of the business, are part of the family, and reflect Feetures' image to the world. It is always about the overall experience regardless of whether it is online or offline. For these reasons, Feetures is able to charge premium prices since the customers are willing to pay for socks with superior fit, comfort, and wearability.

In 2009, Joe Gaither, the youngest son, joined Feetures as a tech rep supporting the sales team. For the next few years, Joe traveled to 49 of the 50 states on behalf of the firm. On his travels, he met thousands of retailers and learned all about Feetures' business-to-business partnerships to make the brand their preferred choice. After extensively learning the wholesale part of Feetures' business, Joe took on a more elevated role on the sales team, managing the sales force in the western United States. Eventually, Feetures earned the position as America's first running sock brand by market share in the running industry. After a few years of managing a part of Feetures' sales force, John decided to relinquish his marketing responsibilities since he wanted to focus more on product development and operations. Accordingly, Joe took on the role of director of marketing. Joe helped create and grow a new marketing department at Feetures, making marketing a larger focus of the organization and, at the same time, developing a direct-to-consumer sales channel. Joe and his team managed key partnerships from creative to digital ad agencies. These partnerships strengthened the brand's position so clients were happy to pay high prices for high-quality products. They successfully developed and created unique cognitive and relational characteristics with customers, suppliers, and other local organizations to access actual or potential resources, exchange information, and develop long-lasting relationships.

No one can deny the power of family management in Feetures as it has generated exclusive strategic resources and capabilities for the firm. The brothers John and Joe are in senior management positions as part of the succession process at Feetures.[36] They demonstrate how strategic shifts often occur during generational transitions in a family business' leadership. While the overall strategy remains the same as when their father began the company, Joe is driving a change in marketing strategy, and John is leading an adjustment in production strategy. As the youngest member of the leadership team, Joe has a deep understanding of social media and the power of the Internet. Hugh's family chose the right strategy and enhanced the business's opportunity to prosper through multiple generations of family ownership, performing successfully in highly competitive markets.

Discussion questions:

1 How do you think Feetures combined market and nonmarket domains to leverage its competitive strategy? What kind of strategy does Feetures follow?
2 What critical resources and capabilities do you think Feetures developed to consolidate its competitive strategy?
3 What are the family business goals in the Feetures family business?

6.9 Case study: An upside down strategy for LEGO[37]

Kjeld Kirk Kristiansen answered the phone while with his wife during a hot Athens summer at the end of August 2004. He knew the situation at LEGO was critical, and he wondered whether this call would announce the fatal denouement—the loss of Kirk Kristiansen's family control over LEGO. Jorgen Vig Knudstorp, selected but not officially announced as the CEO successor, asked Kirk Kristiansen to resign as CEO, saying it was time for him to assume real leadership of the company. He explained they could not continue hiding the real leadership. When the conversation finished, Kirk Kristiansen's wife immediately asked, "Were you fired?" Kirk Kristiansen just looked at her defeated and then lost his gaze in the immensity of Athens.

Kjeld Kirk Kristiansen had selected Knudstorp to succeed him, but everything happened so fast. LEGO was bleeding, but no one—from the board of directors to the employees and the different stakeholders—was able to really understand the critical situation. No one wanted to see the crude reality! The crisis this time was different. By August 31, 2004, the board members who had been very skeptical over the designation of the new inexperienced CEO—Jorgen Vig Knudstorp—finally accepted him as the new leader of LEGO.

The chairman of the board stated, "I am convinced that there always will be a LEGO brand. The question is, who will own it."[38] This resonated among the rest of the board members. There were two main options for LEGO's future: (1) sale, fusion, or partnership to escape the critical strategic, managerial, organizational, and financial situation or (2) LEGO stays an independent family-owned business by reshaping its culture and strategy after cleaning up its financial situation. Actually, Morgan Stanley approached the company with an offer to sell the business for around $1.7 billion. While Kjeld Kirk Kristiansen was emotionally determined to keep the business in the family's hands, the board (his own board) was skeptical about this possibility.

The LEGO story. LEGO was founded by Ole Kirk Kristiansen in 1932 in the Danish town of Billund. During the great depression, the woodworker and carpenter found it hard to make money by producing furniture and began to produce toys. He thought that even in the most critical economic times, parents want to cheer on their children. This was the first successful strategic choice of Ole Kirk Kristiansen. Growing from the wooden toys factory, in 1946, LEGO introduced the first plastic injection-modeling machine for toy production. During the 1950s, Ole and Godtfred, Ole's third son, introduced the new idea of construction bricks and the famous patented stud-and-tube coupling system, which led them to create the modular system we know today as LEGO. The building blocks can be combined in different ways, liberating the creativity of children and adults. The multiple combinations create economies of scale in product development. With time, LEGO introduced the DUPLO line, which are bigger bricks that can be easily assembled by toddlers; added mini figures to their LEGO sets; and expanded into the theme parks. Across several decades, the company experienced acceptable growth rates.

Kjeld Kirk Kristiansen, the third-generation CEO, built an entire organization around LEGO System Play since his appointment in 1979. During his leadership, LEGO doubled in size every five years. The internationalization of the company due to globalization created rapid growth, but the company neglected innovation so they could maintain their global success. The success of LEGO created a unique consensus-oriented culture in the company. Employees were confident in LEGO products, and they knew that the family was behind them to support any crisis. That is, their belief in the product and brand was enough to overcome any difficult situation.

Consequently, the firm was not able to anticipate changes in consumer behavior, sector regulations, market transformations, technology advances, and economic and social trends. By 1993, the growth path suddenly stopped. To address this situation, LEGO's strategy was to invest and diversify the number of products, but the strategic action did not improve the growth curve of the company. By 1998, the company reported its first losses ever. The first nonfamily CEO was appointed, and the strategy of expanding products continued via partnerships with Lucasfilm, new theme parks, and video games. By the beginning of the 2000s, only a few products were profitable, such as Harry Potter, Bob the Builder, and LEGO Bionicle.

In June 2003, a memo from Jorgen Vig Knudstorp to the board of directors stated, "We are on a burning platform." The negative cashflow, high debts, numerous products, and an irresponsible diversification strategy brought LEGO close to collapse.

Kjeld Kirk Kristiansen and Jorgen Vig Knudstorp. In 2003, Kjeld Kirk Kristiansen was back as CEO but selected two inexperienced managers to navigate the company crisis: Jorgen Vig Knudstorp and Jesper Ovesen. However, at this time, the new leadership was not officially announced because the board of directors found Knudstorp to be an unsure individual with no clear vision to hold the CEO title. Kirk Kristiansen helped Knudstorp introduce him to different stakeholders.

While Knudstorp looked for strategic answers to the company's crisis, Ovesen applied a straightforward action plan to reduce expenses by closing factories and conducting layoffs. Kirk Kristiansen tried to maintain firm harmony among senior managers, employees, and stakeholders by managing the internal and external politics. A strange situation started materializing around the leadership. Knudstorp and Ovesen had actual but not formal leadership. Employees still saw Kirk Kristiansen as the leader even when he was, in part, responsible for not anticipating and preventing the actual crisis in LEGO. Kirk Kristiansen represented the family behind LEGO.

The internal strategy of the triumvirate was to make all stakeholders aware of the crisis. At that time, the crisis was not reversible. It had to be taken seriously, and there was an urgent need to design a new business model for LEGO. However, it was not easy for the board of directors, employees, and stakeholders—even for Kirk Kristiansen—to really recognize this crisis. The culture of the company prevented them from seeing it.

Kjeld Kirk Kristiansen's resignation, the official new position for Jorgen Vig Knudstorp as CEO, and the final decision to sell the parks—a decision that Kirk Kristiansen opposed—finally changed the leadership dynamic by the autumn of 2004. The choice of Jorgen Vig Knudstorp as a CEO was a personal decision from Kirk Kristiansen based on trust rather than more objective criteria.

The new vision. One of the main issues for the new CEO, Knudstorp, to resolve was to answer two questions to advance a new strategy: What went wrong at LEGO, and why does LEGO exist? The first action plan to stabilize the company by dramatically reducing costs and making all stakeholders aware of the situation had gone successfully but with huge human, emotional, and economic costs for everyone involved in the family business. Now what?

From the book *Profit from the Core*, Knudstorp recognized the importance of understanding the core business and constantly strengthening it to be profitable. To his surprise, Knudstorp found that Godtfred Kirk Kristiansen, managing director of the LEGO Group from 1957 to 1973 and the third son of the founder Ole Kirk Kristiansen, had the same vision: the need to focus and concentrate on the business at its core. Knudstorp started developing his strategy based on this simple idea of going back to the core and wrote several blogs to transmit the idea to all stakeholders. According to Knudstorp, four things make LEGO unique: brand, brick, construction system, and community (customers passionate for LEGO). Now that Knudstorp found the core of the family business, it was time to develop a strategy.

In the summer of 2005, Kjeld Kirk Kristiansen invited Knudstorp to join BrickFest in Washington DC, where Knudstorp learned something unique about LEGO: it is about CREATIVITY. Creativity was the word to center the new strategy around. LEGO stimulates consumers' creativity. While the future of the company rests on the bricks and the construction system, creativity was a new lens to understand it. LEGO could occupy this small and profitable niche in the market. This required adjusting the value chain from developing the product to focusing on the final customer. Thus, the new vision was "to be the provider of systematically creative, fun, quality tools to foster shapers of the future by letting them build everything possible—and impossible—to imagine." The second strategic stage started by improving the core of the business, building a defensible business core, and rebalancing the financial structure of the business.

Discussion questions:

1   If you were Kjeld Kirk Kristiansen, would you follow your emotional instincts or listen to your board of directors when selecting the CEO?
2   Why do you think LEGO was able to maintain its independence as a family business?
3   What could have happened in a nonfamily business? Would the board of directors keep waiting so long to make a decision to stay independent or sell the company?

Notes

1   Aparicio, G., Basco, R., Iturralde, T., & Maseda, A. (2017). An exploratory study of firm goals in the context of family firms: An institutional logics perspective. *Journal of Family Business Strategy*, 8(3), 157–169.
2   Heath, C., Larrick, R. P., & Wu, G. (1999). Goals as reference points. *Cognitive Psychology*, 38(1), 79–109.
3   The value function reflects family members' preferences for different levels of achievement. The value function depends on changes in wealth relative to a reference situation.
4   Gómez-Mejia, L. R., Haynes, K. T., Nunez-Nickel, M., Jacobson, K. J. L., & Moyano-Fuentes, J., (2007). Socioemotional wealth and business risks in family-controlled firms: Evidence from Spanish olive oil mills. *Administrative Science Quarterly*, 52(1), 106–137.
5   *Tharawat Magazine*. (2018). Au Gant Rouge—A tale of perseverance and innovation. Article retrieved from   www.tharawat-magazine.com/family-business-culture/au-gant-rouge-perseverance-and-inn ovation/
6   *Tharawat Magazine*. (2016). IPORTRAIT: Maison Tamboite—About family and bicycles. Article retrieved from www.tharawat-magazine.com/rise-family-office/portrait-maison-tamboite/
7   *Tharawat Magazine*. (2019). Sparks & Daughters. Information retrieved from www.tharawat-magaz ine.com/vocabulary/sparks-daughters/
https://sparksanddaughters.com/, https://sparksanddaughters.com/our-journey/
8   *Tharawat Magazine*. (2015). The Tan family and the strength of unity. Issue 28. Article retrieved from www.tharawat-magazine.com/tan-family-strength-unity/
9   Basco, R., Rodriguez Escudero, A. I., Martin-Cruz, N., & Barros-Contreras, I. (2021). The combin- ations of market and non-market strategies that facilitates family firm survival. *Entrepreneurship Research Journal*, 11(3), 245–286.
10 Barney, J. B. (1991). Firm resources and sustained competitive advantage. *Journal of Management*, 17(1), 99–120.
11 Habbershon, T., & Williams, M. (1999). A resource-based framework for assessing the strategic advantage of family firms. *Family Business Review*, 12(1), 1–25.
12 Hall, C. (2018). Why family businesses are better at weathering economic downturns. EY Blog. Information retrieved from www.ey.com/en_ae/growth/why-family-businesses-are-better-at-weather ing-economic-downturn
13 Information retrieved from www.heaton.cz/en/we-are-part-of-the-forbes-family-business-ranking- 2022/. Company website: www.heaton.cz/en/
14 Information retrieved from Wal-Mart website https://corporate.walmart.com/about/sam-walton
15 Blombäck, A., & Botero, I. C. (2013). "Chapter 28: Reputational Capital in Family Firms: Understanding Uniqueness from the Stakeholder Point of View." In *Handbook of Research on Family Business*, Second Edition. Cheltenham: Edward Elgar Publishing. Retrieved Mar 2, 2023, from www.elgaronl ine.com/view/edcoll/9781848443228/9781848443228.00044.xml

16 A discussion with Hipp Holding AG. Prof. Dr. Claus Hipp Boyden. *Boyden Leadership Series*, 5(15), 2–5. Article retrieved from www.boyden.com/media/hipp-holding-ag-prof-dr-claus-hipp/img/hipp-holding-ag-prof-dr-claus-hipp.pdf

17 Sirmon, D. G., & Hitt, M. A. (2003). Managing resources: Linking unique resources, management, and wealth creation in family firms. *Entrepreneurship Theory and Practice*, 27(4), 339–358.

18 Interview conducted by the author of this book as part of an international research project on family businesses. The information disclosed in this paragraph was authorized by the interviewee.

19 Basco, R. et al. (2022). Weathering the storm. Family firm strategies in the midst of growing uncertainty. STEP Project Global Consortium and KPMG COVID-19 Report Middle East and Africa.

20 STEP Project Global Consortium and KPMG (2021). Taking the long view. Lessons in endurance from European family businesses. Report retrieved from https://globaluserfiles.com/media/40495_c0aedffab6759b91b81d0b982034ff46177866e7.pdf/o/GM-TL-01299-European-Family-Business-Barometer_V14_Web-1.pdf

21 STEP Project Global Consortium and KPMG (2021). Taking the long view. Lessons in endurance from European family businesses. Report retrieved from https://globaluserfiles.com/media/40495_c0aedffab6759b91b81d0b982034ff46177866e7.pdf/o/GM-TL-01299-European-Family-Business-Barometer_V14_Web-1.pdf

22 Porter, M. E. (1980). *Competitive Strategy: Techniques for Analyzing Industries and Competitors*. New York: The Free Press.

23 Basco, R. (2014). Exploring the influence of the family upon firm performance: Does strategic behaviour matter? *International Small Business Journal*, 32(8), 967–995.

24 Information retrieved from Mitchells website https://mitchells.mitchellstores.com/about-us

25 *Tharawat Magazine*. (2019). Mitchell Stores. Article retrieved from www.tharawat-magazine.com/fbl/mitchell-stores/. Additional information Mitchell website https://shop.mitchellstores.com/

26 Basco, R., Stough, R., & Suwala, L. (2021). *Family Business and Regional Development*. London: Routledge.

27 European family businesses website https://europeanfamilybusinesses.eu/

28 Luxottica is an Italian eyewear conglomerate and the world's largest company in the eyewear industry.

29 Information retrieved from Gore website www.gore.com/about

30 Information retrieved from *EY Family Business Yearbook 2017*. Document with additional information can be downloaded from the following address: https://assets.ey.com/content/dam/ey-sites/ey-com/en_gl/topics/growth/screen-ey-17-002-fby-2017-bkl1705-002-v27-30-new-zealand.pdf

31 Information retrieved from *EY Family Business Yearbook 2017*. Document with additional information can be downloaded from the following address: https://assets.ey.com/content/dam/ey-sites/ey-com/en_gl/topics/growth/screen-ey-17-002-fby-2017-bkl1705-002-v27-05-denmark.pdf

32 Basco, R., Rodriguez Escudero, A. I., Martin-Cruz, N., & Barros-Contreras, I. (2021). The combinations of market and non-market strategies that facilitates family firm survival. *Entrepreneurship Research Journal*, 11(3), 245–286.

33 Information retrieved from *EY Family Business Yearbook 2017*. Document with additional information can be downloaded from the following address: https://assets.ey.com/content/dam/ey-sites/ey-com/en_gl/topics/growth/screen-ey-17-002-fby-2017-bkl1705-002-v27-30-new-zealand.pdf

34 This example discussion is developed solely as the basis for class discussion. This example discussion is not intended to serve as an endorsement, source of primary data, or illustration of effective or ineffective management.

35 This case study discussion is developed solely as the basis for class discussion. This case study discussion is not intended to serve as an endorsement, source of primary data, or illustration of effective or ineffective management.

36 The recent announcement of the Feetures family business's succession planning can be found at the following website: www.endurancesportswire.com/feetures-celebrates-20-years-of-family-owned-business-and-announces-organizational-changes/

37 This case study discussion is developed solely as the basis for class discussion. This case study discussion is not intended to serve as an endorsement, source of primary data, or illustration of effective or

ineffective management. Several references were used to build the case study discussion: (1) Lunde, N. (2012). *The LEGO Miracle*. Jyllands-Postens Forlag. English version of the Book retrieved from https://kontextagency.com/images/sample/Lego_English_sample.pdf, (2) Geislinger, A. (2020). A turnaround case study: How LEGO rebuild and become the top toymaker in the world, and (3) Venables, M. (2013). Behind the legendary LEGO, Part one: The public relations, family values, and product quality. *Forbes*. Article retrieved from www.forbes.com/sites/michaelvenables/2013/03/12/the-state-of-the-lego-part-1/?sh=11b551402b96

38 Lunde, N. (2012). *The LEGO Miracle*. Jyllands-Postens Forlag. The quote comes from the English version translated from the Danish by Mark Kline. Book retrieved from https://kontextagency.com/images/sample/Lego_English_sample.pdf

Part III
Governance in family business

7   Ownership governance in family business

Learning objectives

- Distinguish the different types of family owners in family businesses.
- Understand the importance of formalizing ownership governance.
- Recognize the agency problems that are unique to family businesses.
- Identify the benefit of having shareholder agreements.
- Interpret how family complexity across time affects ownership governance.

7.1 Introduction

Corporate governance refers to formal and informal systems, practices, and processes used to coordinate interactions between the ownership, business, and family entities as well as the rights and responsibilities by which family businesses are directed, managed, and controlled. The aim of corporate governance is to balance and align the multiple and conflicting goals of a firm's many stakeholders. Due to the family's importance as one of the main stakeholders of a family business, family business corporate governance comprises three different yet complementary governance structures: ownership governance, business governance, and family governance.

All family businesses have corporate governance, no matter their size, age, or industry. When a family business is small and consists of one or few family members, the corporate governance system is informal. Even when a firm's governance mechanisms are not highly developed, such informal governance can be very effective. Take, for instance, the hotels and restaurants owned, governed, and managed by the Oostwegel family in the Netherlands. The family has been in business for more than 40 years, and is currently led by Camille, a member of the second generation, who holds the position of owner and general director of Oostwegel Collection.[1] Informal interpersonal relationships among family members have replaced formal governance mechanisms for addressing succession, growth strategies, and new business development issues.[2] However, when the evolution of the ownership, business, and family entities over time increases the complexity of one or more of these entities, family businesses are required to start developing formal corporate governance structures.

At the early stages of a family business, when the founder and family exert significant influence and the firm size is still manageable and governable by a few family individuals, the cost of implementing formal corporate governance could exceed the benefit. However, as the complexity of the business, ownership, and family entities increases, more formality is needed in the business's corporate governance to ensure long-term firm survival and to maintain family cohesiveness. An example of the importance of corporate governance development in a family business can be found in the Wadi Group,[3] a family-run business that started as a small-scale

DOI: 10.4324/9781003273240-10

poultry operation in 1984 and is now a leader in the agribusiness industry with 12 subsidiaries and 10 brands. When the family business faced a growth challenge, it moved from an informal governance structure dominated by owners for owners to a professional structure with specific sub-structures for the ownership, business, and family entities. In addition, the new structure includes family, external, and independent representation to provide advice and support business development.[4]

Consequently, recognizing the complexity of family business corporate governance, this chapter begins by covering ownership governance (the next two chapters, Chapters 8 and 9, focus on business and family governance, respectively). This chapter focuses on ownership structure and governance in family businesses. It addresses the importance of recognizing, implementing, and planning family businesses' ownership structures and governance; describes the types of owners who usually participate in an ownership structure; and outlines the types of ownerships structures that family businesses can develop by considering the complexity of the ownership, business, and family entities.

7.2 Corporate governance in family businesses

Corporate governance gains importance for owners in terms of directing and controlling a business when ownership and management are separated—that is, when owners are not the same as managers and owners delegate the managerial function to managers. In this context, corporate governance reduces agency problems, which are the conflicts of interest inherent in any relationship where managers are expected to act in the owners' and other stakeholders' interests. However, some argue that when the family is the main shareholder in a family business and family members are present in managerial positions, corporate governance loses importance in the family business context because the owners' and managers' interests are intrinsically linked due to their kinship relationships.

It is true that in the family business context, the low separation between ownership and management (family members with overlapping roles as owners and managers) reduces the classic agency problems between principals (owners) and agents (managers), such as conflicts of interest and asymmetric information. It can typically be assumed that the controlling family acts as a monolithic group that pursues its own interests and directly monitors nonfamily executives for possible misbehavior in terms of appropriating the family owners' wealth by not acting in the best interests of the family shareholders.

Even though the classic agency problems are reduced or even eliminated in the family business context, family businesses suffer from other agency problems that are, to a certain extent, exclusive due to family involvement in ownership and business. In this sense, family businesses have to deal with unique and specific agency problems that corporate governance structures can minimize.

- Principal–principal problems

  - *Majority–minority problems* emerge when the majority principal family owners maximize their own wealth but do not act in the interests of minority principal family or nonfamily owners because of conflicts of interest, divergences about family business goals, moral hazard,[5] and asymmetric information.[6] The power of the majority principal family owners over the rest of the shareholders can be used to their own benefit by influencing decision-making. This can happen in any small or medium private family firm when the ownership is unevenly distributed among family members. For instance, this is a typical problem in the context of Arab family businesses, where the inheritance process dictates that male family members receive double what female family members receive because of Sharia law. The unbalanced distribution of shares can complicate family cohesiveness in the generations to come. Majority-minority agency problems can happen in listed firms when family members or a group of family members have dual-class shares, which give them excessive control over the family business via super voting rights. This is the case of Ford Motor Company, founded in 1903 by Henry Ford. Via individual participation or trusts, Ford family members own Class B shares, which account for just 2% of Ford Motor's outstanding stock, but they control 40% of the voting power.[7]

- *Problems related to conflicts of vision* emerge when there are different visions about how to govern and manage the family business and which strategic direction the business should take within the group of family members. The typical family feud emerges when two or more family groups attempt to impose their strategic visions. Family feuds impede decision-making and, ultimately, the quality of the decisions because family members are more concerned about imposing their interests than responding to competitive market challenges. The Feil family, owners of a multibillion-dollar real estate empire, spent more than eight years and millions of dollars in a family dispute. The two sisters of the family filed a lawsuit against their brother, Jeffrey, who managed the company following their father's desires and old-fashioned management principles, for unfairly depriving them of cash (distribution of dividends), abusing the sisters' trust, and not giving them access to financial records and other important information.[8] The brother and his sisters differed in how to govern and manage the family business. Finally, the battle ended with an agreement on a new formula for distributing dividends and organizing the family empire's corporate governance. Conflict of vision can also emerge when there is high cohesiveness among family owners who are majority shareholders and external shareholders are also involved as minority shareholders. The majority group may extract private benefits at the expense of the minority group via managerial talent (e.g., by adding family members to the top management team, thereby blocking other nonfamily members from accessing top positions), executive compensation (e.g., by adjusting family members' compensation indiscriminately without using market parameters), and tunneling benefits (e.g., by transferring profits from controlled companies to the parent company such that family members can extract the benefits for themselves). Take, for example, the legal battle between SAICO, a minority shareholder of SARL Peronnet (a French firm controlled by the Peronnet family), and the directors of Peronnet:

The Peronnet family established a new company, SCI, solely owned by family members. SCI bought some land and took out a loan to build a warehouse. SCI then leased the warehouse to SARL Peronnet, which expanded its business, and used the proceeds to repay the loan. The plaintiff argued that the Peronnet family expropriated the corporate opportunity of SARL Peronnet (namely to build a warehouse), and thereby benefitted itself at the expense of minority shareholders.[9]

- Principal–agent problems

  - *Problems related to altruism* emerge when principals (owners) and agents (managers) are relatives and their familial ties based on mutual trust, support, and benevolence supersede formal contractual relationships. Altruism behavior creates specific principal–agent problems. First, family status prevails over meritocracy, which not only leads to less prepared family members managing the firm but also discourages nonfamily members from engaging in the process of competition. Second, family members are discouraged from controlling themselves or applying sanctions or corrective actions when necessary. Third, incentives are created for free-riding behavior among family members who expect benevolence from the rest of the family members. For instance, Heather Cho was the vice president of Korean Air and daughter of the company's chairman, Cho Yang-ho. During a flight to Seoul, she was served nuts in a bag instead of on a plate. Not only did Heather reprimand and shout at the flight attendant, but she also demanded the plane go back to the gate so she could exit.[10] Even though, in this case, Heather lost her job because of the public nature of her behavior, family members are always part of the power structure and can influence decision-making. In this family, the last conflict emerged when Heather criticized her younger brother, Walter Cho-Won-Tae, who was the chairman of the family holding, Hanjin KAL, by claiming their father "wanted the family to cooperate and run the business together." She threatened her brother that she would join forces with other owners to better control the management of the conglomerate.[11]

- *Problems related to conflicts of interest* occur when principals (owners) and agents (managers) are relatives but the agents have different interests and visions for the firm. Because of the agents' position, they are able to direct strategic actions in a particular way to achieve their own interests at the expense of the rest of the family owners. This is the case when the next generation of family members assumes business leadership but does not have shares as the shares remain in the senior generation's hands. The next generation of family members can act on their own behalf (e.g., via salary compensation) at the expense of the senior generation (who could receive reduced dividends).

- *Problems related to asymmetric information* arise when principals (owners) and agents (managers) are relatives but the agents, who are better positioned to know different aspects of the family business, use the asymmetric information for their own benefit at the expense of the rest of the family owners. For instance, it is common in small and medium family businesses that the sibling who assumes the business leadership has higher psychological ownership to influence the firm's destiny and to use the family business resources for his or her own benefit.

- Agent–agent problems

  - *Power-related problems* occur when one group of agents (managers) and another group of agents (family or nonfamily managers) do not have the same power to discuss, bargain, and decide the best course of strategic action. The most common consequences are undervalued decisions, an unmotivated group of family or nonfamily managers, and difficulties attracting and retaining talented managers. The main problems appear when quasi-family members—nonfamily employees who have been engaged with the current generation since the beginning or early stages—are able to control or influence decision-making and can act to achieve benefits for themselves while calling for the new generation to maintain the status quo and undermining generational changes.

Not all of the abovementioned governance problems are the same in all family businesses; their importance can vary depending on the complexity of the business and the family. The complexity of the business is related to the level of competitiveness within the industry or sector in which the family business operates, the growth strategy implemented, the technological dynamism, and the structure of the business (i.e., a single business, business group, or conglomerate structure). The complexity of the family is related to the structure of the family (e.g., size and the extent to which extended family is embraced), the demarcation of roles, and the intensity of the kinship relationships. Therefore, there is no one-size-fits-all governance structure for all family businesses. Each family business has to create its own structure based on the internal needs that emerge from the complexity of the ownership, business, and family entities and external pressures coming from the rest of the stakeholders.

Corporate governance in a family business aims to maintain the cohesiveness of the family entity by developing structures for accountability, transparency, fairness, and responsibility and to guarantee long-term business survival. The governance and structure of the ownership entity is the first challenge to be addressed in the context of corporate governance in family businesses.

7.3 Ownership structure and governance

The design of the family business ownership structure is one of the most important decisions for a family to exert their influence and execute control over the family business. The ownership structure is the cornerstone of the business and family governance. One well-known right of any owner is to receive dividends proportional to the stake of the business he or she owns. However, the cohesiveness of family shareholders and their relationships with nonfamily shareholders (in case external owners exist) are important because owners are the ultimate decision-makers and the destiny of the family business rests in their hands.

The commitment of the controlling family to the business is demonstrated through responsible ownership behavior. This means that family shareholders have to assume their rights and obligations while balancing the emotional ties that connect past and future generations. The following are among the most important principles for responsible family owners:

- Promote stability in the ownership structure to ensure the continuity of the owning family across generations.
- Design the present and future ownership structures in terms of private versus public ownership, current and future generations, and dual-class shares, among other aspects.
- Respect internal communication, consensual decision-making, and transparency to avoid family conflicts and contradicting messages to the rest of the stakeholders.
- Develop a shared vision of the family business in terms of long-term goals, risk taking, growth, and principles that help the board of directors and managers execute their tasks.
- Lead through the governance structure to ensure the continuity of the family business across generations.
- Understand the specificities of the family business, including the business itself, the industry in which the family business operates, and the family dynamics across generations.
- Formalize different policies and processes for dividends, estate planning, corporate philanthropy, coordination between the board of directors and the top management team, and governance succession, among others.

Committed and cohesive family ownership can provide substantial value in terms of firm performance and continuity. However, education is needed to achieve this level of professionalization in the ownership entity. Everyone in the family understands the right to receive dividends, but only few family members understand the importance of ownership obligations. The dividend fallacy, the false idea that a business always has to distribute dividends and satisfy family members' needs, is common in the second and subsequent generations if the founder generation does not educate their offspring in the logic of ownership and does not define an action plan to create reliable ownership governance. As mentioned in Chapter 4, the case of the Steinberg family in Canada illustrates the importance of educating family members to be responsible owners. In this family-first family business with a culture of nepotism, Mitzi, the daughter of the founder, did not accept being ousted from her management position and, consequently, executed her ownership power to convey her resentment and initiate a family feud. Because of the family conflicts, the family business was taken over by Socanav in 1989.[12]

7.3.1 *Type of owners*

Owners have equal rights, but not all of them contribute to the family business equally. To understand the dynamics of ownership governance and its effectiveness, it is necessary to differentiate the types of owners depending on their behavior: group-oriented behavior and wealth-oriented behavior. Group-oriented behavior refers to the extent to which family owners act to develop a cohesive group with similar goals, values, and expectations. Wealth-oriented behavior, on the other hand, refers to the extent to which owners act to develop and expand family wealth. Figure 7.1 combines the two dimensions to create different types of owners. The group-oriented behavior continuum goes from steward behavior to individualistic behavior, and the wealth-oriented behavior continuum goes from wealth creation to wealth harvesting.

- *Active owners* show their commitment to the family business by assuming their owner roles with responsibility. They actively participate in ownership assemblies, are informed and prepared for their participation, and constantly challenge the status quo with constructive interactions to support long-term family business sustainability. Their aim is to preserve wealth while keeping the cohesiveness of the group of owners. Active owners may or may not work in the business, but they have a wide enough vision about what both the family and the business need.
- *Obstructive owners* demonstrate individualistic behavior to satisfy their own personal interests. They are interested in harvesting the wealth created by the previous generation and/ or imposing their own personal vision on the family business. They tend to be an obstacle to effective ownership governance in terms of ownership cohesiveness and long-term business

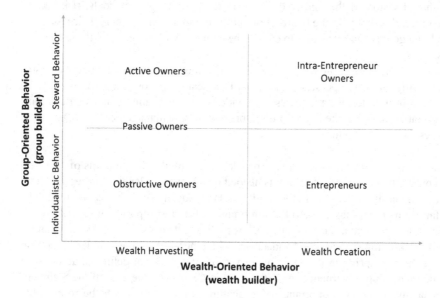

Figure 7.1 Types of family business owners.

survival. Obstructive owners may or may not work in the firm, but their individualist vision prioritizes their ambition over family and business needs.

- *Intra-entrepreneurship owners* have a strong transgenerational entrepreneurship mindset to create new streams of economic, social, and emotional value within the boundaries of the family business. They embrace family cohesiveness by developing a long-term perspective. These owners are important because of their interest in creating new value and diversifying wealth. Intra-entrepreneurship owners usually work in the firm and have a strong business-oriented perspective.
- *Entrepreneurial owners* have a strong desire to make money, but they have low commitment to the family business itself and to family cohesiveness. They direct their entrepreneurial energy to external projects beyond the boundaries of the family business. Some entrepreneurial owners may act independent of the family business, while in other cases, their new businesses become part of the family business as a spin-off strategy.
- *Passive owners* do not work in the business, and their main aim is to cash in on their shares by receiving dividends. They are not wealth builders (but are just harvesting what they have inherited from their parents), and they fluctuate in their behavior as active owners and obstructive owners.

7.4 Ownership assembly or shareholder meeting

An ownership assembly, also called a shareholder meeting, is a meeting held by those individuals who are owners, and the aim of the meeting is to discuss the long-term interests of the family business; control its general progress; and agree on critical business issues, such as approving a contract to buy back company shares. Regardless of the type of family business—private or public—all owners (family and nonfamily owners) should participate and engage in ownership assemblies/shareholders meetings.

All family businesses have ownership assemblies even when they are not formally designed, planned, or prepared. In most family businesses (specifically during the early stage in their lifecycle), ownership meetings may be a mere formality to distribute dividends, to accept and corroborate financial statements, and to agree on other decision-making that requires the owners' authorization or final decision. However, such informality carries an inherent risk. It is common to observe family businesses with ghost ownership assemblies. For instance, some family members do not like to participate in business discussions, arguing that they trust their parents, siblings, or other family members who are more involved in the business or feeling these meetings are boring and not useful. Consequently, important ownership decisions are made and agreements are signed during family dinner meetings without understanding the future implications of such agreements—no communication, no explanation, and no transparency. Those family owners who are less engaged, possess less business knowledge, and trust those who are actively working in the firm are the most vulnerable, compromising their owner rights and their future descendants' rights.

To avoid current and future conflicts among family owners (and nonfamily owners if they exist), it is important to systematically plan ownership assemblies. Any ownership meeting has to have an agenda that is known in advance by all owners and needs to be finalized with meeting minutes to summarize agreements and pending resolutions. The meeting minutes should be recorded, signed, and stored so they are accessible to current and future owners. In other words, family businesses need to professionalize their ownership assemblies.

It is the responsibility of owners to show up prepared for constructive discussions during ownership assemblies. An agenda helps maintain the flow of the discussion within a specific frame. Having a specific agenda is not trivial because there is a tendency to divert ownership conversations toward family problems or operative business issues that are not part of ownership conversations. Ownership assemblies are not forums to treat issues related to the family, which are instead intrinsically part of family assemblies (see Chapter 8 on family governance), or issues related to the business, which have to be handled by the board of directors. The main message is that owners should use their ownership hat during ownership assemblies by assuming the rights and responsibilities of the ownership role.

Depending on the complexity of the ownership, business, and family entities, the topics of the agenda can vary from one family business to another. In general, the main ownership assembly topics are as follows: elect directors of the board, approve major transactions, define and approve auditors, approve financial statements, define the dividend distribution, and interact and communicate with other governance bodies (board of directors, managers, and family).

However, it is important to recognize that in the evolutionary path of any family business, there is a learning process to move into a professional governance structure. When there is high overlap between the ownership, business, and family entities and a low number of owners, the ownership assembly could overlap with the family assembly, which is normal in the early stages. This is the case of the Emirati Al Saud Company, where the seven second-generation siblings and mother are owners. They hold an ownership assembly annually, which focuses on ownership matters, but because all of the owners are also family members, they extend the conversation to family matters.[13] This arrangement works perfectly for the family and the business. However, this situation cannot be maintained for long because the third generation will soon enter into the scene. It is highly recommended that the third generation not participate in the ownership assembly without having shares, but the complexity of the family with three active generations should activate the family assembly.

7.5 Shareholder agreement

The shareholder agreement is an important instrument used by shareholders in private family businesses and, to some extent, in publicly traded family businesses to govern the present and future relationships among multiple owners and, more specifically, among family members of the owning family. The shareholder agreement is a written document that regulates relationships to keep a cohesive group of owners and to maintain the long-term perspective of the owning family to perpetuate their ownership control across generations. Shareholder agreements are more common in private family businesses than in their public counterparts and are generally private documents. The difference between the shareholder agreement and the articles of incorporation, a legal document to formalize the creation of a company, is that the latter is public and defines the general regulations for owning and governing the business when it is created. More specifically, the shareholder agreement defines the ownership rights and responsibilities; the general framework under which family shareholders operate; and under which circumstances family shareholders may sell, buy, and transfer their shares. In other words, it creates obligations and compromises that tie family shareholders together.

Depending on the family and the business, a shareholder agreement could address some of the following topics:

• Creating a board of directors by defining its composition; main tasks; and other internal procedures/mechanisms that could be important, such as selection, rotation, and compensation.
• Protecting key decision-making that could alter the fundamentals of the family business. What percentage of voting rights does decision-making require? There are some important decisions that could affect firm survivability (e.g., mergers and acquisitions, borrowing in

excess of a specific amount, and transferring or selling any part of the business) that require higher consensus among shareholders (70% of the voting rights), whereas other decisions would require a simple majority (51% of the voting rights).

- Identifying the mechanisms for problem-solving or dispute resolution when family owners have to address conflicts.
- Defining the shareholder employment policy that outlines the special rules for family owners to work in the family business.
- Defining the dividend policy with specific criteria to determine the dividends given to shareholders and those reinvested in the business.
- Establishing ownership succession by defining the inheritance process and future ownership structure. There are four potential forms of ownership succession in a family business:
  - First, the aim to abide by classical law transmission where the (national or religious) law imposes how shares are passed from one generation to another.
  - Second, the aim to maintain the principle of equality where each family member receives equal ownership participation in the business.
  - Third, the aim to limit the number of owners via a holding company such that instead of having multiple individual family owners, each family branch creates its own company that owns the holding family business in proportion to the shares inherited.
  - Finally, the aim to take the business-family option in which shares are held in a separate entity, such as a trust, and from this entity, the owning families execute their control over the business.
- Restricting or constraining decisions to buy, sell, and transfer shares to preserve the family business values and identity across generations. Restrictions could be related to the following:
  - The methods or processes used for share valuation, particularly for private family businesses because their shares are not publicly traded. Family owners generally wonder about the value of their shares.
  - The discounts applied to the final value of shares in the case of shareholder exit. Some family businesses penalize family members who want to exit by applying a discount.
  - The payment method applied for shares family members want to sell. If the family business buys back shares, it is important to consider the cash flow of the business to avoid jeopardizing its day-to-day operations.
  - The priority of family owners to buy shares from family members exiting the business.
  - The policy dividends to guarantee the liquidity of the business while respecting the needs and rights of shareholders to receive dividends.
  - Mechanisms for resolving disputes and conflicts related to ownership to ensure the confidentiality of the conflicts—for instance, to guarantee arbitration or other mechanisms to resolve conflicts.

In other words, a shareholder agreement establishes restrictions that can be used to control the growth of the ownership structure across generations; prevent the entrance of external owners to the family business; prioritize the family's control over the business; and anticipate the ownership consequences of unpredictable situations, such as divorce, death, incapacity, and/or misbehavior of an owner.

There is no one single shareholder agreement that fits all family businesses. Even though general legal regimes (country law and regulations) can constrain it, the type of agreement depends on the final aims that the owning family would like to achieve. Some important aims could be keeping ownership of the business in family hands, maintaining all family members as shareholders, preserving the sense of belonging, securing family unity, ensuring shares remain with those family members who are committed to the business, and preventing the entrance of external owners. For instance, returning to the example of Al Saud Company, an Emirati business, when the founder died, the rest of the family members (wife and seven siblings) decided to sign a simple shareholder agreement that, to a certain extent, limited the shareholder right and freedom to sell and transfer the shares. The buy-and-sell agreement, which is one important part of the shareholder agreement, prohibits family members from selling their shares outside the family and discourages the sale of shares even within the family by setting the price of transferred shares at 25% below market value.[14] The aim of this shareholder agreement is threefold: keep family members together around the family business, avoid individual intentions to divide the founder's wealth into smaller parts, and force family members to talk and find consensus.

Any successful shareholder agreement should be inspired by the family's shared vision and should balance the needs of the three entities (ownership, business, and family). Specifically, a shareholder agreement should evolve with family and business complexity across time. In the case of Al Saud Company, the family's shareholder agreement achieved its purpose for all the second-generation members who signed it. However, since 2016, the third generation of family members has started to incorporate into the business and potentially to the ownership, so the old agreement does not necessarily fit the new needs of the ownership, family, and business entities. In this case, the business family intends to update the agreement by considering the new vision of the second and third generations within the family business. At this new stage, the owning family members are questioning the need to encourage family members to stay. Maybe, it is time to let some family members who are not committed and do not have interest in the business to leave their ownership positions. Al Saud Company shows that a shareholder agreement is not a static document that compromises present and future generations. In each generational transition, it is important to put the shareholder agreement up for debate to establish a conversation with new generations and to update the shareholder agreement accordingly.

7.5.1 Benefits of shareholder agreements

The main benefit of having a shareholder agreement is undergoing the process to create it and define a regulatory framework for current and future decision-making. To have an effective shareholder agreement, the process should be transparent and inclusive by giving all family members the chance to be heard so they can express their goals, needs, and expectations. There are several benefits of developing and having a shareholder agreement:

- Protect the family's control over the business when the family wants to perpetuate control over generations. The shareholder agreement governs the sale, transfer, and succession of ownership.
- Prevent future conflicts among family owners.
- Define the governance structure of the family business by coordinating governance across the ownership, business, and family entities.
- Determine courses of action and processes under specific circumstances that can have implications for the ownership, business, and family entities, such as owner death, incapacity, and/or misbehavior; external shocks that can affect family business continuity, marriages, and divorces with consequences to the family business, and strong disagreements among owners and family members.

7.6 Evolutionary approach to ownership governance

Simplifying real life, we can present the evolution of the family ownership structure through different lifecycle stages by considering the challenges and complexity of ownership governance.

- *Owner–manager/founder stage.* The founders who initiate the economic activities are the main owners and are actively involved in the daily activities of the family business. There could be external shareholders, but family members retain control over the family business. Corporate governance is informal and is generally executed via the strong power and influence of the founders. At this stage, the cost of implementing formal corporate governance could be expensive and could slow down decision-making, which is one important competitive advantage of family businesses at this stage. The mutual trust of family owners, even when there are nonfamily owners involved, and the constant informal interpersonal interactions among owners in the business and family arenas reduce governance agency problems by maintaining a shared vision and reducing conflicts of interest, adverse selection, and moral hazard behavior within the owner family.

However, the entrepreneurial characteristics of the owner–manager stage cannot be sustained for long because of several challenges that family businesses encounter in the evolutionary process. At the business level, the main challenges are related to the growth process in terms of accessing financial capital, skilled labor, and experienced and capable managers. The excessive power of one or few family members could be an impediment to growth because it can lock in knowledge or resources, preventing the entrance of external voices. In other words, dominant owners can abuse their power. At the ownership level, the main challenge is related to the entrance of new family members from the upcoming generation. Multiple generations coexisting can create communication problems, which jeopardizes the shared vision among family owners and increases conflicts of interest, adverse selection, and moral hazard behavior. Finally, at the family level, new challenges start emerging because there are new voices operating in the shadows. For instance, in-law family members who influence family members can alter the level of trust among family owners.

When a family business moves forward from the founder generation, the family shareholder group tends to fragment into different subgroups—for instance, large versus small owners based on the percentage of ownership, active versus passive owners based on owners' involvement (or lack thereof) in the business, senior versus next-generation owners based on the generation to which owners belong, and different coalitions and branches. When ownership is fragmented, faultlines—hypothetical dividing lines that split a group into two or more subgroups based on alignment with one or more individual attributes—may emerge. The internal segregation of subgroups could have positive (e.g., diversity of the ideas during debates and conversations, which could help the overall group find innovative solutions to problems) or negative (e.g., conflicts become emotional and personal between subgroups, which can paralyze decision-making) impacts on group processes, performance, and commitment.

- *First-degree multi-generational stage (parent-sibling partnership).* At this stage, the founders coexist as owners with other family members from subsequent generations, such as children or even grandchildren. Ownership begins an atomization process by integrating new family members into decision-making with voice and vote. Centralization of power in decision-making may informally exist when the founders are still active, but the rest of the family members—as owners and/or managers—are preparing to take over the family business. Certain business governance mechanisms are needed, specifically at the ownership level. The most basic mechanism is to create and formalize ownership assemblies or shareholder meetings. The shareholder meeting represents the seed of corporate governance in a family business. It creates the foundation for communication, agreement, and decision-making among family members. Most successful family businesses that follow the classic family business lifecycle start organizing shareholder meetings. The shareholder meeting is a governance body that starts defining regulations for the ownership structure and governance. However, in some cases, the attributes of shareholder meetings are extended to define the specificities of family business relationships, such as the family employment policy and succession planning.

The duration of the first-degree multigenerational stage could be short or long depending on how long the incumbent/senior generation exists (retires or gives away responsibilities to the next generation) and how long it takes the next generations to enter and lead the family business. When siblings start accumulating power via ownership and making decisions via management participation, the family business develops the sibling partnership model.

- *Sibling partnership stage.* At this stage, siblings are the dominant group in the family business, having enough ownership participation and experience in the family business from their ownership and management involvement. The best scenario at this stage is to have formal shareholder meetings. With less influence and pressure from their parents, siblings are ready to prove their maturity to own, govern, and manage the family business. The main challenge is to maintain the level of trust among siblings, specifically between those who work in the family business and those who do not. Communication within shareholder meetings is fundamental to ensure transparency, create a shared vision, and reduce sibling rivalry. Owners have to dedicate time to strengthen the shareholder meeting and to avoid members' overlapping roles from affecting this and other governance bodies at business and family levels. It is time for siblings to keep a high level of cohesiveness and redefine (if necessary) the shareholder agreement, family employment policy, and succession planning.

If the owners' decision is to embrace the family and the subsequent generations, the next stage is the sibling-cousin consortium, the second-degree multigenerational stage, in which the number of family shareholders tends to increase exponentially and multiple generations coexists. The ownership dynamic at this stage is difficult to manage and coordinate. The level of trust is lower, family branches exercise their power in small groups of family members, and agency problems tend to emerge and intensify. Since new challenges appear, new ownership governance solutions are needed.

- *Second-degree multigenerational stage (sibling-cousin consortium).* At this stage, there are multiple family (and in-law) members from different generations as owners. It is important to maintain the nature and spirit of shareholder meetings for two reasons: (1) to keep the cohesiveness among owners by aligning their interests and maintaining their high commitment to the business and (2) to avoid family feuds that can damage the coexistence of multiple family branches. Coordinating a high number of family owners is demanding because shareholder meetings cannot be confused with other governance bodies, such as family assemblies, which have different aims (see Chapter 9). Some family businesses at this stage are public, such as Wal-Mart,[15] whose ownership is distributed among individual family owners (i.e., Walton family members, such as Robson Walton, who owns around 1% of the total shares), nonfamily owners (e.g., Douglas McMillon), and institutional shareholders (some of which are also controlled by the Walton family, such as Walton Enterprise LLC [owns 35% of the total shares] and Walton Family Holding Trust [owns 15% of the total shares]).

Beyond the logical evolutionary process described earlier, the family could also become a business family that manages its wealth via an investment firm, foundation, or trust, with the family business being just one asset. The family is no longer involved in the daily business operations, which are instead under the control of nonfamily members. In this case, it is important to preserve the dynastic wealth of the family. Continuing with the Walton family example, part of the fortune derived from Wal-Mart is invested in low-cost exchange trade funds[16] as a way to diversify the family's wealth.

7.7 Additional activities and reading material

7.7.1 Classroom discussion questions

1 What are the different types of family owners? What are the positive and negative consequences of having each of them in the ownership structure?
2 Why is formalizing shareholder meetings important for family businesses?
3 Do shareholder agreements add value to family businesses? Why is a shareholder agreement necessary when family members trust each other?
4 When do you think the process of writing the shareholder agreement should begin?
5 Does the shareholder agreement change across generations? Why or why not?

7.7.2 Additional readings

1 Clark, E. (2022). Your family business's resiliency depends on its structure. *Harvard Business Review*. Article retrieved from https://hbr.org/2022/10/your-family-businesss-res iliency-depends-on-its-structure
2 Sciorilli Borrelli, S. (2021). Ferragamo family shareholders eye management overhaul. *Financial Times*. Article retrieved from www.ft.com/content/f2e91150-77ad-4474-8e20-28083a6f8fc4
3 Baron, J., & Lachenauer, R. (2021). Build a family business that lasts. *Harvard Business Review*. Article Retrieved from https://hbr.org/2021/01/build-a-family-business-that-lasts

7.7.3 Classroom activity

Aim: Reflect on the importance of the shareholder agreement by engaging in the process of writing one.
Material: Organize the classroom in groups of four or five students and assign the following roles based on the general stage that each group would like take on.

First-Generation Stage	First-Degree Multigenerational Stage
• Manufacturing firm	• Manufacturing firm
• Father and mother (in-law) and three siblings	• Two members of the senior generation (second generation—a woman who works in the firm and a man who does not) and their offspring (third generation)
• It used to be a business-first firm, but in the last 10 years, due to the father's health problems, the founder turned it into a family business-first firm. The children have different views for the future.	• It is a family business-first firm for the eldest sibling's family branch but a business-first firm for the youngest sibling's family branch.

First-Generation Stage	First-Degree Multigenerational Stage
• The father is 73 years old, has 70% of the shares, and is near retirement (against his will) because of some physical problems. He would like to see his business flourish and grow.	• The eldest sibling's family branch has 50% of the firm shares, which are equally distributed among four family members (mother and three offspring). It is this family branch that has influenced the family business via management participation.
• The mother is 70 years old and does not have shares because of her good relationship and supportive role with her husband. She knows all that has been happening with the firm.	• Two of the third-generation members work in the firm and are very interested in the family business and its continuity, seeing their professional careers within the family business boundaries. The third sibling of this family branch does not work in the firm.
• The eldest child is 40 years old and has three children. He has been working in the firm close to his father for more than a decade and possesses 10% of the firm shares. He considers himself the future leader of the family business and plans to assume the CEO role after his father's retirement. He is an active owner but shows some obstructive behavior when negotiating with his siblings.	• Because of their mother's role in the business, they feel that it is their company. They believe their grandfather made a mistake giving 50% of the shares to their uncle (the second family branch).
• The middle child is 35 years old, has two children, does not work in the firm because of poor relationships with his father and eldest sibling, and has 10% of the firm shares. He is a passive owner interested in dividends.	• The youngest sibling's family branch has 50% of the firm shares, which are equally distributed among two family members who do not work in the firm (father and son).
• The youngest child is 30 years old, has one child, began working in the family business after graduating from a top university and gaining some external experience, and has 10% of the firm shares. She has shown great entrepreneurial spirit.	• While the father and son of the second family branch were initially passive owners interested in dividends from the firm, the son recently started showing interest in the business. He works outside the firm and has shown to be a great and respected leader.

Running the classroom exercise: This exercise can be used as an assignment (ask students to prepare a formal shareholder agreement) or an exercise for students during class (ask students to engage in the negotiation process and develop some of the most critical points of any shareholder agreement). Ask each student to take on one role and reflect on the character he or she represents. During this reflection, students should consider the needs, goals, and expectations that each character could have in the particular context described by considering the type of family, sibling position, types of relationships with the business, and experience/education.

Based on the information provided and students' own reflections, students should initiate the debate, discussion, and negotiation process to write a shareholder agreement. The most important topics that a shareholder agreement should cover are listed below. Ask students to write down their agreements.

Most important topics/issues of the shareholder agreement:

- Purpose of the shareholder agreement. Define the purpose of the shareholder agreement to summarize the spirit by which the family shareholders, including the current and future generations, shall be governed. The type of family business (e.g., family-first, business-first, and family business–first) may shape the nature of the shareholder agreement to define the policies and direction of the family business.
- Shareholder rights and responsibilities.
  - Information about the family business.
  - Confidentiality.
  - Annual shareholder meeting. Participation and information.
  - Dividend policy. Distribution/reinvestment of family business' profits based on a pre-determined percentage for reinvesting or distributing (dividends). Is it necessary to have a minimum level of profits to distribute dividends? Below the minimum threshold, dividends will not be distributed.
  - Transfer of shares by shareholders. Who can own shares (e.g., only legal descendants)? What happens with in-laws and adopted children?
  - Family employment. Who can work in the business and under what conditions?
  - Executive compensation. What should family members' compensation be for working in the firm?
- Decision-making at the shareholder level (type of majority needed for important decisions).
  - Decision to sell the entire company.
  - Profit distribution via dividends.
  - Decision to modify the present shareholder agreement.
  - Decision about mergers and acquisitions.
  - Other important decisions.
- Creation of a board of directors.
  - Composition of the board of directors that defines the number of independent board members. Additionally, for nonindependent boards, the composition should define family and nonfamily members. Within the family member group, it is necessary to define the number of family members who work in the firm and who do not work in the firm.
- Sale or transfer of shares.
  - Valuing shares.
  - Discounting shares.
  - Sale of shares by shareholders.
- Conflict resolution.
  - Techniques applied in case of conflict: mediation versus arbitration.

Takeaways: The importance of this exercise is to have students negotiate via role play. The aim is to engage in the process of creating an agreement that can satisfy all shareholders. Students should recognize how important it is to tie the different family business voices together in one agreement that can help all family members navigate the journey of being family business owners. The instructor could ask students to publicly present their agreements and discuss the similarities and differences. Additionally, students can discuss the different approaches they used to negotiate and write the agreements. Differences are going to emerge based on the negotiation power and ability of each of the members involved in the process. The instructor can challenge ideas by having a shareholder agreement as a backup to discuss points not discussed or considered by the groups. The instructor should highlight the consequences of not having a shareholder agreement for the future of a family business if something happens.

7.8 Case for analysis I: The united family behind LEGO[17]

The Kirk Kristiansen family owns LEGO, a company that employed more than 24,000 employees around the world by 2021 and is the world's largest toy company by revenue. The company was founded in 1932 by Ole Kirk Kristiansen, a carpenter who produced household goods and, due to the great depression, shifted to producing wooden toys. LEGO developed and introduced to the market the well-known system of interlocking bricks. The original LEGO bricks were wooden until the company introduced the plastic bricks in 1947.

The ownership and management leadership of the Kirk Kristiansen family was present even during difficult times. The company addressed changes in consumer behavior, the expiration of LEGO's patents, and the introduction of digital games, all of which forced the company to adapt to new market realities several times. Godtfred Kirk Kristiansen, one of Ole's three sons, became the managing director who led LEGO's international expansion. After the company was led by a nonfamily CEO for a period of six years, Kjeld Kirk Kristiansen, Godtfred's son, took over leadership. In the 2000s, the Kirk Kristiansen family developed a plan to have all the family-owner generations represented. One member from each generation appointed one representative to be recognized as the "most active owner." The family's aim was to ensure the continuing success of the company under family leadership. In 2023, Thomas Kirk Kristiansen, a fourth-generation family member, will take over as chairman of the board from his father Kjeld Kirk Kristiansen.

To consolidate their ownership position and ensure a sustainable future for family ownership of the LEGO brand through generations, in the 1980s, the family founded the Kirkbi company, the family's investment company. Today, Kirkbi owns 75% of LEGO, and the charitable Lego Foundation owns the other 25%. There are three fundamental tasks: (1) protect, develop, and leverage the LEGO brand across the family entity; (2) commit to long-term and responsible investment for the family activities; and (3) support family members and prepare them to continue active and engaged ownership for future generations.

The owner family (with its multiple family branches) receives various support from the Kirkbi company, such as human resource, finance, communication, and legal assistance, among others. For instance, the LEGO School is an initiative to prepare the fifth-generation owners of the Kirk Kristiansen family to assume ownership and governance leadership. The fifth generation consists of six girls, representing the children of the fourth generation of the owner family. On the Kirkbi website, the program mission states: "The purpose of the programme is for the next generation to become acquainted with the breadth and future opportunities across the LEGO entities."[18]

Discussion questions:

1 What is the ownership strategy of the Kirk Kristiansen family?
2 Why do you think the Kirk Kristiansen family emphasizes the importance of ownership across generations?

7.9 Case for analysis II: H51—The mission to preserve the Hermès family identity[19]

In 2010, the phone rang, and on the other side was Bernard Arnault, CEO of LVMH Moët Hennessy Louis Vuitton (commonly known as LVMH), who announced that they acquired 17% of the shares in Hermès.[20] Thomas Patrick, a nonfamily CEO (from 2003 to 2014) in Hermès, was shocked by this brief call. LVMH developed a silent strategy to penetrate one of the most prominent luxury houses in the world.

Hermès was found in 1837 by Thierry Hermès, who opened a workshop in the rue Basse-du-Rempart. Hermès has been focused on its customers and products since the beginning. The family business expanded through generations of family members leading the operations of and controlling the company. In 1993, the family business went public, maintaining the brand philosophy of quality and refinement. Six generations have owned, governed, and managed Hermès. Today more than 66% of the shares of the company are in the Hermès family, with Axel Dumas, a member of the sixth generation, as CEO.

This famous battle in the fashion and luxury industry could have cost Hermès its identity in the market. The family company was at risk, but the unity of the family was a crucial value to counter the movement initiated by LVMH. Axel Dumas, the 44-year-old CEO of Hermès persuaded family members to pool their shares in a new private holding company, "H51." The family recognized the importance of uniting and preserving its identity as a family business led by the Hermès family's values and principles. Individual family shareholders lost their independence but gained it as a family group. The Hermès family strategy was to vote as a block to preserve the family vision for the company. The culture of craftsmanship is part of the family's creed, and the family's aim is to preserve it across generations.

The Hermès family declared, "The creation of this holding structure confirms the unity of the family in their commitment to defend the independence of Hermès to preserve its values and culture."[21] To avoid further problems and consolidate the family's control, one important resolution is that the holding company has the first right of refusal when family members decide to sell shares. In addition, no one can sell their shares for 20 years. The Hermès family preserves its values, and family members are proud of their roots, showing strong identification with the company.

From that moment on, the Hermès family was patient enough to legally fight against the LVMH fashion conglomerate. Finally, LVMH and Hermès found some calm when Bernard Arnault agreed to relinquish part of the shareholding in Hermès.

Discussion questions:

1   Do you think it was important to create one family voice to control the family business?
2   How do you think the family behind H51 is able to achieve unified decision-making to preserve the one voice controlling Hermès?

7.10 Case study: "The Factory" of the human misery

Pancho II Fernandez got into his CEO office, which belonged to his father and grandfather, with an expression of triumph on his face. After several months of organizing the final ownership agreement to prune the family ownership tree, almost 80% of the family owners sold their shares for almost nothing, just a few dollars. Even though the family business, The Factory, was in financial crisis according to the accounting books, it has good prospects with a strong strategy and some new blood. So far, Pancho II has basically applied a harvest strategy by extracting the benefits of the family business for his own lifestyle without respecting the other owners' rights.

Pancho II belongs to the third generation of the Fernandez family. His grandfather, an immigrant to Mexico from Spain at the beginning of the 20th century, created the business as a way to survive and navigate the difficult times of being an immigrant. Among 12 brothers and sisters, Pancho II's father, well-known as Pancho I, kept the tradition of the business and kept the family united, using the family business as a tool to embrace all family members. At the end of 1980s, after Pancho I's death, Pancho II found himself as the leader of the business and family patriarch as an implicit mandate.

By that time, there were multiple family shareholders—cousins, uncles, and aunts across several family branches. However, the cake was too small to satisfy all shareholders' expectations. That was why Pancho II decided to prune the ownership tree. Additionally, he did not want to work for the rest of the big and extended family as his father had done before. In his mind, he believed that the firm belonged to him alone and that no one could take the benefits of his CEO work, thereby misunderstanding the basic rights and responsibilities that divide owners and managers.

Changing his expression of triumph to an expression of superiority, Pancho II thought, "Now I can eat my own cake." He played some accounting and emotional tricks to get things done that betrayed the values and beliefs developed by previous family generations. He knew the second part of his strategy would be to displace his two sisters from inheriting their business shares. As he had expected, the two sisters did not claim their inheritance when Pancho I died because they wanted to continue to support their mother's modest lifestyle after her husband's death. Their mother's expenses were managed by Pancho II as his father, Pancho I, did. Thus, displacing his sisters would be an easy task, but he needed to find a solution for his brother to compensate him with some assets and keep him away from business ownership.

Pancho II thought about how the story should continue. "Should I move this company forward and embrace my siblings as shareholders, or should I get rid of them?" He thought the first option would require significant effort to develop new corporate governance and transparency. However, even though the second option would likely be emotionally painful, because it would require him to kick them out of the business, it would be easy to manage the firm on his own and to benefit his own children one day. The phone rang, and he answered, "My loved sister! How are you? I was just thinking on you just now!"

The business. More than 100 years ago, a Spanish immigrant found his place in the world after escaping from poverty on the old continent. The new continent was the dream for Europeans. However, the life of an immigrant was not the dream that someone would have imagined. While resources, land, and privileges were already assigned in the new continent to those families with longer histories in the region's economic and social life, it was full of opportunities for people with an entrepreneurial mindset. Pancho II's grandfather activated his entrepreneurial skills by producing candles and soups with waste from a slaughterhouse.

The production of soap was the main manufacturing activity of The Factory, and the family business achieved its own pace of growth by incorporating machines, building human resources, and extending its commercial network beyond the local community. Its commercial market comprised the regional environment, but this was more than enough for the family business to care for family members. During the first and second generations, the family business had a clear family-first orientation. The company was an instrument to unite the family, take care of family members, and achieve a modest lifestyle.

The third generation continued with the same strategy by simply maintaining and harvesting what the previous generations were able to create. The end of the 1970s and the beginning of the 1980s brought a new dynamic to the sector, and the economy of Mexico changed. The company suffered shocks from several national economic crises, which severely affected the business. The third generation had no interest in growth, and the lack of entrepreneurial skills made it difficult to manage the firm in a context of instability. The result was business stagnation. The third generation was unable to reorient the family business toward modernizing the manufacturing facilities, adopting a consistent and long-term business strategy, and embracing and aligning family shareholders to keep strong unity. What happened in the family business was a secret kept from the rest of the family members. For his own convenience and easy modus operandi, Pancho II used the same approach his father did: no communication, no talking, no transparency.

From an extended family to a nuclear family. During the first and second generations, the family business embraced the extended family. This position was aligned with the Spanish-Mexican collectivistic culture. The family replaced the fragility of the economic and social context, and it became the welfare state. However, by the end of his days, Pancho I started focusing on his own children (four siblings), who had their own nuclear families. The extended family was too large for the business, which was why Pancho II removed family owners from the business to reduce the ownership complexity. Therefore, the family business moved to belonging to the Pancho Fernandez family with the four family branches.

Pancho II's sisters never worked in the firm. Their knowledge about it was very limited since their father never shared any important information with them, which was normal in those times. However, after their father's death, their brother, Pancho II, kept the same culture of secrecy and a chauvinist position even when all the siblings (males and females) were owners.

Discussion questions:

1   What should Pancho II do with his two sisters and brother as owners?
2   Should Pancho II get rid of them? How?
3   Should Pancho II look for a family-business first orientation? How should Pancho II structure ownership governance?

The third generation—movement back. Time passed without any significant change in terms of ownership structure. Pancho II continued managing the firm using the same style as his father but personalized. The family business survived in constant stagnation, lacking a business strategy and ambition to develop something more than what Pancho II received from the previous generation. The lack of growth was compensated for with a creative financial strategy using debts, government grants, external investors, and opaque buy-and-sell agreements between the brothers and sisters. Each of these financial movements helped The Factory survive until the next financial movement.

The great movement. While his mother, Pancho I's wife, was alive and Pancho II kept financially sustaining her, the rest of the siblings maintained a tense silence, a fictional peace. The fourth generation, comprising more than 15 cousins, perceived the tense environment, but the silence prevailed. No one wanted to break the image of an idyllic family—but it was just a fake image!

A few years before Pancho I's wife died, the sisters questioned Pancho II and his brother's administration of the family's wealth. They asked for accountability. This word was not in the brothers' moral dictionary. The rebellion of the sisters had begun. From this moment on, disagreements, fights, and misunderstandings followed one after another across successive events. Pancho II and his brother started a process of family rent seeking in a non-conversational style using legally questionable procedures to take profits and assets for their personal wealth. The sisters were deceived. The only time the mother referred to this situation was as follows: "Panchito has done wrong things, I know, un pinche cabron." Even knowing her boys' behavior, she was afraid to go against her sons in the male-dominated environment. She kept silent!

Over a long period of confusion, manipulation, and emotional extortion, both brothers were able to move the family's wealth into their hands. Both sisters refused to put their brothers on judicial trial to demand their rights. They wanted to defend their rights, wanted to show they were excluded, wanted to be listened to, but they did not want to break up the family even more for the next generations.

When someone asked the sisters why this happened, they mentioned three actions that led to this outcome: they trusted their brothers in excess, they ignored understanding the business world and assuming their rights and responsibilities, and they obeyed an implicit mandate from their father who belonged to a different cultural generation.

Discussion questions:

1 What can Pancho II do to restore his honor and embrace the family again?
2 Is there any possibility to move the family business forward, or should the family business continue with Pancho II's family branch as owners and forget what has happened?

Notes

1 Information retrieved Oostwegel Collection website from www.oostwegelcollection.nl/en/about-oostwegel-collection/
2 The interpretation of the importance of family interpersonal relationships to guide family business governance was taken from the following institutional video: https://vimeo.com/262197648?embedded=true&source=vimeo_logo&owner=20774789
3 WADI Group website www.wadigroup.com/
4 Information retrieved from www.youtube.com/watch?v=sEofec4F7aM
5 Moral hazard is a situation in which a group of family owners has an incentive to increase the firm's exposure to risk because they do not bear the full costs of the risk.
6 When one family member or group of family members has more and better information than other family members—for instance, family members with overlapping roles as owner and managers versus family members who are owners. Managerial positions provide family members more information about the business, putting them in a better position to negotiate and make decisions.
7 Wayland, M. (2022). Bill Ford is doubling down on Ford shares, and quietly amassing more control of his great-grandfather's company in the process. *CNBC*. Article retrieved from www.cnbc.com/2022/01/14/bill-ford-is-doubling-down-on-ford-shares-and-amassing-more-control-of-the-company.html
8 Grant, P. (2017). Real-estate empire survives brutal family battle. *Wall Street Journal*. Article retrieved from www.wsj.com/articles/real-estate-empire-survives-brutal-family-battle-1494932405
9 Simon, J., La Porta, R., Lopez de Silanes, F., & Shleifer, A. (2000). Tunneling. *The American Economic Review*, 90(2), 22–27. Article retrieved from https://dash.harvard.edu/bitstream/handle/1/30747165/w7523.pdf?sequence=1
10 Taylor, A. (2014). CEO's daughter loses job after "nut rage" incident on Korean air flight. *The Washington Post*. Article retrieved from www.washingtonpost.com/news/worldviews/wp/2014/12/09/ceos-daughter-loses-job-after-nut-rage-incident-on-korean-air-flight/
11 Kirk, D. (2019). Korean air heiress criticizes her brother for going against father's wishes. *Forbes*. Article retrieved from www.forbes.com/sites/donaldkirk/2019/12/27/korean-air-heiress-criticizes-her-brother-for-going-against-fathers-wishes/?sh=2f386a7d431a
12 Information retrieved from www.fundinguniverse.com/company-histories/steinberg-incorporated-history/
13 Basco, R., & Brodtkorb, T. (2018). *Saud Bin Majid's Dilemma*. Sharjah, UAE: American University of Sharjah.

14 Basco, R., & Brodtkorb, T. (2018). *Saud Bin Majid's Dilemma*. Sharjah, UAE: American University of Sharjah.

15 The information about Wal-Mart's ownership structure represents the composition as of March 2020.

16 Weiss, M., & Pendleton, D. (2021). *World's Richest Family Reveals $5 Billion Worth of Stock Picks*. Bloomberg. Article retrieved from: www.bloomberg.com/news/articles/2021-09-28/walmart-walton-family-world-s-richest-reveals-stock-picks-worth-5-billion-ku43my3e#xj4y7vzkg

17 This example discussion is developed solely as the basis for class discussion. This example discussion is not intended to serve as an endorsement, source of primary data, or illustration of effective or ineffective management.

18 Information retrieved from the Kirkbi website: www.kirkbi.com/activities/family-support/

19 This example discussion is developed solely as the basis for class discussion. This example discussion is not intended to serve as an endorsement, source of primary data, or illustration of effective or ineffective management.

   Bawden, T. (2011). LVMH's Bernard Arnault persists in his pursuit of Hermès. *The Guardian*. Article retrieved from www.theguardian.com/business/2011/mar/08/mergers-and-acquisitions-retail. The Fashion Law (2017). Hermès vs. LVMH: A timeline of the legal drama. Article retrieved from www.thefashionlaw.com/hermes-vs-lvmh-a-timeline-of-the-drama/#:~:text=%E2%80%93%202001%2D2002%3A%20LVMH%20acquired,keeping%20holdings%20below%205%20percent. Ellison, J. (2015). Lunch with the FT: Axel Dumas. *Financial Times*. Article retrieved from www.ft.com/content/75d8a0da-d228-11e4-a225-00144feab7de.

20 For some legal reasons, the LVMH company was not obligated to inform regulators or disclose how LVMH acquired Hermès shares.

21 Reuters. (2011). Hermes family finalises holding to prevent takeover. Information retrieved from www.reuters.com/article/hermes-idUSWEA546020111214

8 Business governance in family business

Learning objectives

- Distinguish the difference between ownership and business governance.
- Understand the role of the board of directors in family businesses.
- Recognize the importance of board of director composition.
- Identify the most important tasks of the board of directors.
- Interpret business governance across generations.

8.1 Introduction

Just as the ownership entity has its own governance that adds value to the family business, the business entity also needs structure, coordination, and integration with the ownership and family entities.

There is a common perception that business governance is not an essential priority for family businesses. This perception typically stems from the high family involvement in such businesses (high family ownership concentration, family members in managerial positions, and a high level of psychological ownership among family members), which allows family businesses to relax requirements for developing solid business governance or postpone the need to formalize business governance structures. There are several arguments that support this perception. First, family businesses require fewer actions/processes to control nonfamily managers and align nonfamily managers' interests with those of the owning family. Second, family businesses can align goals quickly because of the shared interests and vision developed through the common cognitive structures family members use to interpret the world. Finally, family businesses are able to access and use external resources outside of their direct control because of their family social capital, which links these businesses with their local environments.

However, the aforementioned competitive advantages related to governance may emerge naturally for a short period of time and in some particular moments/periods across the family business lifecycle. As we highlighted in the Chapter 7, family businesses are not exempt from agency problems and tend to carry specific agency problems, such as goal alignment among family owners, altruism, conflicts of interest, and asymmetric information. The complexity of the ownership, business, and family entities across generations requires family business leaders who are engaged in managerial positions and those who have substantial ownership participation to assume the responsibility of developing business governance structures that can help their family businesses consolidate and exploit their competitive advantages.

DOI: 10.4324/9781003273240-11

This chapter focuses on business governance and structure. The chapter addresses the importance for family businesses to create, develop, and maintain business governance as an important mechanism to coordinate, control, and direct their destinies.

8.2 Board of directors

The board of directors is the business governance arena of the family business. Members of the board are elected by the shareholders and represent owners' interests, define the long-term vision and strategy of the firm, control the top management team, and connect the firm with its main and strategic stakeholders.

There are two business governance systems based on country legislation: one-tier and two-tier board systems. The one-tier system, like in the United States, refers to a board of directors comprising a group of individuals with different types of affiliations with the ownership, business, and family entities (e.g., executive, independent, and family board members) who are elected by the owners. The board of directors' primary responsibility is to promote the interests of the shareholders. The two-tier board system, such as in Germany, is composed of two different boards: the management (or executive) board and the supervisory board. While the management board is responsible for the operational and tactical direction of the family business, the supervisory board—similar to the board of directors in the one-tier system—represents the interests of the shareholders, and its main function is to control, oversee, and advise the top management team.

In the family business context, the aim of business governance is to develop efficient cooperation between owners and managers and to create a firewall that avoids family conflicts jeopardizing business competitiveness and, vice versa, business problems affecting family well-being and cohesiveness.

8.2.1 Board of directors' tasks

The board directors represents the interests of the owners (family and nonfamily owners) in the form of a set of business- and family-oriented goals that emerge from shareholder meetings and family assemblies. To represent both owner and family interests, there are five general tasks undertaken by the board of directors:

- *Control tasks* are all actions and activities that board members perform to control and oversee the top management team's behavior to ensure the firm's strategy aligns with the family business's interests and is being successfully implemented to achieve family business goals. Additionally, controls tasks should guarantee the protection of minority shareholders regardless of whether they are family or nonfamily minority owners.
- *Service tasks* are all actions and activities that board members perform to support, advise, counsel, and help the top management team define and implement the firm's strategy. Even though strategy implementation is not part of the board of directors' function, their assistance could be important. Specifically, the board could serve as a form of support to ensure sustainable business growth (new ventures, organic growth, acquisitions, and divestures). Additionally, the board should provide explicit support to family governance (see Chapter 9) to guarantee the continuity of the family (in terms of ownership and management) in the business.
- *Network tasks* are all actions and activities that the board performs to connect the family business with its environment and stakeholders. The aim is to attract resources that are

not controlled by the family or the business but can be exploited by the family business to leverage its strategy and achieve business- and family-oriented goals.

• *Communication tasks* are all actions and activities that the board of directors performs to ensure the board is part of the family business governance structure. This means that the board of directors is responsible for informing and reporting to the other governance bodies (in the ownership and family entities) as well as being informed and reported to by the other governance bodies. Communication tasks are about transparency and accountability to maintain cohesiveness and foster the family business culture by ensuring the adequate flow of information across the governance structures.

• *Succession tasks* are all actions and activities that the board of directors performs to help the owning family develop its transgenerational entrepreneurship vision specifically regarding succession planning. There are several succession tasks in which the board of directors can be engaged: providing counseling on management succession, specifically CEO succession; preparing and developing potential successors; and overseeing the implementation of the succession plan.

Communication across the different governance bodies should be achieved using informal and formal mechanisms. Informal mechanisms are those that are not structured or written but are products of the culture and interpersonal interactions among family members. For instance, when individuals participate in more than one governance body, this creates open avenues of communication between these governance bodies. Formal mechanisms are those that are official and pre-established, such as preparing reports to be shared among the different governance bodies, having special joint/overlapping meetings, creating specific committees, inviting family and/or owner observers to join board meetings, and proposing informal meetings among the boards of the different entities. Informal mechanisms should not replace formal mechanisms but should instead facilitate the communication of the governance bodies across the three entities.

No one board task is more important than the others. All of them are equally important to have an effective board of directors and to achieve its principal aim of representing the interests of the shareholders. However, because of specific characteristics of the family, business, and ownership entities and the overlapping roles of family members, some tasks may be superfluous or become less important for a short time. For instance, when there are two family owners who have equal shares (50% each) and also hold management positions, control tasks could be less important. That is, the control function of the board is no longer a major issue, and the independent members can focus on service, network, and succession tasks.

8.2.2 Types of boards of directors

The effectiveness of the board of directors is related to the board composition and the different types of board members. Different types of board members may exist based on their affiliations with the ownership, business, and family entities. To simplify, Figure 8.1 uses two dimensions to classify board members. On the one hand, family affiliation indicates whether a board member has family or in-law ties with the owning family. On the other hand, business affiliation indicates whether a board member has any kind of business affiliation, such as an employment relationship in the family business (e.g., executive position), or provides some kind of service, such as business consulting or legal services. When combining these family and business affiliations, four types of board members emerge who may or may not have ownership affiliation.

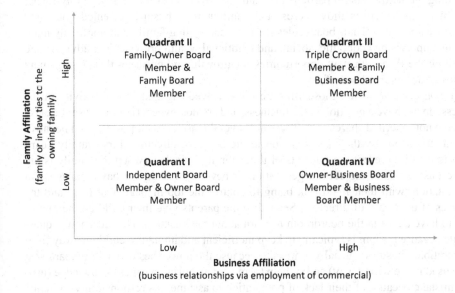

Figure 8.1 Types of board members based on their family, business, and ownership affiliations.

- *Quadrant I* (no family and no business affiliation)
  - *Independent board members* are those who do not have any affiliation or relationship with the ownership, business, or family entities. The benefit of independent board members is their non-biased behavior to interact and communicate with the rest of the board members. Their independence from the ownership, business, and family entities could be useful to constructively communicate ideas, bring external perspectives, and reflect on the different aspects and issues related to the family business. They can serve as final arbiters for decision-making and conflicts in the board room when family members have differences among them. Their primary aim is to represent the interests of the owners and the family as a whole. The main drawback of these board members is that they may not understand the dynamics of corporate governance in the family business, they may have less knowledge about the business itself (e.g., its culture), and they may lack of awareness of family-oriented goals.
  - *Owner board members* are those who have enough ownership participation to have a seat on the board of directors but have neither family nor business affiliation. This is the case when family businesses are listed firms or private firms with external (nonfamily) owners. Owner board members represent their own interests in the business, which may or may not be the same as the interests of the owning family. There are two sub-types of owner board members: relational and transactional. Relational owner board members have long-term investment horizons, sustainable goals over profit-maximization goals, and social ties with the family business, whereas transactional owner board members prioritize profitability by maximizing profit, have short-term investment horizons, and are interested in dividends and stock price if the firm is a publicly listed company.
- *Quadrant II* (family affiliation but no business affiliation)
  - *Family-owner board members* are those who are not involved/engaged in any activity or position in the business but are owners and part of the owning family. They are very important board members because they represent the interests of the owning family members who do not work in the firm but have a high psychological ownership.

Depending on the ownership participation and cohesiveness of the family, family-owner board members' interests move across the continuum of business-oriented goals and family-oriented goals. Their board roles focus on controlling family and nonfamily management; supervising economic, social, and emotional wealth preservation; advising and connecting the firm with new opportunities for growth; and ensuring that management assumes an acceptable level of risk.

- *Family board members* are those who are not involved/engaged in any activity in the business, do not have a position in the business, and are not owners (in most cases because they have not inherited shares yet). There are several reasons (with positive and negative implications) to justify their participation in the board of directors. First, family board members could represent the interests of those family branches (when the family is big and the business is in the second generation or beyond) that do not have management representation, with their main task being to control the top management team and the dynamics of the board of directors. Second, some parents give their children the opportunity to have a seat in the boardroom to learn about the business. This decision is questionable because the aim is typically to keep inefficient and immature children away from the operational business (usually a mistake because the power bestowed by a board seat can be used in the wrong way) and/or help them start acquiring business knowledge (usually a mistake because of their lack of preparation to assume this responsibility). Finally, perhaps the best situation is when a family member who does not have business or ownership affiliation gets a seat because his or her capabilities and abilities could add value to the board of directors and the firm in general because of the family member's experience, education, knowhow, leadership, and/or external network.
- *Quadrant III* (family affiliation and business affiliation)
  - *Triple-crown board members* combine the three types of affiliations (family, business, and ownership). Therefore, in their board roles, they represent different entities' interests to achieve a sustainable business, profitable investments, and a cohesive family. These board members possess unique information and understanding of the functionality of the family business because of their overlapping roles. They are one of the most important types of board members because of their central position to embrace multiple interests and lead the board of directors to a successful stage of development. However, their central position could also lead them to abuse their power, thereby impacting the effectiveness of the board of directors by failing to represent the interests of the owners and the family and instead focusing on their personal interests.
  - *Family-business board members* are family members who work in the family business (generally executives) and are not owners but expect to be part of the ownership in the future by inheriting shares from their parents or other family members. Next-generation family members are the most likely to be in this position, and their roles mix with different interests, such as achieving personal goals (economic or noneconomic goals as well as personal professional goals), proving their legitimacy to the rest of the stakeholders, and representing the interests of their family branches and the rest of the owners. Generally, these board members are highly committed to the firm with strong psychological ownership.
- *Quadrant IV* (business affiliation but no family affiliation)
  - *Owner-business board members* are owners who do not belong to the owning family but work in the firm. Because of their engagement in daily business operations, they have long-term horizons and are highly committed to the family business. Their role is important because they can maintain the business-oriented vision of the board, thereby

avoiding the excessive influence of the family. They are able to add the rationality of the business into boardroom discussions because of their business knowledge.

• *Business board members* are executives of the family business who do not belong to the owning family but are invited to join the board of directors. When their nominations are based on their experience, leadership, and knowledge, they are important board members who bring their internal perspectives of the family business to the main discussions of the board. However, when shareholders appoint them to maintain subordinate relationships to corroborate/approve decisions without questioning and debating ideas (because these business board members are not independent), their effectiveness is lost, and they are no longer able to contribute to the board dynamics.

8.2.3 Board of directors composition

One of the most important decisions at the corporate governance level is to define the composition of the board of directors. This involves determining who is going to be part of this selective group of individuals to represent the interests of the shareholders and the family. The shareholders are responsible for answering this question, which emerges during shareholder meetings. The decision-making process for defining the composition of the board of directions is regulated by the shareholder agreement, in which the general rules for selecting, appointing, amending, and removing board members are established. Decisions regarding the composition of the board of directors are not trivial and determine the quality of the internal dynamics in the boardroom. That is, these decisions affect the extent to which board members' interactions lead to constructive discussions and valuable contributions as well as direct the focus of attention toward the board's tasks.

Knowing that there are different types of board members, some may wonder what the best board of director composition is. There is not a definitive answer, however, because the best composition depends on the complexity and needs of each entity comprising the family business system. Board composition should guarantee positive and constructive dynamics of the board of directors to achieve its main goal, which is to represent the short- and long-term interests of the owners and the family as a whole. When deciding the composition of the board of directors, owners should answer several questions:

• Why does our family business need a board of directors?
• What types of board members does our family business need?
• What should be the focus of attention of the board of directors in terms of their tasks?

Even though board composition is unique for each family business and there is no one-size-fits-all option for family businesses, it is important to understand board composition based on two primary ratios. First, the ratio between independent/dependent directors. Independent directors are those who do not have any family, business, or ownership affiliations with the family business, whereas dependent directors are those who have at least one type of affiliation with the ownership, business, or family. Second, the ratio between family executives and nonexecutives (i.e., family members working in the firm and those who do not). While the former ratio indicates the magnitude of board independence, the latter indicates the power balance between the two factions of family members with potentially different interests.

Both academics and practitioners strongly recommend having independent board members, with the optimal percentage of independent board members ranging from 25% to 35%.[1] This percentage of independent board members enhances job-related diversity (experience, knowledge, and relationships with external stakeholders) and information exchange, both of which improve the quality of discussions in the boardroom and thereby increase the professionalization of the board of directors itself. On the one hand, having a higher percentage of independent board members could generate fractional faultlines that divide the boardroom into sub-groups (internal vs. external) with equal power. This situation may reduce the benefit of having independent voices and increase the likelihood of relational conflicts (generally associated with negative conflicts because relational conflict involves people against people such that problems become personal). On the other hand, a low percentage of independent board members impedes their voices from being heard, which reduces the benefits of having task conflicts (generally associated with positive conflicts because task conflict involves people against problems, such as disagreements about processes, solutions, and decision-making) in the boardroom.

Another important decision in terms of the composition of the board of directors is the proportion of family executive and nonexecutive board members. Even though both types of these directors are family affiliated, they may perform different roles in the boardroom because of their connection (or lack thereof) with the business and ownership entities. Having internal perspectives of the family business, family executive board members are able to recognize family and business needs while representing the interests of the owners. On the other hand, family nonexecutive board members are better positioned to control the top management team to ensure the family business is oriented toward the goals imposed by ownership and family entities. Even though there is not an optimal ratio of family executive board members to nonexecutive board members (it depends on the size of the family and the business), the board of directors should find an equilibrium between both types of board members to avoid the negative consequences of having one sub-group ruling the board's decision-making to its own benefit. The aim of designing board composition is to incorporate different voices to increase the benefits of diversity while avoiding faultlines.[2] For instance, family executive members are more likely to be interested in re-investing the family business's profits in business activities (to grow, expand, or maintain the business's competitiveness) than in distributing dividends. On the contrary, family nonexecutive board members are more likely to be interested in maintaining regular and stable dividend distribution beyond business needs.

8.3 The evolution of the board across the lifecycle of the family business

The board of directors is intrinsically related to the owners' vision. Since the function of the board of directors is to represent the interest of the owners, its functionality and effectiveness depend on the owners' intentions to recognize the importance of the board of directors and delegate it control, advice, network, communication, and succession tasks.

Most of family businesses in the early stages of their lifecycle do not have a board of directors because of the centrality of the owners' power, the owners' involvement in managerial positions, and formal laws exempting small and medium firms from having a board of directors. There is no real need to create a board of directors and delegate it control, advice, network, communication, and succession tasks. Family businesses do not need to have a board of directors to be successful at the early stages of their lifecycle.

However, laws may require a family business to have a board of directors. Nevertheless, mere obligation does not guarantee a successful board of directors. The lack of a real need (or a need recognized by shareholders), high ownership concentration, and overlapping roles of family members across the three entities could create a "compliance board" with one or few individuals who are owners, managers, and family members. That is, some family business have rubber-stamp boards of directors without any important functions for the business or the family.

Regardless of whether a board of directors is required by law, the most important antecedent for creating, developing, and maintaining a successful board of directors is recognizing family and business needs (e.g., family trust and business transparency and accountability) to shift informal governance to more formal governance. These needs emerge from a combination of external and internal forces that may guide family business leaders to create a board of directors. External forces are related to the dynamism and complexity of the sector or industry in which the family business operates. One or a few family owners alone are not able to strategically anticipate the direction of an industry, technology, and/or political and social forces that can both threaten and create opportunities for the family business. In this sense, a board of directors could be a governance body to guarantee family business continuity in the long term. On the other hand, internal forces are related to the complexity of the business and the family. When the business grows and requires mature structures and formal channels of communication, a board of directors can link the ownership and management entities. Additionally, when the family grows, more members assume responsibilities, and these responsibilities overlap across the three entities, the board of directors is an important context to discuss and reflect on the strategic level of the family business, avoiding day-to-day operations and family issues that are not strategic in nature. For instance, when there are several family owners, it could be useful to create a professional board of directors as an intermediary between the ownership (full of family members) and business entities as a way to respect the ownership, business, and family needs and avoid problems between the three entities. Finally, the presence of external owners is another force that may accelerate the need for a board of directors by pushing for the development of formal structures.

When needs are evident and recognized by shareholders, there is likely a progressive change in owners' minds about adjusting the board composition. That is, a family business undergoes a transition process involving learning about and understanding the functions of the board as it moves from having a rubber-stamp board of directors, where the founder and a few board members (most of them with some kind of affiliation with and high subordination to the owner) dominate the decision-making, to a professional board of directors with independent board members and good governance practices and processes. In this sense, a board of directors could provide first-class advice from experienced experts; offer unbiased, fresh, and innovative ideas; reflect a professional image among stakeholders; mediate in family problems from a different perspective; and consolidate the communication mechanisms to represent stakeholders' voices.

Such a transition not only requires the maturity of family members, regardless of their roles across entities, to interpret the lifecycle of the family business but also requires rebuffing the typical myths related to the board of directors. The following are among the most common myths to justify the rejection of a board of directors:

- The owning family does not want to give up control over the business.
- The owning family does not want to share sensitive information to externals or nonfamily members.
- Having a board of directors is an expensive formality for family businesses.
- The family business's success is unquestionable, so it does not need a board of directors.

All of these myths about the board of directors can be refuted because they are a consequence of the family business having a myopic view. These myths mirror the owning family's ignorance about the aims and functions of a board of directors, the owning family's fear to show their governance and managerial weaknesses, and family arrogance. To address these myths, family business leaders have to educate family shareholders and potential shareholders about the benefits of a board of directors for business performance and family cohesiveness.

After implementing an educational plan, the most important step to move the development of a board of directors forward and to rebuff the aforementioned myths is to start incorporating independent directors (directors with no affiliation with the ownership, business, or family). However, the benefits of developing a formal professionalized board of directors do not automatically happen, so the owning family has to work on implementing, respecting, and supporting the board across time. In the long term, a board of directors helps separate and respect the ownership, business, and family needs; supports the top management team in its strategic function; develops a culture of accountability among the top management team; and projects a long-term perspective for the family business in terms of ownership and management transition from one generation to another.

8.4 Board of director practicalities

8.4.1 Number of board members

There is no single number of board members that fits all family businesses. The number should be decided by members of the ownership assembly in coordination with the other governance bodies to create a functional group of individuals committed to adding value to the family business at the strategic level. In general, the size of the board of directors depends on the ownership structure, business complexity, and current and future family size. The general recommendation is to have five to eight board members. For instance, the code of good governance of Carvajal SA, a leading diversified family-owned firm established in Colombia in 1904 by Manuel Carvajal Valencia, defines that the board of directors should include nine members who are elected for a one-year period by members of the ownership assembly. At least three of the members need to be independent directors.[3] The company's board composition has evolved from five family members and the rest of the board members having other types of affiliations in 2017 to six independent board members and the rest of the board members having family affiliation in 2022.

8.4.2 Recruiting board members

Before starting the recruiting process for the board of directors, members involved in the ownership assembly should envision the board of directors' aims by reflecting on why the family business needs a board of directors. Having defined the aims of the board of directors, members of the ownership assembly could explore the board of directors' role in general and the board members' roles in particular. This exercise can help determine the size of the board of directors and its composition. The next step is to develop a list of criteria for each type of director in terms of the knowledge, experience, networks, personal traits, and interpersonal abilities the family business requires. Not all family businesses need the same board members in terms of competencies and capabilities, which ultimately depend on the specific circumstances of the ownership, business, and family entities. The role of the board of directors, its composition, and the criteria for board members' selection have to be explicitly summarized in a document developed by members of the ownership assembly.

Depending on the size of the family business, the recruitment process can be outsourced or performed internally. If the process is carried out internally, owners can start the recruitment process by harnessing their social networks to attract independent members and evaluate potential internal candidates (family-affiliated and/or business-affiliated candidates). The goal is to have a fair selection process to select the best possible independent members and family candidates to fill the positions based on the requirements previously defined by members of the ownership assembly.

For instance, continuing with the Carvajal SA example, Article 26 of the firm's code of good governance[4] defines the most important characteristics that board members should have to be nominated and elected: potential members should (1) identify with the business vision of Carvajal; (2) have relevant experience and education as well as a well-established professional career; (3) demonstrable analytic and managerial skills, business vision, the ability to present their own point of view, and the ability to evaluate top managers; and (4) have a strong external reputation (sector, industry, and society).

8.4.3 *Regulation of the board of directors*

Beyond the initial process to create a board of directors or to move it to a professionalized level, members of the ownership assembly, in collaboration with the board of directors itself, should develop a written document to specify the rights, responsibilities, internal decision-making processes, and roles of board members to regulate the functionality of the board of directors. The aim of this document is to demarcate the boundaries of the board of directors' actions and ensure an effective business governance structure. This document is generally called the code of the good corporate governance.

Even though the governance-regulation document is unique and should fit the family business's specific needs and any relevant laws (e.g., the formality and obligation for listed and non-listed family firms are different[5]), it should contain certain information and requirements:

- The preliminary section covers general aspects related to regulating the board of directors, such as the definition and aims of the board of directors, the scope of the regulation itself, and the boundaries of any applicable laws.
- The next section is the principles of conduct for the board of directors. This section defines and regulates the general behavior of board members and the board of directors as a group within the family business system and in line with the interests of the different shareholders and stakeholders. This section should include ethical principles.
- The structure and powers section establishes the board of directors' internal organization and structure as well as the main tasks to regulate the actions and activities expected from the group.
- The composition section covers the number of board members and types of directors based on their affiliations with the ownership, business, and family entities.
- The next section outlines the nomination, appointment, cessation, and terms of office of board members. It includes internal processes from nomination until replacement and cessation of office. This section could also define the board of directors' remuneration.
- The positions and committees section defines the minimum and main positions that the board of directors should have, such as chairperson, as well as the committees it should include, such as an audit and risk supervision committee and an appointment committee, among others.
- The section on the board of directors' operations defines the structure of board meetings.
- The duties of the board of directors section specifies the obligations of the board of directors in general and in their specific positions as well as the conflicts of interest that they should avoid.

8.5 Additional activities and reading material

8.5.1 Classroom discussion

1 Why could a board of directors be useful for a family business?
2 What types of boards of directors are the most important? Why? When?
3 Is there any composition of the board of directors that can guarantee success?
4 What are the main excuses that family members may use to reject having a board of directors?
5 How should the process of creating a board of directors be navigated in a family business?

8.5.2 Additional readings

1 Goodspeed, W. B. (2020). Does your board of directors have an old boys'/girls' club problem? *Family Business Magazine.* Article retrieved from www.familybusinessmagazine.com/does-your-board-directors-have-old-boysgirls-club-problem
2 Cheng, J. Au, Kevin, Widz, M., & Jen M. (2021). *The Governance Marathon: Dynamic Durability in Entrepreneurial Families Amid Disruptions.* Boston, MA: 2086 Society & the Family Firm Institute. Report retrieved from https://digital.ffi.org/pdf/ffi_the_governa nce_marathon_report.pdf
3 Angus, P. M. (2022). Your family business needs a board. Harvard Business Review. Article retrieved from https://hbr.org/2022/09/your-family-business-needs-a-board

8.5.3 Classroom activity

Aim: Learn the importance of the process for creating corporate governance in a family business.
Material: Organize the classroom into groups of four to five students and assign them family shareholder roles. Below is a list of different types of shareholders that students can select to perform their roles.

Shareholder	Affiliation	Additional Information
#1 (father/ mother)	Family member, owner of 60% of the business's shares and CEO of the business.	He or she is the founder of the family business. He or she is not very interested in creating a board of directors because this could jeopardize his or her power and decision-making. This person thinks the board of directors is a good idea for the next generation when he or she retires.
# 2 (sibling)	Family member, owner of 10% of the business's shares, works in the family business.	The eldest of all the siblings, who started working in the firm just after graduation. Close to the father/mother who is the main shareholder. This person is not going to contradict his or her father/mother so he or she believes a board of directors is not needed. Additionally, this person would like to lead the business, so a board of directors could affect his or her expectations.

Shareholder	Affiliation	Additional Information
# 3 (sibling)	Family member, owner of 10% of the business's shares, and does not work in the family business.	One of the middle children in the family. He or she is not very interested in the business and currently works outside the family business, but this person understands the importance of having a voice in the business. He or she is aware about the eldest sibling's desire to occupy the CEO position.
# 4 (sibling)	Family member, owner of 10% of the business's shares, and does not work in the family business.	The second middle child in the family. He or she is not interested in the business at all. This person is currently launching a firm with his father/mother as the second major shareholder (less than 50% of the business's shares).
# 5 (sibling)	Family member, owner of 10% of the business's shares, and does not work in the family business.	The youngest child. This person suggested creating a board of directors. He or she just graduated with an MBA and is willing to implement new ideas and solutions in the family business.

Running the classroom exercise

- 10 minutes. Once the teams are created and the roles assigned, the first activity is to ask students to have a first meeting to discuss the possibility of creating a board of directors. Ask the students who have the Shareholder #5 role to present the importance of having a board of directors to the rest of the shareholders. Encourage the rest of the shareholders to actively participate in this meeting by asking questions and challenging the need to have a board of directors.
- 5 minutes—pause. Dissolve the meeting and ask the shareholders to reflect on their positions.
- The instructor should share the following statement with the groups: "After three months, at the next ownership assembly, the father/mother agrees to create a board of directors and asks the youngest child to define the next steps to move forward."
- 15 minutes. The youngest child should coordinate the next meeting with the following aims: define the number of board members, describe the selection process for choosing board members, and select the board members based on the nomination lists suggested by each shareholder:

1. Father/mother because he or she is the main shareholder
2. The eldest sibling because of his commitment
3. One of the middle siblings to control the direction of the firm
4. The youngest sibling because of his or her initiative
5. The business's accountant, who is a long-time friend of the family
6. The wife/husband of the eldest sibling because of his or her experience in the industry

7. 65-year-old retired CEO from a successful firm in the international market
8. The current financial manager of the family business because of his or her loyalty
9. One of the main investors in the community because of his or her business knowledge
10. Retired local politician who has collaborated to develop the business ecosystem
11. A professor of family business at the local university
12. A family business consultant

(Based on the selection criteria defined by the group of shareholders, the selection should begin, and the shareholders should come with their final list of the four selected board members)

- 15 minutes—debriefing. The discussion could center on the process that each team decided to use for selection. Does everyone have the same voting rights or not? What different alternatives could have been implemented beyond giving one vote per shareholder? Ask students to reflect on their own selection and discuss the advantages and disadvantages. Additionally, reflect on the different final lists of selected board members. Different processes, negotiation tactics, and criteria could alter the final list of board members.
- 15 minutes. With the final list of board members for each team, discuss the challenges and benefits that each board member (based on their affiliations) could have.

Takeaways: This exercise provides students the chance to experience the difficulties of introducing a board of directors in a family business context in which each family member has different goals, needs, and expectations. How important is it for the shareholders to define and agree on the need to have a board of directors, the process to select and appoint board members, and the consequences of the selection for the family business?

8.6 Case study for analysis I: Al-Wadi Group—Corporate governance[6]

It is said that family businesses are competitive due the complementary skills of their family members. Is this always true in a fast-growing firm or across the generations of a family business? The success story of the Al-Wadi Group illustrates transformation best practices for a family business in which the governance practices, knowledge, and skills of its members complement each other. The roots of this international group go back to the early 1960s when a collaboration between two Lebanese friends, Philip Nasrallah and Musa Freiji, resulted in an Egypt-based agribusiness conglomerate.

The chief financial officer and the group's vice president, Ramzi Nasrallah, noticed a fundamental challenge to firm survival as the firm moved into the second and third generations. After the patriarchs' hard work, these generations needed to maintain and develop the Al-Wadi Group. However, a misperception from the spoiled new generations came into play since they were family members: they believed they deserved the highest pay regardless of their contributions and added value. Hala Freiji, the head of the family council, addressed a similar issue with the younger generations being employed just because their bosses were their fathers, mothers, or close relatives.

On the other hand, some challenges occurred due to the old classical approach of leading the enterprise. For instance, the board of directors' opinion was biased toward the chairman's opinion that the board of directors should only include family members. In such environments, when succession becomes dependent on a few key people—usually the founders, who have the highest power—mix-ups between family and business relationships can arise. Therefore, out of respect for the older members, everyone reacted positively to the imposed opinion despite its adverse effects—mainly when the board members discussed projects, issues, and future plans outside of the work context. For example, the two families used to have family assembly discussions during lunch and dinner, so many things were lost and forgotten, and the majority of the family members were often not present. The firm did not have a clear vision and mission since there was an unclear division between management and the board, especially the chairman and the CEO.

Furthermore, it was very challenging to persuade the founders of Al-Wadi Group to include nonfamily members on the board or to convince the chairman to leave daily activities to an outsider CEO. Additionally, there were no internal audits, and even external audits, which were mandatory, were not fully independent and did not have the trust of the board. Generally, the firm lacked the basic principle of transparency to share information and details about the performance of the Al-Wadi Group via its different communication channels.

Al-Wadi Group's main goal is continuity, sustainability, and growth; as a result, they realized that significant changes had to occur. They started implementing corporate governance. First, they established a clear description for each role, including the responsibilities and limitations, as well as a distinction between the role of a board member and that of a manager. The chairman began gradually relinquishing daily activities to a managerial role. Additionally, restructuring based on business units took place as the leaders empowered the new heads to control each unit in the best possible way. Second, they developed family employment policies governing the hiring of family members. They determined that compensation would be based on experience and added value. Hala Freiji noted that the business was "adding elements to make it fairer to encourage the family members to join—after all, we care to ensure the continuation of the family business, that is what the WADI family and the council is all about."[7] It was initially difficult for the family members to accept strangers (nonfamily members) on the board of directors, and the employees found it difficult to deal with outsiders. Third, Al-Wadi Group began a formal strategic planning process each year with continuous reviews by the board and management to achieve long- and short-term objectives. Succession planning was also integrated at various levels within the organization. Fourth, the business implemented a new core financial system and other modules across the group, which enabled the business to set key performance indicators for the group and apply a balanced scorecard. In this direction, the firm established new internal audit processes led by senior management and the board, the group selected one external audit firm to conduct an audit for the entire enterprise. Finally, the business implemented a form of corporate governance that calls for upstanding, transparent company behavior that leads to ethical decisions that benefit all stakeholders.

All these changes helped protect Al-Wadi Group from bad governance, which may have led to a company breakdown and often results in scandals and bankruptcy.

Discussion questions:

1 Could Al-Wadi Group have survived/grown without introducing the main governance changes?
2 What are the real changes that the new governance adjustments produced in the family business?

8.7 Case study for analysis II: Volkswagen scandal and boardroom politics[8]

Volkswagen Group is a German multinational automotive manufacturing company headquartered in Wolfsburg, Lower Saxony. It designs, manufactures, and distributes passenger and commercial vehicles, motorcycles, engines, and turbomachinery. Volkswagen owns and manages multiple automotive brands, including Skoda, SEAT, Audi, Lamborghini, Ducati, Porsche, Bentley, Bugatti, MAN, and Scania.

Founded in 1937, the Volkswagen board of directors has been responsible for steering the automaker through thick and thin. Volkswagen is governed mainly by family members, with some government and labor influence intervening in the process, and the voting rights are distributed as follows: the Porsche and Piëch families own more than 50% of votes, Lower Saxony owns 20%, and Qatar Holdings owns 17%.

Volkswagen follows an autocratic leadership style as Piëch and Porsche family members own the majority of voting rights. When voting on issues related to Volkswagen, family members gather their votes under one committee and cast their vote as one under a family agreement, giving their vote tremendous power within Volkswagen. Ferdinand Piëch was the chairman of the executive board of Volkswagen Group from 1993 to 2002 and the chairman of the supervisory board of Volkswagen Group from 2002 to 2015 until he was forced to resign in the spring of 2015.

In 2012, shareholders elected Mr. Piëch's fourth wife, Ursula, a former kindergarten teacher, to the company's supervisory board. Many shareholders protested her lack of qualifications and independence, but they had little to no influence, which demonstrates Mr. Piëch's power. However, Mr. Piëch was forced to resign in the spring of 2015 after unsuccessfully trying to oust the company's chief executive, Martin Winterkorn, who was also forced out a few weeks later.

This forced resignation was mainly due to Volkswagen's emissions scandal as it was revealed that Volkswagen had been cheating on emissions tests for years. This revelation has caused a lot of damage to the company's reputation, especially since it is evident that the board was heavily involved in this matter.

Volkswagen's emissions scandal left the board with a lot of work to rebuild the company's image. Not having a strong leadership structure and not having an outsider as chairman deeply compromised Volkswagen's ability to manage the fallout from the crisis. When the crisis struck, Volkswagen had not yet formally appointed a chairman following the resignation of Ferdinand Piëch.

Hans Dieter Pötsch, former Volkswagen group chief financial officer, was confirmed by the full board as the new chairman. After being elected, Pötsch said, "We must overcome the current crisis, but we must also ensure that Volkswagen continues to grow."[9] His remarks suggested that he saw the scandal as a short-term problem but not a sign that there were bigger issues with how Volkswagen was run and governed.

The scandal suggested that Volkswagen's board seemed more concerned with achieving the goals of different stakeholders, such as labor representatives and local officials, than ensuring good governance. Mr. Piëch was obsessed with achieving a dominant global market share, and the government officials and labor representatives wanted Volkswagen to create more jobs, leading all sides to act in agreement with no proper governance. As a result, this situation led to one of the biggest scandals in the automotive industry.

Volkswagen's recent blunder is a major instance of the importance of sound governance. When a company has a proper governance structure that ensures accountability of everyone in the company, it is more likely to operate well and avert costly mistakes.

Discussion questions:

1   What is your opinion about Volkswagen's corporate governance?
2   What principle of corporate governance is the family challenging?

8.8 Case study: In between the board of directors and family shareholders[10]

A few months after her father's death, Jasmin Venvenuti found herself trapped between the board of directors and family shareholders of Amber Holding. The board of directors was not confident in her managerial skills to lead the family business through the difficult time in which it was immersed. The family shareholders were organized in three different branches, which had different perceptions and expectations regarding the direction the family business should take.

Her father committed suicide when the company was nearly financially suffocated and close to bankruptcy. After this event, her mother approached her to assume the new leadership role. She found herself in a transitory position because the board of directors had not fully agreed on whether to appoint her or someone else. The financial situation was extremely difficult. The effect of the COVID-19 pandemic on revenue and her father's decision to preserve all employees caused the firm to have three consecutive years of red numbers.

Jasmin was waiting for the final decision from the consultancy firm about the best candidate for the CEO position. It was the first time in her life that she really desired, with all her love, to continue with the family tradition and lead the family to the next level of growth and development.

The family business. The business was originally founded by Jasmin's grandfather in 1971 and operates in the petrochemical industry. Today, the industry faces very strong competition, with innovation being a key strategic point to maintain a competitive advantage. Because of external pressure, margins are becoming increasingly smaller, so innovation can ensure increased prices to have better margins. The family business has an excellent reputation in the industry's value chain, and the news of the patriarch's death was a shock for all stakeholders. The motto the family business uses is "quality, safety, and consistency." The family business owes much of its success (more than 30 years as the market leader) to Jasmin's father, Don Venvenuti, the former CEO of Amber Holding, and to Mark Owen, the chairman of the board of directors, who is a nonfamily member who worked side by side with Jasmin's father. The Venvenuti family controls 60% of the firm's equity, and the rest of the shares are publicly traded.

The family shareholders. The ownership composition passed to Don Venvenuti's three children in equal proportion (33% each of the 60% that used to belong to Don Venvenuti). Don Venvenuti forced all present and future shareholders to sign an agreement that the 60% of shares would remain in family hands. If family shareholders want to sell their shares, the other family members from the same family branch have the right to buy them. If no one wants to buy them, the other family members can buy the shares. Jasmin, Mack, and Joe are the current shareholders of the 60% of the firm's equity. However, the complexity of the family started to increase, and more than 25 fourth-generation family members are going to become family shareholders sooner or later.

Jasmin worked with her father after graduating from Harvard. However, after a few years of being dedicated to the family business, she decided to have her own family and move to her husband's city where she developed a career at the local bank, eventually achieving a middle managerial position. Today, Jasmin's children are in university. Mack and Joe never worked in the family business, and their interests are economic in nature. The dividends for their shares help them maintain an excellent lifestyle. However, two cousins—Mark's son and Joe's daughter—have shown interest in the company.

Governance structure. The governance structure is composed of eight members, including three family members and five nonfamily members, of which three of these five have to be independent. Don Venvenuti's aim was to guarantee an independent board to guide the destiny of the business, thereby avoiding negative family consequences in case of feuds or conflicts among family members. From the family side, only Jasmin was part of the board of directors while her father was alive, and the other two family chairs were occupied by her father and a family friend. Today, the composition is different: Jasmin, Mack, and Joe sit in the boardroom and represent the different interests of the family.

The family dynamics. While the father was alive, there were respectful and friendly interpersonal relationships among all family members. The father was the guardian of emotions and conversations. Everyone was happy while the money was flowing into their pockets. Jasmin and Don Venvenuti had a unique and special relationship. He wanted to have her in the business and work side by side. Jasmin's decision to leave the family business had a big emotional impact on Don Venvenuti. She was his favorite child, and he wanted her to succeed his position. He convinced her to keep the family chair on the board. Jasmin was his friend and business partner.

However, Don Venvenuti's death completely changed the family dynamics. Without the patriarch, the family's dividends and additional perks were suspended. The father was no longer redistributing the wealth. The mother was financially covered by several investments that he made to guarantee her lifestyle. The family business was not a problem for her, but she knew her husband's emotional attachment of the business. She intervened to convince her daughter to stay as interim CEO while the board of directors decided.

The communication among the siblings was not optimal, and with the new circumstances, it deteriorated. The communication went from the dinner table to the boardroom to informal calls. A conversation could change from being an emotional one to a formal one about the business in just seconds. It was acceptable to talk about the past, their father, their business, and the future anytime and anywhere.

The board of directors. The board of directors assumed the leadership responsibility to oversee the debt situation, which was hidden in the accounting books. At the time, the board was divided into two different factions. One faction led by one independent board member and other board members who represent the minority shareholders wanted Jasmin to continue as CEO. Their arguments were clear and simple: she is competent and well prepared for the position, she has the tacit knowhow from being close to her father, she is committed to the family business, and she carries the same social capital as her father. The other faction representing the majority (which includes Jasmin's brothers) looked for an external CEO with experience to lead the situation and develop a new strategy for Amber Holding.

To address the situation, the board of directors brought in an external firm specialized in recruiting top managers to help them with the decision, which would be ratified by the board of directors based on an internal voting system. The external consultancy brought two main candidates to the table after several months of searching and evaluating. The first candidate was Jasmin Venvenuti, and the second candidate was an external ex-CEO of an international family business. Among his or her achievements, the nonfamily candidate was able to revive a family business, but the business is no longer a family business as it was sold to external investors. The consultancy firm selected the external candidate, the nonfamily member, as the CEO.

The eight members of the board of directors (Jasmin was not in the group since she was waiting for the final decision, and her mother occupied her chair) stayed in silence for five long minutes. The ice was broken by Jasmin's mother . . .

Discussion questions:

1 What is your opinion about the composition of the board of directors? To what extent does it represent the interests of the owners?

2 If you were Don Venvenuti, would you have a different board of directors? What are the advantages and disadvantages of having family members, external members who represent the minority, and independent members?
3 How should the family shareholders behave in this situation?
4 What do you think the mother's speech was after knowing the final decision? Do you think the mother convinced her sons to select her daughter as the next CEO?

Notes

1 Basco, R., & Voordeckers, W. (2015). The relationship between the board of directors and firm performance in private family firms: A test of the demographic versus behavioral approach. *Journal of Management & Organization*, 21(4), 411–435.
2 Basco, R., Campopiano, G., Calabrò, A., & Kraus, S. (2019). They are not all the same! Investigating the effect of executive versus non-executive family board members on firm performance. *Journal of Small Business Management*, 57 (Issue sup2), 637–657.
3 Explore the board of directors composition of Carvajal SA on their website www.carvajal.com/inversi onistas/gobierno-corporativo/junta-directiva/
4 Information retrieved from the Carvajal SA website: www.carvajal.com/inversionistas/gobierno-corp orativo/codigo-de-buen-gobierno/
5 If the reader is interested in exploring different types of documents that regulate the board of directors for private and public firms, Wal-Mart's corporate governance guidelines can be downloaded at the following link: https://cdn.corporate.walmart.com/50/0e/4edaab334942a353ad813be0a4e9/ corporate-governance-guidelines.pdf. Additionally the good governance code for Carvajal SA can be explored at this website www.carvajal.com/inversionistas/gobierno-corporativo/codigo-de-buen-gobierno/
6 This example discussion is developed solely as the basis for class discussion. This example discussion is not intended to serve as an endorsement, source of primary data, or illustration of effective or ineffective management. This example discussion includes information from different sources: (1) Al Wadi website www.wadigroup.com/, (2) Saleh, H. (2014). Family businesses: Sons, daughters, and outsiders. *Financial Times*. Article retrieved from www.ft.com/content/c41b0648-3a61-11e4-bd08-00144feabdc0, and (3) Al Wadi video, educational video downloaded from the International Finance Corporation, video retrieved from www.youtube.com/watch?v=sEofec4F7aM&t=4s
7 Saleh, H. (2014). Family businesses: Sons, daughters and outsiders. *Financial Times*. Article retrieved from www.ft.com/content/c41b0648-3a61-11e4-bd08-00144feabdc0
8 Information retrieved from www.cnbc.com/2015/10/04/volkswagens-uniquely-awful-governance-at-fault-in-emissions-scandal.html,
    www.nytimes.com/2015/09/25/business/international/problems-at-volkswagen-start-in-the-boardr oom.html, and
    www.ft.com/content/e816cf86-6815-11e5-a57f-21b88f7d973f. Several references were used to write this example: Stewart, J. B. (2015). Problems at Volkswagen start in the boardroom. *The New York Times*. Article retrieved from www.nytimes.com/2015/09/25/business/international/probl ems-at-volkswagen-start-in-the-boardroom.html. Milne, R., & Bryant, C. (2015). Boardroom politics at heart of VW scandal. *Financial Times*. Article retrieved from www.ft.com/content/e816cf86-6815-11e5-a57f-21b88f7d973f
9 Ewing, J., & Ivory, D. (2015). Volkswagen U.S. Chief knew of potential emissions problems in 2014. *The New York Times*. Article retrieved from www.nytimes.com/2015/10/08/business/international/vol kswagen-diesel-emissions-fix.html
10 This case study discussion is developed solely as the basis for class discussion. This case study discussion is not intended to serve as an endorsement, source of primary data, or illustration of effective or ineffective management.

9 Family governance in family business

Learning objectives

- Distinguish the difference between ownership, business, and family governance.
- Understand the roles, duties, and responsibilities of family members in family governance.
- Recognize the different types of family governance structures.
- Identify the most important written instruments for family governance.
- Interpret family governance across generations.

9.1 Introduction

Family governance is the third pillar that forms family business governance, along with ownership and business governance. Family governance occupies a unique space because it attempts to regulate an entity—the family—that is typically self-regulated culturally and uses different logic than the business and ownership entities. However, family governance does not attempt to regulate family life or emotional interpersonal relationships. Instead, the goal is to coordinate and organize family matters and individual/group interactions with the ownership and business entities. Consequently, family governance is defined as a system of rules, practices, and processes to regulate the relationships between the family, ownership, and business entities in the best interests of the shareholders and the family in general to preserve the family business across generations.

The main aim of family governance is to guarantee family cohesion, which refers to the emotional bonding that family members have with each other because it represents the necessary conditions for family businesses' long-term survival. At the early stage of the family business lifecycle, family businesses have informal mechanisms (processes and actions) that affect the relationship between the family and the business. In some contexts and particular moments of the lifecycle, these informal mechanisms are enough to coordinate the family and business entities. However, as the complexity of the family increases, because of the growing number of family members across generations and the interpersonal relationships among family members, the informal mechanisms are no longer efficient to reduce conflicts, keep open and transparent communication, develop consensus, and prepare the family for the responsibility to lead economic projects.

If the intention is to own, govern, and manage a family business across generations, the family entity needs to develop its own governance rules, actions, and processes to coordinate the relationship between the family and the business. The aim of this chapter is to discuss the benefits and challenges of family governance for family businesses. This chapter addresses how

DOI: 10.4324/9781003273240-12

the nature of family cohesion and the different family business lifecycle stages shape formal family governance, which may vary in terms of governance body and instruments.

9.2 Types of family cohesion

Not all families are alike because they differ in terms of the cohesion that ties family members to each other. There are different types of family cohesion based on two dimensions: the source of cohesion and the type of bonding. The source of family cohesion refers to the similarity between members' interests and consists of family-oriented or business-oriented cohesion. The type of bonding refers to the processes by which relationships are developed and includes emotional-oriented or financial-oriented bonding. Combining both dimensions—source of cohesion and type of bonding—Figure 9.1 shows four types of family cohesion.[1]

- *Family emotional cohesion* is the basic state of business families based on altruistic behavior and entails a common story, actions, and processes to satisfy family members' needs, and love that binds family members to each other.
- *Family financial cohesion* is the state of business families based on economic principles that intertwine family wealth and the economic exchange of relationships to bind family members to each other.
- *Business emotional cohesion* is the state of business families bas on the business as a centri-petal force to develop a common identity, sense of belonging, and commitment that bind family members each other.
- *Business financial cohesion* is the state of business families based on selfishness and the coordination of financial and economic investments that guarantee economic needs to bind family members each other.

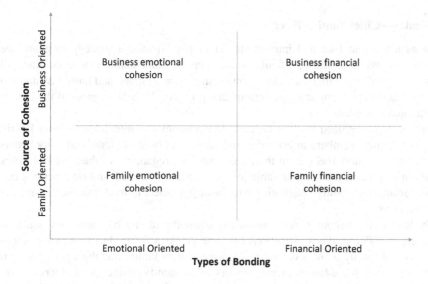

Figure 9.1 Types of family cohesion.

Source: Adapted from Pieper, T., & Astrachan, J. H. (2008). *Mechanisms to Assure Family Business Cohesion: Guidelines for Family Business Leaders and Their Families*. Kennesaw, GA: Cox Family Enterprise Center.

To some extent, all of these types of cohesion are present in a business family, but one of them tends to dominate family interpersonal relationships and, consequently, affects the relationship between the family and the business. The particular type of cohesion that binds business family members to each other is a fundamental part of family governance as it shapes the rules, actions, and processes that are developed, implemented, and maintained to regulate the family–business relationship.

Family governance mechanisms have to adjust to the type of family cohesion that prevails in each family context. For instance, the control aim of overseeing economic principles and preserving family wealth is higher in families with business financial cohesion than in families with family emotional cohesion. The family governance mechanisms that work for one family business do not necessarily work for other family businesses because family governance mechanisms have to adapt to the cohesion that binds family members.

However, the types of family cohesion that prevail in the family business context are not static but dynamic and can change across the family business lifecycle. For instance, a generational change can alter the cohesiveness dynamics of a family business, and, consequently, the family governance mechanisms have to be adapted. Mitchell Stores (men's and women's specialty stores) are family owned and operated by the second and third generations of Mitchells. The brothers, Jack and Bill, complemented each other in leading the successful story of the Mitchell Stores, having a strong business emotional connection. To guarantee the business's success across generations, they created a family council to embrace all family members and their in-laws. For the Mitchell family, the family council is the mechanism that keeps harmony and unity as well as keeps family members informed and included. In this case, the family council serves to maintain the family's and the business's emotional cohesion.

Therefore, when implementing or adapting family governance, family business leaders have to answer two main questions: (1) what types of cohesion drive my business family, and (2) what cohesion dimensions are important for the next generation? Overall, family governance should define mechanisms that guarantee and enhance business family cohesion.

9.3 Family leader—Chief family officer

As important as a CEO to lead and implement the family business's strategy to guarantee business survival across generations, a family leader plays a fundamental role to embrace all family members (regardless of their roles in the ownership, management, and family entities) to ensure one vision and implement strategic actions that preserve the cohesiveness of the family in each generational transition.

Family leaders are recognized by their capacity to communicate, interact with other family members, engage family members in activities and actions, uphold the family identity across generations, and make others feel part of the family business regardless of their position/roles in each of the entities. Family leaders are able to keep the family united, and their actions can be informal or formal (i.e., through institutions) by inspiring others to work together in support of the family business.

The family leader role becomes more important when the family business moves across generations because different types of factions can emerge. As a family business grows, there are different types of family owners or groups of owners, new family members (in-laws) can be added to the business, some family members work in the family business and others do not, there are differences in terms of political and religious beliefs, and different generations are often present. As the diversity of the family increases, family leaders have to manage these differences.

For instance, Karen Bichin, a fourth-generation owner of ABC Recycling Company in Canada,[2] was able to lead the family transformation to ensure a smooth transition from the third to the fourth generation. Karen is involved in community activities on the behalf of the family and the firm and is responsible for keeping the family united. She served as the facilitator in developing the family governance structure (family council, shareholder meetings, and family assembly), developed projects to compile and publish the family history, and organized events for the 100th anniversary of the family business. Karen acts as a values-keeper in the family and is passionate about perpetuating the legacy of

> Joseph Yochlowitz who began scratching out a living as a junk peddler and backyard scrap dealer. His sons, Daniel and Charlie, soon joined him in his labour and by the 1920's the family business was established on Main Street as Service Auto Wrecking.[3]

9.4 Family governance viewed across an evolutionary perspective

Family governance exists in small, medium, and big family businesses dominated by one family owner or a group of family owners who are highly involved in the business. In some family businesses, family governance is formal, well defined, and clearly integrated with ownership and business governance. For instance, Franz Haniel & Cie. GmbH is a 100% family-owned business that was founded in Germany in 1756. Family members only pass shares from one generation to another. To sustain the family model, family governance is critical. There are more than 750 shareholders who elect 30 members to the family advisory board, which links the family and the firm. The advisory board elects four family members to represent their interests on the supervisory board (board of directors).[4] No family members work in the family business group, but the family implements governance to control the destiny of the business.

However, in other family businesses, family governance is not formal or explicit but instead informal. Even informal mechanisms are still sufficient to manage the family–business relationship. For instance, parents may informally define the procedures by which children can join the business, or they may informally transmit the values and principles that the family uses to govern and manage the business. At the dinner table, family members may discuss business issues and make important decisions. In private conversation, a couple may decide about financial issues that affect the family and the business. Taken together, all these actions are the first manifestations of family governance.

When the complexity of the family increases because of the number of family members and their overlapping roles across the three entities, it is necessary to shift informal family governance procedures to formal ones. The formality of family governance is a necessary condition for family businesses to survive longer while maintaining family cohesiveness. Figure 9.2 shows the relationship between family complexity and the degree of formality of family governance. The degree of family governance formality increases with time assuming that the family complexity varies from one generation to another (Line A in Figure 9.2). Even though this may be a common pattern of family governance evolution, in real life, variation exists. For instance, when business families decide to prune the tree and keep ownership concentrated in one or few family branches with the intention to control the complexity of the family, the pressure to increase formality stays constant (Line B in Figure 9.2), and family governance does not need to be changed in the short term.

There is not one successful form of family governance, so each family should structure it to fit both family and business needs. Independent of the specific structure, process, and protocols, family governance should achieve some general goals:

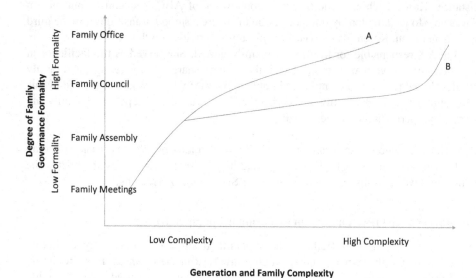

Figure 9.2 Family governance evolution.

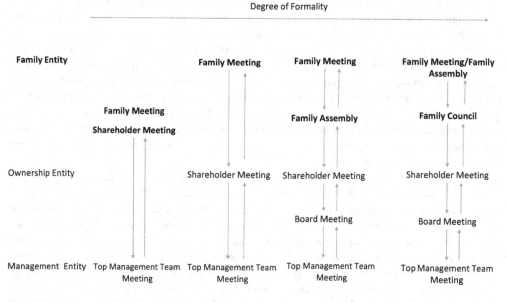

Figure 9.3 Degree of formality of the family governance structure.

- Demarcate decision-making among the ownership, management, and family entities. Independent of individuals' overlapping roles, each entity should develop its own structure for decision-making.
- Improve the channels of communication to embrace all participants in their respective governance body. The family can communicate its vision, values, and long-term perspective, and

the other way around, family members can be informed about important issues at the owner-ship and business levels.
- Have a transparent process for decision-making to reach consensus and unify the family voice across the three entities.
- Limit and constrain family members' expectations, which could help align collective and individual interests.
- Have clear rules to address family issues in relation to the ownership and business entities and to anticipate, manage, and resolve conflicts.

Each family business has to recognize its current and future family complexity in terms of active generations, number of family members, and quality of interpersonal relationships as well as the types of family cohesion that prevail in the family context. Based on this self-evaluation, fam-ilies will be able to introduce and implement different types of family governance mechanisms from more informal structures, such as family meetings, to more formal structures with family councils and family offices. The next section discusses the most important family governance mechanisms (Figure 9.3).

9.4.1 Family meetings

Family meetings are informal family reunions that can occur spontaneously at the dinner table or be pre-arranged events where family members discuss business issues and/or any other issues related to the implications of the family in the business or the business in the family. This family governance arrangement occurs because of the interpersonal interactions among family members. Family interactions define the system of rules, practices, and process by which the family governs and directs the business.

It is important for any business family to move from traditional spontaneous family interactions to formal meetings because this helps family members with overlapping roles rec-ognize that there is one arena where family members can discuss, share, and confront ideas and make decisions about the family–business relationship. Family meetings should be inten-tionally organized to maintain a minimum level of formality, taking into consideration that the tasks and subgoals of these meetings may be diverse but that the basic aim is to maintain and develop the cohesiveness of the family by aligning goals, recognizing needs, and setting real-istic expectations.

Basic formality for family meetings requires leaders to define the number of meetings per year as well as the agenda, composition, and participants for every meeting. Depending on the size of the family, the number of informal meetings could range from two to four per year. The agenda should be created for each individual meeting by prioritizing the most important issues to be discussed and agreed upon with the rest of the family members. Additionally, discussions and agreements should be documented using classic family meeting minutes. The aim is to document conversations, discussions, and agreements.

Some may wonder why it is necessary to have a written agenda and decision-making resolutions when only a few family members who love each other reach an agreement. The basic idea is that a verbal agreement is not enough to fully recognize what each partici-pant understood about a resolution. Even more important, as time passes and each family member interacts with other individuals (and in-law family members emerge in the inter-pretation process), a verbal agreement may not be clear or may no longer be accepted. Participants may also change their interpretations in different ways. Decisions should be documented and signed; then, it is more difficult for family participants to reinterpret or retract decisions.

Finally, the family should decide who is going to participate in family meetings. To make this decision, there are two main questions to answer: (1) members from which generations should participate and (2) should in-law family members actively participate? There are no correct answers to these questions, and the answers should fit the family's particular needs and the underlying purpose of family meetings. However, there are certain guidelines that business families can follow to reach the best decision. If the aim is to create a cohesive family and to develop a transgenerational family entrepreneurial mindset, including all family members across generations is important. This decision is not easy for those who hold significant power and use it for their own benefit because this means sharing information and control and being accountable in front of others. In the long run, family meetings are important because they help all family members communicate and be heard. The most common practice is to open family meetings to those family members who are related by consanguinity (i.e., blood kinship) and are at least 18 years old. Regarding family members related by affinity (i.e., in-laws, such as through marriage relationships), there is no unified position about the pros and cons of including them, so each family needs to decide whether to include in-laws in their family meetings. The advantages of doing so are opening up transparent communication among all family members (i.e., those related by both consanguinity and affinity) and avoiding informal communication and manipulation. The disadvantages are that family problems are exposed to all family members and could become public, it is more difficult to reach consensus when family member related by both consanguinity and affinity are involved, and family members related by affinity can paralyze family meetings.

Formal meetings are not going to eliminate the informal interactions among family members, but formal meetings constitute official mechanisms to discuss, debate, and agree among family members. This means that formal meetings are the best arena to discuss and share family business issues with the rest of the family members, to make decisions that tie all family members together, to resolve problems and misunderstandings between family members, to anticipate needs that could emerge from the family–business relationship across time, and to create realistic expectations in the family–business relationship.

The two main challenges for creating and maintaining formal family meetings are defining the aim of these meetings as a governance mechanism and demarcating the boundaries of decision-making. In other words, these challenges relate to how family meetings are coordinated and integrated with the family business's corporate governance, which combines ownership and business governance (each entity has its own governance mechanisms). Because family meetings occupy a sui generis position in the governance structure, coordination with the other two governance entities tends to be informal and led by family leaders who have overlapping roles.

The following are the most important topics to discuss in family meetings:

- Discuss the family–business relationship and desirable family involvement in the business via ownership, governance, and management.
- Resolve family conflicts that could affect the well-being of the family, ownership, and business entities in the long term.
- Develop activities to ensure the cohesiveness of the family.
- Educate family members on what it means to be part of a business family.
- Reflect on succession topics and the continuity of the family in the business.
- Develop and define the main family values and align interests and goals among family members.

The effectiveness of family meetings lies in having a manageable and committed number of family members. The rule of thumb is to have no more than seven family members at family meetings (even though this number can be adjusted based on the specific family circumstances and communication style). In any case, having the appropriate number of family members ensures participants are able to exchange ideas, share different points of view, and implement effective mechanisms for decision-making. In this sense, family meetings are the first step to prepare the family for the next level of formality and to create the family assembly. Family assemblies are necessary when the number of family members increases and family meetings are no longer productive and efficient. Due to the number of family members, the organization of an assembly is predetermined and coordinated with formal procedures to guide debates and decision-making.

9.4.2 Family assembly

A family's structure, composition, and quality of relationships change across time because of the family lifecycle. The complexity of the family increases due to the incorporation of new family members, the multiple overlapping roles across the three entities, and the less intense emotional bonds among family members. When families begin experiencing the shift from a nuclear family to a family with different branches as brothers and sisters start to create their own families, family assemblies replace family meetings. In this context, family assemblies have the same aim as family meetings, which is to preserve the cohesiveness of the family and define the relationship between the family and the business. There are four main roles for a family assembly:

- The *communication role* accounts for all actions and activities to inform the ownership and management entities about decisions made during a family assembly. These channels also enable the family to be informed by the ownership and management entities about decisions they are responsible for, such as current and prospective strategies and the economic and financial situation of the business. If a family council is in place, (see Section 9.4.3), members of the family assembly should select the family council members and maintain a channel of communication between the two institutions.
- The *educational role* accounts for all actions and activities developed with the aim of educating family members about being part of a business family. Education topics vary from one family to another but generally include financial and business education, communication and leadership skills, and the responsibilities of being a family owner, among other topics that can help family members better understand their role as part of a business family.
- The *socialization role* accounts for all actions and activities to preserve and maintain the family legacy and to develop transgenerational entrepreneurial spirit in the next generation of family members. This role encompasses preserving the values and principles of the business family that inspire the family business and defining family goals as a group that will then be transmitted to the ownership assembly.
- The *conflict-resolution role* accounts for all actions and activities to reduce tension and resolve family conflicts before they are transferred to the ownership or business entity. This is an important role for the family assembly to ensure family and business coexistence and avoid cross-conflicts between entities.

9.4.3 Family council

The lifecycle of the family implies that a family grows through different family branches incorporating new family members (via consanguinity and affinity) across generations. In some families, the number of family members increases exponentially, making it impossible to maintain family functioning via simple family assemblies. There is a threshold level (in terms of family size) after which diseconomies of scale manifest through interpersonal conflicts, emotional costs, and high efforts for reaching consensus. Therefore, in this situation, the quality of the decision-making process deteriorates, and the efficiency of the group decreases. Family assemblies comprising more than 15–20 individuals and several family branches are typically no longer productive.

Members of the family assembly should anticipate that the complexity of the family will slow down these meetings' effectiveness, so new rules, practices, and processes are needed to regulate the relationships between the family, ownership, and management entities. Parallel to family assemblies, the family council gains importance in streamlining the family decision-making process. Based on an agreed-upon procedure for appointing family council members, members of the family assembly have to select a group of family representatives responsible for operative and decision-making tasks. In other words, the family council represents the family's interests in the institutional relationships with the ownership and business entities.

A common way to organize the family council is to select representatives from each family branch plus senior family members who can add value to the family council. The composition of the family council can comprise equal representation for each family branch such that each family branch contributes with the same number of representatives, meaning that the power is balanced. In contrast, the composition of the family council could follow an ownership logic such that each family branch contributes representatives according to its ownership power.

The family council takes on communication, educational, guarantor, and conflict-resolution roles. At this stage of family governance development, the family council is responsible for developing the family chapter or constitution, which includes the family's core values, strategy, and governance structure for navigating affairs related to the business as well as a set of policies that limit the family's arbitrariness over the business. In this sense, it is the responsibility of the family council to prepare, discuss, and propose family policies, such as family employment, succession, and conflict-resolution policies, among others, to members of the family assembly.

9.4.4 Family policies

Family policies help present and future family members understand their ownership, business, and family relationships. Policies differ from family to family, but the main goal of having written policies is to maximize individual relationships across the three entities by addressing issues before they become personal and emotional. Additionally, family policies serve to clarify expectations for all family members independent of their positions across the three entities and the specific roles they perform. There are different family policies, but the three most important are the family employment policy, the succession policy, and the conflict-resolution policy.

- The *family employment policy*, as a formalized document, aims to establish the processes and procedures by which family members can enter the family business and develop their professional careers in it. It helps family members align their expectations with the types of relationships the family would like to have with the business. The family employment policy should describe the conditions under which family members can access (be hired by) the business as well as how and when this can happen. The main reason to have an agreed-upon document developed by the family (through the family assembly or family council) is because not all family members can work in the family business, so it is important to ensure that the most competent and committed family members can access it.

A family employment policy should be a written document with at least three sections. First, the purpose and philosophy section defines the general boundaries that should be used to interpret the policy itself and the spirit with which it was created. Second, the general conditions section describes the actions and practical processes for family members to be considered as potential candidates to work in the firm. It outlines the conditions to be hired, evaluated, and fired. It is important to clarify the career path that a family member could expect if he or she decides to join the business. Finally, the family support section describes how the family will economically and emotionally support potential candidates before they can access the business by funding their studies; connecting them with external stakeholders; and taking any other actions to develop the skills, knowledge, and capabilities of those family members who would like to join the business.[5]

- The *succession policy* is a written document that attempts to embrace the common vision of the family around the process of transitioning the ownership, governance, and management of the business to the next generation of family members. The succession policy document should not be confused with the succession planning document. While the succession policy is a document that attempts to outline the general guidelines of succession, such as the purpose and philosophy of the business family, the succession plan (see Part IV, which includes Chapters 10, 11, and 12) attempts to define the processes and actions to achieve the family's succession goals in terms of ownership, governance, and management. This means a family business could have several succession plans across generational changes, but one succession policy, which is more or less stable across generations.

- The *conflict-resolution policy* is the basic document to define the guidelines to achieve timely, equitable, and satisfactory resolutions of conflicts among family members. The aim is to develop conflict-resolution mechanisms in a cost-effective manner with less impact to the business and with the intention to reduce conflict recurrence across generations that may jeopardize the cohesiveness of the family and the long-term sustainability of the business. This policy should anticipate the common problems that any family business may experience across generations (e.g., nepotism, entitlement, goal alignment, and asymmetric information among family members) and the unique problems that the family could experience due to culture or religion (e.g., polygamy and inheritance laws, among others). Problem anticipation should be complemented with the process that families should follow to address general and specific problems in terms of resolution, accountability, and monitoring.

9.4.5 Family wealth governance

Having successful family businesses also implies that families have to manage, organize, and monitor their wealth to preserve, consolidate, and grow it over time. For some families, the family business is one source of wealth, and there are multiple other assets that these families have beyond the direct control of the family business. Regardless of whether a family has one or multiple sources of wealth, family wealth governance has to be defined because family members have different expectations, goals, and needs.

The type of governance structure that business families should use to govern their wealth depends on several considerations. First, a business family needs to consider the size and complexity of its

Table 9.1 Summary of the three governance structures

Area of Composition	Family Meeting	Family Assembly	Family Council
Composition	Open to family members who have or may have influence in the family and the business. Depending on the family and family culture, in-laws may be part of these meetings.	Open to all family members of a minimum age (generally 18 years old), and the inclusion of in-laws depends on the family culture.	Just a few family members designated by members of the family assembly to ensure all family branches and generations are represented. It has the ultimate decision-making for the family as a whole.
Generation	Most common in between the first and second generations when the family business starts the process of governance formalization.	Most common in between the second and third generations when the number of family members increases and more formality is necessary.	Most common in between the second and third generations and beyond when family branches are consolidated and the number of family members increases the complexity of decision-making.
Level of formality	Low	Medium	High
Size	No more than 7 individuals.	No more than 15 or 20 individuals who are able to respect each other and maintain good communication.	Between 5 to 9 family members who represent the different family branches.
Meeting frequency	Generally an extension of social family meetings but with more formality in the meetings themselves by having an agenda, minutes, and formalized agreement documents that all family members approve.	At least 2 or 3 meetings per year that may or may not overlap with social family meetings. It is important to have an explicit agenda, minutes, and agreement documents signed by all family members.	Between 3 to 9 meetings per year. A family member has to assume the chair of the family council and implement formalities, such as having an explicit agenda, minutes, and agreement documents signed by all family members.
Responsibilities	Communication and consensus. Coordinate the relationships between the family, ownership, and business entities.	Organize the family as a business family and coordinate the decision-making for issues related to the business, ownership, and family wealth. Look for consensus among family members.	Coordinate the family, ownership, and business relationships; improve communication; and develop instruments to formalize the family–business relationship, such as the family constitution and different policies. Be part of succession planning.

Table 9.1 (Continued)

Area of Composition	Family Meeting	Family Assembly	Family Council
Overlap with the other governance body	Because of the overlapping roles among the group of family members, informality is part of the interactions among different corporate governance bodies, such as shareholder meetings and the board of directors.	When first implementing family assemblies, because of family members' overlapping roles, formal and informal channels of communication among different governance bodies alternate. However, formal communication and coordination should be prioritized.	The family assembly and family council generally coexist, and the communication channels between them should guarantee decision-making transparency. It is the family council that maintains communication with the business and ownership governance bodies.
Pros	Agile decision-making because of the high level of trust and flow of information. It works when the family is very small, there is high role overlap across the three entities, and there is a clear leader to guide the process.	Family assemblies help families improve their communication, discuss conflicting topics, educate family members, and define the meaning of being a business family.	The high formalization and family representation in a small group of family members make business families more entrepreneurial and thus better able to recognize and exploit opportunities.
Cons	The process is subject to arbitrariness because of asymmetric information and unbalanced power among members with different roles across the three entities.	If the family grows quickly, family assemblies lose effectiveness very fast because the cost of coordination is excessive, discussions become less productive, and difficulties reaching consensus and agreements arise.	Since the family delegates decision-making to a small group of family members, agency problems are more likely to occur, such as asymmetric information and conflicts of interest. It is necessary to implement procedures (accountability and transparency) to prevent inappropriate behavior that can jeopardize family economic, social, and emotional endowments.

wealth to define whether more or less formal governance constellations are needed, which entail different costs (e.g., administrative and organizational costs) and benefits (e.g., maintaining family cohesiveness and preserving wealth across generations). Second, a business family needs to consider the size of the family and the prospect of family growth in the next generational stage. Third, a business family needs to consider the level of control family members would like to have over their assets. Finally, a business family needs to consider the extent to which family members (and family branches) would like to have their wealth beyond the family business.

Some family members (family branches) prefer to maintain simple control over their family wealth. The family as a whole has the family business as a source of wealth, so each family member (or family branch) has to manage his or her own wealth from the family business in the form of dividends. Family members (family branches) use ownership, business, and family corporate governance to manage the family business as a source of wealth. In other words, each family member (or family branch) directly uses the governance mechanisms to control his or her portion of wealth linked to the family business. However, if the family business produces important profits, there are several dispersed family investments accumulated across generations, there are legal (tax) or strategic reasons to preserve the wealth in the business or alternative assets or institutions, and there is typically the intention to preserve the business family identity. In other words, coordinating the tied family wealth would require special attention.

A new family governance mechanism is necessary to avoid the lack of coordination of and control over family wealth, address potential conflicts of interests (e.g., some family members subordinate family interests to their own personal interests, while others take excessive risk), and protect the intrinsic value of the family name among stakeholders. Therefore, the decision to implement family wealth governance mechanisms is not without costs because additional governance structures, decision-making processes, and human resources are needed to serve the interests of the family, preserve wealth across generations, and formalize the management and governance of family wealth.

The simplest governance solution is the family office (single-family office or multiple-family office), which aims to manage family wealth-related affairs by providing services to family members individually or collectively. This organization is different from both the family and the business and is tasked with managing family wealth. The aim of the family office is to maintain family cohesiveness by creating an intermediary figure between family members (their interests, needs, and goals) and the family as a whole to manage family assets. The main responsibility is to coordinate all aspects related to family wealth, such as investment management planning, risk diversification, family and individual tax issues (tax planning), control over assets, transparency, information sharing and reporting to all family members, and family philanthropic actions. There are different types of family offices, and their roles depend on the aim for which the owners created them. One of the top family offices by total assets is Walton Enterprise LLC, which supports the business, personal, and philanthropic activities for multiple generations of the Walton family (founding family of Wal-Mart).

Depending on the type of family office (based on the family's aims, level of wealth, and strategy), the following comprise some of the most important services offered by the family office:

* *Wealth management and investments*: investing advice and strategy, financial statements and reporting, private equity and debt, risk management, and manager and bank coordination.
* *Wealth and succession planning*: succession planning, estate planning, prenuptial and last wills, life insurance, gift insurance, and the transfer of wealth as gifts during lifetime.
* *Charity and philanthropy management*: giving strategy, foundation administration, philanthropic planning, philanthropic projects, and fundraising.
* *Family governance*: next-generation development, conflict-resolution mechanisms, and family-event coordination.
* *Security*: personal security, protection of assets, and cybersecurity.

- *Tax and legal assistance*: tax returns and administration, international relations, real estate structures, asset protection planning, and legal advice and regulation.
- *Administrative and accounting support*: budgeting, document filing, invoice and credit card payments, bookkeeping, and cash flow management.
- *Lifestyle management*: trophy assets, art management, travel and coordination of vehicles, concierge services, private secretary.
- *Real estate services*: insurance, real estate management, and real estate acquisition.
- *Trust and corporate services*: family shareholdings and nomination, trust coordination, company incorporation.

The second more formal structure is to create a trust and/or foundation where there is high delegation of management and control. In a family trust, there are commonly three parties involved: the grantor(s) (who transfer assets into the trust), trustees (who manage the assets in the trust on behalf of the beneficiaries), and the beneficiaries (who receive some type of financial benefit from the trust). As with any other governance structure to preserve and grow family wealth and reduce the possibility of family conflicts jeopardizing family wealth across generations, there are pros and cons to establishing a trust. Among the pros, the firm is protected from family conflicts and family wealth is protected from excessive lifestyle choices, easy fragmentation of wealth and control is avoided, family interests are aligned (or at least interests are forced to be aligned), there can be tax advantages, economies of scale can be realized across family investments, a better diversification strategy can be achieved, and philanthropic actions can be coordinated. Some of the main cons, in most of legislations, are the lack of the control mechanisms over trustees, excessive costs (e.g., the costs of having professional wealth managers as trustees and structure costs), conflicts of interest, and different visions on how to manage the wealth (conservative or entrepreneurial).

9.4.6 Family chapter or constitution

One of the most important instruments that family governance has to develop along with the different policies (e.g., family employment policy and conflict-resolution policy) is the family constitution. The family constitution is a written document that emotionally embraces family members to guide a concerted family vision and actions that link the family, ownership, and business entities. The family constitution's level of detail and sophistication differ based on the complexity of the family, ownership, and business entities. However, it is important to recognize that the family constitution is not a legal document according to most national legislations, and for this reason, the document does not have legal implications but instead attempts to tie family members together to maintain trusting relationships and ensure a high level of cohesiveness.

The document should contain a set of rules and regulations that constrain how families own, govern, and manage the family business and family wealth. There are different types of constitutions in terms of the details of the rules and regulations—from a simple form defining the spirit of being a business family and how the family and business should interact to a more thorough document that covers the most important policies and governance structure details. There are four general parts of the family constitution regardless of the level of detail:

- The *family section* covers the mission, values, philosophy, family goals, and principles for developing family governance (structure and policies).

- The *ownership section* encompasses the principles related to ownership obligations and responsibilities (mechanisms to agree on dividends and policies for disputing resolutions) and specific processes for owner exit (e.g., buy-and-sell agreement), family business valuation, and business dissolution.
- The *business section* contains the business vision, values, and goals; business governance coordination (e.g., eligible board of director characteristics and code of conduct); and rules and regulations to coordinate the family–business relationship from family employment to conflict-resolution mechanisms.
- The *family wealth section* defines the family wealth strategy and governance structure (e.g., family office) to manage family wealth according to explicit family values and principles.

However, the family constitution by itself is not what works as a mechanism for families to regulate the family–business relationship by maintaining a shared vision and a cohesive family. Instead, what serves as this mechanism is the process by which the family constitution is developed as all family members should be embraced to finalize this document and come to a shared consensus. This process is the real learning mechanism that demarcates the boundaries of individual and collective actions in relation to ownership, business, and family wealth affairs. The process is what helps family members understand the meaning of being part of a business family, the individual and collective roles within the family business system, and their individual and collective obligations and responsibilities. Finally, the process and the family constitution distinguish the boundaries of family members' expectations and align individual expectations with family expectations as a group of individuals who share a common past and project their future together.

9.5 Additional activities and reading material

9.5.1 Classroom discussion questions

1 Does initial family cohesion shape the use and the development of family governance?
2 Why is it important to develop family governance even when the family is small and not very complex?
3 How does family governance affect the ownership and management entities? To what extent does family decision-making have implications for the other entities?
4 What are the main elements family leaders should consider when developing their family governance structure?
5 Do you think the family constitution is a living document? Should it be adjusted when families move across generations? Why? What kind of elements could change/vary and/or remain stable?

9.5.2 Additional readings

1 Kruppa, M. (2022). Traditional family offices emerge as unlikely venture capitalists. *Financial Times*. Article retrieved from www.ft.com/content/35030a02-df4c-474a-8306-8dee53f62252
2 Jaffe, D. T., & Grubman, J. (2020). The two pillars of governance in family enterprises: A straightforward understanding of complex systems. *FFI Practitioner*. Article retrieved from https://ffipractitioner.org/the-two-pillars-of-governance-in-family-enterprises-a-straightforward-understanding-of-complex-systems/

3 Braverman, B. (2022). 5 best practices for your family office. *Family Business Magazine*. Article retrieved from www.familybusinessmagazine.com/5-best-practices-your-family-office

9.5.3 Classroom activity

Aim: Engaging in the process to develop a family business constitution.

Material: Organize the classroom into groups of five students and read the Al Saud Company case study (discussion case study in Chapters 9 and 12). Ask two students to assume the roles of Sheikh Sultan (second generation) and Sheikh Saud (third generation) to lead the process of creating and developing the family constitution for the Al Saud Company family business. The rest of the family members should assume other family roles by considering the interests they may have.

• Before starting the process, all group members should answer this question: Why does the company need a new constitution to replace the family chapter they already have? This question should define the spirit of the constitution for family members.
• Define the structure of the family constitution by defining the sections and subsections.
• Write the content of each section and subsection based on the agreement/consensus of the family members.

Running the classroom exercise. Let students discuss the structure and content of the document to reach consensus about what is important and not important to add in the family constitution. This could take 45–50 minutes because students should discuss and write out their main ideas. Leave the last 15 minutes to engage all students in a constructive guided discussion by the instructor. Below are the most important questions that can help guide the class discussion:

• What are the mission, vision, and values for the family? To what extent is it important to define this in the context of this family business?
• Is the family's last name socially important in the context in which the Al Saud Company is embedded? Is it necessary to address this issue with family members?
• Should the constitution contain the general philosophy for family employment?
• What about succession, next-generation development, entry, senior-generation exit, and future engagement?
• Is there any ownership policy to define the ownership structure across generations? What about dividends and reinvestment policies?
• Are there any regulations for family members' (family branches') exit? Should the company keep the tradition of preserving and keeping family members together across generations, penalizing the exit of shareholders? Is it time to change this regulation?
• What family governance structure should the constitution promote? What should the aim of the family governance structure be?

Takeaways: This exercise provides students the chance to experiment with the difficulties of agreeing on common points to define the frame of reference for family life as a business family and the relationship of the family with the ownership and business entities. The family has a very simple family chapter (constitution) that mainly addresses the conflict that could arise if family members decide to exit. However, the rest of the important elements of any family constitution were informally managed by the second generation of family members. The third generation and, eventually, the fourth generation need to make substantial changes to address the family's complexity. A new, more comprehensive constitution is needed to address the general challenges of Al Saud Company.

9.6 Case for analysis I: The family organization behind Al Handal International Group (HIG)[6]

HIG is a third-generation family business with humble beginnings in Iraq when Haji Noori Ayyed Al Handal began his entrepreneurial career in the early 1940s. In the 1990s, the second generation shifted part of the operations to the United Arab Emirates, looking for a stable country to internationalize. Today, from its headquarters in Dubai, the group operates several companies in the banking, real estate development, tourism, and hospitality sectors, among others.

HIG is a business group owned, governed, and managed by the Al Handal family. The integration of the family in the business has gradually professionalized to consolidate the family business-first orientation. The company has moved from the autocratic leadership of the founder to a meritocratic approach with a family governance structure to the latest movement to create their family office (Al Handal family office). The aim of the recent creation of the family office is to separate business wealth from family wealth and initiate an investing vehicle for the family.

The family governance changes were triggered by the death of one member from the second generation who generated several problems and conflicts among the family business owners, including legal battles. The family developed its own family constitution that helps family members regulate their expectations regarding the business and their intentions to initiate their professional careers in the family business. The family constitution focuses on the family's story to transmit the principles and values of the founder to the new generation, the vision of the family as a family in business, the expected communication among family members, and the main processes and activities to keep the family united. For instance, the family members meet two times per year to share, discuss, and exchange ideas and experiences at the personal level, group level, and family and business level.

Being a big family (with several siblings in the second generation and even more cousins in the third generation), those family members who are working in the company possess the biggest shares of the company. The family employment policy is the most important instrument to coordinate and lead the uncomfortable conversation with family members regarding their roles in the family business. Omar Al Handal, managing director at HIG, stated that "instilling in the next generation the family values and a sense of collective pride in the mission of the business is fundamental to future engagement."[7]

Discussion questions:

1 Family governance has to take into account the soft and hard issues of being a family in business. How is the Al Handal family dealing with this?
2 Explore the HIG website and have a look at the business and family governance sections. For instance, as of December 2022, the board of directors had seven members, five of whom were family members. What would be your recommendation for the family to continue structuring its family governance?

9.7 Case for analysis II: Merck—A family transcending generations[8]

"All you have to do is make sure that this heritage is passed on in one piece to the next generation"—Dr. Frank Stangenberg-Haverkamp, chairman of the board and 11th-generation family member.

A united family that has navigated a more than 350-year-old journey from Engel Apotheke (a local pharmacy in the town of Darmstadt, Germany) to Merck & Co Inc., Merck is a listed German multinational company with a presence in more than 66 countries and about 60,000 employees. The Merck family owns around 70% of the company via the E. Merck OHG holding company, and the rest of the company's ownership is public. There are around 204 family shareholders (the family firm is in its 13th family-owned generation), and not one of the family members has more than 3% of the total shares.

Discussion question:

1   How is the Merck family able to maintain cohesiveness across generations and align family members' goals to control and govern the long-term destiny of this complex business?

The Merck family developed a dual system of corporate governance that includes the business governance system and the family governance system. These two governance systems are not independent and communicate with each other. Beyond the classical governance structure for a listed company, Merck has carefully designed the family governance system to embrace all family members, thereby attempting to organize the complexity of the family, keep open communication, increase members' sense of belonging, and manage interpersonal conflicts.

- *Family shareholder meetings* (currently involving more than 200 family members) are used to inform family owners about the business as well as to ensure family members know each other and maintain their personal ties and commitment to the business. Family shareholders are responsible for electing representative members for the family board.
- The *family board* is a governance body formed of 13 family members elected by family owners at shareholder meetings (family members are trained to assume the role of family board member). The aim of the family board is to represent the interests of the family (owners) in the company in terms of controlling and supervising strategic oversight of the business. For some decision-making, the family board has veto power, such as for financial operations (e.g., merger or acquisition) that would require the owners' approval. The family board meets more frequently than members at family shareholder meetings—around 10 times per year. The family board is also responsible for selecting five of its members to represent the family in the supervisory board.
- The *board of partners* (acts as a supervisory board) is formed of nine members (five family members and four nonfamily members), and its aim is to supervise and control the managerial team and strategic implementation and execution. Of course, this group guarantees alignment between family interests and business interests.

Additionally, the Merck family has its own constitution that outlines the principles to guarantee the family–business relationship. The first constitution was written in 1888, and it is revised every 10 years to address upcoming challenges due to the family's evolution. It covers the most important rights and responsibilities for family members according to their roles (and overlapping roles) across the three entities (ownership, business, and family). It is about transparency, legal rights, differences between ownership and management, and the buy-and-sell agreement. For instance, family members can only sell their family business shares to other family members but at a discount of 20% of the market value.

Discussion questions:

2   What do you think about the strict separation between the operational management of the business and the family owners? Do you think this is a good solution for all family businesses?

3   What are the pros and cons of the family governance structure defined by the Merck family?

9.8 Case study: Al Saud Company and the first serious crisis[9]

The Al Saud Company is a family firm established in the late 1970s by Sheikh Saoud Bin Khalid Bin Khalid Al Qassimi in the Emirate of Sharjah in the newly established country of the United Arab Emirates (UAE). The new country enjoyed rapid development, and Sheikh Saoud took part in the boom by opening a firm that did business in the construction and real estate sectors. As the years passed, the company continued to grow, benefiting from the opportunities offered by the rapid growth of the UAE and the surrounding Gulf Cooperation Council (GCC) region. Local entrepreneurial families have played an important role in contributing to the UAE's development and supporting the ruler's direction for the country's strategic growth. After the death of the patriarch, Sheikh Saoud, in 2005, there was a shift in the family ownership distribution, and a family charter was drawn up to ensure the family remained united through the firm. Two brothers, Sheikh Saoud' sons, Majid and Sultan, took control of business operations. Majid became the chair of the firm, and Sultan took over as the managing director.

Sultan joined the firm in the late 1990s to spend time with his father. During this time, Sultan also learned a lot about the business. As any other family business in its first generation in the cultural context of the Gulf, the figure of the founder was immense, and communication moved around the figure of the patriarch. The father aligned family members' interests while maintaining family cohesiveness, but when the patriarch died, leadership needed to be rebuilt. Sultan wondered, "Now what!? How we can preserve the cohesiveness of the family to support the family business continuity?" It was the first thought that came to Sultan after his father's death. Where do we have to go as a family and as a firm? How can we really ensure our father's mandate to keep the family united and the business as a tool for this purpose?

Family business story. The origins of the family firm can be traced to Dallal Street in Colaba, Mumbai (then known as Bombay), where Sheikh Saoud spent part of his childhood living in humble circumstances with his grandmother, Ummi Mariam. He had moved to India for medical care that was unavailable in Sharjah at that time. After spending seven years in Mumbai and two years in Sharjah, at the age of 14, he moved to Kuwait, spending time with his mother, Fatima; his grandmother, Mariam; and his maternal uncle, Ibrahim. In 1964, he got married after returning to Sharjah to work in the accounting department of the Kuwaiti Office in Dubai.

Settling in Sharjah, he started his own business building small shops in the rapidly developing coastal districts, renting rooms above the shops, and finally building apartments for middle-income families. Sheikh Saoud's business was developing at a time of rapid economic growth in the Emirate of Sharjah. He was able to recognize opportunities and exploit them. In the beginning, Sheikh Saoud accepted risks as a necessity in his attempt to escape from poverty and to create, expand, and then consolidate his firm, earning a respected name in society throughout the process. Sheikh Saoud and his wife Sheikha Na'ma had seven children. All the children were granted shares in the firm from the time of their birth.

The business. When the firm began operations in the 1970s, it focused on the real estate and construction sectors. However, over the years, this model has been diversified through the redirection of profits into stock investments. While real estate and construction were focused within the Emirate of Sharjah, stock investments were focused within the GCC region. Sheikh Saoud developed a specific investment strategy to diversify risk across firms, industries, and countries within the region and to ensure stability while exploiting opportunities. However, Sheikh Saoud's investment strategy was developed for a world that lacked the instant communication technologies of today, so his regional focus was necessary for him to gain familiarity with the main stakeholders and their investment positions across the region. In some cases, he invested in companies to access their financial statements and other records. With this long-term strategy, Sheikh Saoud had mapped a network of the influential investors across GCC countries, allowing the firm to capture economic opportunities in the region while operating with businesses and individuals who were known entities.

During the 2000s, there were significant changes in the firm's business model. First, there was a shift in business activities as a source of income from construction to stock investments. Sultan convinced his father to refocus the business model by internationalizing the firm's stock investments beyond GCC countries. Currently, stock investments are the most important source of income for the firm. As the stock portfolio grew, construction activity was correspondingly reduced in importance as the sector became more and more competitive, requiring significant new investments as well as specialized knowledge to participate and thereby potentially exposing the firm to correspondingly high risk.

The current generation is managing the firm under the motto "do not take unnecessary risk." This attitude is a part of the business culture even though there is some resistance from non-executive family members who would prefer to move into investments that offer higher returns or begin new business activities, such as construction and mall administration. So far, Majid and Sultan have been able to adhere to their motto and block risky initiatives from other family members, crediting their conservative approach for minimizing the firm's troubles during the 2008 downturn.

The first crisis. In 2004, the family faced a crisis. Sheikh Saoud fell ill, and it was suddenly apparent that the issue of succession had not been adequately addressed, leaving the future of the firm uncertain. Due to Sharia law, male family members hold shares representing higher percentages of firm ownership than female family members. In fact, it is not uncommon in the region for male family members to buy the shares of female family members, leaving control of firms entirely in the hands of male descendants. The Al Saud Company, however, defied this local tradition, leaving female family members with their shares in the firm, albeit representing lower percentages of firm ownership than their male counterparts (see Tables 9.2). While this decision is progressive in terms of gender equality, it exacerbated issues related to firm unity and control by increasing the number of shareholders and increasing the potential for exponential expansion as the family tree continued to develop more branches.

Table 9.2 Ownership composition before and after Sheikh Saoud's death

Owner	Before	After
Sheikh Saoud	20%	-
Sheikha Na'ma	10%	12.5%
Majid (eldest)	12%	15.9%
Majd	6%	7.9%
Nourah	6%	7.9%
Khalid	12%	15.9%
Sultan	12%	15.9%
Layla	6%	7.9%
Abdulaziz	12%	15.9%

Even though the family was united, holding social family meetings and having strong interactions among them, the father managed conversations about the firm and opened and closed communication channels in his own particular way due to his hierarchical communication style with a high level of conformity. That is, no one disagreed with their father's decisions and opinions. The father was the individual who maintained family unity and controlled family wealth.

Discussion question:

1   What type of family governance can Sheikh Sultan design for the family to keep the family united while maintaining a profitable business?

Second generation—New leadership. Since Sheikh Saoud's death, the firm and family cohesion required by Majid and Sultan's vision has been maintained under Sultan's leadership in the family sphere, assisted by Sheikha Na'ma, who took on an important role in settling contentious issues through her embodiment of Sheikh Saoud's legacy.

The rest of the shareholders had minimal impact on the business's daily decision-making. In the particular context of the UAE and considering the sectors in which the family firm competes, risk was the main concern. Therefore, there were two important issues to maintain the health of the firm: (1) preventing the firm from taking on financial risks that could threaten the wealth at the root of the firm and (2) maintaining a sufficient return from that wealth to keep the family united around the firm as the best vehicle to manage the family's wealth. Majid and Sultan understood the need to control risk and, consequently, developed a clear investment strategy in this sense.

Majid, having extensive experience in the business and being the eldest male in the second generation, took primary responsibility for overseeing the business, while Sultan managed and successfully strengthened the relationship between the family and the firm. Sultan persuaded family members to define specific spaces for interacting and discussing both family issues and business issues. For instance, he implemented annual family shareholder meetings as a way to keep the family informed about business activities and to debate relevant issues related to the management of the business, the ownership structure, and the relationship between the family and the business.

When Sultan and Majid became the leaders of the firm, they not only managed and controlled the daily operations, but they were also able to control voice in the ownership meetings with the support of their mother. They established a family charter to ensure the firm and the family would stay together, even convincing family members to restore company assets that Sheikh Saoud had distributed before passing away. Sheikh Saoud believed that "arrows when apart are fragile but bound together are unbreakable," a saying attributed to Ma'n ibn Za'ida, an eighth-century Arab general who was also important to Sultan. Sultan has been the primary peacemaker between the family members, who—like in any family—have had their share of disagreements. An important part of the family constitution is the buy-and-sell agreement, which prohibits family members from selling their shares outside the family and even discourages sales of shares within the family by setting the price of transferred shares at 25% below market value.

Despite its restrictions, the charter enjoys broad support among the siblings because it is seen as honoring and preserving Sheikh Saoud's legacy, and no family members have been so dissatisfied with the management of the firm that they have availed themselves of the buy-and-sell agreement.

Discussion questions:

2 Do you think the new family governance mechanisms were effective for keeping the cohesiveness of the family?
3 What threats could the family face in the near future? Do you think these threats would require changes in the family business governance?

Notes

1 Pieper, T., & Astrachan, J. H. (2008). *Mechanisms to Assure Family Business Cohesion: Guidelines for Family Business Leaders and Their Families*. Kennesaw, GA: Cox Family Enterprise Center.
2 Additional information from the company website: www.abcrecycling.com/about-us/the-story-of-abc-recycling
3 Stone, D. (2009). Communication and commitment. *Family Business Magazine*. Article retrieved from www.familybusinessmagazine.com/communication-and-commitment-0
4 Information retrieved from the company website: www.haniel.de/company/
5 An example of family employment policy is the SABI—Family Employment Policy. Information can be retrieved from www.aidaf.it/wp-content/uploads/2014/09/FamilyBusinessGovernance_Handbook_English.pdf
6 This example discussion is developed solely as the basis for class discussion. This example discussion is not intended to serve as an endorsement, source of primary data, or illustration of effective or ineffective management. Information retrieved from www.youtube.com/embed/ancD_6Z9OyU?rel=0, https://alhandal.me/about#LeaderMessage, and Clemens, D. (2021). Al Handal International Group: A culture of giving and the Family Office Interview with Omar Al Handal, Managing Director at Al Handal International Group, Dubai Office. *Tharawat Magazine*. Article retrieved from www.tharawat-magazine.com/stories/al-handal-culture-of-continuity/
7 Clemens, D. (2021). Al Handal International Group: A Culture of Giving and the Family Office Interview with Omar Al Handal, Managing Director at Al Handal International Group, Dubai Office. Tharawat Magazine. Article retrieved from www.tharawat-magazine.com/stories/al-handal-culture-of-continuity/
8 This example discussion is developed solely as the basis for class discussion. This example discussion is not intended to serve as an endorsement, source of primary data, or illustration of effective or ineffective management. Bhatnagar, N. (2019). 350 years of family business: Lessons from Merck. ISBI Insight. Article retrieved from https://isbinsight.isb.edu/350-years-of-family-business-lessons-from-merck/
9 This case study discussion is developed solely as the basis for class discussion. This case study discussion is not intended to serve as an endorsement, source of primary data, or illustration of effective or ineffective management. Basco, R., & Brodtkorb, T. (2020). *Saud Bin Majid's Dilemma*. Sharjah: American University of Sharjah.

Part IV
Succession in family business

10 Ownership, governance, and management succession

Learning objectives

- Distinguish the different types of succession that family businesses have to face.
- Understand succession as an event and as a process.
- Recognize the pre- and post-succession periods in the succession process.
- Identify actions and activities during the pre- and post-succession periods.
- Interpret the barriers for intra-family management succession.

10.1 Introduction

Succession is one of the most important challenges for family business continuity because the owning family's intention to pass the business from one generation to another and create a family legacy around the business may collide with reality. The tensions between family members' intentions and reality manifest as a lack of having a prepared and mature successor or even incumbent, a lack of strategic direction of the owning family as the main shareholder, and/or a lack of interest from the next generation to assume family business leadership, among others. Therefore, family intention is not enough to guide all participants through the succession process. Intention needs to be transformed into individual and collective behavior, which requires coordinated actions and processes toward the succession goal. Therefore, succession is about managing and orchestrating a process that embraces different participants, and leading this process requires unique abilities and competencies to direct interpersonal relationships and to handle financial, economic, and strategic issues across ownership, governance, and management.

Succession is a broad concept and can be interpreted differently by family members with different roles across the ownership, management, and family entities. While for some stakeholders, succession is an event that entails family wealth being transferred from one generation to the next, for other stakeholders, succession is a process with different steps that involves participants transmitting leadership from one generation to another. Consequently, the main question that emerges for participants is, succession of what?

For the purpose of this chapter, succession is an event and a process related to the transfer of ownership and/or leadership (governance and management), and it is intrinsically related to the individuals involved. Succession could be viewed narrowly as involving one or few individuals (e.g., successor and incumbent) or more broadly as embracing all stakeholders who are directly or indirectly affected by succession.

Succession is a challenging issue that requires significant attention from family businesses to ensure a sustainable business, a cohesive family, and consolidated wealth. The aim of this chapter is to introduce the fundamental concepts of succession in family businesses by reflecting

DOI: 10.4324/9781003273240-14

on the different types of succession, the complexity of succession, and the barriers to intra-family succession.

10.2 Succession of what?

Succession can have different meanings for families, and these meanings depend on the generational stage of the family, business, and ownership entities and on the complexity of the family–business relationship. However, for all families, succession is the point of departure and point of arrival in terms of ownership, governance, and management. Succession is a transgenerational family intention (of one individual or of a group of individuals) to own, govern, and manage the family business across generations as well as a form of behavior (actions and processes) to achieve this transgenerational goal. While succession intention is a good predictor of succession behavior, two questions guide succession: who and where are we as a family and family business, and who and where would we like to be as a family and family business?

Ownership succession is the most important transgenerational intention for business families because owners exercise effective control over the business, and ownership confers the power to decide the destiny of the family business across generations. We can interpret family ownership as a continuum with two ends (Figure 10.1). On the right side of the continuum is a fully family-owned business where the family (one or more family members) owns 100% of the shares, and on the left side of the continuum is a nonfamily business without family ownership of shares or where the family owns a minority portion of the shares (this is the succession option for the family exit strategy). In between these ends, there are different degrees of family ownership where a family (one or several family members) partially owns a business. In a private family business, the family should own more than 50% of the business to exercise effective control, whereas in a public firm, this percentage could be lower than 50% but should still be high enough to maintain voting rights to exercise effective control over the business. For instance, the Ford family owns only a tiny portion of Ford Motor Company stock since the family diluted its

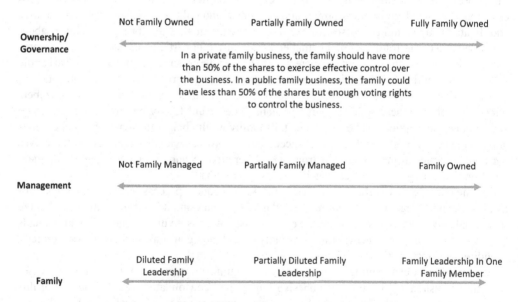

Figure 10.1 Configurations of ownership, governance, management, and family succession.

position when the company went public in the middle of 1955. However, Ford family members possess specific types of shares, giving them more than 40% of the voting rights. Ownership succession is intrinsically linked to governance succession because the ownership structure of a business determines the structure and dynamic of the business's corporate governance.

In addition to ownership succession (and its implications for governance succession), management succession is another transgenerational issue and is related to the operative (day-to-day) control over the business. Management succession is about shifting business leadership from one generation to another (or to external nonfamily members) to define the operative and strategic control over the business. Management succession can also be seen as a continuum with two ends (Figure 10.1). On the right side of the continuum is a family-managed business where the top management team is mainly formed by family members. On the left side is a nonfamily-managed business where family members are not involved in day-to-day operative and strategic decisions (strategic implementation). In between both ends, there are several combinations of family involvement that result in partially family-managed businesses.

Finally, succession is also about family succession. Family succession means there is a leadership shift from one generation to another on issues related to family wealth and family business matters as well as a new family structure and relationships. In any family business succession, there is a reconfiguration of roles and, consequently, a reconfiguration of interpersonal relationships through which new family leaders emerge. Family leadership could overlap with business leadership (a common situation in most family businesses) or not (i.e., family business leaders are not family leaders). Family succession can be seen as a continuum with two ends (Figure 10.1). On the right side of the continuum, family leadership rests in one family member. This is the common form of succession in families with hierarchical family structures and authoritarian cultures. For instance, in Middle Eastern or Asian families, families tend to pass leadership from one member to another because of cultural tradition, such as the primogeniture approach. This is even more common in families with very informal family governance. On the left side of the continuum, family leadership is diluted among several family members. In this case, the participative family culture may not only determine the type of leadership but also the formality of family governance. A formal family governance structure helps business families dilute leadership among several family members across different governance arenas.

Any family business should reflect on what ownership, governance, management, and family structures exist today and what ownership, governance, management, and family structures are needed in the future (next generations). Therefore, family business succession requires a specific understanding of the combination of ownership, governance, management, and family issues by considering what the business family is today and what it would like to be in the future.

Ownership, governance, management, and family succession could occur simultaneously or at different moments of time. The moment of time that each succession occurs is contingent on different family business characteristics, external forces, and specific circumstances. Among the family business characteristics, the most common are the complexity of each entity (ownership, business, and family), the formal and informal mechanisms for interactions, and the number of generations and family members that succession may affect. For instance, while preparing for succession, the Al Fahim family in Saudi Arabia decided to consolidate all of its economic activities into one holding—a risky move because doing so implied embracing the family in one structure and professionalizing the family–business relationship. Mohammed Abdul Rahim Al Fahim, CEO of the Paris Gallery Group, expressed this idea about the succession changes: "I do not believe, however, that everyone understood everything they agreed upon in this partnership." He also highlighted the following:

Some family members certainly didn't see the whole picture and didn't understand the responsibilities they would have to shoulder and the sacrifices they would have to make for such a combined venture to succeed. They just saw themselves as family members who were entitled to the business and its assets. We put in place a board of directors, which consisted of my brothers and me. My father didn't want to be a member. He wanted to leave it to us because he trusted us.[1]

External forces refer to the political and economic events that can trigger or constrain family business succession. For instance, new laws and regulations could increase or reduce inheritance tax and may thus accelerate or delay ownership succession for tax advantages. Finally, there are specific circumstances that could alter the dynamics of family business succession by accelerating or delaying the succession process, such as the illness of an important family member, poor family business performance, and the dilution of ownership/new owners due to unexpected inheritance. For instance, the COVID-19 pandemic has accelerated succession in family businesses across the world by increasing family members' awareness of the need to have a succession plan or by suddenly triggering ownership, governance, and management succession.[2]

10.2.1 Types of succession in family business

The most common intention for families is to maintain high ownership control over their businesses and, if possible, direct influence over management. The combination of family ownership and family management is the best option for business families to directly control the destiny of their family businesses. Ownership and management make families the power to preserve and increase the economic, social, and emotional benefits of being linked to a business.

The extreme option is to maintain a fully family-owned and family-managed business. Family-owned and managed business succession has some advantages, such as continuity of the family legacy, preservation of family values and principles in the business, transfer of implicit knowledge from one generation to another, and conservation of family commitment to the business. However, there are several challenges, such as nominating and selecting the next leaders from a limited pool of candidates, educating the next generation of family members, managing conflicts among the increasing number of family members, implementing better and more formal governance structures, and managing growth and expansion by balancing the distribution/reinvestment of family business benefits.

Beyond the family-owned and managed option, there are several succession alternatives for family businesses that involve sharing control (ownership) and management with external individuals (nonfamily members) or other institutions (investors). Involving external nonfamily individuals or institutions could have advantages for family businesses—for instance, pruning the tree by removing family members or family branches that are not committed to the business, receiving new capital to finance expansion and increase liquidity, reducing risk with external partners, and increasing pressure to avoid certain family behaviors (e.g., altruism) that could reduce the competitiveness of the business. However, this option could also raise several challenges for family businesses—for instance, increasing conflicts of interest (e.g., goal discrepancy in terms of return expectations, management compensation, and the strategic direction of the business, among others) between family and nonfamily owners; increasing pressure for an ownership exit strategy, which can increase emotional problems and thus harm the business; and boosting the cost of coordinating ownership, management, and family priorities.

Becoming a public family business is an option when the intention is to open the ownership of the business. Initial public offering (IPO) is a possibility for some businesses, but it requires significant organizational changes, which should be aligned with well-known corporate governance practices (at the ownership, business, and family levels). Among the best advantages of this option are increased market pressure for developing transparent and professional business and family governance mechanisms, the existence of a market for selling shares (the value of the business is known in case family members would like to exit), the opportunity to finance growth and expansion, and the chance to develop a more market-oriented business culture. The risks of this option are that the family loses influence in the business and is no longer able to impose its own values and principles. Additionally, the excessive pressure from the market for short-term performance (instead of long-term performance) may shock the family culture. Finally, classical agency problems (principal–agent and principal–principal conflicts) tend to emerge.

In some countries, such as the United Arab Emirates, there is governmental pressure and high incentives for family businesses (most of them huge family conglomerates due to excessive protection from the government) to become public family businesses.[3] The implicit aim of this new legislation is to preserve the competitiveness of local family businesses by using the market logic to reduce nepotism, the tribal culture of doing business, and authoritarian leadership practices, all of which did successfully contribute to the economic development of the country but are no longer effective in its new knowledge- and entrepreneurial-based economy.

Opening ownership to nonfamily individuals and institutions is one succession option for family businesses, but it is generally combined with opening management to external individuals (nonfamily members) or passing leadership to nonfamily members. Relaxing family management via external nonfamily members and integrating them into operative decision-making is an option that comes with firm growth and development. This option has advantages: the strategic implementation lies in a diversified group of professionals; there is a wider pool of talent for managerial positions and, eventually, for the management successor; the renewal of management talent is not limited to family options; and nonfamily members could help the family business balance family-oriented and business-oriented goals. These benefits of incorporating nonfamily members into the top management team are not without challenges—for instance, selecting appropriate managers from the labor market, fitting nonfamily members into the family business culture, handling faultlines between the family and nonfamily managers, aligning nonfamily managers' goals with family goals, and managing nonfamily managers' expectations due to the potential glass ceiling for their careers.

Ownership and management succession options could be the result of an explicit, deliberative, and consensual agreement among family members or could emerge as a reaction to external circumstances beyond the family's control. That is, family businesses reconfigure their ownership, management, and family structures because of unpredicted events, specific circumstances, and/or the natural evolution of each entity. For instance, an external financial crisis alongside a liquidity crisis in the business could force a family business to incorporate external (nonfamily members) into its ownership. This is the case of the shoemaker Clarks, a UK family business established in 1825. In 2021, the family lost control of the company, selling 51% of shares to a Hong Kong-based investor after being hit hard by the COVID-19 pandemic and failing to adopt 21st-century trends fast enough.[4] Additionally, internal forces can also precipitate changes. The exponential growth of family members across generations could force family businesses to take specific directions regarding ownership and management. However, via their governance structures, families and their family businesses should be able to anticipate possible future events and specific circumstances stemming from the complexity of the family and lifecycle evolution of each entity by planning for succession.

10.2.2 Exit strategy (from a family business to a nonfamily business)

When business families want to exit ownership and management, there are several options available for them. One of the most common exit strategies is the management buyout option whereby current nonfamily managers become owners and continue the business activities. This option has several advantages for families who would like to offer continuity to their businesses as it projects a responsible image in society, provides stability to the rest of the stakeholders, and produces a less traumatic change for employees. However, sometimes, this succession option is not easy to implement, and several challenges can emerge. For instance, financial issues can necessitate that third parties lend money to the new managers, there can be a lack of agreement on the value of the business between family members and buyers, emotional conflicts can arise when determining the final price, and achieving the expected goals can require a long process. This was the succession option for Baltic Amadeous, the first private information technology firm in Lithuania founded by a group of friends at the end of the 1980s, which is today a leading company in the region with an international presence. The founders developed the business together but instead of having a family business structure (ownership, governance, and management combined with multiple family branches), they preferred to sell the business to the current management team. In 2018, Andžej Šuškevič and Vytautas Kaminskas became the main shareholders.

Another option beyond management buyout is to sell the business to financial or strategic buyers. Financial buyers are speculative in nature and focus on the final return that a business can produce when it is sold again in the near future via an IPO or to other investors. On the other hand, strategic buyers who are less speculative are generally other businesses that would like to acquire a family business for strategic reasons and tend to have a long-term view for the acquisition. For example, this was the case when Luxotica, the largest eyewear manufacturer in the world controlled by the Del Vecchio family, acquired the Carinelli family business group Tecnol in 2011. The CEO of Luxottica stated, "This operation perfectly fits into our long-term growth strategy."[5] With both options, the number of potential buyers can be high so business families can benefit from maximizing the selling price of their family businesses. However, having financial buyers could have several consequences for business continuity as well as implications for stakeholders since such buyers are likely going to introduce several changes to improve firm productivity, such as structural adjustments and operative, administrative, and labor cost reductions. Strategic buyers tend to introduce less radical changes and, to a certain extent, tend to keep the conditions and cultures of family businesses.

10.3 Complexity in family business succession

Family business succession is complex because it requires considering the current and future dynamics of the three entities, their interactions, the individuals involved, and the external context in which the family business operates and the family dwells.

*   *Altering individual needs, expectations, and goals.* At the individual level, succession alters participants' positions across the three entities and, consequently, their roles in the family business system. This means that succession shapes individuals' needs, expectations, and goals. The next generation of family members' expectations change as they move from the beginning of their careers in their 20s to more senior positions and having family responsibilities on their hands. In this sense, with succession, each family member has to adjust his or her role and consequently his or her needs, expectations, and goals. It is difficult to anticipate

the direction of these new needs, expectations, and goals, but it is necessary to anticipate such changes when drawing up the succession plan. The higher the complexity of the family, the more difficult it is to address family members' needs, expectations, and goals across the succession process.

- *Succession means changes.* Succession implies changes in the status quo for different individuals across the ownership, business, and family entities. Family members are moved from their comfort zones (positions). For some members, succession means significant changes (economic, social, and emotional changes), and for other individuals, succession means small changes that alter their economic or social interpersonal relationships. Any succession entails decisions to keep the status quo or alter it. Because of the uncertainty these changes can produce in individuals' lives, some family members may resist them, so the succession plan should anticipate the psychological forces associated with being afraid of change.
- *Lack of a planning culture in the family entity.* Ownership, governance, management, and family succession requires concrete plans to recognize the succession point of departure and point of arrival to keep a cohesive family and sustainable business across generations. However, planning is not always part of the family culture, so there is often a tendency to postpone it until succession is imminent because of specific circumstances or events.
- *Technical and structural complexity.* Depending on the complexity of the ownership, business, and family entities, specific knowledge may be needed to coordinate the different aspects of succession. Aspects related to interpersonal relationships, organizational and management matters, and legal and tax issues need to be considered. In some cases, one or few family members cannot address all of these issues, thereby requiring a multidisciplinary approach with the participation of external professionals to support the process.
- *Lack of/imperfect capital markets.* Specifically in private family businesses, the main succession problem is defining the value of the family business. Succession could increase family owners' appetite to know the value of their participation. The problem of liquidity (family firms are fully or highly illiquid) is combined with asymmetric information (transparency regarding the real financial wealth of the family business) and psychological ownership (the increased valuation that owners give to the assets they possess), which makes it challenging to identify and agree upon the value of the family business.
- *Uncertain process.* Since succession is a process, it will take some business families longer to complete. The longer the process, the more uncertain the outcome in terms of ownership, governance, management, and family succession. Uncertainty could affect the competitiveness of the family business. For instance, when one of the family business's competitive advantages lies in the current leader's close relationships with suppliers, a delay and subsequent lack of definition in nominating, selecting, and training the future successor may affect and alter these strategic relationships.

10.3.1 Barriers to intra-family management succession

The intention to pass management leadership from one family generation to another is one of the main aims of the incumbent generation to ensure the continuity of the family legacy. Intra-family management succession occurs when both the incumbent leaders who relinquish managerial leadership and the successors who take over management leadership are family members. For some families, family management represents the main mechanism to perpetuate the family values and principles in the business and to project the family interests across generations. Family involvement in management provides meaning to members of the current generation by enabling them build on the previous generation's economic, social, and emotional wealth and to project the family's vision for future generations.

Intra-family management succession is one of the most critical issues for families that would like to keep family members involved in business operations and directly influence the business's day-to-day decision-making. However, there are several barriers that families may have to address to ensure continuity during intra-family management succession.

- **Individual factors**
  - *Abilities, skills, and capabilities of potential successors to take on management leadership.* It is important to recognize to what extent potential family members are prepared to assume management leadership. Are they equipped with the knowledge, experience, skills, and abilities to continue the family legacy? Are they eager to increase the family's economic, social, and emotional wealth?
  - *Motivation of potential successors to join the family businesses.* Families need to acknowledge to what extent potential successors have real motivation to develop their professional careers within the boundaries of the family business while serving the family.
  - *Unexpected losses/health issues (successor and/or incumbent) that can change the dynamics of interpersonal relationships and the succession plan.* Families need to notice to what extent mechanisms exists that will ensure the continuity of the family business under unexpected circumstances and facilitate the transfer of the tacit knowhow and knowledge that has accumulated across generations.
  - *Incumbent generation's inability to exit (let the business go).* The incumbent generation's inability to let the business go could postpone succession and perpetuate the transition indefinitely. When the incumbent generation is not ready to transfer management to the next generation, members may use different excuses, such as the next generation not being ready to assume leadership, the incumbent generation not having financial security for retirement, and the incumbent generation's psychological attachment to the business, among others.
  - *Unexpected personal changes that can alter the succession process, such as divorce, marriage, and stepchildren.* In some situations, the most important individuals involved in the succession process may alter their marital status, or new unexpected family members may appear on the scene.
- **Relational factors**
  - *Dynamics of parent–child (incumbent–successor) relationships are crucial for successful succession.* The quality of the interpersonal relationships among members of the two generations who have to work together affect the level of conflict (both positive and negative) that can alter, accelerate, or slow the succession process.
  - *Dynamics of interpersonal relationships among family members who are not directly involved in the succession process but could be affected by it.* For instance, siblings who are or will be owners but do not work in the business and in-law family members could have indirect effects on succession by generating noise in the process though their behavior or communication styles. This barrier emerges when there is a lack of trust between the successor(s) and the rest of the family members and a lack of commitment to potential successor(s) among family members.
  - *Fictional consensus as a mechanism to keep the family united.* Some business families prefer mutual agreement as a way to avoid conflicts instead of looking for the optimal solution that could lead to better results but would entail friction and conflicts. This

mean that families do not necessarily select the most profitable or effective solution for their businesses but instead choose a solution that may satisfy all family voices to avoid conflicts.

- **Familial factors**
  - *Lack of family governance structure to address intra-family management succession.* Precarious family governance may jeopardize the cohesion of the family to support the managerial transition from one generation to another. Governance could help families improve communication, reach agreement and consensus, and educate family members on their responsibilities as owners and managers.
  - *Lack of family cohesion to sustain family commitment to the business.* Lack of cohesion and commitment means that the family does not have a common long-term vision to navigate succession challenges or the energy to compromise and find solutions to achieve successful outcomes.
- **Financial factors**
  - *Tax problems in relation to ownership succession.* Tax issues can generate problems during intra-family management succession in terms of timing, ownership structure, and governance solutions. When ownership and management succession are handled in parallel, technical and legal issues could alter the flow of management succession.
  - *Lack of market to sell family business shares and/or lack of liquidity of the family or family business to purchase shares (to prune the family ownership tree).* This barrier could force family members who are not committed to the business to stay on as owners. These unsatisfied owners may alter the dynamics of the ownership, business, and family entities with their needs, expectations, and goals, thereby preventing the alignment of interests with the rest of the family members.
  - *Family business financial problems and lack of sustainable business model.* Business-related issues, such as financial problems, the attractiveness of the industry, and the complexity of the business itself, among others, could affect successors' enthusiasm, increase conflicts between generations, and postpone the intra-family management succession decision because successors are skeptical about whether to join the family business or not.
  - *Increased business complexity that makes it too difficult to keep management in family hands.* Sometimes a business becomes so complex and difficult to manage that the possibility of handing over operative leadership (day-to-day decision-making) to family members is difficult if not impossible. In this case, alternative forms of family control are needed.
  - *Small business scale that affects successors' interests.* Sometimes the small scale of a family business makes successors unable to see themselves managing it. The small business scale clashes with such successors' ambitions and with the rest of the family members' desire to earn enough returns (via dividends) from their investments.
- **Processual factors**
  - *Lack of planning and developing alternatives actions for contingencies.* When intra-family management succession is a spontaneous and unplanned event, unexpected results may arise. The final outcome of succession with no planning is subject to different challenges, such as a lack of clear roles for family participants; poor communication; incongruence between participants' needs, expectations, and goals; unsuccessful preparation of the incumbent to exit; and a lack of development of the successor to enter. Additionally, there are no alternative actions to guide decision-making to cope with unforeseen contingencies. For instance, the incumbent's health issues could affect

the transfer of leadership, and the potential successor may not be ready or prepared to assume the leadership role.

- **Contextual factors**
  - *External shocks (economic, cultural, and political) altering the succession process.* External shocks can slow down and even paralyze the succession process. Such shocks can also accelerate the management transfer, thereby leading to a premature succession that the successor and the rest of the family participants and stakeholders are not ready for.
  - *Sector/industry changes that may affect participants' willingness to join the business.* The attractiveness and future prospects of the sector/industry may affect family members' desire to stay on as owners and to support the succession process. They could also make the successor reevaluate his or her decision to join the firm or not.
  - *Stakeholders' trust in the new generation of family members.* Family businesses are usually strongly embedded in their regional economic structures, and their social capital acts as their competitive advantage. Thus, external stakeholders could determine, constrain, and otherwise influence the pace of the management succession process. In some family businesses, external support from stakeholders is a determinant of intra-family management succession.

10.4 Succession process perspective

The view of succession as a process describes a set of informal and formal actions, events, and interactions that drive the ownership, governance, management, and family transition from one generation to another (see Figure 10.2).

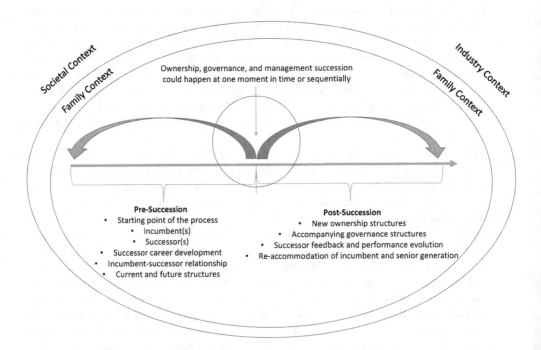

Figure 10.2 Succession process.

- *Types of succession.* The events of ownership, governance, and management succession can happen simultaneously at one particular moment of time or in a sequence of steps. In some cases, ownership, governance, and management succession are completed at the same time, but this situation is not common because each has a different pace, requires different decisions, and involves different individuals. For instance, all three forms of succession may be completed at once due to the unexpected loss of an incumbent who was an owner–manager, with the event triggering ownership, governance, and management succession simultaneously. This was the case for Ulrich, owner of the Florax Group, a pharmaceutical firm in the Netherlands, who—on his deathbed—asked his eldest son to sell the business as he had planned and financially take care of his brother and mother. The complicated relationship between the brothers persuaded Ulrich that the best option would be to sell the firm. The father's death changed the dynamics of the business: new ownership, new governance, and new management. Sjak, one of the Ulrich's son, ultimately decided to continue with the business and keep the family tradition, and he ended up buying his mother's and brother's shares.[6] However, it is more common for ownership, governance, and management succession to occur at different moments of time, the sequence of which varies from one family business to another. The order is not irrelevant and should respond to the family's and business's needs to achieve a successful succession outcome. For example, in some family businesses, management succession is the first step followed by governance succession and finalizing with a new ownership structure, while in others, ownership succession is first followed by governance and management succession.
- *Succession process.* No matter the timing of the different types of succession, the succession process has the pre- and post-succession periods. The pre-succession period involves what happens before the succession-triggering event(s) and how the family, business, and relevant individuals prepare themselves for succession. The post-succession phase entails what happens after the succession-triggering event(s) and how the family, business, and relevant individuals fit into the new family and business contexts.
- *The pre-succession period* includes all actions and interactions that are necessary to coordinate and prepare each entity and the associated members for succession.
  - *Starting point of the process.* It is important to identify the gravity center of succession—the family, the business, or both simultaneously. Fundamental questions may emerge: Who are we as a business family? Where would we like to go as a business family? How can we achieve our desires as a family? What is the role of the family business in our family? What kind of family business do we currently have, and what would we like to have in the next generation? Succession planning can help a family increase family members' involvement in and commitment to the business and recognize the shift it will experience during succession and its relationship with the business. Most likely, the governance bodies are the main arenas to discuss and coordinate succession planning. However, when there is no family governance or it is not mature enough, it could be important to implement mechanisms to formalize the discussion and have a written roadmap for succession. Succession means reaching consensus among family members to overcome the challenges of transferring ownership, governance, and management from one generation to another. It requires developing the family's shared vision while promoting family harmony and cohesiveness.
  - *Incumbents.* Regardless of the formality of the succession planning, it is important to recognize who the incumbents are and their intentions and commitment toward their exit. Ownership, governance, and management succession mean economic (loss of power), financial (loss of income), social (loss of status in the business community), and emotional

(loss of identity) changes for incumbents. Succession should address the fear, anxiety, and uncertainty of the incumbents to improve the quality of the process. However, any action to address these issues requires previous knowledge of the incumbent's personality. Additionally, the number of incumbents, incumbents' relationships, firm size and performance, and the complexity of the family all affect an incumbent's approach to succession.

- *Successor(s)*. As important as the incumbents are the successors in terms of the selection criteria and development programs. The number of successors, their commitment, motivation, and abilities and capabilities all need to be considered. Individuals who do not demonstrate commitment and motivation and those chosen based on cultural imperatives, such as the primogeniture rules, require different approaches to train, educate, and coach them as successors than those who freely assume the responsibility to continue the family legacy. The dynamics of the succession process change when the successor is a nonfamily member because the potential candidate needs to develop a cultural and emotional fit with members from each of the three entities (ownership, governance, and management).
- *Successor career development*. Business families need to define the conditions/requirements to access the succession nomination (e.g., education and outside work experience), the actions to train the successor, and the professional career path the successor needs to follow in the family business. All of these actions are important in helping successors develop their capabilities, abilities, and skills; gain credibility and legitimacy among family members and other stakeholders; build internal and external relationships; gain self-confidence; and shape their own identities. Some of these aspects of succession career development are also important when a nonfamily member will become the future leader of the family business.
- *Incumbent–successor relationship*. This aspect is one of the most important to take into consideration when planning for and practicing the execution of succession. The quality of this relationship matters (in terms of mutual respect, communication, and trust, among others) to smooth the learning process, transmit tacit knowledge, share key social connections (stakeholders), and manage the generational gap.
- *Current and future ownership structures*. In the pre-succession period, it is important to recognize the current and future ownership structures. In this sense, succession should develop and implement all mechanisms to ensure the future ownership structure the family desires. This means contemplating tax issues, liquidity to buy shares from family shareholders who would like to exit, and the possibility of lending money to family owners to acquire other family members' shares.
- *Post-succession period*. Succession does not end with the ownership, governance, and management transfer. Instead, it continues beyond the effective transfer or reorganization of ownership, governance, and management. The post-succession period thus entails overseeing the new family–business relationship and intervening when unexpected succession outcomes or circumstances arise.
  - *New ownership structure*. After ownership reorganization, a new power structure emerges (conferred by property) as well as shifts in terms of roles within the ownership, management, and family entities. A learning process starts for all family members as they adjust their roles to their new positions.
  - *Accompanying changes in the governance structures*. Succession implies changes in the ownership, business, and family governance structures. The new governance structures should satisfy the complexity of needs, expectations, and goals of the next generation and

senior family members. Since new structures, positions, and roles are in place, timing is crucial for developing strong new governance.

- *Successor feedback and performance evaluation.* The post-succession period requires implementing procedures for successor development, support, and evaluation. These procedures could be more formal when governance structures exist and the board of directors can coordinate them in collaboration with the family council. They can also be more informal when the family business does not have formal structures and interactions between the senior generation and next generations are enough to share feedback and evaluate performance.
- *Incumbent and senior generations' adjustment to their new positions and roles.* In the same way successors receive feedback and performance evaluations, family members from the senior generation who changed positions and roles also need to receive feedback, support, and training (if necessary) to satisfactorily fulfill the needs, expectations, and goals in their new lifecycle stage (retirement or partial retirement).

- *Context.* Succession can be constrained by being embedded in different contexts—namely, the family, industry, and societal contexts.
  - *The family context* is characterized by family culture, family interpersonal dynamics, family commitment, and family complexity (in terms of structure). The family is the nearest institution that may affect the dynamics of the succession process and its outcomes. It represents the strongest institutional force in directing the successor process and the associated activities and actions.
  - *The industry context* refers to the focal industry's internal dynamics and complexity in terms of competition, innovation, regulation, and entrance barriers, among others, all of which can accelerate or slow the succession process and/or constrain the associated actions and activities. For instance, the prospect of industry evolution in relation to innovation may require the successor development program to refine successors' abilities, skills, and capabilities to successfully lead the family business in the future.
  - *The societal context* refers to broader dimensions, such as culture, social norms, ethics, religion, and laws, that—to a certain extent—affect the direction of the succession process because succession should be accepted within the context in which it occurs to ensure legitimacy.

10.5 Additional activities and reading material

10.5.1 Classroom discussion questions

1 What types of succession do family businesses have to face?
2 What are the most common barriers that can prevent intra-family management succession?
3 Why is it important to consider succession as a process instead of as an event?
4 Is succession in family businesses more complex than in nonfamily businesses? Why?
5 Do you think succession should be planned in advance? Who is responsible for this planning?

10.5.2 Additional readings

1 Gapper, J. (2022). How to succeed with a family business succession. *Financial Times.* Article retrieved from www.ft.com/content/38379d99-1ae9-4cf2-9863-312549dd9e83
2 Jaskiewicz, P., De Massis, A., & Dieleman, M. (2021). The future of the family business: 4 strategies for a successful transition. *The Conversation.* Article retrieved from https://theconve rsation.com/the-future-of-the-family-business-4-strategies-for-a-successful-transition-156191

3 Matthews, H. (2017). It's uncomfortable, but family businesses need succession planning. *The Guardian*. Article retrieved from www.theguardian.com/small-business-network/2017/oct/02/family-businesses-succession-planning-littles-chauffeurs

10.5.3 Classroom activity

Aim: Reflect on the succession process.

Material: Ask students watch the movie *The Inheritance* directed by Per Fly before coming to class.

Instruction during class: Divide the classroom into groups with four to five members in each group.

- Ask students to reflect on the succession process.
- Ask students to prepare a business consultant report to highlight the problems the family business faces and the consequences of the highlighted problems.
- Ask students to prepare a business consultant report to define a succession plan for the family business. What could the father have done before to successfully address succession?

Takeaways: The Inheritance can help students understand the complexity of family business succession and the barriers, processes, actions, activities, and contexts that leaders should consider when the time to discuss, plan, and implement succession arrives. In this exercise, students can assume the role of a family business consultant to reflect on any mistakes and what kinds of actions could have been taken to successfully guide the family in the succession process.

10.6 Case for analysis I: The global pasta—Barilla[7]

Barilla is a family-owned Italian food group with an international presence. Guido Barilla, chairman of Barilla Group, expressed the essence of the family business as follows: "Basically, we are pasta makers and bakers; this is the line of work our family has pursued over the last four generations, with the help of outstanding coworkers. It is the only line of work we can and try to improve every day."[8]

It is interesting to observe the family's identification with the business after four generations. What has happened in the Barilla family? Existing more than 150 years, Barilla is a well-known brand around the world. Everything started in 1877 when Prieto Barilla opened the family's first pasta and bread shop in Parma, which was passed to his sons, Gualtiero and Riccardo, before War World I. Under their leadership, the family's first pasta factory was opened. In the third generation, two brothers, Gianni and Pietro, expanded the business beyond their locality and further developed the business after World War II.

However, at the end of the 1960s, the company suffered some crises, and Gianni sold the business. In 1971, Barilla was divested to the US multinational W.R. Grace group, but day-to-day control was in the hands of Pietro Barilla. Finally, it was Pietro's passion for the past and for his family tradition that drove him to buy back the business in 1979 at the risk of the economic, social, and emotional wealth the family had created around the business.

In 1993, Pietro passed away, and his three sons Luca, Paolo, and Guido and one daughter, Emanuela, became owners. The three boys took over leadership of the consolidated business. Pietro left an important wake in the company and, of course, in the family, specifically in his children's interpersonal relationships. It is common for the brothers to ask themselves what their father would think about this project or product and what he would have done if he were alive.

Pietro's children have different personalities, but they have been able to work as a consolidated team. The reason for this successful partnership is the great mission the previous generations left for all of them, which is the mandate to maintain the family tradition, move their family business forward, and focus on the core of the business. This is the glue that binds the interpersonal relationships together. Even more, the three brothers and their sister serve as directors of Barilla Holdings.

Discussion questions:

1 Why do you think it is important to have an upper-level mission beyond the economic goals of productivity and performance in a family business to maintain healthy interpersonal relationships?
2 How important is it in family businesses to develop a culture that embraces economic, social, and emotional goals? Why?

10.7 Case for analysis II: Succession to succeed in the Middle East[9]

Most family businesses in the Middle East, specifically in the Gulf area, grew at a high speed alongside the region's economic development from exploiting natural resources. There were opportunities everywhere, and debt was the main engine to finance growth. This was the case for the business developed by the Al Fahim family.

The family business established by Abdul Rahim Abdul Razzak Ali Al Fahim in the 1960s started as a cosmetics and beauty distributor. Paris Gallery emerged in the middle of the 1990s when Al Fahim's sons, four brothers, consolidated all of the family's economic activities into one holding. Even with the challenges that this entailed, the strength of family ties prevailed, and the family designed a plan to become a leading luxury retailer.

In 1996, when Mohammed Abdul Rahim Al Fahim, the second son of the family business founder, moved back to the region after his educational experience in the United States, graduating with a degree in business administration and a minor in marketing and gaining his own business experiences, his parents convinced him to join the business, and he was sent to Saudi. Ten years later, he began taking on different positions in the family business until he was appointed CEO in 2006.

The major change in 2006 was the lack of structure, organization, and strategy in a context of huge debt and family conflicts. Mohammed Abdul Rahim Al Fahim described the situation as follows:

There was no policy, no system, no [official] decision making process. There was no clear responsibility from top to bottom; everybody was responsible and everybody was not accountable at the same time. Everybody had the authority and on the other hand, nobody had to be accountable to authorities.[10]

Mohammed Abdul Rahim Al Fahim developed strong leadership and demonstrated remarkable foresight. A revolution was initiated in the family and in the business to transform and modernize the family business. The process started capturing family members' needs, goals, and expectations. Mohammed recalled,

We asked everybody what their ambitions were and what they wanted in life. Then we asked them what they expected from the company. Interestingly there were many incongruities between what they wanted in their lives and what they wanted from the business.

The new leadership and changes started from the family's aspirations as a business family. Mohammed developed a governance structure to support the family–business relationship and lead growth to take the family business to the next level. In a personal reflection, Mohammed recognized that while his goal was to put a new structure in place within a year-and-a-half, it took him several years. The most difficult part during the company's CEO succession was identifying those individuals who were willing to change and those who would sabotage the succession process because of their desire to keep the status quo.

Discussion questions:

1   Why do you think Mohammed had to fight with individuals to introduce changes in the business and family?
2   Do you think each succession transition has to refocus the structure of family business relationships? Why?

10.8 Case study: How far can U-Haul go from here?[11]

It was end of the 1970s after the family's last session with a psychologist and family expert when L.S. Shoen still had the same question without an answer: What is the best next step to successfully transfer the family business—U-Haul—to the second generation? Having 13 children from several marriages had created a dilemma for L.S. Shoen, whose maximum desire was to transfer U-Haul ownership, governance, and management to the next generation and give continuity to what he and his first wife had created.

About the U-Haul business. U-Haul was founded in the 1940s by Leonard Samuel Schoen and his wife. Son of a farmer who lost his land during the Great Depression, he worked here and there for several years to pay for college. Without finishing college, he entered the US Navy during War World II. It was during that time, when moving from one military base to another, that L.S. Shoen discovered the need to borrow trailers to carry all of one's personal things. The business opportunity he envisioned was a national company that would provide reliable trailers to anyone so they could move their personal belongings. With some money, he brought and built some trailers and painted the company name on them. The family business empire of trailer dealerships had begun. By mid-1950, his dealer network extended from one side of the United States to the other. In the 1960s, the family business became the preeminent do-it-yourself trailer rental company in North America.

There were two major crises for U-Haul during the 1970s. The first one was during the oil crisis at the beginning of the 1970s with the first oil shock. Because its dealer network was based on gasoline stations and most stations shut down during that time, the family business needed a new business model. The second crisis was when the Ryder System company in Miami became a powerful competitor threatening U-Haul's industry leadership. How did U-Haul address these external shocks?

The family business implemented the so-called Grand Diversification Plan. First, the company was forced (because of the gasoline stations shutting down) to invest in their own rental centers, which represented a huge investment (financially). Then, the family business converted their rental centers into stores where everything could be rented from jet skis to champagne fountains. With this strategy, the family business went beyond the core of its business. The company started losing its own competitive advantages and, at the beginning of the 1980s, U-Haul's revenues sank.

The family. L.S. Shoen's first wife died very young at the age of 35. Together, they had six children: Sam, Mike, and Joe followed by Mark, Mary Anna, and Paul. One year after his first wife's death, he married a woman named Suzanne, whom he would eventually divorce. Joe and Mark did not have a good relationship with their stepmother. In this second marriage, the couple had four girls and one boy. Even though L.S. Shoen tried to keep the peace at home while building the organization, the rivalry among siblings soon came, and this spread to the family business. L.S. Shoen divorced Suzanne and got married two more times before his death.

Family business succession. L.S. Shoen planned to hand over his business to his children, and they were fully instructed in running the company. He gave company stock to each of his children since the beginning, and he also distributed shares to the most loyal employees who became top managers. At one particular point in time, he held only 2% of the company.

L.S. Shoen was aware of his children's rivalry. To address this issue, he gave his children some positions in the business through which he thought he could teach them their family business roles as owners and managers. There were two factions. On one side were Joe and Mark, who worked in a business L.S. Shoen acquired as a teaching instrument (an amusement park called Legend City) so the children could learn managerial skills. On the other side were Sam and Mike, who went to college. Sam's aim to be a doctor and Mike's aim to be a lawyer created Joe's expectation that he would keep the business for himself. However, L.S. Shoen expected to offer succession to Sam after his graduation. Indeed, Sam joined the business after becoming a doctor and earning a Harvard MBA. While Sam became head of East Coast field operations, Joe, who also earned a Harvard MBA, was appointed head of international operations. These managerial changes happened during the external shocks (oil crisis and new competitors).

With the Great Diversification Plan, U-Haul leadership crashed. Joe and Mark accused Sam of being incompetent when dealing with the business environment and questioned their father's decisions. Tensions increased, and the family business environment become conflictive.

Discussion questions:

1 L.S. Shoen already defined ownership succession by distributing ownership among his children and loyal employees. How should have L.S. Shoen acted regarding management succession?
2 How should have L.S. Shoen coordinated governance succession as well?

The fatal ending. After the final meeting with the family therapist, L.S. Shoen decided to promote Sam to president and CEO while he remained as chairman. This decision precipitated Joe's and Mark's resignations, and they went on to establish a new business, a printing house, whose most important customer was U-Haul. When the strategic (diversification) and financial (less revenue and even losses) situation became critical, all family members became alarmed. With some family support in a shareholder meeting, Joe and Mark forced L.S. Shoen to step aside and receive a pension as salary. The new structure of the business was Sam as CEO and Joe as chairman. The board of directors was formed by four members: Sam, Joe, and two brothers (Paul and Jim), who were on the Joe and Mark side of the dispute.

With the new management structure, the company reverted the investment and action plan related to diversification and focused on the core business by renovating its fleet of trucks. However, the distribution of power was not the best solution, and problems kept coming up between Sam and Joe. Sam quit one year after agreeing to the new structure (1987). The three levels of decision-making—ownership, governance, and management—were under different groups of power and were fragile in terms of avoiding conflicts and maintaining decision-making consistency.

For example, Joe and Mark's sister, Katrina, who supported them in restructuring the business's management and governance, changed her mind in 1988 and started supporting Sam and L.S. Shoen, who started to negotiate the sale of the business to various investment companies. From then on, the family business was involved in all kinds of crises (suspicion of murder, family conflicts, betrayals, and so forth) stemming from the family. Nevertheless, with a focus on the core business, U-Haul successfully navigated the strategic and financial situation.

With some legal movement, Joe cemented his control; kept the chairman position; cut out his father's retirement compensation; and created a new composition for the board of directors with seven board seats, four of which were reserved for nonfamily members. In 1993, the company began to trade on the New York Stock Exchange.

Discussion questions:

3 If you were L.S. Shoen, would you have organized and executed succession planning? Prepare a succession plan for L.S. Shoen.

Notes

1 Lee, J. (2017). The pains and gains of family business governance. *Tharawat Magazine*. Article-Interview retrieved from www.tharawat-magazine.com/pains-gains-family-business-governance/
2 SPGC–KPMG Report. (2021). Mastering and comeback. How family businesses are triumphing over COVID-19. Report retrieved from STEP Project Global Consortium: https://globaluserfiles.com/media/40495_61100e368148fe983b5ee499fdd18a78d806fa01.pdf/o/GM-TL-01270_Family-Business-Survey-Report_V21_Web.pdf
3 Kerr, S. (2021). UAE pushes merchant families to open up to competition. *Financial Times*. Article retrieved from www.ft.com/content/116b083a-1811-4501-ad9b-2f6a3183db3e
4 Taylor, N. (2021). Clarks heir slams family for taking eye off the ball at retailer, praises new owner. *Fashion Network*. Article retrieved from www.fashionnetwork.com/news/Clarks-heir-slams-family-for-taking-eye-off-the-ball-at-retailer-praises-new-owner,1269885.html
5 Luxottica (2011). Luxottica to acquire Tecnol, a leading eyewear company in Brazil. An ideal platform for growth in Latin America is added to the Luxottica Group. Press release retrieved from www.luxottica.com/sites/luxottica.com/files/2011_12_1_press_release_brazil_eng.pdf
6 Steenbeek, R., van Helvert, J., & Knobel, J. D. (2022). "Chapter 7: Florax Group: When Unintended Succession Leads to Unfulfilled Promises". In Jeremy Cheng , Luis Díaz-Matajira , Nupur Bang , Rodrigo Basco , Andrea Calabrò , Albert James, & Georges Samara (Eds.), *Family Business Case Studies Across the World*. Cheltenham: Edward Elgar Publishing.
7 This example discussion is developed solely as the basis for class discussion. This example discussion is not intended to serve as an endorsement, source of primary data, or illustration of effective or ineffective management.
8 Barilla website. Information retrieved from www.barilla.com/en-us
9 This example discussion is developed solely as the basis for class discussion. This example discussion is not intended to serve as an endorsement, source of primary data, or illustration of effective or ineffective management. Several sources were used to develop this story: (1) Capital Finance International (2015–2016). CFI.co Meets the CEO of Paris Gallery Group: Mohammed Abdul Rahim Al Fahim. Winter. Article retrieved from https://cfi.co/wp-content/uploads/2016/02/profile-paris-gallery.pdf, (2) Trenwith, C. (2013). Paris Gallery's sweet smell of success. *Arabian Business*. Article retrieved

from: www.arabianbusiness.com/gcc/paris-gallery-s-sweet-smell-of-success-502771, and Lee, J. (2017). The pains and gains of family business governance. *Tharawat Magazine*. Article retrieved from www.tharawat-magazine.com/pains-gains-family-business-governance/

10 Trenwith, C. (2013). Paris Gallery's sweet smell of success. *Arabian Business*. Article retrieved from: www.arabianbusiness.com/gcc/paris-gallery-s-sweet-smell-of-success-502771

11 This case study discussion is developed solely as the basis for class discussion. This case study discussion is not intended to serve as an endorsement, source of primary data, or illustration of effective or ineffective management. Adelson, A. (1989). Gains at U-Haul dampened by feud in owning family, *New York Times*. Article retrieved fromwww.nytimes.com/1989/01/31/business/gains-at-u-haul-dampened-by-feud-in-owning-family.html

Additional information retrieved fromwww.company-histories.com/AMERCO-Company-History.html

11 The incumbent generation in family business succession

Learning objectives

- Distinguish different types of incumbent and senior generations.
- Understand the different succession strategies.
- Recognize the importance of succession planning.
- Identify the different types of retirement styles.
- Interpret the role of passive family members and transgenerational value creation.

11.1 Introduction

Any succession should start with understanding who the senior generation is. The current generation is the dominant family generation whose family members have enough power to impose the family's and business's strategic agendas and prevail in decision-making because they own a significant portion of the family business and/or occupy key positions at the governance and management levels. The importance of the senior generation lies in its capacity to influence decision-making, specifically related to ownership, governance, and management succession issues. Even in multigenerational family businesses (family businesses in which two or more generations coexist), one generation is more dominant than the others.

The generational stage, the number of family members, and the quality of corporate governance are three main dimensions that determine succession failure or success and/or facilitate or constrain the plan to address succession. The generational stage and number of family members are two critical dimensions affecting the complexity of any succession. A more advanced generational stage and a higher number of family members from different generations increase the role overlap of family members and make it difficult to reach consensus on the succession plan. However, the existence of corporate governance structures could facilitate the succession planning and process. Actually, the most critical situation in family business succession happens when there is no corporate governance and the current generation has to discuss, reflect on, and agree on the succession process. Building succession planning on informal mechanisms is likely to lead to failure or a process that may harm participants. While some exceptions could exist, informal succession mechanisms are only likely to succeed in small families with high cohesiveness and a strong communication style.

The aim of this chapter is to put succession into perspective from the incumbent (i.e., the senior) generation's view. When analyzing the senior generation, it is important to distinguish different individuals who are implicitly or explicitly part of the succession process. While it is easy to recognize the incumbent or group of incumbents as part of the senior generation, there are several other family members who could foster or inhibit the succession process—for instance,

DOI: 10.4324/9781003273240-15

family owners who are not directly involved in management or in-laws whose influence is not visible in the main discussions or decisions but whose voices indirectly influence other members' behavior toward the family. Additionally, in multigenerational family businesses, the predecessor generation of the current generation whose members are still active or have significant ownership (and thus power) in the family business could influence succession.

11.2 Senior generations across time

Succession differs in family businesses depending on the generation that owns, governs, and manages the family business across time because each generational stage has different challenges while planning and navigating the succession process.

11.2.1 Founder generation

When the senior generation is the founder generation, succession has some unique characteristics because a founder has his or her own psychological attachment to the business, which could have different meanings for the founder's life. Succession tends to be centralized in his or her person due to the lack of governance structure (or an incipient structure). The founder makes succession decisions, chooses what information to share, and visualizes the future of the family business. Informal mechanisms and personalized communication play important roles in navigating the succession process. The founder accumulates power and legitimacy to direct and guide succession. In this situation, succession tends to be more chaotic (because of the lack of transparency) with top-down communication and tends to be more confrontational with the upcoming generation. However, this does not mean that succession will fail under these circumstances. Even more, in some cases, the founder is able to manage the process by him- or herself to achieve satisfactory results. Nevertheless, in this context, the family business is too dependent on one individual.

Additionally, the number of founders could affect the succession dynamics. When there is more than one founder, the quality and types of relationships may determine the complexity of succession. Kinship relationships among founders add emotion among members of the current generation as they make decisions, plan, and take action related to succession. For instance, this could occur when two siblings who founded a business together have to agree on succession. Although the siblings could have a unique relationship in terms of trust, confidence, and mutual respect as business partners, succession could be a point of conflict as they have to decide on future aspects related to ownership, governance, and management. Both of the siblings have likely formed their own nuclear families, so in-laws are part of their family lives, and they likely have their own children. Over time, each founder adjusts his or her own needs, goals, and expectations, which may not necessarily be aligned with the family business's interests.

When founders have a friendship relationship, that represents another type of family business with specificities around succession. The friendship relationship that sustains the founders as partners could be affected by the family-oriented position that emerges when founders start reflecting on their own succession. A friendship- and trust-based partnership among founders cannot be directly transferred to the next generation. In this case, the succession process requires unique decisions to give continuity to the family business, or the founders need to consider exiting by implementing a management buyout. This form of succession requires formalizing corporate governance to guarantee the succession transition and business continuity.

11.2.2 Second generation

When the second generation is the senior generation that owns, governs, and manages the family business, succession is critical due to the complexity of the family and the lack of (or rather immature) governance structures to convey and fulfill participants' various needs, expectations, and goals. In the second generation, the first step of succession requires effort to align goals among family members and to strengthen the family–business relationship. Without consensus about what the business family is and what type of family business members would like to have, succession could become chaotic and confrontational, breaking the family into small groups with different interests. Therefore, having governance structures is a fundamental condition to anticipate the quality of the succession process and ensure the expected outcomes.

When corporate governance is in place and ownership, business, and family governance structures are developed, governance bodies exist that can discuss, reach consensus, plan, and implement actions related to succession. Coordinating these multiple governance bodies is an important part of the succession process to maintain the cohesiveness of the family and the continuity of the business. However, the main challenge emerges when the second generation has to deal with succession in the absence of a governance structure. While informal mechanisms among participants may work to maintain information exchange and decision-making between the family and the business, these informal mechanisms may or may not be enough to sustain and coordinate succession and its complexity. If the senior generation expects that informal mechanisms will not be enough for succession, it is a good opportunity for families to develop corporate governance. That is, succession can be an excuse to implement corporate governance. This was the example discussed in Chapter 10 when Mohammed Abdul Rahim Al Fahim, CEO of the Paris Gallery family business, developed family and business governance structures to lead his own succession transition.

11.2.3 Third and further generations

Some family businesses arrive at the third and subsequent generations by embracing all family members (a high number of family owners across multiple family branches), while others implement the pruning strategy by removing family branches that are less committed to or interested in the business. The pruning strategy implies reducing the number of family shareholders and concentrating ownership in one or few family members or family branches. This strategy attempts to simplify the ownership structure and reduce the family complexity, and its dynamics are similar to the early stages of development (when the family firm belongs to the founder or a small group of family members). For example, the Schantz Organ Company in the United States, which was founded in 1873 by A. J. Tschantz (later Schantz), is today managed by Vic Schantz, a member of the fourth generation. Over the last 30 years, the family business repurchased the third generation's shares, and the outstanding shares went from 2,250 to 511.[1]

If the family business arrives at the third or subsequent generation by embracing all family members, the key issue it faces is the extent to which the current corporate governance is enough to support the succession process. Without consolidated corporate governance, there are three options available. First, the riskiest option is to maintain the status quo and keep using informal mechanisms to address succession. It is a risky option because of the number of participants and multiple generations involved in the process with different expectations, needs, and goals. Even when clear, strong leadership exists, most decisions are imposed and not decided on via a consensus process. Thus, in the long term, when the leader passes away, many family members may not recognize the previous succession decisions and may deny or question them. In this context, interpersonal conflicts due to a lack of goal alignment, conflicts of interest, and opportunistic behavior are the classic dynamics.

The second option is to initiate a process to formalize the family business's corporate governance while engaging in the succession process. This entails working on the corporate governance structures and succession plan/process in parallel. This option was discussed in the previous subsection (on the second generation), and it follows the same principles; however, the challenge of starting to implement the corporate governance structures in the third generation is dealing with a bigger and more complex family. In addition, this option entails addressing many governance and succession issues at the same time, such as communication, education, conflict-management resolution, and structures and rules, among others, such that families can get lost during this process.

The final option is when a family business arrives at this stage with formal, consolidated, and mature corporate governance structures. In this context, the family and the business anticipated the challenges of succession by developing mechanisms that would help navigate succession from planning to implementation.

11.3 Succession strategies

After analyzing succession in terms of the different generational stages, there are three general strategies to address the challenges of succession, each of which has advantages and disadvantages.

11.3.1 Keep relying on informal mechanisms to address succession

The strategic option of relying on informal mechanisms based on interpersonal relationships and nonstructured communication channels has advantages and disadvantages. This succession strategy is effective when the number of participants is small, there is high family cohesion, the business is not complex, there is one potential successor candidate with skills and abilities to continue the business, and the successor has high support from passive family owners. This option is common in small and medium family businesses during the transition period from the first generation to the second generation or in subsequent generations after pruning family ownership. Informal mechanisms are not costly and are cemented in interpersonal trust, and there are long-lasting relationships among family members.

Beyond the advantages that informal mechanisms provide for planning and coordinating succession, the family business is susceptible to suffering the so-called imbalance effect. The imbalance effect refers to when the ownership, business, and family entities mature at different paces, and the entities are not able to support each other while maintaining a stable equilibrium. Neither the family nor the business develops a culture, structures, or procedures to support business growth and manage the family complexity across generations. If the family grows across generations and the modus operandi is to rely on informal mechanisms to address succession, the family business is likely condemned to suffer a generational shock followed by multiple conflicts that may eventually jeopardize business continuity and family cohesiveness. For example, take the story of two brothers who founded a family dinner theater in Delaware in the United States. During succession, they kept ownership and some decision-making responsibilities, while the day-to-day operations were delegated to second-generation family members. The informality of this succession prevented the real transfer of decision-making that would have enabled the family business to adjust to new customer needs. One of the grandsons referred to the situation as follows: "Because of its inability to change directions, the business unfortunately came to a screeching halt in 2008." The business was ultimately sold putting, the family members out of work.[2]

11.3.2 Formalize corporate governance to address succession

Some families, at the time of confronting succession issues, are able to recognize the need to develop (by creating or improving) their governance structure so they can agree on a succession plan and guide the succession process. The advantage of this succession strategy is that the three entities (ownership, business, and family) are able to evolve simultaneously due to their common path to maturity. By developing the necessary corporate governance that succession requires, family businesses are able to create the learning mechanisms to develop the next-generation leadership. These learning mechanisms are the communication channels that align expectations, needs, and goals among family participants and embrace the alignment between the family and the business. The Al Saud Company in the United Arab Emirates took this approach for its informal management transition from the first generation to the second generation. The family introduced several corporate governance mechanisms, including shareholder meetings and a charter, to keep the family united.

The disadvantage of this option for business families is that family members and stakeholders have to work simultaneously on several fronts. In some cases, the energy, time, and money to develop both succession and corporate governance to achieve positive results make this strategy a burden. The family business is vulnerable to external shocks that can alter the process to address corporate governance issues and succession issues in parallel.

11.3.3 Pruning the family ownership tree

Pruning the family ownership tree is a classic strategy families use to avoid conflicts, reduce family complexity, and maintain concentrated ownership and decision-making. It liberates the business from those family members (family branches) who are less committed to the economic activities, have different strategic views than the dominant group, or would simply like to cash out their shares.

The advantage of this strategy is keeping ownership concentrated by reducing the number of shareholders with different roles and different interests. In this sense, ownership is kept by those family members who are committed to the continuity of the business. Additionally, this option can be a problem-solving strategy when family members (or family branches) are not able to own, govern, and manage the business together because of conflicts, incompatible personalities, or merely different interests.

The disadvantage of this option stems from conflicts among family owners when discussing and implementing the pruning strategy, which could consume valuable resources, such as time and money, as well as affect emotions and, consequently, interpersonal relationships. Conflicts related to the strategy itself emerge when passive family owners do not want to sell or when the group of passive owners suspects some hidden intentions from active family members. Even when all family members agree to this strategy, buyers and sellers are likely to confront conflicts related to the price or value of shares, the valuation method used, and the liquidity needed to make this option effective. Finally, this strategy can create emotional conflicts for current and future generations because members of the pruned family branches could continue to be attached to the business as part of their identities.

There are two hidden risks of using this strategy. First, if the strategy is used to avoid consensus, postpone the creation of governance structures, and/or keep an autocratic culture, the short-term benefits from bypassing action to address succession confront long-term problems from maintaining a culture of poor communication and the inability to develop consensus. Second, this strategy can destroy family relationships when family members from the pruned branches continue feeling attached to the business and, even worse, when the next generation of family members from the pruned branches feel they were excluded from the family business without their consent.

11.4 Plan the succession process

Developing a plan to address succession is the most recommended strategic action for family businesses. A strategic plan for succession is an instrument to generate consensus among family members and stakeholders, establish clear boundaries to frame family members' expectations, and avoid conflicts that can jeopardize business continuity and family cohesion. By developing a succession plan, families attempt to create a road map for actions and a framework for decision-making.

There is no specific way to develop a succession plan, and it could have different degrees of details. The written document is important, but even more important is the process the family goes through to agree on the plan and gain support from all family members. Planning is a strategic process in itself for the family business to formalize decision-making. If the family business has mature corporate governance, then the different governance bodies should be involved in developing the succession plan. Mature corporate governance with clear structures and policies constrains the succession plan because principles exist to regulate the family–business relationship and demarcate family members' expectations. In this context, the succession plan should be specific to address the family business's particular situation, which could be intra-family management and ownership succession, management buyout succession, or family exit succession (total or partial).

However, when there is no corporate governance, the succession plan could be used to create a task force of family members and nonfamily members to discuss, define, and create the path for moving the family business from one generation to the next. In this case, the succession plan is more demanding because general and specific consensus related to succession (ownership, governance, and management) are needed followed by the respective action plans.

Even though there are important advantages to addressing succession with an explicit plan, the disadvantage of this option is the bureaucratic approach to decision-making. Such an approach could clash with the agile decision-making that traditionally characterizes family businesses. Additionally, because a succession plan is not always necessary, initiating an unnecessary process could be costly in terms of money and time.

The incumbent generation has a significant influence on the existence, development, and implementation of a succession plan, which depends on the preferred retirement style. Indeed, succession depends on members of the incumbent generation seeing themselves as having different roles after retirement—of course, if retirement is an option. The paradox of being a founder is being succeeded by someone. Holly Branson, daughter of Virgin billionaire Richard Branson, joined the firm in her 40s. At that moment, she thought, "I never ever thought I'd be working in the family business, but it was a great opportunity."[3] However, Richard is not someone who is going to retire and leave his position. In an interview with the *New York Times*, Richard reflected on this topic:

Richard: You don't automatically assume that your child is going to come into the company. If one of them ended up wanting to come and work with this, obviously that's lovely. But the key thing was that they found what they wanted to do in life. It's great that Holly, from the company's point of view, and from the 80,000 people who work for it, is becoming a figurehead. I'm not going to be able to be the figurehead forever.

Journalist: Is that a formal announcement of succession planning?

Richard: No. I don't think I'll ever retire.[4]

Therefore, in the succession process and when developing a succession plan, it is important to be aware of incumbents' retirement style because their behavior shapes succession itself.

11.5 Type of incumbent based on their retirement styles

The incumbent or group of incumbents actively involved in the family business are the most important actors because their attitudes toward succession, their family business visions, and their intentions to assist with succession could affect the succession process and succession outcomes.

To analyze an incumbent's exit, the problem can be simplified by considering two main rationalities that may have an important influence on the role an owner and/or founder will perform before, during, and after succession: his or her financial readiness to let go and mental readiness to let go.[5] The financial readiness to let go refers to the incumbent's financial and economic position when retiring. The mental readiness to let go refers to the incumbent's emotional and psychological position when changing his or her role. When combining these two dimensions, four paths for incumbents emerge (Figure 11.1).

1 *Quadrant I—Imperative decision to stay.* Incumbents who are neither financially nor mentally prepared to let go are most likely going to stay actively involved in their family businesses.

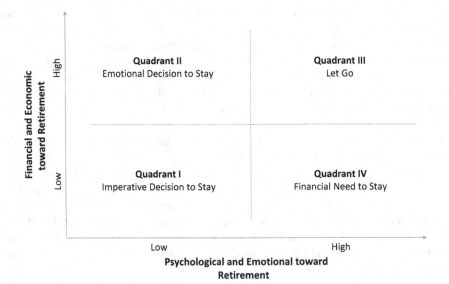

Figure 11.1 Incumbent's exit.

Source: Adapted from Leonetti, J. M. (2008). *Exiting Your Business, Protecting Your Wealth: A Strategic Guide for Owners and Their Advisors*. New Jersey: John Wiley.

This is a critical situation, especially when the incumbent has not separated his or her own wealth from the business, and there is no financial retirement plan. To address this situation, it is necessary to know why the incumbent is not financially and mentally prepared and whether there is time to work on both the financial and psychological dimensions of retirement. The succession process should define a plan of action to prepare the incumbent for exit and his or her own retirement. The aim is to guarantee the incumbent's readiness to let the next generation continue the business or implement any other succession alternative, such as selling the business. It is important to recognize the consequences for the succession process of having an incumbent without an exit path. Such consequences include interpersonal conflicts with the next generation, the existence of two different chains of commands (incumbent and successor), excessive control over the next generation, and the next generation's decisions being undermined. However, not all consequences of this path are negative. The incumbent could support the next generation by assisting and advising them and by passing on tacit knowledge and social capital (network of relationships), all of which are competitive strategic resources in a family business.

2   *Quadrant II—Emotional decision to stay.* Incumbents who are financially prepared to let go but not mentally ready to leave may decide to stay and not cut off from the business. It is necessary to recognize and understand the reasons for such a lack of mental readiness. For instance, it could be that the next generation of family members is not prepared to assume full leadership yet, the incumbent could have high personal attachment to the family business, retirement is not an option yet because of the incumbent's young age, or retirement is a scary option for the incumbent. Each reason requires a different approach to mentally prepare the incumbent for the succession process (before or after the transfer of ownership and management succession), and a succession plan should address this approach explicitly.

3   *Quadrant III—Let it go.* Incumbents who are financially and psychologically prepared to let go will most likely retire. This is the best option because the incumbent has the freedom to plan his or her exit, coordinate the succession process with the next generation of family members, and even define alternative solutions (e.g., management buyout) in case no one from the next generation wants to be engaged with the family business in any of its forms (ownership, governance, or management).

4   *Quadrant IV—Financial need to stay.* Incumbents who are mentally prepared to let go but not financially ready may stay longer in cohabitation with successors. The incumbent could be forced to stay longer to prepare him- or herself financially in collaboration with the next generation or forced (because of age or health problems) to sell the business at the highest price possible to move into the new life stage—retirement. This situation could be critical depending on the age and health of the incumbent and the extent to which there are potential successors in the next generation. Some incumbents have to stay longer in their position because their work (salary) is the main source of family income.

Intrinsically related to the incumbent's financial and mental readiness to let go as his or her retirement style is the incumbent's exit style. The incumbent's exit style[6] refers to how members of the incumbent generation will leave their current positions and develop different engagements with the next generation of family members or nonfamily members during and after succession.

•   *The monarch exit style.* This style refers to those incumbents who do not want to leave their positions. Their positions and roles have meaning in terms of power, legitimacy, and recognition among different stakeholders. Some incumbents believe that their family businesses are their kingdoms where they can impose their rules. Most likely, in such cases, the family business culture is hierarchical, vertical, and strongly dependent on the incumbent. In this context, succession may not be a topic of conversation among family members, and consequently, succession planning never takes place. Even though these family businesses tend to be successful under the control of the respective incumbent, who is able to bond family members together in the family business context, when unexpected events push the incumbent from his or her position (death or illness), chaos typically seizes the family business. Family members are not able to interact with each other without the presence of the incumbent. They have to face ownership, governance, and management succession suddenly, but they are not able to collaborate effectively, maintain constructive conversations, and develop problem-solving mechanisms because they were never trained to assume the succession responsibilities. Succession outcomes under the monarch exit style are uncertain. For example, Barry Sr. of the Bingham family still controlled his family media empire in the United States at the age of 80, at which point he sold the family business. His son Barry Jr., who had managed the firm for several years, felt betrayed. His father never retired and kept the power and ultimate decision-making until the end. After Barry Sr. made wrong decisions to accommodate both the family's and the business's needs in an emotional manner and without a succession plan, the board of directors was paralyzed due to family factions with different interests.[7]

- *The general exit style.* This exit style refers to those incumbents who are going to retire and are able to recognize when it is time to transfer leadership to the next generation due to family and business pressures. However, these incumbents may not be personally and/or mentally ready for such a change in their lives. Because of their past success, they may wait for the next generation to call them back to the office and lead the destiny of their family businesses again. The main challenge for the next generation under the general exit style is to address the loyal quasi-family members who are still working in the family business but who respond and are loyal to the senior generation. This group of nonfamily members who have been working in the family business for a long time will likely be the main supporters of the retired generation to come back to restore the past. This was the case for Ratan Tata, who announced his retirement two years before turning 75. Cyrus Mistry was offered the position of deputy chairman in 2011 so he could work closely with Ratan before officially taking over as executive chairman of Tata Sons and Tata Group. Cyrus Mistry's position as a deputy chairman lasted only four years as he was ousted by the board in 2016, leading to Ratan Tata assuming the chairman position again.

- *The ambassador exit style.* This exit style refers to those incumbents who are ready to retire from their day-to-day activities but are still committed to the family business. Because of their experience, know-how, and extensive social networks, incumbents with an ambassador style are diplomatic and represent the family business across different contexts and with different stakeholders. They are likely to make a progressive exit, delegating operative actions and decision-making to the next generation and assuming a new role without interfering in the new family business leadership. Their new role is to represent the interests of the family business beyond the boundaries of the family business in the family, industry, sector, and region in which the family business dwells. It is common for an incumbent to move from the CEO position (active day-to-day operations) to a board of director role during succession. These incumbents have the opportunity to be ambassadors of the family business to connect it with stakeholders and to be stewards of the family business culture. For instance, Sulaiman Abdulkadir Muhaidib, a member of the second generation of Al Muhaidib Group, became chairman in 1997 after working in the company with his father since 1976. Today, his role is to embrace the third and fourth generations in the business culture to perpetuate his father's legacy.

- *The governor exit style.* This style refers to those incumbents who recognize the end of their functions in office and publicly announce their retirement. They do not have any romantic intentions to go back and understand that their contribution to their family business is done in this position and that it is time to move the business forward to the next generation. Once the announcement is public, the family and the business have to initiate succession preparation, which could add pressure to the family business system and alter interpersonal relationships. If there are corporate governance structures, an orderly succession transition could unfold. However, a smooth transition may not occur if the current incumbent was not able to establish corporate governance mechanisms and develop a succession plan. For example, after working in the family business for more than 20 years, Sultan Sooud Al Qassemi, second generation in Al Saud Company, decided to step down from his managerial position to give room to the next generation of family members and pursue new professional aims. He is now an Emirati columnist and researcher and is the founder of Barjeel Art Foundation.
- *The inventor/entrepreneur exit style.* This style refers to those incumbents for whom innovation/entrepreneurship was and is their main meaning for having a family business. Their dream is to succeed with the next invention or business idea and move on. The leader position is not important, and when the time arrives, they are ready to pass leadership to the next generation and continue creating their inventions within or outside the firm or start a new business. The main succession challenge is to preserve their know-how to continue contributing to the family business's success and organize the structure of the family business for future generations. For example, Osmo Suovaniemi, innovator and founder of the biotechnology firm Biohit in Finland in 1988, opted for an external successor because none of his three children wanted to take over his management role.[8] His intention was to keep inventing, patenting, and developing new businesses. At the age of 66, Osmo announced his resignation as president and CEO of Biohit position, which was taken over by Jussi Heiniö, an internal manager of the firm. Osmo Suovaniemi did not leave Biohit but instead continued to be actively involved in developing innovations in his new role as chairman of the board of scientific advisors.[9]
- *The transition leader.* This style refers to those incumbents who assume leadership during succession to transfer the ownership, governance, and management to the next generation and to ensure a successful process. They are able to adapt their roles across the succession process (coach, advisor, or consultant) before and after succession. Additionally, they are committed to the governance structures and the consensus approach to ensure the expected succession outcomes are achieved. For example, in the case of the Mitchells family business, which specializes in men's and women's stores, the third generation comprises seven grandsons, six of whom lead Mitchells stores today. Bob and Russ Mitchell are co-CEOs, and Andrew Mitchell-Namdar is responsible for marketing and visual services. The company's management succession was developed based on an agreed-upon succession plan. The last step was to transfer ownership from the second generation to the third generation. The second generation remains active as consultants in the business.[10]

11.6 Passive family members

While the incumbent (or group of incumbents) is an important actor in succession, the rest of the family members, depending on their positions, can foster or constrain the succession process. Their roles cannot be underestimated, and their consensus is always needed to make the succession process successful.

Any succession path means changes in family members' positions across the three entities (ownership, management, and family) and their overlapping areas. The main question to reflect on is, to what extent are the succession process and expected outcomes aligned with the individual needs, expectations, and goals of each family member? This question is important because family members who feel betrayed, harmed, or displaced during succession are likely going to resist changes, slow down the succession process, and eventually paralyze succession.

During succession, changes in family members' positions across the three entities also imply changes in the ownership and governance structures. Succession means that some family members have to step down from their governance seats and let other family members occupy the governance structures. Therefore, the succession process is also about the redistribution of power and decision-making positions across the ownership, governance, and management structures. That is, beyond the core changes of succession, there are peripheral succession changes that represent new adjustments to decision-making and power. The succession process and succession plan should embrace the peripheral issues of succession, which are just as relevant as the managerial leadership shift from one generation to another. The peripheral issues of succession should be aligned with and support the managerial leadership shift.

The generational stage of the family business could be an important determinant of the importance of the peripheral issues of succession and the actions needed to address them. At the early generational stages, ownership and management succession monopolize all the attention by defining the new ownership and governance structures and the management leadership. In such cases, the dynamics of peripheral succession are a consequence of ownership and management succession. Even though this approach is generally effective, the risk is not considering passive family members (e.g., family members not directly involved in the business and in-laws) and upcoming generation (family members who are not owners yet but are forming their impressions and beginning to understand the family business) during succession. This situation could break the cohesiveness of the family in the near future. It is always a good option to embrace all family members during succession and to communicate succession decisions and the rationality behind them even when formal governance bodies exist.

When family businesses move beyond the early generational stages and governance structures are in place, the succession discussion across governance bodies includes peripheral succession. The explicit changes from ownership and management succession are linked to the peripheral issues of succession to ensure a smooth process and successful outcomes. There is a shift in the conversation that requires a focus not only on the business but also on the family. This is the time when most families start renewing their identities, defining themselves as a family in business, and projecting their transgenerational family values.

11.7 Transgenerational value creation

Family wealth tends to have a complex evolution, which has to be considered when planning succession. At early generational stages, family wealth is mainly invested and concentrated in the family business. This high level of family ownership concentration implies high risk for the family due to the lack of diversification. The family business's economic activities focus on one or a few (related or unrelated) sectors.

As the accumulation of family wealth continues within the boundaries of the family business, families tend to look for alternative investment opportunities for their wealth. Some families opt for reinvesting in the same family business to finance growth strategies within the same industry. Other business families look for alternative investments (diversification by acquiring or creating new businesses to move toward a conglomerate or family business group). In both cases, family wealth is still concentrated in business activities that the family controls, governs, and/or manages.

If wealth creation continues and the family business is successful, business families initiate a new step as investors by trying to diversify their family wealth. In this sense, families own, govern, and manage the family business (or the conglomerate or family business group) and are also responsible for their portfolio investments. The alternative investments could be managed by the same family business (using the family business as a platform), by an outsourced firm that administrates the wealth, or by a family office that canalizes all matters related to family wealth (Chapter 9 addresses the family office as part of the family governance structure).

Therefore, in each generational change, succession should not only involve redefining ownership, governance, and management but also planning how to preserve and administrate family wealth. At particular moments in some business families' lifecycles, succession means talking about family wealth (the investment and diversification strategy) and the family business (ownership, governance, and management succession).

The final stage for some families is to manage their wealth with the family business as just another (albeit important) investment in their family portfolios. For instance, the Swedish Wallenberg family: "The family's activities are mainly connected to the Wallenberg Foundations, investor AB, FAM AB and associated holdings. SBE, founded by Andre Oscar Wallenberg in 1856, continues to play a central role in the family's activities."[11] One extreme is when the family sells the business from which it generated its wealth, but the family preserves its business identity. The business family typically decides to preserve its wealth in a new organization, such as a trust, foundation, or family office. In these cases, succession is about preserving and growing family wealth across generations by keeping the cohesiveness of the family via the identity of the original family business as the seed of the family wealth. This is the case of Leitz, a German manufacturer of office products founded by Lois Leitz. The fourth generation of family members sold the family business to the Esseltre Group, but most of the family members decided to stay together via a family office.[12]

11.8 Additional activities and reading material

11.8.1 Classroom discussion questions

1 Why does the current generation matter for succession?
2 Are senior generations the same across different family business life stages? What kinds of challenges for succession planning arise from different senior generations?
3 What are the most common succession strategies?
4 What are the successor retirement styles? How do these retirement styles affect ownership and management succession?
5 How important are passive family members before, during, and after succession?

11.8.2 Additional readings

1 SPGC-KPMG (2020). The courage to choose wisely. Why the succession decision may be a defining moment in your family business. Report retrieved from https://globaluserfiles. com/media/40495_f8c01b1ce1a8c10b81123ab0b1eb27fd9a1697be.pdf/o/GM_IB_0670_S tep-Article_V17_web.pdf
2 Jaffe, D., & Allred, S. (2023). Succession is a journey, not a plan. *Family Business Magazine*. Article retrieved from www.familybusinessmagazine.com/succession-journey-not-plan

3 Perdue, M. (2019). Chain of command violations: Three traps for the family business. *FFI Practitioners*. Article retrieved from https://digital.ffi.org/pdf/wednesday-edition/ 2019/february/february-06/chain-of-command-violations-three-traps-for-the-family- business.pdf

11.8.3 Classroom activity

Aim: Create a consultant report on how to address and manage different types of incumbents during succession.

Material: Ask students to select a family business incumbent from their experience (their own family business) or use public incumbents for this exercise. Alternatively, the instructor could provide names or case studies for this task to simplify students' data collection or select one or several movies or series (e.g., the *Succession* TV series). Students should then collect as much information as possible to describe and interpret the incumbent's personality, retire- ment style, exit style, and consequences for the family and the business.

Instruction during class: Break the classroom into groups of four to five members.

- Ask students to reflect on the incumbent's personality, retirement style, and exit style.
- Ask students to reflect on the positive and negative consequences of the incumbent's characteristics for succession for the particular case.
- Ask students to design some strategic actions to reduce the negative impact of the incum- bent on succession.

Result: Beyond the specific personality, retirement style, and exit style, it is important to high- light the cultural context when interpreting the negative and positive consequences of current incumbents for succession. An open discussion among and between groups could help students think critically about the incumbent's role as well as about possible solutions to guide succession within different contexts.

11.9 Case for analysis I: Holly in her father's shoes[13]

Is Virgin Group a family business? The answer could be no, or it could be yes. Richard Branson, a well-known entrepreneur, started Virgin in 1970 as a mail-order record retailer. Today, Virgin Group comprises successful and innovative businesses in different sectors, including mobile telephones, travel, financial services, leisure, music, health and wellness, and space tourism. It employs more than 71,000 in 35 countries.

Richard is not alone in Virgin Group. His daughter, Holly, is highly involved in the business. Holly is Richard and Joan Branson's daughter, who joined her father's business after finishing her education (medical and physiology degrees) and pursuing her own professional career. One day, her father said to her, "Why don't you take a year off and go to work at Virgin?"[14] Even though it was not in her plan to work in the family business, she agreed to the one-year challenge with the promise of going back to her passion—medicine. However, she never went back to medicine.

After a year-long intensive internship across all Virgin companies, she joined Virgin's man- agement leadership team, where she managed the companies' people, culture, and purpose. She worked for more than ten years on making sure that work–family balance was prioritized. Today, in the company, it is possible to talk about unlimited holidays, motherhood and pater- nity policies, and other actions that tend to improve Virgin employees' quality of life. Everyone feels valued and trusted. Holly is now the chief purpose and vision officer, working on specific projects and launching new businesses. Additionally, she chairs Virgin Unite, Virgin's nonprofit foundation.

But what is Branson's business? It is said that Branson does not have a board position in any of the companies within the Virgin Group. He is an entrepreneur rather than a businessman in the conventional sense. Actually, his most iconic firms have other major shareholders, and in most of the cases, he simply licenses the brand. Richard is the figurehead of the company, and in his own words, he reflected on succession: "I don't think I will ever retire."

Discussion questions:

1 Do you think Holly is going to replace Richard as the face of Virgin Group?
2 How do you see this succession process? What part of succession is complete, and what part remains?

11.10 Case for analysis II: What's next? Retirement[15]

John Nils Nordstrom started working summers in the stock room of the family business. Moving around the business with his dad, Elmer, and grandfather, John W., was common for John N. Nordstrom, and he eventually developed a career working in the business.

Nordstrom was founded as a shoe store by John W. Nordstrom and Carl F. Wallin in Seattle in 1901. In the 1930s, Wallin sold his stake in the business to John W. Nordstrom's sons, who had inherited their father's shares in the late 1920s. Brothers Everett, Elmer, and Lloyd expanded the business, and in 1968, they handed it over to the third generation. The third generation of family members included Bruce, Jim, and John as well as Jack, Lloyd's son-in-law. This group assumed leadership of the family business and took it public in 1971 (called Nordstrom Inc.). They also opened the company's management to nonfamily members. The ascension of the company continued, and in 1995, the co-leadership of the third generation of the Nordstrom family moved to a governance position. In that same year, the fourth generation arrived to take over the business. Bill, Blake, Dan, Erik, Jim, and Pete Nordstrom—the fourth generation— were all between the ages of 31 and 34.

John Nils remembered when his brother passed away, which led him to pay close attention to his own health. Even before retirement, he dedicated time to his physical and mental health. Looking for new challenges, John Nils found aviation. Before his retirement, he bought a de Havilland Beaver single-wing plane and prepared for the exams to get a license. John Nils described this new passion as follows:

I love the challenge of it. When I was going to retire, I needed something to challenge me other than playing bridge or golf or whatever it was. I wanted something that I really had to work at. With flying, you have to study and pass tests and all that stuff. I like that.[16]

His retirement was planned and arrived just when the company needed a new change of leadership because consumer behavior started to shift and the digitalization era was coming. The third-generation member Bruce Nordstrom, John Nils's brother, reflected, "We were getting old. This is a young person's business, you have to adapt to change, you have to look at it fresh."[17] Finding a new passion and recognizing the need to step down helped John Nils navigate the next step of his personal life. He is happy not being involved in the day-to-day operations of the family business but is following the younger generation as it runs and leads the company. He is enjoying spending time with his kids and grandkids and being part of the Nordstrom family legacy.

Discussion questions:

1 Why do you think it is important to prepare the incumbent generation for retirement?
2 How did John Nils Nordstrom find his way to give meaning to the next chapter of his life?
3 Can you imagine different types of retirement that could link the incumbent generation's personal lives with the family and business entities?

11.11 Case study: Can I stay a bit more with all of you? Group Olive Mendoza[18]

"I will never ever retire." The sentence that Alfonso, the second generation of the Group Olive Mendoza, announced in front of his three children, which now rumbles in Carmen's, Juan's, and Ricardo's heads. Each of the children knows it is time for their father to retire and finally designate the next leader of the company. However, their father is determined to continue in his position.

The children are happy with their father still moving around and having his say, but the situation is creating some tension among the three children, and because of his authority, their father still influences decision-making. Even though the three siblings recognize the tension and are able to apply their leadership at different times and in different situations, their father centralizes the power, and his visibility represents the voice of the family in front of stakeholders.

The origins of the family. Like many other families in the Cuyo region in Argentina, the Martinez family-owned olive farmland, which was passed down from one generation to another. However, in the early 1980s, one of Mario Martinez's six siblings, Alfonso, proposed the family build a factory to press olives. Under Alfonso's leadership, the entrepreneurial idea was successfully implemented in the market. In the following years, the company increased its production volume, introduced innovations, and diversified its business activities.

In the late 1990s, when succession approached Mario, Alfonso decided to prune the tree and bought his father's and siblings' shares. Therefore, Alfonso moved the evolution of the family business backward to become the sole owner of the family business. In Alfonso's words, this strategic ownership action to concentrate ownership in one family branch "was carried out with respect to the family and it was a consensual decision with my father and siblings."

With time, Alfonso's children incorporated into the business and developed their professional careers. Today, Carmen, Juan, and Ricardo occupy the chief financial officer, quality and purchasing manager, and production and marketing head positions, respectively. Group Olive Mendoza is a vertically integrated group that covers the full cycle of the olive—from land management to olive byproducts. Today, it is the largest oil mill in Latin America focusing on the production of olive oil. Financially, the company is characterized by a high level of sales ($21 million in 2018) and a low EBITDA[19]/sales margin, with a 1.6% average for the last five years. This margin and, thus, the results of the company are highly influenced by the price of olive oil.

The second and third generations. Alfonso Martinez, a member of the second generation, reinvented his father's business activities by proposing the construction of a factory to produce olive oil. Alfonso was the fourth of six siblings and the one who did not study. So, from an early age, he worked with his father while dedicating time to supervising the olive farms.

For Alfonso, who just turned 74 years old, the best success is the fact that his three children—the next generation of family members—are involved in the business. He is proud when mentioning his children. Just as Alfonso did, the third generation has moved the family business forward by introducing new entrepreneurial ideas, such as the subsidiary Olive Mendoza, which is a theme park focused on olives. The family is also implementing several new initiatives, such as Mendoza Energy, through which the company is going to produce its own source of energy.

The company also recently invested more than $6 million in a new oil press with the most advanced technology and recent innovation. Overall, it is one of the most efficient and advanced olive oil mills in Latin America.

Governance structure and succession. The family leads the management and governance structures. While Alfonso, Carmen, Juan, and Ricardo are the top managers, they also make up the board of directors. To address the continuity of the family business across generations, the family prepared a family constitution that defines the mechanisms to resolve conflicts, procedures to maintain family unity and keep the family–business relationship stable, and guidelines future generations of family members have to follow to join the family business. The family constitution sets the stage for family–business relationships.

Although the family constitution explicitly states that the retirement age for family members is 70 years old, Alfonso is still responsible for certain (important) decisions. Operative decisions have been delegated to his three children, all of whom occupy managerial positions.

Management and governance succession have been unfolding for a long time and at a slow pace. However, ownership succession has been stagnant. The father, Alfonso, still owns the majority of the family business shares and, consequently, keeps the final decision-making authority in his hands. Each of the third generation of family members owns only 2% of the family business.

Discussion questions:

1 What is your opinion about the ownership, governance, and management succession that Olive Mendoza has developed so far?
2 What kind of challenges can you anticipate for the family in the years to come?
3 How do you interpret Alfonso's behavior? What type of incumbent is he?
4 Alfonso is waiting for the right time to designate the next CEO. Is this a good strategy? What would be your suggestion?

Notes

1 Pearl, J. A. (2010). Should you prune your family tree? *Family Business Magazine*. Article retrieved from www.familybusinessmagazine.com/should-you-prune-your-family-tree
2 Dahl, D. (2011). Succession stories: The good, the bad, and the ugly. *Inc. Magazine*. Article retrieved from www.inc.com/articles/201103/succession-stories-keeping-the-business-in-the-family.html
3 Gelles, D. (2018). Richard and Holly Branson: A father–daughter conversation. *The New York Times*. Article retrieved from www.nytimes.com/2018/06/29/business/richard-holly-branson-virgin-corner-office.html
4 Gelles, D. (2018). Richard and Holly Branson: A father–daughter conversation. *The New York Times*. Article retrieved from www.nytimes.com/2018/06/29/business/richard-holly-branson-virgin-corner-office.html
5 Leonetti, J. M. (2008). *Exiting Your Business, Protecting Your Wealth: A Strategic Guide for Owners and Their Advisors*. New Jersey: John Wiley.
6 Sonnenfeld, J. A., & Spence, P. L. (1989). The parting patriarch of a family firm. *Family Business Review*, 2(4), 355–375.
7 Jones, A. S. (1986). The Binghams, after the fall. *The New York Times*. Article retrieved from www.nytimes.com/1986/12/21/business/the-binghams-after-the-fall.html
8 Kontinen, T. (2014). Biohit: A global, family-owned company embarking on a new phase. *Entrepreneurship Theory and Practice*, 38(1), 185–207. https://doi.org/10.1111/j.1540-6520.2011.00488
9 Biohit OUJ website. Information retrieved from www.globenewswire.com/en/news-release/2010/06/10/172218/0/en/NEW-PRESIDENT-AND-CEO-FOR-BIOHIT-OYJ.html

10   Mitchells family business website. Information retrieved from https://mitchells.mitchellstores.com/about-us

11   Wallenberg website. Information retrieved from https://wallenberg.com/en/ecosystem

12   Canessa, B., Escher, J., Koeberle-Schmid, A., Preller, P., & Weber, C. (2018). *The Family Office: A Practical Guide to Strategically and Operationally Managing Family Wealth.* Cham, Switzerland: Palgrave Macmillan.

13   This example discussion is developed solely as the basis for class discussion. This example discussion is not intended to serve as an endorsement, source of primary data, or illustration of effective or ineffective management.

14   Gelles, D. (2018). Richard and Holly Branson: A father–daughter conversation. *The New York Times.* Article retrieved from www.nytimes.com/2018/06/29/business/richard-holly-branson-virgin-corner-office.html

15   This example discussion is developed solely as the basis for class discussion. This example discussion is not intended to serve as an endorsement, source of primary data, or illustration of effective or ineffective management. Bromwich, J. E. (2019). Inside the Nordstrom Dynasty. *The New York Times.* Article retrieved from www.nytimes.com/2019/10/23/style/nordstrom-family-department-stores.html. Additional information retrieved from www.nordstrom.com/browse/about/nordy-podcast?breadcrumb=Home%2FAbout%20Us%2FNordy%20Podcast

16   Worcester, A., & Matthews, T. (2017). The Nordstrom Family Brand. *425 Business Magazine.* Article retrieved from www.425business.com/lifestyle/the-nordstrom-family-brand/article_c413519d-2992-5d46-9fc3-5c61cbc33989.html

17   Kian, K. (2020). How Bruce Lee can help young leaders adapt and overcome obstacles. *Forbes.* Article retrieved from www.forbes.com/sites/forbescoachescouncil/2020/05/07/how-bruce-lee-can-help-young-leaders-adapt-and-overcome-obstacles/?sh=a63fe62e9a75

18   This case study discussion is developed solely as the basis for class discussion. This case study discussion is not intended to serve as an endorsement, source of primary data, or illustration of effective or ineffective management.

19   Earnings before interest, taxes, depreciation, and amortization.

12 The next generation in family business succession

Learning objectives

- Distinguish the different types of succession careers for the next generation of family members.
- Understand the Disney effect for the next generation of family members.
- Recognize the different types of succession for the next generation of family members.
- Identify the importance of succession intentions in the next generation of family members.
- Interpret the next generation of family members' succession reactions to market and nonmarket pressures.

12.1 Introduction

The next generation is the group of family members who are part of the owning family, mainly descendants of the incumbent generation and their in-laws, and are going to occupy the most important positions to lead the ownership, business, and family entities in the near future. In some family businesses, generational leadership happens in a sequence where one generation precedes another generation with relatively low overlap between both generations. That is the case, for instance, when the founder and second generations demarcate the transition to pass ownership, management, and family leadership from one generation to another. For example, after a five-year succession transition, in 2020, Camille Jr. assumed management leadership of Oostwegel Collection, a family business started in 1980 by Camille Sr. and his wife Judith, who were the first to renovate a castle for tourists (turning it into a hotel and restaurant) in the catering and hospitality industry. Oostwegel Collection hotels and restaurants provide unique experiences by inspiring customers in places that connect the past with the present.[1]

However, in other family businesses, the sequence of the transition is blurred because several generations of family members coexist in key positions across the ownership, management, and family entities and decision-making is shared among family members from different generations. For instance, Randall and Brad Lange, who are fourth-generation twins in a business dedicated to farming and winemaking in California, work with their five children in the family business. Marissa, Randall's eldest daughter, is the president of the winery; her brother handles international sales; one of her cousins works in the treasury; and two other cousins work on the viticulture operations.

Regardless of whether a family business is mono- or multigenerational, it is a common mistake to associate the next generation and the successor when talking about succession in family businesses. The successor is the family member of the upcoming generation who is going to assume the primary business leadership role. In a small or medium family business, this could be

DOI: 10.4324/9781003273240-16

the CEO position—for instance, Camille Jr. in Oostwegel Collection. In a big or listed company, this could be the chairperson position on the board of directors—for instance, Marta Ortega (Amancio Ortega's daughter of Inditex, the biggest fast fashion group in the world) assuming the leadership of the board of directors.

Despite the importance and visibility of the successor in any succession process (when there is an intention to transfer managerial leadership), succession also deals with the key positions and roles across ownership, governance, and management that the rest of the members from the next generation are going to assume. Therefore, succession implies preparing the organization for the next generation of family members and training them to assume the next generation of leadership regardless of their positions.

The aim of this chapter is to provide a broad view of succession from the next generation's perspective, which includes the successor's perspective (generally the business leader) and the perspectives of the rest of the next generation of family members who are going to assume other important roles in the new family business structure.

12.2 The Disney effect in family business succession

The Disney effect is a common phenomenon worldwide that refers to those next-generation family business members who are interested in the family business but do not see room for their contributions (how to add value to the family business) except for running for leadership (management) positions. This is a myopic vision of family business succession because it focuses all possible contributions on a management leadership career without considering other alternative career paths.

The Walt Disney movie *The Lion King* showcases today's stereotypes regarding succession career paths in a family business. In one scene, Simba, the son of Mufasa (the king), is introduced as Mufasa's heir to the throne of the Pride Lands kingdom. This is an iconic scene as it symbolizes the ritual of a successor stepping into the family business to assume the leadership role, indicating that the animals (stakeholders and shareholders) can rest assured as they have a successor.

Today's stereotype of family succession erroneously associates succession with the transition of top managerial positions from one generation to another. Most business families focus on selecting, training, and developing their next-generation leaders. While the next generation of family business typically interprets succession as a leadership transition that confers power, prestige, and influence over the family, business, and society, incumbents (the older generation currently in charge of the family business) generally interpret succession as a projection of their own legacy to guarantee business and managerial continuity.

Unfortunately, the Disney effect creates complex dynamics in family businesses by increasing intrapersonal and interpersonal conflicts, shrinking the boundaries of succession conversations, excluding other family members from the succession process, and limiting family participation and engagement in the family business. Since a family business's succession refers to ownership, governance, and management succession, the next generation of family members could develop different career paths to make their contributions to the family business.

To broaden the conversation and start planning succession, it is important for families to redirect their focus by answering the following question: *how can the next generation develop a cohesive family and a sustainable business?* Answering this question may help relax the urgency to find, develop, and establish the next management leader and to have a more holistic perspective of succession regarding how the generation of family members can integrate and add value to the family business. A holistic approach usually requires cultural changes at the family level to adjust and direct family members' behavior and mindset toward succession. In this sense, several actions and activities could be developed:

- Increase all family members' interest in and commitment to the family business by engaging them in constructive conversations so they can express their expectations, goals, needs, and emotions.
- Understand the different positions that emerge in the ownership, business, and family entities and the positions' importance for future family cohesiveness and business sustainability.
- Visualize different career paths for the next generation of family members so they can occupy specific positions and be trained to successfully navigate the journey.
- Develop a new culture of family business succession in which the family business is more important than specific family members.
- Avoid building the family business identity around the myth of the older generation being heroes and instead develop the idea that each generation is responsible for adding value to the family business in different ways.

The educational approach to embrace the next generation of family members implies explicitly recognizing the different positions that next-generation family members can pursue within the family business depending on the family and business complexity. All family members must broaden their perspectives to collectively understand that the functioning of the family business is not limited to the main managerial leadership role itself but to the different roles across the family, ownership, and business entities. There are different positions and roles that the next generation of family members can occupy:

- *Responsible owner of the family business.* In this role, family members develop constructive attitudes and behaviors to commit to the shareholders and stakeholders of the family business. Take, for instance, the case of the Seaman Corporation, a manufacturer of industrially coated fabrics. Under Richard Seaman's leadership, the Seaman family redefined its shareholder role by shifting from the traditional owner role to the shareholder steward role, which entails a broader meaning for being a family shareholder (education, commitment, participation, and engagement) beyond the classical economic logic of harvesting annual dividends.[2]
- *Member or chairperson of the board of directors.* Increased work experience inside and outside the family business can lead to a long-lasting career inside the firm. These family members have developed capabilities and gained legitimacy to occupy a seat on the board of directors and may eventually become a chairperson. For example, Marta Ortega, second generation, developed a professional career as a manager, member of the board of directors, and a nonexecutive chairperson of the family business group Inditex, a Spanish multinational clothing brand that is among the fastest-growing fashion groups in the world.
- *Member of the family council or other family governance body.* Building and understanding interpersonal relationships in the family and business are essential for multigenerational family businesses. Managing interpersonal relationships is vital when seeking a position on the family council to professionalize family governance. For example, Kathy Munson, a third-generation shareholder of the centennial firm Crescent Electricity Supply, has dedicated her energy to creating and developing family governance. She had several leadership positions in family governance and worked on the original council charter for her business family, which was ratified in 2005.

- *Head, board member, or committee member of the family office.* Wealthy families typically choose to create their own family offices to manage different aspects of their wealth and serve the interests of family members. For example, Ali and Emine Sabanci prioritized professionalizing ESAS, the largest family office in Turkey. The professionalization process for the Sabanci family meant bringing nonfamily members into the management structure and creating strong family governance for their diversified assets both inside and outside Turkey.[3]
- *Family philanthropist or champion of social impact.* Philanthropy can help families materialize their values and beliefs through actions to help others in their local communities. To become a family philanthropist, a family member needs to embrace other family members and interpret the family philosophy to give back and generate an impact in the community. For example, Ana Milton took over her grandfather's philanthropic legacy in the José Milton Foundation. The José Milton Foundation was established by the patriarch of the Milton family, architect and entrepreneur José Milton, who developed his family business career in Florida in the United States.[4]
- *CEO or part of the top management team.* Next-generation family members who would like to lead need to acquire skills, abilities, and capabilities to assume managerial leadership positions in their family businesses. For example, with his brother Prieto, Giovanni Ferrero assumed the co-leadership position of his family's luxury chocolatier business (producing the well-known Ferrero Rocher chocolates and Kinder Eggs) after completing his studies in Brussels and the United States. In 2011, after the death of his brother, he became sole CEO until 2017, when he stepped down as CEO to assume the chairman position focusing on the family business's corporate strategy.
- *Entrepreneur by creating a spinoff of the family business or an independent venture.* New career paths have emerged in today's entrepreneurial societies to support next-generation family members in fulfilling their entrepreneurial dreams and ambitions. For example, Mohammed Azhar Sajan, who was initially reticent to start working in his family business, has successfully developed and led Casa Milano (a luxurious supplier of exquisite European brands to achieve high-end interior spaces), a spinoff of Danube Group in the United Arab Emirates (UAE).[5]

12.3 Managerial succession

Most business families intend not only to own their businesses and perpetuate family control but also to influence business decision-making by keeping top management positions in family hands. This is a natural intention in the family entity because parents expect their children to inherit managerial leadership and give continuity to the business across generations. However, it is a mistake to think that children always want to pursue a professional career in the business and that parents' managerial capabilities are naturally transferred from one generation to another. The selection, training, and development of next-generation leaders become crucial for family business continuity. When the family does not have any next-generation family members who want to join the business or the next generation does not have the managerial and leadership capabilities to assume the top management position, a nonfamily management transition plan should be activated.

12.3.1 Successor intentions

Potential successors' intentions to join the family business or not are an important determinant of the type of succession process the family business needs to develop. Indeed, intentions precede behavior. Intentions capture the motivational and ability dimensions that influence potential successors' behavior to join the family business or not.[6] Intentions are not spontaneous but are instead influenced by successors' attitudes, perceived behavioral control or self-efficacy, and perceptions of subjective norms.

Attitudes toward succession refer to the degree to which next-generation family members have a favorable or unfavorable view (evaluation or appraisal) of joining the family firm. Successors' attitudes are ultimately influenced by their behavioral beliefs, which refer to the subjective probability that a behavior is going to produce a specific outcome (e.g., success or failure to assume the successor responsibility) or experience (knowledge or skills that successors develop from embarking on this journey).

In addition to attitudes, the next generation of family members' intentions is determined by their family management self-efficacy, which refers to these family members' beliefs about their ability to manage family interpersonal relationships and family dynamics. Control beliefs are based on past experience dealing with family members; previous succession experience in the family (previous generation); secondhand information about succession; and others' experiences, which increase or decrease the perceived difficulty of succession. The more family members believe they can manage the family relationships across the ownership, business, and family entities, the higher their intentions to join the family business. However, excess confidence in one's own skills and capabilities to manage, lead, and be entrepreneurial could have an opposite effect on successors' intentions to join the family business by triggering successors to look for professional career opportunities outside the family business.[7]

Finally, the social factor of subjective norms, which comprise the code of behavior in a group of people or in a larger context, such as a country or region, also determines succession intentions in next-generation family members. Specifically, normative beliefs, as one dimension of subjective norms, are the basis for next-generation family members' perceived subjective norms, which refer to the probability that certain reference groups of individuals (e.g., family, friends, or acquaintances) will approve or disapprove of next-generation family members' decision to join the family business or not. Next-generation family members' perceptions of what other people who are important to them think about their joining the family business matter for interpreting the pressures coming from their close surroundings. In most cases, family members and individuals from their close environments (friends or religious groups) positively affect successors' intentions to join their family businesses because of the supportive conditions these reference groups create and their social acceptance.

Therefore, behavioral, control, and normative beliefs that affect potential successors' attitudes, self-efficacy, and perceived subjective norms have to be understood and interpreted in the context of family and business complexity. In the family context, the most important factors related to complexity are family culture, birth order, family size, and parent–child relationships. In the business context, the most important factors related to complexity are firm size, the sector and its lifecycle, and the types of products and services provided.

12.3.2 *Parent–child relationships*

From a psychological view, self-efficacy to manage family and nonfamily members is one of the most important successor beliefs. How is self-efficacy developed? In general, self-efficacy is built through individuals' exposure to or reflection on their own past performance, observation of others' behaviors, encouragement provided by others, and their emotional management of their own and/or others' performance.[8] Because parents are in a position to significantly influence their children, especially their succession intentions, the specific type of parent–child relationship could affect successors' self-efficacy to manage their family businesses.

There are four types of interpersonal relationships with different degrees of parental involvement and consequences for the next generation of family members' self-efficacy.

- *Instrumental assistance* refers to parental involvement to support their children's skills and develop their abilities to pursue succession. Parents are committed and devote time and effort to teach their children the specificities of owning and managing a family business. For instance, this situation appears when parents bring their children to work with them and parents assume direct supervision and close contact.
- *Career-related modeling* refers to the guidance parents provide their children by demonstrating family business responsibilities, roles, and tasks. Children's learning from their parents' experience unfolds via conversations, mutual interactions, and mutual reflection on the parents' behavior and performance. This situation refers to the business-related conversations between parents and children that may arise at home or in any other context.
- *Verbal encouragement* refers to parents' approval of their children's achievements and professional development. It entails parents' praise and encouragement associated with the development of the next generation of family members (in terms of education, practical experience, and achievements). This situation emerges when parents want to legitimize their children in relation to the family business's main stakeholders. For example, Sir James Waters, from Waters Group, a family-owned construction, property, services, and development business in the United Kingdom, referred to his son in the following way: "My youngest son is, to my great pride, following my career route. He's working on site at the moment, loving every minute, getting up early in the morning and getting home exhausted, which is exactly what a 25-year-old should be doing!"[9]
- *Emotional support* refers to the help parents provide children to develop, encourage, and manage their emotions (e.g., fears, doubts, and excitement, among others) to pursue succession. This situation emerges when parents support their children from a psychological and emotional position via conversations, coaching, or any other type of interaction that helps children control and manage their emotions.

There is no one parent–child relationship for each incumbent–successor relationship. There are multiple points of interaction between parents and children with different degrees of parental involvement in relation to succession. These multiple interactions shape next-generation family members' succession intentions by boosting or hindering successors' intentions to join the family business or not. The four types of parental involvement are not good or bad by themselves, but their effect on successors' succession intentions vary depending on contextual (e.g., the urgency of having a new leader, the children's birth order, the cultural specificities, and the family communication style, among others) and relational (e.g., trust, emotions, power, and psychological determinants) factors.

12.3.3 Successor career-path intentions

Another alternative to guide potential successors' career paths is to analyze their expectations and schemas toward the family business. Successors are immersed in societal and family contexts that influence their intentions and eventually their behavior. However, these influences are not direct. Rather, successors are independent individuals who confront the forces of their environments (e.g., cultural forces) with their own expectations and cognitive schemas. While expectations reflect successors' feelings and beliefs about their participation in the family

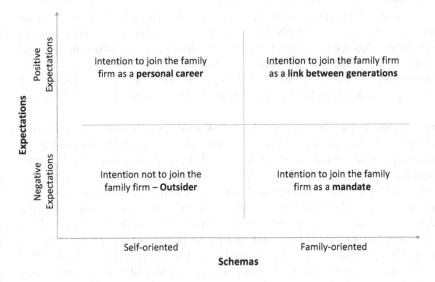

Figure 12.1 Successors' career-path intentions.

business, schemas are the mental structures that successors use to organize knowledge and information to predict the future and visualize their career paths.

Both intentions and schemas can be used to predict potential successors' behavior toward the family business. As Figure 12.1 shows, expectations toward the family business can be positive or negative depending on the information collected, personal past experiences, observations of others' behavior, and stories transmitted across generations. Schemas can be framed by either a self-orientation (egoist position emphasizing personal goals and needs) or a family orientation (collectivist position emphasizing family goals and needs). Combining these two dimensions, Figure 12.1 shows four types of career-path intentions.

1   Positive expectations and a self-oriented schema lead to successors who intend to join the family business as a way to develop their personal careers. A personal career could be linked to the family business itself (alignment of interests), but most likely, successors in this quadrant see the family business as a means to achieve personal recognition and visibility and as a trampoline for other achievements, such as political aspirations. This is the case for Devansh Jain, the next-generation entrepreneur of the Inox Group family business in India, who followed his own initiative and established Inox Wind Ltd. as a new business within the group, which is now the largest renewable energy firm in the world.[10]
2   Positive expectations and a family-oriented schema result in potential successors who intend to join the family business as a way to contribute to family business goals and the family legacy as well as connect previous and future generations. Successors in this quadrant see the family business as something that is beyond themselves. The family business is a means to ensure family cohesion and business sustainability. For instance, Marc Puig Guasch, CEO and president of Puig, a fragrance and fashion company founded in 1914, recalled his experience when he decided to join the family business: "Although I worked for a while for another company, I had no doubt my family wanted me to work at our company and that's how they raised me. I prepared myself to do that."[11] The decision was to keep the family tradition and embrace his father's legacy.

3   Negative expectations and a self-oriented schema lead to potential successors who do not intend to join the family business because they do not see the family business as a vehicle to achieve their personal needs and goals. Working in the family business is not an option on their career paths. They are outsiders. For example, Sunil Vachani's father and siblings started a business that produced electronics under the brand Weston in India. However, after studying business in London, Sunil opted to go his own way in 1993 rather than join the family business and founded Dixon Technologies with money borrowed from his father.[12]

4   Negative expectations and a family-oriented schema result in potential successors who intend to join the family business even though they are skeptical about the family business in terms of its economic and financial performance and are concerned about the dynamics of family interactions (i.e., conflicts). Their negative expectations are balanced by an emotional connection with the family business and a collective culture oriented toward family members. Kimberly Go, a third-generation member and business consultant at Premier Family Business Consulting, transitioned through this quadrant at the beginning of her career. She was thought to be obedient and thoughtful in the context of her Filipino-Chinese family. However, she was not motivated to run a business and told her father that she did not want to lead the family business. After going abroad to finish her studies, her family called her back to join the family business. She reflected on this situation as follows: "The family business is part of our family legacy and I decided I should get to know our business, understand it, and see if the work was a good fit for me. I struggled with this decision."[13]

12.4 Successor commitment

The commitment, engagement, and obligation toward the family business that restricts next-generation family members' freedom make up another important dimension that shapes the succession plan and guides successors during the succession process. There are different types of commitment, which are based on family members' motivation to join the family business or not:[14]

- *Normative commitment* is rooted in successors' obligation toward the family and the business. Successors feel and know that their professional career paths should be undertaken within the boundaries of the firm. Working in the firm is a mandate for these successors regardless of their wishes or desires. Societal culture and family culture play an important role in shaping normative commitment. For instance, in cultures with a high level of power distance (the power in the society/organization is distributed unequally among members), such as in Arab countries, normative commitment becomes a common reason for successors to join the family business, especially the eldest male in a family. Culture is just one dimension that can affect successors' commitment, but there are others, such as gender, birth order, family legacy, and economic reasons, that drive successors' feelings of obligation to join the family business or not. These potential successors feel they "ought to" pursue a career in the family business.
- *Affective commitment* is rooted in successors' emotional connection with the family business (emotional attachment). Successors' personal goals are aligned with the family business, and they strongly identify with the family business. In this sense, successors have the desire to be part of the family business and contribute to it by guaranteeing its continuity. While the family culture is an important determinant of this type of commitment, parent–child

interaction plays an important role in developing successors' emotional connection with the family business. These potential successors feel they "want to" pursue a career in the family business.

- *Calculative commitment* stems from a cost–benefit analysis that potential successors conduct when comparing career paths inside and outside the family business. In other words, potential successors attempt to rationalize their career-path decisions by considering different economic, social, and emotional advantages and disadvantages of joining the family business or not. For instance, when a potential successor analyzes the job market, he or she evaluates the competitive salary, work conditions, legitimacy of the position, and the time to achieve a career, among other things. The potential successor then compares this information to the conditions provided by working in the family business to make a final decision. These potential successors feel they "may want to" pursue a career in the family business.
- *Imperative commitment* emerges from potential successors' lack of confidence in their abilities and capabilities to develop a successful career outside the family business. The family business context is the successors' comfort zone, which provides them security to develop their careers. These potential successors feel they "need to" pursue a career in the family business.

Knowing the types of commitment that motivate potential successors, it is possible to plan actions to counteract the negative effects or increase the positive effects of each successor's commitment. For instance, affective commitment is an excellent motivator that predisposes potential successors to dedicate significant effort, time, and energy to developing their careers within the family business. However, an excess of affective commitment could distort reality about the family business such that potential successors ignore the darker side of working with family members, hidden family stories, and latent conflicts. Potential successors underestimate the meaning of working in the family business and the challenges stemming from this decision. In turn, successors could face a high level of disappointment when developing their professional careers, which could affect their performance and interpersonal relationships with other family members.

12.5 Successor entry and career paths

Any succession plan has to develop the entry mode for the successor and actions to prepare the successor to assume managerial leadership. There are numerous approaches to define when the successor should join the family business and what initial position he or she should occupy to develop a professional career. These decisions depend on the individual, his or her interpersonal relationships, and family- and business-level factors.

At the individual level, factors related to the potential successor's personal characteristics or attributes (e.g., honesty, loyalty, and generosity, among others), traits (e.g., openness, conscientiousness, extroversion, agreeableness, and neuroticism), and emotional and professional maturity could accelerate or delay his or her entry and career path. At the interpersonal relationship level, the quality of the successor–incumbent relationship, the age difference between the successor and incumbent, and the urgency of having a successor could affect the successor's entry mode and career path. Finally, the complexity of the family (family size, interpersonal dynamics, and formal family governance mechanisms) and business (firm size, industry dynamics, and formal business governance mechanisms) are also determinants of the successor's entry mode and career path.

There are some important considerations for any succession entry and career path:

- *Established conditions for entry.* Some family businesses introduce strict conditions for potential successors to work in the family business. These conditions are mainly related to educational background (type of formal education the potential successor has to have) and previous experience (outside or entrepreneurial work experience before joining the family business). These conditions could be formally incorporated into the family constitution, informally discussed among individuals from the senior generation, or merely be the consequences of a developmental process. In small and medium family businesses, the conditions for entry are typically informal. Take, for instance, the case of Jan Ryde, a fifth-generation family member who joined the family business Hästens, a Swedish manufacturer of handmade beds founded in 1852. After earning degrees in science and engineering and working as a science and technology lecturer, Jan Ryde returned to the family business, where he worked with his father for more than 30 years.[15] On the contrary, big family businesses tend to develop strict protocols and conditions that family members have to follow to join the family business. This is the case for the family-owned centennial business Carvajal based in Colombia.[16] The aims of imposing certain criteria for education and practical experience before a successor can enter the family business include developing skills and capabilities, accumulating general knowledge, increasing managerial responsibilities, understanding the job and hierarchy logic within the organization, proving potential motivation and leadership, confronting the reality of the job market, and gaining legitimacy by achieving one's own success.
- *Entry mode.* The main dilemma in any intra-family managerial succession is deciding the position the successor should take and the career path he or she should follow. While some family businesses require potential successors to start in lower positions and climb from there, others opt for successors to enter the middle or top managerial level. This decision depends on the potential successor's age and previous experience and on the specific knowledge (tacit) he or she needs to possess. A young or more inexperienced successor would likely start in an operative position. An experienced successor with a long career would likely start by occupying a top management position. For instance, Kenneth joined his father's business, Ringling Bros. and Barnum & Bailey Circus, in 1970. Kenneth incorporated the circus into a bigger project called Feld Entertainment. Kenneth's three daughters (Nicole, Alana, and Juliette) also joined the family business. To support succession, Kenneth put his daughters in the best positions for them based on their skills and capabilities, stepped back from active decision-making, and added a nonfamily member as chief operating officer to whom the daughters reported.[17]
- *Successor grooming.* Grooming refers to the set of actions and activities undertaken to develop successors' autonomy, competence, and legitimacy. When creating an internal career path, the successor development approach should focus on the successor's skills, capabilities, and interpersonal relationships and, to a lesser extent, the tasks and specificities of the positions across the organization. Felix and Jens Fiege, cousins of the fifth generation of their family business, were prepared to assume their ownership and managerial responsibilities in the family logistic company at a young age. Their fathers, two brothers of the senior generations, decided early on to prepare the next generation and followed a step-by-step process to develop their sons' skills and capabilities. The cousins' grooming process started at home followed by external experience and a clear career within the family business.[18]
- *Successor development.* Regardless of the method (training, coaching, counseling, or instructing), the aim of successor development is to build successors' skills and capabilities,

improve their productivity, and enhance their performance. Combining both the development (supporting successors' continued growth) and performance (tracking successors' goals and achievements) approaches, successors can benefit by building leadership skills, setting realistic expectations to lead and ensure family cohesion and business sustainability across generations, promoting accountability while embracing all stakeholders, transmitting the family values that make the family business unique, and aligning their goals with those of the family business.

12.6 Model of change in family business succession

Succession means changes. Some changes are inevitable and part of ownership, business, and family evolution. This is particularly true for the family entity and its complexity because the number of family members generally increases across generations, and family members shift their positions across the three entities (ownership, business, and family). Today's children without ownership and work experience in the business are tomorrow's parents, owners, and leaders. Therefore, family members' needs, expectations, and goals are not the same before and after succession because succession shapes the power distribution in the family based on new ownership and managerial structures. Beyond evolutionary changes, which are the consequences of family, business, and ownership evolution, there are other changes that are explicitly implemented by incumbents and successors to adapt the ownership, business, and family entities to new and future challenges. While some family businesses introduce radical strategic and structural changes during succession, others opt for incremental changes or simply no changes at all.

To better understand the impact of succession in family businesses, the model of change in family business succession (Figure 12.2) helps clarify past succession processes as well as predict future succession processes.

During any succession, there are two main types of pressures:

1 *Nonmarket pressures* entail those forces stemming from the family that may alter the status quo of the ownership and business entities. Every family has a natural evolutionary development path related to the number of family members (new births and the incorporation of in-laws), and families are divided into different branches. Evolutionary changes alter family members' roles, power, interpersonal relationships, actions, and activities. Families have to organize these dimensions by themselves, which can strengthen or hinder family ties, commitment, and the family legacy.
2 *Market pressures* entail those forces coming from within and outside the sector in which the firm competes. These forces include economic, social, cultural, political, and legal factors that can change competition within the industry and affect firm competitiveness in the short or long term.

To some extent, all family businesses are likely to be affected by market and nonmarket pressures that push them to change their competition models (i.e., how they compete) and their family–business interactions. However, these pressures do not automatically produce changes in a family business. Rather, changes emerge depending on how the successor and other next-generation family members view the status quo.

The level of the status quo represents the extent to which the new generation of family members recognizes market and nonmarket pressures and introduces (or not) changes on the family side to maintain family cohesiveness, on the ownership side to adjust individuals' power and relationships, and/or on the business side to maintain firm competitiveness and sustainability.

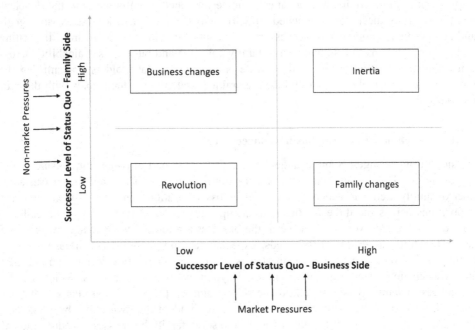

Figure 12.2 Model of change in family business succession.

Source: Adapted from Basco, R., & Brodtkorb, T. (2020). Al Saud Company case study. *Saud Bin Majis's Dilemma.* Sharjah, UAE: American University of Sharjah.

The next generation of family members tends to evaluate market and nonmarket pressures in terms of expected outcomes. The status quo is the specific cognitive bias the next generation uses to judge market and nonmarket pressures and their impact on the ownership, business, and family entities. Consequently, they use the status quo to gauge whether the expected outcomes for changing or not are in the gain or loss domain, which, ultimately, defines the action or behavior they implement. The status quo represents next-generation members' intentions to maintain or change the structure and values of the current system, and it defines the magnitude of the changes.

However, the status quo for the family and business entities is different. The market- and nonmarket-related levels of the status quo for the next generation of family members differ from each other because the market and nonmarket pressures stem from two different institutions (institutional logics) with unique states of affairs. Figure 12.2 combines the level of the status quo from next-generation family members' perspective in relation to market and nonmarket pressures. Thus, when the level of the status quo in the family (or in the business) is high, changes in the family–business relationship (or in the business) are unlikely to occur or will just be marginal. Conversely, when the level of the status quo in the family or in the business is low, changes tend to occur and are more radical. The combination of market and nonmarket pressures and the level of the status quo create four quadrants of successor behaviors:

1 *Inertia—high family and business status quo.* The new generation of family members is not able to recognize market and nonmarket pressures, or if they do recognize these pressures, they decide not to introduce changes in either the family or the business. The new generation prefers to maintain the status quo and follows a harvest strategy.

2 *Family changes—low family status quo and high business status quo.* The new generation
   of family members is able to recognize nonmarket pressures (from the family side) and
   decides to introduce changes to avoid challenges that may jeopardize family cohesiveness.
   The changes mainly relate to the structure and coordination of the family–business relationship, such as changes to family and ownership governance mechanisms. Changes are made
   in the family entity while maintaining the status quo on the firm side in terms of business
   governance, firm strategy, and business model. For instance, Mishal Kanoo, who leads the
   Kanoo Group in Dubai,[19] brought in nonfamily members, which helped improve the level of
   corporate governance. The transition to welcoming nonfamily members on the board has not
   been easy, but family members have gradually started accepting these changes.[20]

3 *Business changes—high family status quo and low business status quo.* The new generation
   of family members is able to recognize market pressures and decides to introduce changes
   to preserve business competitiveness in the market. However, the new generation prefers
   to maintain the status quo on the family side by not introducing changes in the family governance structure or in family–business coordination. This is the case of Gina Rinehart,
   daughter of Lang Hancock (who founded Hancock Prospecting Group in Australia) and one
   of the richest women in the world. She transformed the family business when her father died
   by assuming the executive chairman position in 1992. Under her leadership, "the Hancock
   Group has diversified from prospecting to become a miner, and further investing in iron ore,
   gold, copper, potash, met coal, cattle, dairy and property."[21] However, she did not anticipate the problems that would arise with her own children. In 2015, she was forced by the
   Australian Supreme Court to hand over control of the family trust (as trustee). The Hope
   Margaret Hancock Trust was created by her father with Gina's children as the beneficiaries,
   and it controlled 25% of Hancock Prospecting's shares. Her children initiated litigation in
   2011 when Gina extended the vesting of the trust to 2068.[22]

4 *Revolution—low family and business status quo.* The new generation of family members is
   able to recognize that market and nonmarket pressures may jeopardize family cohesiveness
   and firm survivability. Because of the low-status quo, the next generation decides to introduce changes on both the family side (family governance structure, family constitution, and
   family–business coordination procedures, among others) and the business side (new business
   model, strategic changes, and digitalization, among others). For example, in the LangeTwins
   Family Winery and Vineyards, a revolution started at the end of the fourth generation and
   continued into the fifth generation. At the age of 67, the twins, Randall and Brad Lange,
   expanded their main activity of farming to winemaking. The eldest of the fifth generation,
   Marissa, helped the twins start the winery. With the entrance of the fifth generation, the
   family introduced governance structures to ensure family harmony and firm continuity. The
   family now has an advisory board with external members and a family council. Additionally,
   the family created its own family charter (or constitution).[23]

12.7 Next-generation ownership succession

Ownership succession is about the shift/change in ownership structure from one generation to
another. As discussed in Chapter 11, ownership succession is a discussion that starts with the
incumbent generation and ends with a new ownership structure. The new ownership structure
could take different forms:

* The new ownership structure embraces the new generation of family members as owners
  because the incumbent generation decides to transfer ownership to the subsequent generation.

- The new ownership structure excludes the next generation of family members because the incumbent generation decides to sell the business to nonfamily members (e.g., a management buyout operation).
- The new ownership structure excludes only part of the next generation of family members (not all next-generation family members become owners) because the incumbent generation decides to apply the prune strategy or some family branches decide to exit.

A new ownership structure means changes in power and, consequently, in the dynamics of interpersonal relationships. To understand this, it is necessary to recognize the general development or potential evolution of ownership structures. There are three general paths to define a family business's future ownership structure. All family members should agree upon the ultimate structure, and the final decision should fall within the focal country's laws.

First, the family can prune the family ownership tree. When the incumbent generation decides to prune the family ownership tree, this decision ultimately affects the ownership rights of future generations. Some next-generation family members will no longer be part of the family business, which has implications for their economic, social, and emotional endowments. To avoid misunderstandings and potential resentment, which may devolve into conflicts among family members and undermine family cohesiveness, making a consensual decision to prune the tree across generations and communicating that decision to everyone involved are important. The most critical part of this decision is managing the psychological ownership that members of the next generation may maintain even when they are no longer owners. For instance, a family conflict could emerge when next-generation family members from pruned branches maintain high ownership attachment and their family branches were expelled without clear communication of the circumstances and final decision.

Second, the family can expand the ownership structure by incorporating the next generation (in alignment with the focal country's laws) without having an ownership strategy. The decision to not plan the ownership structure across generations and let the legal system impose its logic about the transfer of wealth from one generation to another could have several implications that families need to acknowledge. When inheritance law regulates ownership transfer from one generation to another, ownership composition and individuals' power change based on the law but not necessarily based on the strategic needs of the family business. For instance, Sharia law in Arab countries stipulates that sons inherit twice as much as daughters, which has implications for ownership structures and power distribution. Families in this context need to ask, is this a good decision for our family business in terms of family cohesion and firm continuity? In other countries, there is no gender separation for wealth inheritance, so all children can receive equal parts regardless of their gender. While equal distribution of shares is fair, it could also be a problem for family business continuity. For example, passive family owners could constrain the business agenda for family members who are highly involved in the business and thus destroy value in the long term at the expense of short-term dividend distribution.

Finally, the family can expand the ownership structure through an ownership strategy by stipulating different ownership percentages for family members or family branches. To avoid the possible demagogy of passive family owners—when a group of passive owners seeks the support of other shareholders by appealing to their desires and prejudices rather than using rational arguments—the alternative is to look for a middle solution between pruning the tree and abiding by inheritance law to determine the new ownership structure. For instance, in some family businesses, the incumbent generation agrees to a specific ownership distribution, which may assign larger ownership participation to active family members and lower participation to passive family members (compensating them with other types of wealth). This solution entails some advantages and disadvantages. While it concentrates ownership in those family members who are engaged in the business to keep agile decision-making, it could break the family dynamics because next-generation family members who would like to incorporate into the business in the near future have less ownership participation and power. That is, future-generation family members who would like to be involved in the business are penalized with a lower level of ownership than their same-generation peers.

Regardless of the ownership structure chosen for the next generation, the succession strategy should outline actions to educate the next generation of owners and potential owners about their ownership roles and how to be responsible owners. A responsible owner in a family business should be aware of dividend payments and the long-term sustainability of the business, the social implications of the business activities, and the cohesiveness of the family. Ownership education involves a wide range of topics from economic and financial matters to emotional and relational issues.

- Owners should be educated to understand their positions across the ownership, business, and family entities; their roles and responsibilities; as well as the limitations and boundaries of their functions in each position, specifically in the ownership position.
- An ownership position should be accompanied by an understanding of the financial and economic aspects of the business. For instance, owners should be able to understand basic economic and business technical concepts and to read and interpret a financial statement, among other technical skills and abilities. This specific education can be provided through the family governance structure with ad hoc workshops, or potential owners can take courses or participate in external educational events.
- Owners need to go beyond economic and financial literacy to also learn about emotional intelligence so they can understand and manage the dynamics of the family business and interpersonal relationships. Even though emotional development is the responsibility of the nuclear family and is unique for each family branch, it could be addressed by family governance to help family members develop the emotions that link the family with the business. Implementing a conversational culture and open communication will help develop healthy emotions and control negative emotions.
- Owners also need to obtain entrepreneurial education to avoid or reduce rent-seeking behavior among next-generation family members. Entrepreneurial education refers to cultivating behavior to create economic, social, and emotional value for the family business. This also implies learning to work and make decisions with the rest of the family members.

12.8 Next-generation governance succession

Next-generation governance succession is about how different next-generation family members join and transfer governance positions during and after succession. Beyond the primary business leader position (managerial position) and the ownership structure and composition and depending on the size and complexity of the family and the firm, the governance structure and composition also require attention when moving from one generation to another.

When the governance structure emerges and is developed during the succession process, there is an opportunity to engage the next generation to design and plan the business and family governance structures to address the upcoming family business challenges. This engagement increases the next generation's commitment to the family business, represents an educational learning mechanism for the next generation, and develops a stewardship culture. When the family business has already implemented a governance structure, during the succession process, governance succession is about expanding the structure if necessary and replacing and moving family members across governance positions.

Incorporating the new generation of family members into the governance structure also implies a new power structure. While some positions are preestablished because of decisions related to ownership and management succession, there are other positions next-generation family members can fill to join and contribute to the family business. The room available for the next generation depends on the type and structure of the corporate governance. As with the main management successor, the next generation of family members who are going to join the governance structure require an entry and career path. The entry and career path should detail the entry conditions, the entry path itself, grooming the next generation, and coaching using external or internal coaches.

12.9 Additional activities and reading material

12.9.1 Classroom discussion questions

1 What are the different ways next-generation family members can contribute to the family business?
2 What is the Disney effect, and how can families minimize this effect among the next generation of family members?
3 How do succession intentions to join the family business form? What dimensions affect succession intentions?
4 How can market and nonmarket changes be explained during and after succession?
5 What are the important elements in a succession plan when discussing ownership and management succession for the next generation of family members?

12.9.2 Additional readings

1 Kislik, L. (2022). How to prepare the next generation to run the family business. *Harvard Business Review*. Article retrieved from https://hbr.org/2022/09/how-to-prepare-the-next-generation-to-run-the-family-business
2 Castro, A., & Krawchuk, F. (2022). Plan a smooth succession for your family business. *Harvard Business Review*. Article retrieved from https://hbr.org/2022/09/plan-a-smooth-succession-for-your-family-business
3 Basco, R., Hamdan, R., & Vyas, A. (2021), Succession intention for the United Arab Emirates NexGens, Sharjah, UAE, available at: https://familyfirmblog.files.wordpress.com/2021/08/succession-intention-report-final-v2-spreads-1.pdf

12.9.3 Classroom activity

Aim: Understand succession intentions in the family business context.
Material: Each group of students has to interview a next-generation family member (friend, family member, or relative) who belongs to a business family but is not officially working in the family business. The data could be anonymized to preserve the confidentiality of the interviewee and his or her family.
Group work:

• *Interview preparation*:

  • Select the interviewee. It is important for the group to decide the potential reasons and characteristics the interviewee has to fulfill to be selected.

- Collect secondary data to know more about the individual that will be interviewed, his or her family, and the family business.
- Schedule the interview.
- Prepare the questions. The questionnaire should serve as a framework for conducting the interview, but the interview should be kept open to allow the interviewee to freely tell his or her story.
- The interview should not be longer than 45 minutes and should be recorded.
- Transcribe the interview (use any software available in the market to perform this task).

- *Material interpretation:*

  - Analyze the interview to discover next-generation succession experience related to the following areas:

    - Intentions
    - Past experience
    - Emotions
    - Behavior
    - Psychological aspects
    - Problems
    - Challenges

- Each group has to present a consultant-style report to interpret the interviewee's succession intentions (maximum five pages). The target of the report should be the business family to help them plan and reflect on the family business challenges. As a suggestion, it should contain the following:

  - A description of the successor and his or her succession intentions.
  - Dimensions and factors that may constrain his or her decision.
  - Consequences for the successor, his or her interpersonal relationships (incumbent–successor), and the family business.
  - A holistic proposal to address current problems and anticipate any potential problems.

Running the classroom exercise: Each group has five minutes to present its report. The presentation should be followed by a class discussion (feedback, comments, and ideas) about the situation.

Takeaways: The group of students has the opportunity to learn more about succession intentions. What are these intentions? How do these intentions form? What affects succession intentions? The exercise is specifically useful for next-generation family members to share their experiences and learn that their feelings are, to some extent, similar to other next-generation family members. Additionally, this exercise helps next-generation family members reflect on how to address problems, issues, and challenges.

12.10 Case for analysis I: Succession in the luxury house of Zegna[24]

Act I—end of 2019. In an interview with the *Financial Times,*[25] Gildo Zegna, fourth generation of the Zegna family business,[26] declared the family business had no interest in going public and, even more, highlighted the intention of the family to welcome the next generation. Edoardo Zegna, Gildo's son, had been working for the company for more than three years, which placed him on the succession career path. He studied at Georgetown University, and before joining the family business, he worked at Everlane as a head of product and at Gap Inc. as a men's concept designer.

Zegna is a family business in the textile industry and is one of the world's largest luxury menswear brands. More than 150 years old, the company was founded by Ermenegildo Zegna and his brothers Edoardo and Mario, who opened a wool mill in northern Italy in 1910. Since its founding, the company's competitive advantages have stemmed from its focus on imported natural fibers and English machinery to produce high-quality fabrics. The second generation—Ermenegildo Zegna's sons, Aldo and Angelo—continued with the company's previous success and expanded the business to ready-made suits.

Since the end of the 1980s, the third generation of family members has gotten into the family business. Gildo Zegna, Angelo's son, became the CEO of the group in 2006, and his cousin Paolo became the chairman of the board of directors. Today, the company is vertically integrated and controls the whole process from sheep to store. The message of the company is as follows: "Led by Gildo Zegna as Chairman and CEO, the Group designs, creates and distributes luxury menswear and accessories under the Zegna brand and womenswear, menswear and accessories under the Thom Browne brand."[27]

Today, the third and fourth generations are involved in governance (board of directors) and managerial positions. Gildo thinks his son has brought new ideas and an understanding about consumer demand for traceability, service, and speed. There are several challenges the company has to address, such as innovation, tough competition in the luxury market, customers' behavior to move to causal wear, digital transformation, and sustainability. The Zegna Group is reorganizing its structure and strategy to put the customer at the center of its universe. In 2018, Edoardo Zegna, Gildo's son, assumed the position of innovation and consumer strategy director to transition and be part of the organizational changes.

Discussion questions:

1 Why do you think the Zegna family is not interested in going public?
2 What does the family's intention to keep the firm as a private family business mean for the fourth generation, including Edoardo Zegna, Gildo's son? What are the succession consequences and implications?

Act II—beginning of 2022. On December 21, 2021,[28] Ermenegildo Zegna Group went public on the New York Stock Exchange.[29] It was a strategic move for the company and, to a certain extent, a shock for the luxury industry's competition. The company was rebranded, eliminating the founder name "Ermenegildo" and consolidating all brands under the Zegna name. Gildo highlighted that the company decided to go public to scale its current growth strategy and refocus on the future of the company. The deal gave the company $769 million to expand its retail stores, expand products by offering more leisurewear, and boost its digital presence.

The Zegna family continues to control the company, retaining more than 60% of the ownership stake. In addition, several members of the board of directors are family members. Before going public, Edoardo Zegna was appointed chief marketing and sustainability officer. This movement put the company into direct competition with other leading luxury firms, such as LVMH and Gucci.

Discussion questions:

3 What does the move to go public mean for the Zegna Group's management succession?
4 How do you think this could have impacted Edoardo Zegna's succession intentions?
5 How do you think the succession process has changed as the company went from being a private family-owned company to a public company controlled by a family?

12.11 Case for analysis II: The succession race at LVMH[30]

Bernard Arnault has not yet officially nominated and announced a successor for the family empire Louis Vuitton Moët Hennessy (LVMH). LVMH is a French holding specialized in luxury goods. It emerged as a merger of two family businesses in 1987, Louis Vuitton (founded in 1954) and Moët Hennessy (it was also the result of a merger between two centennial family businesses in France, Moët & Chandon and Hennessy, in 1971). Coming from a wealthy family, in 1984, Bernard acquired a bankrupt company that owned Christian Dior. From this first movement, he built the LVMH empire by merging and acquiring several firms with recognized brands, such as Loewe, Sephora, and Kenzo, to name a few.

It looks like Bernard Arnault, who is 73 years old and the richest man in the world, is preparing the next step in his long succession to step down from the leadership position as LVMH CEO. He has been running the company for more than four decades. In January 2023, Bernard Arnault's eldest daughter, Delphine, 47, was promoted to run Christian Dior as CEO from her current position as executive vice president of Louis Vuitton. It is said that Delphine is the potential candidate to take over her father's leadership. She joined the family business in 2000 after working at the McKinsey consultancy firm and studying at the London School of Economics. In 2003, she became the first woman to join the board of directors. Arnault explained this internal strategic move as follows: "Under Delphine's leadership, the desirability of Louis Vuitton products advanced significantly, enabling the brand to regularly set new sales records. Her keen insights and incomparable experience will be decisive assets in driving the ongoing development of Christian Dior."[31]

However, Delphine is not alone. There are four other siblings actively working in the family business in senior positions. Her brother Antoine, 45 years old, is responsible for running the holding company that controls LVMH and his father's fortune. Three other stepsiblings from Arnault's second wife also have important jobs within the family business. Alexander, 30 years old, is an executive at Tiffany. Frederic Arnault, 28 years old, is CEO of TAG Heuer. Finally, the youngest child, Jean Arnault, 24 years old, heads marketing and product development for Louis Vuitton's watch division.

All his children are in the succession race. All of them are assuming responsibilities within the company and acquiring the skills and capabilities needed to lead the family business. Actually, in 2022, the company raised the age limit to occupy the CEO position from 75 to 80 years old, showing the challenges Arnault has been facing to hand over the family business. The competition is tough because there are five competitive and smart candidates. It is said that the proposed change in the CEO age limit will give his children time to mature and gain experience. However, there are other nonfamily managers who can also succeed Bernard, such as Antonio Belloni, Michael Burke, and Nicolaz Bazire. Actually, with the new changes in the leadership structure, Michael Burke, who was responsible for Louis Vuitton, is going to work with Bernard Arnault (side by side), but no additional information has been provided about his responsibilities or position.

Discussion questions:

1 How would you describe the succession in LVMH? Do you think there is a real plan behind the succession process, or is it more informal?
2 Do you think the five siblings are competing? Do you think this competition is important for the family business? What could be the consequences of this competition in the future?
3 What other actions would you take to moderate the competition and avoid negative consequences (e.g., rivalry) among the brothers and sisters?

12.12   Case study: Al Saud Company managing changes from the second generation to the third[32]

[This story is a continuation of the case study from Chapter 9] Al Saud Company, founded by Sheikh Saoud Bin Khalid Bin Khalid Al Qassimi in the Emirate of Sharjah in the late 1970s, successfully transitioned ownership, governance, and management from the first generation to the second generation in the middle of the 2000s. The second generation was aware of the transition challenges and developed a minimal formal family governance structure to keep the family united and cohesive. Having two sons that took over the leadership—Majid became the chair of the firm, and Sultan took over the managing director position—the family business continued its successful trajectory under the buoyant economy in the UAE.

By applying a conservative strategy of growing organically and avoiding unnecessary risks, the company was able to weather the 2008 financial crisis without troubles, while most similar companies in the UAE and the Gulf suffered from being financially leveraged. However, the most important challenge for the Al Qassimi family is going to come. Like any other family in the Gulf region, the number of family members in the Al Qassimi family is increasing exponentially across generations and changing the dynamics of the family and the firm. Majid and Sultan's father had left a clear message when he was alive: "I would like Saud succeed me." Saud, Majid's son, occupies a prominent position among the siblings and cousins—the eldest son of the eldest son—which has a special meaning in Arab culture.

After the 2008 crisis, when looking at the company's horizon, Majid and Sultan visualized the need to start planning the next succession. Both of them intended to reduce their participation in the company's daily decision-making for different reasons. While Majid was approaching the retirement age, Sultan had different ambitions and wanted to develop his Barjeel Art Foundation further. Just before Sheikh Saud Bin Majid started his undergraduate studies, his father and uncle made clear their desire to see Saud join the firm by following an informal yet agreed-upon plan among the family leaders.

Saud has been trained to handle business operations and family relationships by his uncle, Sultan. In 2011, after finishing his university degree in finance, he worked at HSBC in Dubai and then at a local bank before joining Abraaj Capital for 18 months, which included six months in Singapore. Saud gradually got into the family business by working side by side with his father and uncle, who helped him navigate the learning process to manage an Arab family business in the Gulf region.

Little by little, Saud has been managing more and more things within the family business, assuming more responsibilities, and making key decisions with his father and uncle as mentors and coaches. As his experience, knowledge, and career have progressed, his father and uncle have moved further away from the day-to-day operations, thereby giving visibility to the future new leader. By the end of 2022, Saud is a well-recognized manager and is leading the path of the family business.

However, Saud is facing a tough situation as he will have to manage a large number of shareholders while keeping the family united. He is optimistic about the future of the firm but believes that some changes are needed to maintain the unity of the family while implementing new initiatives to consolidate the firm's strategic position. As the family and number of shareholders continue to grow, the business will need to produce more income to satisfy these shareholders' expectations. If the income produced through Majid and Sultan's risk-averse strategies fails to keep up with these expectations, that will pose a risk to the future of the firm.

In the last decade, the economy in the UAE has changed, and the competition is tougher today. New laws and regulations are opening the country to new competitors, which has made the benefits of running a business lower than ever. The government has already introduced a value-added tax, and the country is expected to have a corporate tax by 2023. The national UAE government is trying to move the economy from being based on natural resources to being based on knowledge and entrepreneurship, thus producing uncertainty for today's businesses. There will be more and new opportunities in the future UAE economy but not the same opportunities that Saud's grandfather had when the country was in its initial stage. During that time, the country was emerging from the desert and needed committed family businesses to develop all the infrastructure and to open all business sectors and industries to local Emirates. In the new context, Saud will need to manage tradition and innovation to maintain the family and the business together and give continuity to his grandfather's project. If the shareholders believe they can get a higher return by managing their investments differently, then even the 25% penalty for selling their shares will not keep them from cashing out of the family business.

Today, the grandmother and all the siblings of the second generation (seven) maintain ownership in their hands. The third generation comprises more than 30 family members, some of whom are mature enough to start engaging with the family business. However, there is no strategy for developing the next generation of family members. The main action to start engaging the third generation in business matters was taken at the 2016 annual meeting. All owners agreed that the children of the current shareholders, who represent the future of the firm, should attend annual meetings as observers (no voice and no vote). However, this decision was affected by the COVID-19 pandemic as several shareholder meetings were cancelled and there were fewer interactions among family members.

Saud reflected on the daunting task he had inherited:

> How can a young man with a young man's limited experience in business and even in life manage the future of a firm and a family? How can I integrate the interests of the first, second, and third generations into a new balance between my family and our family business? How can I introduce necessary changes while maintaining respect for the legacies of our founder and the second generation of managers? What kind of family business structure and governance should I develop? How [can I] educate my cousins to be responsible owners if my uncles and aunts still keep the ownership? How [can I] invite my cousins to join the family business at different levels and positions when my uncles and aunts keep the vertical communication and the seniority culture?

It seems Saud is trapped between the senior generation and the third generation, preventing him from introducing changes and reshaping the family business. The senior generation still holds ownership of the company, which means it maintains the power, status, and cultural voice to direct decision-making and communication. Saud can lead the family business operations but not the family or the family–business relationship, which are still under the control of the second generation.

Discussion questions:

1 What kind of commitment to join the family business do you think Saud has? Do you think his commitment to join the family business has changed over time?
2 What kind of successor career-path intentions do you think Saud has?
3 Based on the model of change in family business succession, in which quadrant do you think Saud is? Why? Where do you think he needs to be to fully lead the family business into the next stage of development?

Notes

1 Information retrieved from Oostwegel Collection website www.oostwegelcollection.nl/en/about-oostwegel-collection/

2 Seaman, R. (2020). Redefining ownership as shareholder stewardship. *Family Business Magazine*. Article retrieved from www.familybusinessmagazine.com/redefining-ownership-shareholder-stewardship

3 ESAS Holding website. Information retrieved from www.esas.com.tr/en/our-firm

4 José Milton Foundation website. Information retrieved from www.miltonphilanthropy.org/

5 Gulf Business. (2020). Dubai-based young entrepreneur Azhar Sajan on plans ahead for his company Casa Milano. Article retrieved from https://gulfbusiness.com/dubai-based-young-entrepreneur-azhar-sajan-plans-ahead-company-casa-milano/

6 Ajzen, I. (1991). The theory of planned behavior. *Organizational Behavior and Human Decision Processes*, 50(2), 179–211.

7 Zellweger, T., Sieger, P., & Englisch, P. (2012). *Coming Home or Breaking Free? Career Choice Intentions of the Next Generation in Family Business*. St. Gallen: Ernst & Young. Basco, R., & Gómez González, J. (2022). Antecedents of next generation succession intention in family businesses: A cross-country analysis. *European Journal of International Management*, forthcoming. Article retrieved from https://doi.org/10.1504/EJIM.2022.10051782

8 Bandura, A. (1977). Self-efficacy: Toward a unifying theory of behavioral change. *Psychological Review*, 84, 191–215. https://doi.org/10.1037/0033-295X.84.2.191; Bandura, A. (1982). Self-efficacy mechanism in human agency. *American Psychologist*, 37(2), 122–147. https://doi.org/10.1037/0003-066X.37.2.122

9 Campden, F. B. (2022). Sir James Waters: "Integrity underpins everything we do". Article retrieved from www.campdenfb.com/article/sir-james-wates-integrity-underpins-everything-we-do

10 Beech, J. (2021). Devansh Jain of INOX Group on powering family business and renewable energy growth. *Campden FB*. Article retrieved from www.campdenfb.com/article/devansh-jain-inox-group-powering-family-business-and-renewable-energy-growth

11 Beech, J. (2021). Marc Puig Guasch on family business growth, succession and the legacy of his father Mariano Puig Planas. *Campden FB*. Article retrieved from www.campdenfb.com/article/marc-puig-guasch-family-business-growth-succession-and-legacy-his-father-mariano-puig-planas

12 Rehaan Khaneja blog. Information retrieved from www.rehaankhaneja.com/post/interview-with-sunil-vachani-chairman-dixon-technologies

13 Go, K., & Chung, P. (2022). "I'm Never Working for My Family Business." What I learned from my transition to my family business and becoming a family advisor. *NEXTGEN Practice Insight*. Article retrieved from https://ffipractitioner.org/im-never-working-for-my-family-business-what-i-learned-from-my-transition-to-my-family-business-and-becoming-a-family-advisor/

14 Sharma, P., & Irving, G. P. (2005). Four bases of family business successor commitment: Antecedents and consequences. *Entrepreneurship Theory and Practice*, 29(1), 13–33.

15 The Brander. (2022). Jan Ryde—One man's dream of a better world. Article retrieved from www.thebrander.com/en/lifestyle/hastens

16 International Finance Corporation. (2018). *IFC Family Business Governance Handbook*. International Finance Corporation is a Member of the World Bank Group. Document retrieved from www.ifc.org/wps/wcm/connect/2c93b2cb-dec6-4819-9ffb-60335069cbac/Family_Business_Governance_Handbook.pdf?MOD=AJPERES&CVID=mskqtDE

17 Dahl, D. (2011). Succession stories: The good, the bad, and the ugly. *Inc. Magazine*. Information retrieved from www.inc.com/articles/201103/succession-stories-keeping-the-business-in-the-family.html

18 Kuma, P. (2011). Joined at the Hip. *Campden FB*. Article retrieved from www.campdenfb.com/article/joined-hip

19 The headquarters of the centennial Usuf Bin Ahmed Kanoo Group in Manama and led by Khalid Mohammed Kanoo.

20 Sophia, M. (2019). The family man: How Mishal Kanoo is changing and growing his 129-year-old family business. *Forbes*. Article retrieved from www.forbesmiddleeast.com/leadership/ceo/the-family-man

21 Roy Hill family business website. Information retrieved from www.royhill.com.au/about/our-board/

22 Foulsham & Geddes website. Information retrieved from www.fglaw.com.au/the-hope-margaret-hancock-trust/

23 Hall, A. (2017). Old vines lead to new fruit. *Family Business Magazine*. Article retrieved from www.familybusinessmagazine.com/article-download/14705

24 This example discussion is developed solely as the basis for class discussion. This example discussion is not intended to serve as an endorsement, source of primary data, or illustration of effective or ineffective management.

25 Sanderson, R. (2019). Gildo Zegna: Tailoring masculinity for changing tastes. *Financial Times*. Article retrieved from www.ft.com/content/de5969a4-1a72-11ea-9186-7348c2f183af

26 Zegna Group website. Information retrieved from www.zegnagroup.com/en/

27 Zegna Group website. Information retrieved from www.zegnagroup.com/en/our-road/

28 Hirsch, L., & Friedman, V. (2021). Zegna's I.P.O. path raises question: Is this the next big fashion trend?. *The New Work Times*. Article retrieved from www.nytimes.com/2021/12/19/business/dealbook/zegna-spac-ipo-stock-market.html

29 The company went public by using a special product called Special Purpose Acquisition (SPAC) created by Investindustrial Acquisition Corp. led by Segio Ermotti.

30 This example discussion is developed solely as the basis for class discussion. This example discussion is not intended to serve as an endorsement, source of primary data, or illustration of effective or ineffective management.

31 Neate, R. (2023). LVMH billionaire Bernard Arnault appoints daughter to run Dior. *The Guardian*. Article retrieved from www.theguardian.com/business/2023/jan/11/bernard-arnault-appoints-daughter-delphine-dior-chief-executive-lvmh

32 Certain details in this case have been disguised. This case study discussion is developed solely as the basis for class discussion. This case study discussion is not intended to serve as an endorsement, source of primary data, or illustration of effective or ineffective management.

Index

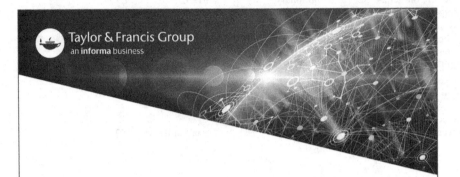

Printed in the United States
by Baker & Taylor Publisher Services

Printed in the United States
by Baker & Taylor Publisher Services